Redemption and Dialogue

Redemption and Dialogue

Reading *Redemptoris Missio* and *Dialogue and Proclamation*

edited by

William R. Burrows

The Catholic Foreign Mission Society of America (Maryknoll) recruits and trains people for overseas missionary service. Through Orbis Books, Maryknoll aims to foster the international dialogue that is essential to mission. The books published, however, reflect the opinions of their authors and are not meant to represent the official position of the society.

Commentaries copyright ©1993 by William R. Burrows and Orbis books for the individual authors; text of *Redemptoris Missio* copyright © 1990 Typis Polyglottis Vaticanis; text of *Dialogue and Proclamation* copyright 1991 Typis Polyglottis Vaticanis.

Published by Orbis Books, Maryknoll, New York, U.S.A.

Manufactured in the United States of America.

Library of Congress Cataloging-in-Publication Data

Redemption and dialogue : reading Redemptoris missio and Dialogue and proclamation /
    edited by William R. Burrows.
        p.   cm.
    Includes bibliographical references
    ISBN 0-88344-935-8 (pbk.)
    1. Catholic Church. Pope (1987-   :   John Paul II).   Redemptoris missio.
2. Catholic Church — Missions — Papal documents.   3. Missions — Theory —
Papal documents.   4. Catholic Church — Missions.   5. Missions — Theory.
6. Dialogue and proclamation.   I. Burrows, William R.   II. Dialogue and
proclamation.   1994.   III. Catholic Church.   Pope (1978-   :   John Paul II).
Redemptoris missio.   1994
BV2180.R39   1994
266'.2 — dc20

                                                                    94-11990
                                                                       CIP

Contents

List of Abbreviations

AA   *Apostolicam Actuositatem*, Vatican Council II decree on the lay apostolate.

AAS   *Acta Apostolicae Sedis* (official gazette of record for papal and Vatican curial statements).

AG   *Ad Gentes*, Vatican Council II decree on the missionary activity of the church, 7 December 1965.

BIRA Bishops' Institute of Interreligious Affairs of the Federation of Asian Bishops' Conferences

CBCI Catholic Bishops' Conference of India

CDF   Congregation for the Doctrine of Faith

CEP   Congregation for Evangelization of Peoples

CIC   *Codex Iuris Canonic* ("Code of Canon Law" of the Roman Catholic Church).

CL   *Christifideles Laici*, apostolic exhortation of John Paul II, 30 December 1988.

CT   *Catechesi Tradendi*, apostolic exhortation of John Paul II, 16 October 1979.

DEV   *Dominum et Vivificantem*, encyclical letter of John Paul II, 18 May 1986.

DH   *Dignitatis Humanae*, Vatican Council II declaration on religious liberty, 7 December 1965.

DM   *Divos in Misericordia*, encyclical letter of John Paul II, 30 November 1980.

D&M   *Dialogue and Mission*, statement of the Pontifical Secretariat for Non-Christians, "Attitudes of the Catholic Church Towards the Followers of Other Religions" in "Reflections and Directives on Dialogue and Mission," *AAS* 84 (1984) 816-28.

DP   *Dialogue and Proclamation*, statement of the Congregation for the Evangelization of Peoples and the Pontifical Council on Inter-Religious Dialogue, *Bulletin of the Pontifical Council on Inter-Religious Dialogue* 26 (No. 2, 1991) 210-250.

DS   *Denzinger-Schönmetzer, Enchiridion Symbolorum: Definitionum et Declarationum de Rebus Fidei et Morum* (collection of classical offical Roman Catholic declarations on matters of faith and morals, numerous editions, Freiburg im Breisgau, Herder).

DV   *Dei Verbum*, Vatican Council II dogmatic constitution on revelation, 18 November 1965.

ES   *Ecclesiam Suam*, encyclical letter of Paul VI, 16 August 1964.

FD   *Fidei Donum*, encyclical letter of Pius XII, 21 April 1957.

FC   *Familiaris Consortio*, apostolic exhortation of John Paul II, 22 November 1981.

EN   *Evangelii Nuntiandi*, apostolic exhortation of Paul VI on evangelization, 8 December 1975.

EP   *Evangelii Praecones*, encyclical letter of Pius XII, 2 June 1951.

FABC Federation of Asian Bishops' Conferences

GS   *Gaudium et Spes*, Vatican Council II pastoral constitution on the church in the contemporary world, 7 December 1965.

LG   *Lumen Gentium*, Vatican Council II dogmatic constitution on the church, 21 November 1964.

MC   *Mystici Corporis*, encyclical letter of Pius XII, 29 June 1943.

MD   *Mulieris Dignitatem*, apostolic letter of John Paul II.

MI   *Maximum Illud*, apostolic exhortation of Benedict XV, 30 November 1919.

MM   *Mater et Magistra*, encyclical letter of John XXIII, 15 May 1961.

NA   *Nostra Aetate*, Vatican Council II declaration on the relationship of the church to non-Christians, 28 October 1965.

OT   *Optatam Totius*, Vatican Council II decree on priestly formation, 28 October 1965

PCID   Pontifical Council for Interreligious Dialogue

PO   *Presbyterorum Ordinis*, Vatican Council II decree on priestly life and ministry, 7 December 1965.

POP   *Populorum Progressio*, encyclical letter of John XXII, 26 March 1967.

PP   *Princeps Pastorum*, encyclical letter of John XXIII, 22 November 1959.

RE   *Rerum Ecclesiae*, encyclical letter of Pius XI, 28 February 1926.

RH   *Redemptor Hominis*, encyclical letter of John Paul II, 4 March 1979.

SA   *Slavorum Apostoli*, encyclical letter of John Paul II, 2 June 1985.

SNC   Secretariat for Non-Christians

SRC   *Sollicitudo Rei Socialis*, encyclical letter of John Paul II, 30 December 1987.

UR   *Unitatis Redintegratio*, Vatican Council II decree on ecumenism, 21 November 1964.

Foreword

William R. Burrows

THE GENESIS OF THIS BOOK

When Pope John Paul II's encyclical *Redemptoris Missio* (RM) was issued in the midst of the Gulf Crisis of late 1990 and early 1991, I was often asked by friends and colleagues, even the *New York Times*, whether the encyclical signaled a new tough Vatican line in relation to other religious traditions, especially Islam. "No," I replied, "from what I read, it mainly addresses internal Catholic problems." Today I would qualify and refine that analysis slightly, but I still believe that it is basically true.

There is a twofold focus in RM: (1) it seeks to correct what Pope John Paul II considers "errors" on the part of certain theologians, especially those who reduce Christian mission to a form of humanitarian rescue mission, on the one hand, and Christ's office to something less than constitutive for salvation, on the other hand; and (2), then, within that context, it seeks to clarify the Roman dogmatic magisterium's position (a) on mission and evangelization and (b) on such issues as interreligious dialogue and the church's role in God's plans for human salvation, development, and liberation. Subsequent readings, conversations with knowledgeable theologians, and a visit to Rome several months after RM and *Dialogue and Proclamation* (DP) were published, confirm my sense that this is the case.

In the theological world, the two statements are not uncontroverted. First, RM and DP have been criticized for attempting to decide questions on which some feel a variety of orthodox views are possible. Second, some question whether RM and DP are internally consistent. Paolo Suess's article, "A Confused Mission Scenario: A Critical Analysis of Recent Church Documents and Tendencies" (*Concilium* 1994/2, pp. 106-17), can be read as an accessible summary of both families of critiques.

As discussions proceeded from suggestions of members of the Maryknoll Advisory Committee to Orbis that we do a book on RM and/or DP, it became clear from the opinions of a wide range of missiologists consulted that the two Roman statements merited attention. I began thinking about what kind of book would do justice both to the richness and — it must be said — lacunae and problems in RM and DP. The book you hold in your hands is the result.

The attempt in *Redemption and Dialogue* is also twofold. The first goal is to make available the text of and reliable, authoritative commentary on each document. Parts One and Two do this. Fathers Zago and Dupuis summarize and explicate the thrust of these documents in their commentaries. The second goal of this book is to make available a range of critical opinions on RM and DP from persons involved in various aspects of mission and scholarship. This is the aim of Part Three.

I wish to thank the eleven men and women from around the globe who responded to the invitation to contribute. Unless I am mistaken, only one of them — in addition to myself — is a citizen of the United States. And he was born in Korea. They range from scholars to rural pastors, and embrace positions that range from agreement with the spirit and substance of RM and DP to serious reservations.

In several chapters, substantial shortening of essays had to be performed. In at least one case — the article by Augustine Kanjamala — the shortened version omits several pages of statistics, and this abridgment may diminish the probative weight that his statistics give to his theological analysis of mission in India.

A WORD ON GENERIC LANGUAGE AND ITS ABSENCE

Some readers will note with alarm the presence of traditional grammatical conventions in *Redemptoris Missio* and *Dialogue and Proclamation*, which they consider "sexist." In weighing what was permissible editorial alteration, I considered making the language of both texts "inclusive." On the one hand, the official text of RM is in Latin, and I could have justified my alterations as a retranslation of these passages. The case was different with DP. Although it avoids sexist language to a great extent, the working language of its drafting process was apparently Italian. It was issued simultaneously in English, Italian, and French. The issuing offices could have edited the English text *fully* to reflect contemporary North American sensitivities toward sexist language. They did not.

In the end, after no little consultation, I decided to publish both texts in their official English versions. Although many readers will object to the abundance of masculine pronouns when generic terms are available — as, indeed, I do myself — the issuing offices knew that such grammatical usages in English are controversial, yet chose to follow them. They seem willing to bear the consequences, and I see no reason not to let them.

In seeking guidance from non-North Americans on sexist language, I was told several times that the generic language question is not one in which persons in such places as India and Africa want to follow the lead of the United States on an a priori basis. Many feel that American crusades to alter language usage cloys as much as the traditional usages. In the process of consulting on this language question, one of the most interesting things I learned was that, although English has become an international language that offers many non-native speakers of the language access to international discussions, American attempts to make everyone use English in the ways feminist discussions have shaped American usages are often viewed as a new form of cultural imperialism. Accordingly, except for simplifying reference styles and correcting minor grammatical and punctuation errors in the original, the documents published here conform to the officially released English texts.

A NOTE ON ABBREVIATIONS

Because *Redemptoris Missio* and *Dialogue and Proclamation* (as well as other official Roman documents) are cited so often in this volume, we shall usually refer to them as "RM" and "DP." When giving citation references to these documents, we shall give article numbers in parentheses *without* the abbreviations when it is clear from the context to which document they refer; abbreviations are added when it is ambiguous.

Numerous other ecclesiastical documents are referred to in *Redemption and Dialogue,* and we have tried to use abbreviations in citing them also. Consult the list of abbreviations on pp.vii-viii for full titles of documents referred to.

Part One

Redemptoris Missio

1

Redemptoris Missio

An Encyclical Letter on the Permanent Validity of the Church's Missionary Mandate

Pope John Paul II

Outline of the Encyclical

Introduction

Chapter I
Jesus Christ, the Only Savior
"No one comes to the Father, but by me"
    Faith in Christ is Directed to Man's Freedom
    The Church as Sign and Instrument of Salvation
    Salvation in Christ is Offered to All
    "We cannot but speak"

Chapter II
The Kingdom of God
    Christ Makes the Kingdom Present
    Characteristics of the Kingdom and Its Demands
    In the Risen Christ God's Kingdom is Fulfilled and Proclaimed
    The Kingdom in Relation to Christ and the Church
    The Church at the Service of the Kingdom

Chapter III
The Holy Spirit, the Principal Agent of Mission
    Sent Forth "to the end of the earth"
    The Spirit Directs the Church's Mission
    The Holy Spirit Makes the Whole Church Missionary
    The Spirit is Present and Active in Every Time and Place
    Missionary Activity is Only Beginning

Chapter IV
The Vast Horizons of the Mission *ad gentes*
   A Complex and Ever Changing Religious Picture
   Mission *ad gentes* Retains Its Value
   To All Peoples, in spite of Difficulties
   Parameters of the Church's Mission *ad gentes*
   Fidelity to Christ and the Promotion of Human Freedom
   Directing Attention toward the South and the East

Chapter V
The Paths of Mission
   The First Form of Evangelization is Witness
   The Initial Proclamation of Christ the Savior
   Conversion and Baptism
   Forming Local Churches
   "Ecclesial Basic Communities" as a Force for Evangelization
   Incarnating the Gospel in Peoples' Cultures
   Dialogue with our Brothers and Sisters of other Religions
   Promoting Development by Forming Consciences
   Charity: Source and Criterion of Mission

Chapter VI
Leaders and Workers in the Missionary Apostolate
   Those Primarily Responsible for Missionary Activity
   Missionaries and Religious Institutes *Ad Gentes*
   Diocesan Priests for the Universal Mission
   The Missionary Fruitfulness of Consecrated Life
   All the Laity are Missionaries by Baptism
   The Work of Catechists and the Variety of Ministries
   The Congregation for the Evangelization of Peoples and Other Structures for
      Missionary Activity

Chapter VII
Cooperation in Missionary Activity
   Prayer and Sacrifice for Missionaries
   "Here I am, Lord! I am Ready! Send Me!"
   "It is More Blessed to Give than to Receive"
   New Forms of Missionary Cooperation
   Missionary Promotion and Formation among the People of God
   The Primary Responsibility of the Pontifical Mission Societies
   Not only Giving to the Missions but Receiving from Them as Well
   God Is Preparing a New Springtime for the Gospel

Chapter VIII
Missionary Spirituality
   Being Led by the Spirit
   Living the Mystery of Christ, "the One who was Sent"
   Loving the Church and Humanity as Jesus Did
   The True Missionary is the Saint

Conclusion

Text of the Encyclical

Venerable Brothers,
Beloved Sons and Daughters,
Health and the Apostolic Blessing!

INTRODUCTION

1. The Mission of Christ the Redeemer, which is entrusted to the Church, is still very far from completion. As the second Millennium after Christ's coming draws to an end, an overall view of the human race shows that this mission is still only beginning and that we must commit ourselves wholeheartedly to its service. It is the Spirit who impels us to proclaim the great works of God: "For if I preach the Gospel, that gives me no ground for boasting. For necessity is laid upon me. Woe to me if I do not preach the Gospel!" (1 Cor 9:16). In the name of the whole Church, I sense an urgent duty to repeat this cry of Saint Paul. From the beginning of my Pontificate I have chosen to travel to the ends of the earth in order to show this missionary concern. My direct contact with peoples who do not know Christ has convinced me even more of the *urgency of missionary activity*, a subject to which I am devoting the present Encyclical.

The Second Vatican Council sought to renew the Church's life and activity in the light of the needs of the contemporary world. The Council emphasized the Church's "missionary nature," basing it in a dynamic way on the Trinitarian mission itself. The missionary thrust therefore belongs to the very nature of the Christian life, and is also the inspiration behind ecumenism: "that they may all be one . . . so that the world may believe that you have sent me" (Jn 17:21).

2. The Council has already borne much fruit in the realm of missionary activity. There has been an increase of local Churches with their own Bishops, clergy and workers in the apostolate. The presence of Christian communities is more evident in the life of nations, and communion between the Churches has led to a lively exchange of spiritual benefits and gifts. The commitment of the laity to the work of evangelization is changing ecclesial life, while particular Churches are more willing to meet with the members of other Christian Churches and other religions, and to enter into dialogue and cooperation with them. Above all, there is a new awareness that *missionary activity is a matter for all Christians,* for all dioceses and parishes, Church institutions and associations.

Nevertheless, in this "new springtime" of Christianity there is an undeniable negative tendency, and the present Document is meant to help overcome it. Missionary activity specifically directed "to the nations" (*ad gentes*) appears to be waning, and this tendency is certainly not in line with the directives of the Council and of subsequent statements of the Magisterium. Difficulties both internal and external have weakened the Church's missionary thrust toward non-Christians, a fact which must arouse concern among all who believe in Christ. For in the Church's history, missionary drive has always been a sign of vitality, just as its lessening is a sign of a crisis of faith.[1]

---

1. Cf. Paul VI, *Message* for World Mission Day, 1972, *Insegnamenti* X (1972), 522: "How many internal tensions, which weaken and divide certain local churches and institutions, would disappear before the firm conviction that the salvation of local communities

Twenty-five years after the conclusion of the Council and the publication of the Decree on Missionary Activity *Ad Gentes,* fifteen years after the Apostolic Exhortation *Evangelii Nuntiandi* issued by Pope Paul VI, and in continuity with the magisterial teaching of my predecessors,[2] I wish to invite the Church to *renew her missionary commitment.* The present Document has as its goal an interior renewal of faith and Christian life. For missionary activity renews the Church, revitalizes faith and Christian identity, and offers fresh enthusiasm and new incentive. *Faith is strengthened when it is given to others!* It is in commitment to the Church's universal mission that the new evangelization of Christian peoples will find inspiration and support.

But what moves me even more strongly to proclaim the urgency of missionary evangelization is the fact that it is the primary service which the Church can render to every individual and to all humanity in the modern world, a world which has experienced marvelous achievements but which seems to have lost its sense of ultimate realities and of existence itself. "Christ the Redeemer," I wrote in my first Encyclical, "fully reveals man to himself. . . . The man who wishes to understand himself thoroughly . . . must . . . draw near to Christ. . . . The Redemption that took place through the Cross has definitively restored to man his dignity and given back meaning to his life in the world" (RH; *AAS* 71, pp. 274f.).

I also have other reasons and aims: to respond to the many requests for a document of this kind; to clear up doubts and ambiguities regarding missionary activity *ad gentes,* and to confirm in their commitment those exemplary brothers and sisters dedicated to missionary activity and all those who assist them; to foster missionary vocations; to encourage theologians to explore and expound systematically the various aspects of missionary activity; to give a fresh impulse to missionary activity by fostering the commitment of the particular Churches — especially those of recent origin — to send forth and receive missionaries; and to assure non-Christians and particularly the authorities of countries to which missionary activity is being directed that all of this has but one purpose: to serve man by revealing to him the love of God made manifest in Jesus Christ.

3. *Peoples everywhere, open the doors to Christ!* His Gospel in no way detracts from man's freedom, from the respect that is owed to every culture and to whatever is good in each religion. By accepting Christ, you open yourselves to the definitive Word of God, to the One in whom God has made himself fully known and has shown us the path to himself.

The number of those who do not know Christ and do not belong to the Church is constantly on the increase. Indeed, since the end of the Council it has almost doubled. When we consider this immense portion of humanity which is loved by the Father and for whom he sent his Son, the urgency of the Church's mission is obvious.

On the other hand, our own times offer the Church new opportunities in this field: we have witnessed the collapse of oppressive ideologies and political systems; the opening of frontiers and the formation of a more united world due to an increase in communications; the affirmation among peoples of the Gospel values which Jesus made incarnate in his own life (peace, justice, brotherhood, concern for the needy);

---

is procured through cooperation in work for the spread of the Gospel to the farthest bounds of the earth!"

2. Cf. Benedict XV, Apostolic Letter *Maximum Illud* (30 November 1919); *AAS* 11 (1919), 440-455; Pius XI, Encyclical Letter *Rerum Ecclesiae* (28 February 1926); *AAS* 18 (1926), 65-83; Pius XII, Encyclical Letter *Evangelii Praecones* (2 June 1951); *AAS* 43 (1951), 497-528; Encyclical Letter *Fidei Donum* (21 April 1957); *AAS* 49 (1957), 225-248; John XXIII, Encyclical Letter *Princeps Pastorum* (28 November 1959): *AAS* 51 (1959), 833-864.

and a kind of soulless economic and technical development which only stimulates the search for the truth about God, about man and about the meaning of life itself.

God is opening before the Church the horizons of a humanity more fully prepared for the sowing of the Gospel. I sense that the moment has come to commit all of the Church's energies to a new evangelization and to the mission *ad gentes*. No believer in Christ, no institution of the Church can avoid this supreme duty: to proclaim Christ to all peoples.

CHAPTER I

JESUS CHRIST, THE ONLY SAVIOR

4. In my first Encyclical, in which I set forth the program of my Pontificate, I said that "the Church's fundamental function in every age, and particularly in ours, is to direct man's gaze, to point the awareness and experience of the whole of humanity toward the mystery of Christ" (RH; *AAS* 71, p. 275).

The Church's universal mission is born of faith in Jesus Christ, as is stated in our Trinitarian profession of faith: "I believe in one Lord, Jesus Christ, the only Son of God, eternally begotten of the Father. . . . For us men and for our salvation he came down from heaven: by the power of the Holy Spirit he became incarnate from the Virgin Mary, and was made man." [3] The Redemption event brings salvation to all, "for each one is included in the mystery of the Redemption and with each one Christ has united himself for ever through this mystery" (RH 13). It is only in faith that the Church's mission can be understood and only in faith that it find its basis.

Nevertheless, also as a result of the changes which have taken place in modern times and the spread of new theological ideas, some people wonder: *Is missionary work among non-Christians still relevant?* Has it not been replaced by interreligious dialogue? Is not human development an adequate goal of the Church's mission? Does not respect for conscience and for freedom exclude all efforts at conversion? Is it not possible to attain salvation in any religion? *Why then should there be missionary activity?*

"No one comes to the Father, but by me" (Jn 14:6)

5. If we go back to the beginnings of the Church, we find a clear affirmation that Christ is the one Savior of all, the only one able to reveal God and lead to God. In reply to the Jewish religious authorities who question the Apostles about the healing of the lame man, Peter says: "By the name of Jesus Christ of Nazareth whom you crucified, whom God raised from the dead, by him this man is standing before you well. . . . And there is salvation in no one else, for there is no other name under heaven given among men by which we must be saved" (Acts 4:10, 12). This statement, which was made to the Sanhedrin, has a universal value, since for all people — Jews and Gentiles alike — salvation can only come from Jesus Christ.

The universality of this salvation in Christ is asserted throughout the New Testament. Saint Paul acknowledges the Risen Christ as the Lord. He writes: "Although there may be so-called gods in heaven or on earth — as indeed there are many 'gods' and many 'lords' — yet for us there is one God, the Father, from whom are all things and for whom we exist, and one Lord, Jesus Christ, through whom are all things and through whom we exist" (1 Cor 8:5-6). One God and one Lord are asserted by way of

---

3. Nicene-Constantinopolitan Creed, *DS* 150.

contrast to the multitude of "gods" and "lords" commonly accepted. Paul reacts against the polytheism of the religious environment of his time and emphasizes what is characteristic of the Christian faith: belief in one God and in one Lord sent by God.

In the Gospel of Saint John, this salvific universality of Christ embraces all the aspects of his mission of grace, truth and revelation: the Word is "the true light that enlightens every man" (Jn 1:9). And again, "no one has ever seen God; the only Son, who is in the bosom of the Father, he has made him known" (Jn 1:18; cf. Mt 11:27). God's revelation becomes definitive and complete through his only-begotten Son: "In many and various ways God spoke of old to our fathers by the prophets; but in these last days he has spoken to us by a Son, whom he appointed the heir of all things, through whom he also created the world" (Heb 1:1-2; cf. Jn 14:6). In this definitive Word of his revelation, God has made himself known in the fullest possible way. He has revealed to mankind *who he is*. This definitive self-revelation of God is the fundamental reason why the Church is missionary by her very nature. She cannot do other than proclaim the Gospel, that is, the fullness of the truth which God has enabled us to know about himself.

Christ is the one mediator between God and mankind: "For there is one God, and there is one mediator between God and men, the man Christ Jesus, who gave himself as a ransom for all, the testimony to which was borne at the proper time. For this I was appointed a preacher and apostle (I am telling the truth, I am not lying), a teacher of the Gentiles in faith and truth" (1 Tim 2:5-7; cf. Heb 4:14-16). No one, therefore, can enter into communion with God except through Christ, by the working of the Holy Spirit. Christ's one, universal mediation, far from being an obstacle on the journey toward God, is the way established by God himself, a fact of which Christ is fully aware. Although participated forms of mediation of different kinds and degrees are not excluded, they acquire meaning and value *only* from Christ's own mediation, and they cannot be understood as parallel or complementary to his.

6. To introduce any sort of separation between the Word and Jesus Christ is contrary to the Christian faith. Saint John clearly states that the Word, who "was in the beginning with God," is the very one who "became flesh" (Jn 1:2, 14). Jesus is the Incarnate Word — a single and indivisible person. One cannot separate Jesus from the Christ or speak of a "Jesus of history" who would differ from the "Christ of faith." The Church acknowledges and confesses Jesus as "the Christ, the Son of the living God" (Mt 16:16); Christ is none other than Jesus of Nazareth; he is the Word of God made man for the salvation of all. In Christ "the whole fullness of deity dwells bodily" (Col 2:9) and "from his fullness have we all received" (Jn 1:16). The "only Son, who is in the bosom of the Father" (Jn 1:18) is "the beloved Son, in whom we have redemption. . . . For in him all the fullness of God was pleased to dwell, and through him to reconcile to himself all things, whether on earth or in heaven, making peace by the blood of his Cross" (Col 1:13-14, 19-20). It is precisely this uniqueness of Christ which gives him an absolute and universal significance, whereby, while belonging to history, he remains history's center and goal (GS 2): "I am the Alpha and the Omega, the first and the last, the beginning and the end" (Rev 22:13).

Thus, although it is legitimate and helpful to consider the various aspects of the mystery of Christ, we must never lose sight of its unity. In the process of discovering and appreciating the manifold gifts — especially the spiritual treasures — that God has bestowed on every people, we cannot separate those gifts from Jesus Christ, who is at the center of God's plan of salvation. Just as "by his incarnation the Son of God united himself in some sense with every human being," so too "we are obliged to hold that the Holy Spirit offers everyone the possibility of sharing in the Paschal Mystery in a manner known to God" (GS 22). God's plan is "to unite all things in Christ, things in heaven and things on earth" (Eph 1:10).

Faith in Christ is Directed to Man's Freedom

7. The urgency of missionary activity derives from the *radical newness of life* brought by Christ and lived by his followers. This new life is a gift from God, and people are asked to accept and develop it, if they wish to realize the fullness of their vocation in conformity to Christ. The whole New Testament is a hymn to the new life of those who believe in Christ and live in his Church. Salvation in Christ, as witnessed to and proclaimed by the Church, is God's self-communication: "It is love which not only creates the good, but also grants participation in the very life of God: Father, Son and Holy Spirit. For he who loves desires to give himself" (DM 7).

God offers mankind this newness of life. "Can one reject Christ and everything that he has brought about in the history of mankind? Of course one can. Man is free. He can say 'no' to God. He can say 'no' to Christ. But the fundamental question remains: Is it legitimate to do this? And what would make it legitimate?"[4]

8. In the modern world there is a tendency to reduce man to his horizontal dimension alone. But without an openness to the Absolute, what does man become? The answer to this question is found in the experience of every individual, but it is also written in the history of humanity with the blood shed in the name of ideologies or by political regimes which have sought to build a "new humanity" without God (MM IV).

Moreover, the Second Vatican Council replies to those concerned with safeguarding freedom of conscience: "the human person has a right to religious freedom . . . all should have such immunity from coercion by individuals, or by groups, or by any human power, that no one should be forced to act against his conscience in religious matters, nor prevented from acting according to his conscience, whether in private or in public, whether alone or in association with others, within due limits" (DH 2).

Proclaiming Christ and bearing witness to him, when done in a way that respects consciences, does not violate freedom. Faith demands a free adherence on the part of man, but at the same time faith must also be offered to him, because the "multitudes have the right to know the riches of the mystery of Christ — riches in which we believe that the whole of humanity can find, in unsuspected fullness, everything that it is gropingly searching for concerning God, man and his destiny, life and death, and truth. . . . This is why the Church keeps her missionary spirit alive, and even wishes to intensify it in the moment of history in which we are living" (EN 53). But it must also be stated, again with the Council, that "in accordance with their dignity as persons, equipped with reason and free will and endowed with personal responsibility, all are impelled by their own nature and are bound by a moral obligation to seek truth, above all religious truth. They are further bound to hold to the truth once it is known, and to regulate their whole lives by its demands" (DH 2).

The Church as Sign and Instrument of Salvation

9. The first beneficiary of salvation is the Church. Christ won the Church for himself at the price of his own blood and made the Church his co-worker in the salvation of the world. Indeed, Christ dwells within the Church. She is his Bride. It is he who causes her to grow. He carries out his mission through her.

The Council makes frequent reference to the Church's role in the salvation of mankind. While acknowledging that God loves all people and grants them the possibility of being saved (cf. 1 Tim 2-4; LG 14-17; AG 3), the Church believes that God has established Christ as the one mediator and that she herself has been established

---

4. Homily for celebration of the Eucharist in Krakow (10 June 1979); *AAS* 72 (1979) 1202.

as the universal sacrament of salvation (LG 48; GS 43; AG 7, 21). "To this catholic unity of the people of God, therefore . . . all are called, and they belong to it or are ordered to it in various ways, whether they be Catholic faithful or others who believe in Christ or finally all people everywhere who by the grace of God are called to salvation" (LG 13). It is necessary to keep these two truths together, namely, the real possibility of salvation in Christ for all mankind and the necessity of the Church for salvation. Both these truths help us to understand the *one mystery of salvation,* so that we can come to know God's mercy and our own responsibility. Salvation, which always remains a gift of the Spirit, requires man's cooperation, both to save himself and to save others. This is God's will, and this is why he established the Church and made her a part of his plan of salvation. Referring to "this messianic people," the Council says: "It has been set up by Christ as a communion of life, love and truth; by him too it is taken up as the instrument of salvation for all and sent on a mission to the whole world as the light of the world and the salt of the earth" (LG 9).

Salvation in Christ is Offered to All

10. The universality of salvation means that it is granted not only to those who explicitly believe in Christ and have entered the Church. Since salvation is offered to all, it must be made concretely available to all. But it is clear that today, as in the past, many people do not have an opportunity to come to know or accept the Gospel revelation or to enter the Church. The social and cultural conditions in which they live do not permit this, and frequently they have been brought up in other religious traditions. For such people salvation in Christ is accessible by virtue of a grace which, while having a mysterious relationship to the Church, does not make them formally part of the Church but enlightens them in a way which is accommodated to their spiritual and material situation. This grace comes from Christ; it is the result of his Sacrifice and is communicated by the Holy Spirit. It enables each person to attain salvation through his or her free cooperation.

For this reason the Council, after affirming the centrality of the Paschal Mystery, went on to declare that "this applies not only to Christians but to all people of good will in whose hearts grace is secretly at work. Since Christ died for everyone, and since the ultimate calling of each of us comes from God and is therefore a universal one, we are obliged to hold that the Holy Spirit offers everyone the possibility of sharing in this Paschal Mystery in a manner known to God" (GS 22).

"We cannot but speak" (Acts 4:20)

11. What then should be said of the objections already mentioned regarding the mission *ad gentes*? While respecting the beliefs and sensitivities of all, we must first clearly affirm our faith in Christ, the one Savior of mankind, a faith we have received as a gift from on high, not as a result of any merit of our own. We say with Paul, "I am not ashamed of the Gospel: it is the power of God for salvation to every one who has faith" (Rom 1:16). Christian martyrs of all times — including our own — have given and continue to give their lives in order to bear witness to this faith, in the conviction that every human being needs Jesus Christ, who has conquered sin and death and reconciled mankind to God.

Confirming his words by miracles and by his Resurrection from the dead, Christ proclaimed himself to be the Son of God dwelling in intimate union with the Father, and was recognized as such by his disciples. The Church offers mankind the Gospel, that prophetic message which responds to the needs and aspirations of the human heart and always remains "Good News." The Church cannot fail to proclaim that

Jesus came to reveal the face of God and to merit salvation for all mankind by his Cross and Resurrection.

To the question, *"why mission?"*, we reply with the Church's faith and experience that true liberation consists in opening oneself to the love of Christ. In him, and only in him, are we set free from all alienation and doubt, from slavery to the power of sin and death. Christ is truly "our peace" (Eph 2:14); "the love of Christ impels us" (2 Cor 5:14), giving meaning and joy to our life. *Mission is an issue of faith*, an accurate indicator of our faith in Christ and his love for us.

The temptation today is to reduce Christianity to merely human wisdom, a pseudo-science of well-being. In our heavily secularized world a "gradual secularization of salvation" has taken place, so that people strive for the good of man, but man who is truncated, reduced to his merely horizontal dimension. We know, however, that Jesus came to bring integral salvation, one which embraces the whole person and all mankind, and opens up the wondrous prospect of divine filiation. *Why mission?* Because to us, as to Saint Paul, "this grace was given, to preach to the Gentiles the unsearchable riches of Christ" (Eph 3:8). Newness of life in him is the "Good News" for men and women of every age: all are called to it and destined for it. Indeed, all people are searching for it, albeit at times in a confused way, and have a right to know the value of this gift and to approach it freely. The Church, and every individual Christian within her, may not keep hidden or monopolize this newness and richness which has been received from God's bounty in order to be communicated to all mankind.

This is why the Church's mission derives not only from the Lord's mandate but also from the profound demands of God's life within us. Those who are incorporated in the Catholic Church ought to sense their privilege and for that very reason their greater obligation of *bearing witness to the faith and to the Christian life* as a service to their brothers and sisters and as a fitting response to God. They should be ever mindful that "they owe their distinguished status not to their own merits but to Christ's special grace; and if they fail to respond to this grace in thought, word and deed, not only will they not be saved, they will be judged more severely" (LG 14).

CHAPTER II

THE KINGDOM OF GOD

12. "It is 'God, who is rich in mercy' whom Jesus Christ has revealed to us as Father: it is his very Son who, in himself, has manifested him and made him known to us" (DM 1). I wrote this at the beginning of my Encyclical *Dives in Misericordia,* to show that Christ is the revelation and incarnation of the Father's mercy. Salvation consists in believing and accepting the mystery of the Father and of his love, made manifest and freely given in Jesus through the Spirit. In this way the Kingdom of God comes to be fulfilled: the Kingdom prepared for in the Old Testament, brought about by Christ and in Christ, and proclaimed to all peoples by the Church, which works and prays for its perfect and definitive realization.

The Old Testament attests that God chose and formed a people for himself, in order to reveal and carry out his loving plan. But at the same time God is the Creator and Father of all people; he cares and provides for them, extending his blessing to all (cf. Gen 12:3); he has established a covenant with all of them (cf. Gen 9:1-17). Israel experiences a personal and saving God (cf. Dt 4:37; 7:6-8; Is 43:1-7) and becomes his witness and interpreter among the nations. In the course of her history, Israel comes to realize that her election has a universal meaning (cf. for example Is 2:2-5; 25:6-8; 60:1-6; Jer 3:17; 16:19).

Christ Makes the Kingdom Present

13. Jesus of Nazareth brings God's plan to fulfillment. After receiving the Holy Spirit at his Baptism, Jesus makes clear his messianic calling: he goes about Galilee "preaching the Gospel of God and saying: 'The time is fulfilled, and the Kingdom of God is at hand; repent and believe in the Gospel'" (Mk 1:14-15; cf. Mt 4:17; Lk 4:43). The proclamation and establishment of God's Kingdom are the purpose of his mission: "I was sent for this purpose" (Lk 4:43). But that is not all. Jesus himself is the "Good News," as he declares at the very beginning of his mission in the synagogue at Nazareth, when he applies to himself the words of Isaiah about the Anointed One sent by the Spirit of the Lord (cf. Lk 4:14-21). Since the "Good News" is Christ, there is an identity between the message and the messenger, between saying, doing and being. His power, the secret of the effectiveness of his actions, lies in his total identification with the message he announces: he proclaims the "Good News" not just by what he says or does, but by what he is.

The ministry of Jesus is described in the context of his journeys within his homeland. Before Easter, the scope of his mission was focused on Israel. Nevertheless, Jesus offers a new element of extreme importance. The eschatological reality is not relegated to a remote "end of the world," but is already close and at work in our midst. The Kingdom of God is at hand (cf. Mk 1:15); its coming is to be prayed for (cf. Mt 6:10); faith can glimpse it already at work in signs such as miracles (cf. Mt 11:4-5) and exorcisms (cf. Mt 12:25-28), in the choosing of the Twelve (cf. Mk 3:13-19), and in the proclamation of the Good News to the poor (cf. Lk 4:18). Jesus's encounters with Gentiles make it clear that entry into the Kingdom comes through faith and conversion (cf. Mk 1:15), and not merely by reason of ethnic background.

The Kingdom which Jesus inaugurates is the Kingdom of God. Jesus himself reveals who this God is, the One whom he addresses by the intimate term "Abba," Father (cf. Mk 14:36). God, as revealed above all in the parables (cf. Lk 15:3-32; Mt 20:1-16), is sensitive to the needs and sufferings of every human being: he is a Father filled with love and compassion, who grants forgiveness and freely bestows the favors asked of him.

Saint John tells us that "God is love" (1 Jn 4:8, 16). Every person therefore is invited to "repent" and to "believe" in God's merciful love. The Kingdom will grow insofar as every person learns to turn to God in the intimacy of prayer as to a Father (cf. Lk 11:2; Mt 23:9) and strives to do his will (cf. Mt 7:21).

Characteristics of the Kingdom and Its Demands

14. Jesus gradually reveals the characteristics and demands of the Kingdom through his words, his actions and his own person.

The Kingdom of God is meant for all mankind, and all people are called to become members of it. To emphasize this fact, Jesus drew especially near to those on the margins of society, and showed them special favor in announcing the Good News. At the beginning of his ministry he proclaimed that he was "anointed . . . to preach good news to the poor" (Lk 4:18). To all who are victims of rejection and contempt Jesus declares: "Blessed are you poor" (Lk 6:20). What is more, he enables such individuals to experience liberation even now, by being close to them, going to eat in their homes (cf. Lk 5:30; 15:2), treating them as equals and friends (cf. Lk 7:34), and making them feel loved by God, thus revealing his tender care for the needy and for sinners (cf. Lk 15:1-32).

The liberation and salvation brought by the Kingdom of God come to the human person both in his physical and spiritual dimensions. Two gestures are characteristic of Jesus's mission: healing and forgiving. Jesus's many healings clearly show his great compassion in the face of human distress, but they also signify that in the Kingdom there will no longer be sickness or suffering, and that his mission, from the very beginning, is meant to free people from these evils. In Jesus's eyes, healings are also a sign of spiritual salvation, namely liberation from sin. By performing acts of healing, he invites people to faith, conversion and the desire for forgiveness (cf. Lk 5:24). Once there is faith, healing is an encouragement to go further: it leads to salvation (cf. Lk 18:42-43). The acts of liberation from demonic possession — that supreme evil and symbol of sin and rebellion against God — are signs that indeed "the Kingdom of God has come upon you" (Mt 12:28).

15. The Kingdom aims at transforming human relationships; it grows gradually as people slowly learn to love, forgive and serve one another. Jesus sums up the whole Law, focusing it on the commandment of love (cf. Mt 22:34-40; Lk 10:25-28). Before leaving his disciples, he gives them a "new commandment": "Love one another; even as I have loved you" (Jn 13:34; cf. 15:12). Jesus's love for the world finds its highest expression in the gift of his life for mankind (cf. Jn 15:13), which manifests the love which the Father has for the world (cf. Jn 3:16). The Kingdom's nature, therefore, is one of communion among all human beings — with one another and with God.

The Kingdom is the concern of everyone: individuals, society, and the world. Working for the Kingdom means acknowledging and promoting God's activity, which is present in human history and transforms it. Building the Kingdom means working for liberation from evil in all its forms. In a word, the Kingdom of God is the manifestation and the realization of God's plan of salvation in all its fullness.

In the Risen Christ God's Kingdom is Fulfilled and Proclaimed

16. By raising Jesus from the dead, God has conquered death, and in Jesus he has definitively inaugurated his Kingdom. During his earthly life, Jesus was the Prophet of the Kingdom; after his Passion, Resurrection and Ascension into heaven he shares in God's power and in his dominion over the world (cf. Mt 28:18; Acts 2:36; Eph 1:18-21). The Resurrection gives a universal scope to Christ's message, his actions and whole mission. The disciples recognize that the Kingdom is already present in the person of Jesus and is slowly being established within man and the world through a mysterious connection with him.

Indeed, after the Resurrection, the disciples preach the Kingdom by proclaiming Jesus Crucified and Risen from the dead. In Samaria, Philip "preached good news about the Kingdom of God and the name of Jesus Christ" (Acts 8:12). In Rome, we find Paul "preaching the Kingdom of God and teaching about the Lord Jesus Christ" (Acts 28:31). The first Christians also proclaim "the Kingdom of Christ and of God" (Eph 5:5; cf. Rev 11:15; 12:10), or "the Kingdom of our Lord and Savior Jesus Christ" (2 Pt 1:11). The preaching of the early Church was centered on the proclamation of Jesus Christ, with whom the Kingdom was identified. Now, as then, there is a need to unite *the proclamation of the Kingdom of God* (the content of Jesus's own "kerygma") and *the proclamation of the Christ-event* (the "kerygma" of the Apostles). The two proclamations are complementary; each throws light on the other.

The Kingdom in Relation to Christ and the Church

17. Nowadays the Kingdom is much spoken of, but not always in a way consonant with the thinking of the Church. In fact, there are ideas about salvation and mission which can be called "anthropocentric" in the reductive sense of the word, inasmuch as they are focused on man's earthly needs. In this view, the Kingdom tends to become something completely human and secularized; what counts are

programs and struggles for a liberation which is socioeconomic, political and even cultural, but within a horizon that is closed to the transcendent. Without denying that on this level too there are values to be promoted, such a notion nevertheless remains within the confines of a kingdom of man, deprived of its authentic and profound dimensions. Such a view easily translates into one more ideology of purely earthly progress. The Kingdom of God, however, "is not of this world . . . is not from the world" (Jn 18:36).

There are also conceptions which deliberately emphasize the Kingdom and which describe themselves as "Kingdom-centered." They stress the image of a Church which is not concerned about herself, but which is totally concerned with bearing witness to and serving the Kingdom. It is a "Church for others" just as Christ is the "man for others." The Church's task is described as though it had to proceed in two directions: on the one hand promoting such "values of the Kingdom" as peace, justice, freedom, brotherhood, etc., while on the other hand fostering dialogue between peoples, cultures and religions, so that through a mutual enrichment they might help the world to be renewed and to journey ever closer toward the Kingdom.

Together with positive aspects, these conceptions often reveal negative aspects as well. First, they are silent about Christ: the Kingdom of which they speak is "theocentrically" based, since, according to them, Christ cannot be understood by those who lack Christian faith, whereas different peoples, cultures and religions are capable of finding common ground in the one divine reality, by whatever name it is called. For the same reason they put great stress on the mystery of creation, which is reflected in the diversity of cultures and beliefs, but they keep silent about the mystery of redemption. Furthermore, *the* Kingdom, as they understand it, ends up either leaving very little room for the Church or undervaluing the Church in reaction to a presumed "ecclesiocentrism" of the past, and because they consider the Church herself only a sign, for that matter a sign not without ambiguity.

18. This is not the Kingdom of God as we know it from Revelation. The Kingdom cannot be detached either from Christ or from the Church.

As has already been said, Christ not only proclaimed the Kingdom, but in him the Kingdom itself became present and was fulfilled. This happened not only through his words and his deeds: "Above all . . . the Kingdom is made manifest in the very person of Christ, Son of God and Son of Man, who came 'to serve and to give his life as a ransom for many' " (Mk 10:45; LG 5). The Kingdom of God is not a concept, a doctrine, or a program subject to free interpretation, but is before all else a *person* with the face and name of Jesus of Nazareth, the image of the invisible God (GS 22). If the Kingdom is separated from Jesus, it is no longer the Kingdom of God which he revealed. The result is a distortion of the meaning of the Kingdom, which runs the risk of being transformed into a purely human or ideological goal, and a distortion of the identity of Christ, who no longer appears as the Lord to whom everything must one day be subjected (cf. 1 Cor 15:27).

Likewise, one may not separate the Kingdom from the Church. It is true that the Church is not an end unto herself, since she is ordered toward the Kingdom of God of which she is the seed, sign and instrument. Yet, while remaining distinct from Christ and the Kingdom, the Church is indissolubly united to both. Christ endowed the Church, his Body, with the fullness of the benefits and means of salvation. The Holy Spirit dwells in her, enlivens her with his gifts and charisms, sanctifies, guides and constantly renews her (LG 4). The result is a unique and special relationship which, while not excluding the action of Christ and the Spirit outside the Church's visible boundaries, confers upon her a specific and necessary role; hence the Church's special connection with the Kingdom of God and of Christ, which she has "the mission of announcing and inaugurating among all peoples" (LG 5).

19. It is within this overall perspective that the reality of the Kingdom is understood. Certainly, the Kingdom demands the promotion of human values, as well as those which can properly be called "evangelical," since they are intimately bound up with the "Good News." But this sort of promotion, which is at the heart of the Church, must not be detached from or opposed to other fundamental tasks, such as proclaiming Christ and his Gospel, and establishing and building up communities which make present and active within mankind the living image of the Kingdom. One need not fear falling thereby into a form of "ecclesiocentrism." Pope Paul VI, who affirmed the existence of "a profound link between Christ, the Church and evangelization" (EN 15), also said that the Church "is not an end unto herself, but rather is fervently concerned to be completely of Christ, in Christ and for Christ, as well as completely of men, among men and for men." [5]

The Church at the Service of the Kingdom

20. The Church is effectively and concretely at the service of the Kingdom. This is seen especially in her preaching, which is a call to conversion. Preaching constitutes the Church's first and fundamental way of serving the coming of the Kingdom in individuals and in human society. Eschatological salvation begins even now in newness of life in Christ: "To all who believed in him, who believed in his name, he gave power to become children of God" (Jn 1:12).

The Church, then, serves the Kingdom by establishing communities and founding new particular Churches, and by guiding them to mature faith and charity in openness toward others, in service to individuals and society, and in understanding and esteem for human institutions.

The Church serves the Kingdom by spreading throughout the world the "Gospel values" which are an expression of the Kingdom and which help people to accept God's plan. It is true that the inchoate reality of the Kingdom can also be found beyond the confines of the Church among peoples everywhere, to the extent that they live "Gospel values" and are open to the working of the Spirit who breathes when and where he wills (cf. Jn 3:8). But it must immediately be added that this temporal dimension of the Kingdom remains incomplete unless it is related to the Kingdom of Christ present in the Church and straining toward eschatological fullness (EN 34).

The many dimensions of the Kingdom of God [6] do not weaken the foundations and purposes of missionary activity, but rather strengthen and extend them. The Church is the sacrament of salvation for all mankind, and her activity is not limited only to those who accept her message. She is a dynamic force in mankind's journey toward the eschatological Kingdom, and is the sign and promoter of Gospel values (GS 39). The Church contributes to mankind's pilgrimage of conversion to God's plan through her witness and through such activities as dialogue, human promotion, commitment to justice and peace, education and the care of the sick, and aid to the poor and to children. In carrying on these activities, however, she never loses sight of the priority of the transcendent and spiritual realities which are premises of eschatological salvation.

Finally, the Church serves the Kingdom by her intercession, since the Kingdom by its very nature is God's gift and work, as we are reminded by the Gospel parables

---

5. Address at the opening of the Third Session of the Second Vatican Council (14 September 1964), *AAS* 56 (1964) 810.

6. Cf. International Theological Commission, *Select Themes of Ecclesiology on the Occasion of the Twentieth Anniversary of The Closing of the Second Vatican Council* (7 October 1985) 10, "The Eschatological Character of the Church: Kingdom and Church."

and by the prayer which Jesus taught us. We must ask for the Kingdom, welcome it and make it grow within us; but we must also work together so that it will be welcomed and will grow among all people, until the time when Christ "delivers the Kingdom to God the Father" and "God will be everything to every one" (cf. 1 Cor 15:24, 28).

CHAPTER III

THE HOLY SPIRIT,
THE PRINCIPAL AGENT OF MISSION

21. "At the climax of Jesus's messianic mission, the Holy Spirit becomes present in the Paschal Mystery in all of his divine subjectivity: as the one who is now to continue the salvific work rooted in the sacrifice of the Cross. Of course Jesus entrusts this work to human beings: to the Apostles, to the Church. Nevertheless, in and through them the Holy Spirit remains the transcendent and principal agent for the accomplishment of this work in the human spirit and in the history of the world" (DEV 42).

The Holy Spirit is indeed the principal agent of the whole of the Church's mission. His action is preeminent in the mission *ad gentes,* as can clearly be seen in the early Church: in the conversion of Cornelius (cf. Acts 10), in the decisions made about emerging problems (cf. Acts 15) and in the choice of regions and peoples to be evangelized (cf. Acts 16:6ff.). The Spirit worked through the Apostles, but at the same time he was also at work in those who heard them: "Through his action the Good News takes shape in human minds and hearts and extends through history. In all of this it is the Holy Spirit who gives life" (DEV 64).

Sent Forth "to the end of the earth" (Acts 1:8)

22. All the Evangelists, when they describe the Risen Christ's meeting with his Apostles, conclude with the "missionary mandate": "All authority in heaven and on earth has been given to me. Go therefore and make disciples of all nations . . . and lo, I am with you always, to the close of the age" (Mt 28:18-20; cf. Mk 16:15-18; Lk 24:46-49; Jn 20:21-23). This is *a sending forth in the Spirit,* as is clearly apparent in the Gospel of John: Christ sends his own into the world, just as the Father has sent him, and to this end he gives them the Spirit. Luke, for his part, closely links the witness the Apostles are to give to Christ with the working of the Spirit, who will enable them to fulfill the mandate they have received.

23. The different versions of the "missionary mandate" contain common elements as well as characteristics proper to each. Two elements, however, are found in all the versions. First, there is the universal dimension of the task entrusted to the Apostles, who are sent to "all nations" (Mt 28:19); "into all the world and . . . to the whole creation" (Mk 16:15); to "all nations" (Lk 24:47); "to the end of the earth" (Acts 1:8). Secondly, there is the assurance given to the Apostles by the Lord that they will not be alone in this task, but will receive the strength and the means necessary to carry out their mission. The reference here is to the presence and power of the Spirit and the help of Jesus himself: "And they went forth and preached everywhere, while the Lord worked with them" (Mk 16:20).

As for the different emphases found in each version, Mark presents mission as proclamation or kerygma: "Preach the Gospel" (Mk 16:15). His aim is to lead his readers to repeat Peter's profession of faith: "You are the Christ" (Mk 8:29), and to say with the Roman centurion who stood before the body of Jesus on the Cross: "Truly this man was the Son of God!" (Mk 15:39). In Matthew, the missionary emphasis is placed on the foundation of the Church and on her teaching (cf. Mt 28:19-20; 16:18). According to him, the mandate shows that the proclamation of the Gospel must be completed by a specific ecclesial and sacramental catechesis. In Luke, mission is presented as witness (cf. Lk 24:48; Acts 1:8), centered especially on the Resurrection (cf. Acts 1:22). The missionary is invited to believe in the transforming power of the Gospel and to proclaim what Luke presents so well, that is, conversion to God's love and mercy, the experience of a complete liberation which goes to the root of all evil, namely sin.

John is the only Evangelist to speak explicitly of a "mandate," a word equivalent to "mission." He directly links the mission which Jesus entrusts to his disciples with the mission which he himself has received from the Father: "As the Father has sent me, even so I send you" (Jn 20:21). Addressing the Father, Jesus says: "As you sent me into the world, so I have sent them into the world" (Jn 17:18). The entire missionary sense of John's Gospel is expressed in the "priestly prayer": "This is eternal life, that they know you the only true God, and Jesus Christ whom you have sent" (Jn 17:3). The ultimate purpose of mission is to enable people to share in the communion which exists between the Father and the Son. The disciples are to live in unity with one another, remaining in the Father and the Son, so that the world may know and believe (cf. Jn 17:21-23). This is a very important missionary text. It makes us understand that we are missionaries above all because of *what we are* as a Church whose innermost life is unity in love, even before we become missionaries *in word or deed.*

The four Gospels therefore bear witness to a certain pluralism within the fundamental unity of the same mission, a pluralism which reflects different experiences and situations within the first Christian communities. It is also the result of the driving force of the Spirit himself: it encourages us to pay heed to the variety of missionary charisms and to the diversity of circumstances and peoples. Nevertheless, all the Evangelists stress that the mission of the disciples is to cooperate in the mission of Christ: "Lo, I am with you always, to the close of the age" (Mt 28:20). Mission, then, is based not on human abilities but on the power of the Risen Lord.

The Spirit Directs the Church's Mission

24. The mission of the Church, like that of Jesus, is God's work or, as Luke often puts it, the work of the Spirit. After the Resurrection and Ascension of Jesus, the Apostles have a powerful experience which completely transforms them: the experience of Pentecost. The coming of the Holy Spirit makes them *witnesses* and *prophets* (cf. Acts 1:8; 2:17-18). It fills them with a serene courage which impels them to pass on to others their experience of Jesus and the hope which motivates them. The Spirit gives them the ability to bear witness to Jesus with "boldness." [7]

When the first evangelizers go down from Jerusalem, the Spirit becomes even more of a "guide," helping them to choose both those to whom they are to go and the places to which their missionary journey is to take them. The working of the Spirit is manifested particularly in the impetus given to the mission which, in accordance with Christ's words, spreads out from Jerusalem to all of Judea and Samaria, and to the farthest ends of the earth.

The Acts of the Apostles records six summaries of the "missionary discourses"

---

7. The Greek word *parrhesia* also means enthusiasm or energy; cf. Acts 2:29; 4:13, 29, 31; 9:27-28; 13:46; 14:3; 18:26; 19:8, 26; 28:31.

which were addressed to the Jews during the Church's infancy (cf. Acts 2:22-39; 3:12-26; 4:9-12; 5:29-32; 10:34-43; 13:16-41). These model speeches, delivered by Peter and by Paul, proclaim Jesus and invite those listening to "be converted," that is, to accept Jesus in faith and to let themselves be transformed in him by the Spirit.

Paul and Barnabas are impelled by the Spirit to go to the Gentiles (cf. Acts 13:46-48), a development not without certain tensions and problems. How are these converted Gentiles to live their faith in Jesus? Are they bound by the traditions of Judaism and the law of circumcision? At the first Council, which gathers the members of the different Churches together with the Apostles in Jerusalem, a decision is taken which is acknowledged as coming from the Spirit: it is not necessary for a Gentile to submit to the Jewish Law in order to become a Christian (cf. Acts 15:5-11, 28). From now on the Church opens her doors and becomes the house which all may enter, and in which all can feel at home, while keeping their own culture and traditions, provided that these are not contrary to the Gospel.

25. The missionaries continued along this path, taking into account people's hopes and expectations, their anguish and sufferings, as well as their culture, in order to proclaim to them salvation in Christ. The speeches in Lystra and Athens (cf. Acts 14:15-17; 17:22-31) are acknowledged as models for the evangelization of the Gentiles. In these speeches Paul enters into "dialogue" with the cultural and religious values of different peoples. To the Lycaonians, who practiced a cosmic religion, he speaks of religious experiences related to the cosmos. With the Greeks he discusses philosophy and quotes their own poets (cf. Acts 17:18, 26-28). The God whom Paul wishes to reveal is already present in their lives; indeed, this God has created them and mysteriously guides nations and history. But if they are to recognize the true God, they must abandon the false gods which they themselves have made and open themselves to the One whom God has sent to remedy their ignorance and satisfy the longings of their hearts. These are speeches which offer an example of the inculturation of the Gospel.

Under the impulse of the Spirit, the Christian faith is decisively opened to the "nations." Witness to Christ spreads to the most important centers of the eastern Mediterranean and then to Rome and the far regions of the West. It is the Spirit who is the source of the drive to press on, not only geographically but also beyond the frontiers of race and religion, for a truly universal mission.

The Holy Spirit Makes the Whole Church Missionary

26. The Spirit leads the company of believers to "form a community," to be the Church. After Peter's first proclamation on the day of Pentecost and the conversions that followed, the first community takes shape (cf. Acts 2:42-47; 4:32-35).

One of the central purposes of mission is to bring people together in hearing the Gospel, in fraternal communion, in prayer and in the Eucharist. To live in "fraternal communion" (*koinonia*) means to be "of one heart and soul" (Acts 4:32), establishing fellowship from every point of view: human, spiritual and material. Indeed, a true Christian community is also committed to distributing earthly goods, so that no one is in want, and all can receive such goods "as they need" (cf. Acts 2:45; 4:5). The first communities, made up of "glad and generous hearts" (Acts 2:46), were open and missionary: they enjoyed "favor with all the people" (Acts 2:47). Even before activity, mission means witness and a way of life that shines out to others (EN 41-42).

27. The Acts of the Apostles indicates that the mission which was directed first to Israel and then to the Gentiles develops on many levels. First and foremost, there

is the group of the Twelve which as a single body, led by Peter, proclaims the Good News. Then there is the community of believers, which in its way of life and its activity bears witness to the Lord and converts the Gentiles (cf. Acts 2:46-47). Then there are the special envoys sent out to proclaim the Gospel. Thus the Christian community at Antioch sends its members forth on mission; having fasted, prayed and celebrated the Eucharist, the community recognizes that the Spirit has chosen Paul and Barnabas to be "sent forth" (cf. Acts 13:1-4). In its origins, then, mission is seen as a community commitment, a responsibility of the local Church, which needs "missionaries" in order to push forward toward new frontiers. Side by side with those who had been sent forth, there were also others, who bore spontaneous witness to the newness which had transformed their lives, and who subsequently provided a link between the emerging communities and the Apostolic Church.

Reading the Acts of Apostles helps us to realize that at the beginning of the Church the mission *ad gentes,* while it had missionaries dedicated "for life" by a special vocation, was in fact considered the normal outcome of Christian living, to which every believer was committed through the witness of personal conduct and through explicit proclamation whenever possible.

The Spirit is Present and Active in Every Time and Place

28.   The Spirit manifests himself in a special way in the Church and in her members. Nevertheless, his presence and activity are universal, limited neither by space nor time (DEV 53). The Second Vatican Council recalls that the Spirit is at work in the heart of every person, through the "seeds of the Word," to be found in human initiatives — including religious ones — and in man's efforts to attain truth, goodness and God himself (AG 3, 11, 15; GS 10-11, 22, 26, 38, 41, 92-93).

The Spirit offers the human race "the light and strength to respond to its highest calling"; through the Spirit, "mankind attains in faith to the contemplation and savoring of the mystery of God's design"; indeed, "we are obliged to hold that the Holy Spirit offers everyone the possibility of sharing in the Paschal Mystery in a manner known to God" (GS 10, 15, 22). The Church "is aware that humanity is being continually stirred by the Spirit of God and can therefore never be completely indifferent to the problems of religion" and that "people will always . . . want to know what meaning to give to their life, their activity and their death" (DEV 54). The Spirit, therefore, is at the very source of man's existential and religious questioning, a questioning which is occasioned not only by contingent situations but by the very structure of his being (DEV 54).

The Spirit's presence and activity affect not only individuals but also society and history, peoples, cultures and religions. Indeed, the Spirit is at the origin of the noble ideals and undertakings which benefit humanity on its journey through history: "The Spirit of God with marvelous foresight directs the course of the ages and renews the face of the earth" (GS 26). The Risen Christ "is now at work in human hearts through the strength of his Spirit, not only instilling a desire for the world to come but also thereby animating, purifying and reinforcing the noble aspirations which drive the human family to make its life one that is more human and to direct the whole earth to this end" (GS 38). Again, it is the Spirit who sows the "seeds of the Word" present in various customs and cultures, preparing them for full maturity in Christ (LG 17; AG 3, 15).

29.   Thus the Spirit, who "blows where he wills" (cf. Jn 3:8), who "was already at work in the world before Christ was glorified" (AG 4), and who "has filled the world, . . . holds all things together (and) knows what is said" (Wis 1:7), leads us to

broaden our vision in order to ponder his activity in every time and place (DEV 53). I have repeatedly called this fact to mind, and it has guided me in my meetings with a wide variety of peoples. The Church's relationship with other religions is dictated by a twofold respect: "Respect for man in his quest for answers to the deepest questions of his life, and respect for the action of the Spirit in man." [8] Excluding any mistaken interpretation, the interreligious meeting held in Assisi was meant to confirm my conviction that "every authentic prayer is prompted by the Holy Spirit, who is mysteriously present in every human heart." [9]

This is the same Spirit who was at work in the Incarnation and in the life, death and Resurrection of Jesus, and who is at work in the Church. He is therefore not an alternative to Christ, nor does he fill a sort of void which is sometimes suggested as existing between Christ and the Logos. Whatever the Spirit brings about in human hearts and in the history of peoples, in cultures and religions serves as a preparation for the Gospel (LG 16) and can only be understood in reference to Christ, the Word who took flesh by the power of the Spirit "so that as perfectly human he would save all human beings and sum up all things" (GS 45; DEV 54).

Moreover, the universal activity of the Spirit is not to be separated from his particular activity within the Body of Christ, which is the Church. Indeed, it is always the Spirit who is at work, both when he gives life to the Church and impels her to proclaim Christ, and when he implants and develops his gifts in all individuals and peoples, guiding the Church to discover these gifts, to foster them and receive them through dialogue. Every form of the Spirit's presence is to be welcomed with respect and gratitude, but the discernment of this presence is the responsibility of the Church, to which Christ gave his Spirit in order to guide her into all the truth (cf. Jn 16:13).

Missionary Activity is Only Beginning

30. Our own time, with humanity on the move and in continual search, demands *a resurgence of the Church's missionary activity.* The horizons and possibilities for mission are growing ever wider, and we Christians are called to an apostolic courage based upon trust in the Spirit. *He is the principal agent of mission!*

The history of humanity has known many major turning points which have encouraged missionary outreach, and the Church, guided by the Spirit, has always responded to them with generosity and farsightedness. Results have not been lacking. Not long ago we celebrated the millennium of the evangelization of Rus' and the Slav peoples, and we are now preparing to celebrate the five hundredth anniversary of the evangelization of the Americas. Similarly, there have been recent commemorations of the centenaries of the first missions in various countries of Asia, Africa and Oceania. Today the Church must face other challenges and push forward to new frontiers, both in the initial mission *ad gentes* and in the new evangelization of those peoples who have already heard Christ proclaimed. Today all Christians, the particular Churches and the universal Church, are called to have the same courage that inspired the missionaries of the past, and the same readiness to listen to the voice of the Spirit.

---

8. Address to Representatives of Non-Christian Religions, Madras (5 February 1986), *AAS* 78 (1986) 767; Cf. *Message to the Peoples of Asia*, Manila (21 February 1981), 2-4, *AAS* 73 (1981) 392f.; Address to Representatives of Other Religions, Tokyo (24 February 1981), 3-4, *Insegnamenti*, IV/1 (1981), 507f.

9. Address to the Cardinals of the Roman Curia (22 December 1986) 11; *AAS* 79 (1987) 1089.

CHAPTER IV

THE VAST HORIZONS
OF THE MISSION *AD GENTES*

31. The Lord Jesus sent his Apostles to every person, people and place on earth. In the Apostles the Church received a universal mission — one which knows no boundaries — which involves the communication of salvation in its integrity according to that fullness of life which Christ came to bring (cf. Jn 10:10). The Church was "sent by Christ to reveal and communicate the love of God to all people and nations" (AG 10).

This mission is one and undivided, having one origin and one final purpose; but within it, there are different tasks and kinds of activity. First, there is the missionary activity which we call *mission ad gentes,* in reference to the opening words of the Council's Decree on this subject. This is one of the Church's fundamental activities: it is essential and never-ending. The Church, in fact, "cannot withdraw from her *permanent mission of bringing the Gospel* to the multitudes — the millions and millions of men and women — who as yet do not know Christ the Redeemer of humanity. In a specific way this is the missionary work which Jesus entrusted and still entrusts each day to his Church" (CL 35).

A Complex and Ever Changing Religious Picture

32. Today we face a religious situation which is extremely varied and changing. Peoples are on the move; social and religious realities which were once clear and well-defined are today increasingly complex. We need only think of certain phenomena such as urbanization, mass migration, the flood of refugees, the dechristianization of countries with ancient Christian traditions, the increasing influence of the Gospel and its values in overwhelmingly non-Christian countries, and the proliferation of messianic cults and religious sects. Religious and social upheaval makes it difficult to apply in practice certain ecclesial distinctions and categories to which we have become accustomed. Even before the Council it was said that some Christian cities and countries had become "mission territories"; the situation has certainly not improved in the years since then.

On the other hand, missionary work has been very fruitful throughout the world, so that there are now well-established Churches, sometimes so sound and mature that they are able to provide for the needs of their own communities and even send personnel to evangelize in other Churches and territories. This is in contrast to some traditionally Christian areas which are in need of re-evangelization. As a result, some are questioning whether it is still appropriate to speak of *specific missionary activity* or specifically "missionary" areas, or whether we should speak instead of *a single missionary situation*, with one single mission, the same everywhere. The difficulty of relating this complex and changing reality to the mandate of evangelization is apparent in the "language of mission." For example, there is a certain hesitation to use the terms "missions" and "missionaries," which are considered obsolete and as having negative historical connotations. People prefer to use instead the noun "mission" in the singular and the adjective "missionary" to describe all the Church's activities.

This uneasiness denotes a real change, one which has certain positive aspects. The so-called return or "repatriation" of the *missions* into the Church's mission, the insertion of *missiology* into ecclesiology, and the integration of both areas into the

Trinitarian plan of salvation, have given a fresh impetus to missionary activity itself, which is not considered a marginal task for the Church but is situated at the center of her life, as a fundamental commitment of the whole People of God. Nevertheless, care must be taken to avoid the risk of putting very different situations on the same level and of reducing, or even eliminating, the Church's mission and missionaries *ad gentes.* To say that the whole Church is missionary does not preclude the existence of a specific mission *ad gentes,* just as saying that all Catholics must be missionaries not only does not exclude, but actually requires that there be persons who have a specific vocation to be "life-long missionaries *ad gentes.*"

Mission "ad gentes" Retains Its Value

33. The fact that there is a diversity of activities *in the Church's one mission* is not intrinsic to that mission, but arises from the variety of circumstances in which that mission is carried out (AG 6). Looking at today's world from the viewpoint of evangelization, we can distinguish *three situations.*

First, there is the situation which the Church's missionary activity addresses: peoples, groups and sociocultural contexts in which Christ and his Gospel are not known, or which lack Christian communities sufficiently mature to be able to incarnate the faith in their own environment and proclaim it to other groups. This is mission *ad gentes* in the proper sense of the term (AG 6).

Secondly, there are Christian communities with adequate and solid ecclesial structures. They are fervent in their faith and in Christian living. They bear witness to the Gospel in their surroundings and have a sense of commitment to the universal mission. In these communities the Church carries out her activity and pastoral care.

Thirdly, there is an intermediate situation, particularly in countries with ancient Christian roots, and occasionally in the younger Churches as well, where entire groups of the baptized have lost a living sense of the faith, or even no longer consider themselves members of the Church, and live a life far removed from Christ and his Gospel. In this case what is needed is a "new evangelization" or a "re-evangelization."

34. Missionary activity proper, namely the mission *ad gentes,* is directed to "peoples or groups who do not yet believe in Christ," "who are far from Christ," in whom the Church "has not yet taken root" (AG 6, 23, 27) and whose culture has not yet been influenced by the Gospel (EN 18-20). It is distinct from other ecclesial activities inasmuch as it is addressed to groups and settings which are non-Christian because the preaching of the Gospel and the presence of the Church are either absent or insufficient. It can thus be characterized as the work of proclaiming Christ and his Gospel, building up the local Church and promoting the values of the Kingdom. The specific nature of this mission *ad gentes* consists in its being addressed to "non-Christians." It is therefore necessary to ensure that this specifically "missionary work that Jesus entrusted and still entrusts each day to his Church" (CL 35) does not become an indistinguishable part of the overall mission of the whole People of God and as a result become neglected or forgotten.

On the other hand, the boundaries between *pastoral care of the faithful, new evangelization* and *specific missionary activity* are not clearly definable, and it is unthinkable to create barriers between them or to put them into water-tight compartments. Nevertheless, there must be no lessening of the impetus to preach the Gospel and to establish new Churches among peoples or communities where they do not yet exist, for this is the first task of the Church, which has been sent forth to all peoples and to the very ends of the earth. Without the mission *ad gentes,* the Church's very missionary dimension would be deprived of its essential meaning and of the very activity that exemplifies it.

Also to be noted is the real and growing *interdependence* which exists between these various saving activities of the Church. Each of them influences, stimulates and assists the others. The missionary thrust fosters exchanges between the Churches and directs them toward the larger world, with positive influences in every direction. The Churches in traditionally Christian countries, for example, involved as they are in the challenging task of new evangelization, are coming to understand more clearly that they cannot be missionaries to non-Christians in other countries and continents unless they are seriously concerned about the non-Christians at home. Hence missionary activity *ad intra* is a credible sign and a stimulus for missionary activity *ad extra*, and vice versa.

To All Peoples, in spite of Difficulties

35. The mission *ad gentes* faces an enormous task, which is in no way disappearing. Indeed, both from the numerical standpoint of demographic increase and from the sociocultural standpoint of the appearance of new relationships, contacts and changing situations, the mission seems destined to have ever wider horizons. The task of proclaiming Jesus Christ to all peoples appears to be immense and out of all proportion to the Church's human resources.

The difficulties seem insurmountable and could easily lead to discouragement, if it were a question of a merely human enterprise. In certain countries missionaries are refused entry. In others, not only is evangelization forbidden but conversion as well, and even Christian worship. Elsewhere the obstacles are of a cultural nature: passing on the Gospel message seems irrelevant or incomprehensible, and conversion is seen as a rejection of one's own people and culture.

36. Nor are *difficulties* lacking *within* the People of God; indeed these difficulties are the most painful of all. As the first of these difficulties Pope Paul VI pointed to "the lack of fervor [which] is all the more serious because it comes from within. It is manifested in fatigue, disenchantment, compromise, lack of interest and above all lack of joy and hope" (EN 80). Other great obstacles to the Church's missionary work include past and present divisions among Christians (AG 6) de-christianization within Christian countries, the decrease of vocations to the apostolate, and the counter-witness of believers and Christian communities failing to follow the model of Christ in their lives. But one of the most serious reasons for the lack of interest in the missionary task is a widespread indifferentism, which, sad to say, is found also among Christians. It is based on incorrect theological perspectives and is characterized by a religious relativism which leads to the belief that "one religion is as good as another." We can add, using the words of Pope Paul VI, that there are also certain "excuses which would impede evangelization. The most insidious of these excuses are certainly the ones which people claim to find support for in such and such a teaching of the Council" (EN 80).

In this regard, I earnestly ask theologians and professional Christian journalists to intensify the service they render to the Church's mission in order to discover the deep meaning of their work, along the sure path of "thinking with the Church" (*sentire cum Ecclesia*).

Internal and external difficulties must not make us pessimistic or inactive. What counts, here as in every area of Christian life, is the confidence that comes from faith, from the certainty that it is not we who are the principal agents of the Church's mission, but Jesus Christ and his Spirit. We are only co-workers, and when we have done all that we can, we must say: "We are unworthy servants; we have only done what was our duty" (Lk 17:10).

Parameters of the Church's Mission "ad gentes"

37. By virtue of Christ's universal mandate, the mission *ad gentes* knows no boundaries. Still, it is possible to determine certain parameters within which that mission is exercised, in order to gain a real grasp of the situation.

(a) *Territorial limits*. Missionary activity has normally been defined in terms of specific territories. The Second Vatican Council acknowledged the territorial dimension of the mission *ad gentes* (AG 6), a dimension which even today remains important for determining responsibilities, competencies and the geographical limits of missionary activity. Certainly, a universal mission implies a universal perspective. Indeed, the Church refuses to allow her missionary presence to be hindered by geographical boundaries or political barriers. But it is also true that missionary activity *ad gentes*, being different from the pastoral care of the faithful and the new evangelization of the non-practicing, is exercised within well-defined territories and groups of people.

The growth in the number of new Churches in recent times should not deceive us. Within the territories entrusted to these Churches — particularly in Asia, but also in Africa, Latin America and Oceania — there remain vast regions still to be evangelized. In many nations entire peoples and cultural areas of great importance have not yet been reached by the proclamation of the Gospel and the presence of the local Church (AG 20). Even in traditionally Christian countries there are regions that are under the special structures of the mission *ad gentes*, with groups and areas not yet evangelized. Thus, in these countries too there is a need not only for a new evangelization, but also, in some cases, for an initial evangelization.[10]

Situations are not however the same everywhere. While acknowledging that statements about the missionary responsibility of the Church are not credible unless they are backed up by a serious commitment to a new evangelization in the traditionally Christian countries, it does not seem justified to regard as identical the situation of a people which has never known Jesus Christ and that of a people which has known him, accepted him and then rejected him, while continuing to live in a culture which in large part has absorbed Gospel principles and values. These are two basically different situations with regard to the faith.

Thus the criterion of geography, although somewhat imprecise and always provisional, is still a valid indicator of the frontiers toward which missionary activity must be directed. There are countries and geographical and cultural areas which lack indigenous Christian communities. In other places, these communities are so small as not to be a clear sign of a Christian presence; or they lack the dynamism to evangelize their societies, or belong to a minority population not integrated into the dominant culture of the nation. Particularly in Asia, toward which the Church's mission *ad gentes* ought to be chiefly directed, Christians are a small minority, even though sometimes there are significant numbers of converts and outstanding examples of Christian presence.

(b) *New worlds and new social phenomena*. The rapid and profound transformations which characterize today's world, especially in the southern hemisphere, are having a powerful effect on the overall missionary picture. Where before there were stable human and social situations, today everything is in flux. One thinks, for example, of urbanization and the massive growth of cities, especially where demographic pressure is greatest. In not a few countries, over half the population already

---

10. Address to the members of the Symposium of the Council of the European Episcopal Conferences (11 October 1985), *AAS* 78 (1986) 178-189.

lives in a few "megalopolises," where human problems are often aggravated by the feeling of anonymity experienced by masses of people.

In the modern age, missionary activity has been carried out especially in isolated regions which are far from centers of civilization and which are hard to penetrate because of difficulties of communication, language or climate. Today the image of mission *ad gentes* is perhaps changing: efforts should be concentrated on the big cities, where new customs and styles of living arise together with new forms of culture and communication, which then influence the wider population. It is true that the "option for the neediest" means that we should not overlook the most abandoned and isolated human groups, but it is also true that individuals or small groups cannot be evangelized if we neglect the centers where a new humanity, so to speak, is emerging, and where new models of development are taking shape. The future of the younger nations is being shaped in the cities.

Speaking of the future, we cannot forget the young, who in many countries comprise more than half the population. How do we bring the message of Christ to non-Christian young people who represent the future of entire continents. Clearly, the ordinary means of pastoral work are not sufficient: what are needed are associations, institutions, special centers and groups, and cultural and social initiatives for young people. This is a field where modern ecclesial movements have ample room for involvement.

Among the great changes taking place in the contemporary world, migration has produced a new phenomenon: non-Christians are becoming very numerous in traditionally Christian countries, creating fresh opportunities for contacts and cultural exchanges, and calling the Church to hospitality, dialogue, assistance and, in a word, fraternity. Among migrants, refugees occupy a very special place and deserve the greatest attention. Today, there are many millions of refugees in the world and their number is constantly increasing. They have fled from conditions of political oppression and inhuman misery, from famine and drought of catastrophic proportions. The Church must make them part of her overall apostolic concern. Finally, we may mention the situations of poverty — often on an intolerable scale — which have been created in not a few countries, and which are often the cause of mass migration. The community of believers in Christ is challenged by these inhuman situations: the proclamation of Christ and the Kingdom of God must become the means for restoring the human dignity of these people.

(c) *Cultural sectors: the modern equivalents of the Areopagus.* After preaching in a number of places, Saint Paul arrived in Athens, where he went to the Areopagus and proclaimed the Gospel in language appropriate to and understandable in those surroundings (cf. Acts 17:22-31). At that time the Areopagus represented the cultural center of the learned people of Athens, and today it can be taken as a symbol of the new sectors in which the Gospel must be proclaimed.

The first Areopagus of the modern age is the *world of communications*, which is unifying humanity and turning it into what is known as a "global village." The means of social communication have become so important as to be for many the chief means of information and education, of guidance and inspiration in their behavior as individuals, families and within society at large. In particular, the younger generation is growing up in a world conditioned by the mass-media. To some degree perhaps this Areopagus has been neglected. Generally, preference has been given to other means of preaching the Gospel and of Christian education, while the mass-media are left to the initiative of individuals or small groups and enter into pastoral planning only in a secondary way. Involvement in the mass-media, however, is not meant merely to strengthen the preaching of the Gospel. There is a deeper reality involved here: since the very evangelization of modern culture depends to a great extent on the influence of the media, it is not enough to use the media simply to spread the Christian message and the Church's authentic teaching. It is also necessary to integrate that message into the "new culture" created by modern communications. This is a complex issue, since the "new culture" originates not just from whatever content is eventually expressed, but from the very fact that there exist new ways of communicating, with new languages, new techniques and a new psychology. Pope Paul VI said that "the split between the Gospel and culture is undoubtedly the tragedy of our time" (EN 20), and the field of communications fully confirms this judgment.

There are many other forms of the "Areopagus" in the modern world toward which the Church's missionary activity ought to be directed; for example, commitment to peace, development and the liberation of peoples; the rights of individuals and peoples, especially those of minorities; the advancement of women and children; safeguarding the created world. These too are areas which need to be illuminated with the light of the Gospel.

We must also mention the immense "Areopagus" of culture, scientific research, and international relations which promote dialogue and open up new possibilities. We would do well to be attentive to these modern areas of activity and to be involved in them. People sense that they are as it were traveling together across life's sea, and that they are called to ever greater unity and solidarity. Solutions to pressing problems must be studied, discussed and worked out with the involvement of all. That is why international organizations and meetings are proving increasingly important in many sectors of human life, from culture to politics, from the economy to research. Christians who live and work in this international sphere must always remember their duty to bear witness to the Gospel.

38. Our times are both momentous and fascinating. While on the one hand people seem to be pursuing material prosperity and to be sinking ever deeper into consumerism and materialism, on the other hand we are witnessing a desperate search for meaning, the need for an inner life, and a desire to learn new forms and methods of meditation and prayer. Not only in cultures with strong religious elements, but also in secularized societies, the spiritual dimension of life is being sought after as an antidote to dehumanization. This phenomenon — the so-called "religious revival" — is not without ambiguity, but it also represents an opportunity. The Church has an immense spiritual patrimony to offer mankind, a heritage in Christ, who called himself "the way, and the truth, and the life" (Jn 14:6): it is the Christian path to meeting God, to prayer, to asceticism, and to the search for life's meaning. Here too there is an "Areopagus" to be evangelized.

Fidelity to Christ and the Promotion of Human Freedom

39. All forms of missionary activity are marked by an awareness that one is furthering human freedom by proclaiming Jesus Christ. The Church must be faithful to Christ, whose Body she is, and whose mission she continues. She must necessarily "go the same road that Christ went — namely a road of poverty, obedience, service and self-sacrifice even unto death, from which he emerged a victor through his Resurrection" (AG 5; LG 8). The Church is thus obliged to do everything possible to carry out her mission in the world and to reach all peoples. And she has the right to do this, a right given her by God for the accomplishment of his plan. Religious freedom, which is still at times limited or restricted, remains the premise and guarantee of all the freedoms that ensure the common good of individuals and peoples. It is to be hoped that authentic religious freedom will be granted to all people everywhere. The Church strives for this in all countries, especially in those with a Catholic majority, where she has greater influence. But it is not a question of the religion of

the majority or the minority, but of an inalienable right of each and every human person.

On her part, the Church addresses people with full respect for their freedom (DH 3-4; EN 79-80; RH 12). Her mission does not restrict freedom but rather promotes it. *The Church proposes, she imposes nothing.* She respects individuals and cultures, and she honors the sanctuary of conscience. To those who for various reasons oppose missionary activity, the Church repeats: *Open the doors to Christ!*

Here I wish to address all the particular Churches, both young and old. The world is steadily growing more united, and the Gospel spirit must lead us to overcome cultural and nationalistic barriers, avoiding all isolationism. Pope Benedict XV already cautioned the missionaries of his time lest they "forget their proper dignity and think more of their earthly homeland than of their heavenly one" (MI). This same advice is valid today for the particular Churches: Open the doors to missionaries, for "each individual Church that would voluntarily cut itself off from the universal Church would lose its relationship to God's plan and would be impoverished in its ecclesial mission" (EN 62).

Directing Attention toward the South and the East

40. Today missionary activity still represents the greatest challenge for the Church. As the end of the second Millennium of the Redemption draws near, it is clear that the peoples which have not yet received an initial proclamation of Christ constitute the majority of mankind. The results of missionary activity in modern times are certainly positive. The Church has been established on every continent; indeed today the majority of believers and particular Churches is to be found no longer in Europe but on the continents which missionaries have opened up to the faith.

The fact remains however that the "ends of the earth" to which the Gospel must be brought are growing ever more distant. Tertullian's saying, that the Gospel has been proclaimed to all the earth and to all peoples,[11] is still very far from being a reality. The mission *ad gentes* still in its infancy. New peoples appear on the world scene, and they too have a right to receive the proclamation of salvation. Population growth in non-Christian countries of the South and the East is constantly increasing the number of people who remain unaware of Christ's Redemption.

We need therefore to direct our attention toward those geographical areas and cultural settings which still remain uninfluenced by the Gospel. All who believe in Christ should feel, as an integral part of their faith, an apostolic concern to pass on to others its light and joy. This concern must become as it were a hunger and thirst to make the Lord known, given the vastness of the non-Christian world.

CHAPTER V

THE PATHS OF MISSION

41. "Missionary activity is nothing other and nothing less than the manifestation or epiphany of God's plan and its fulfillment in the world and in history; in this history God, by means of missions, clearly accomplishes the history of salvation" (AG 9, cf. 10-18). What paths does the Church follow in order to achieve this goal?

Mission is a single but complex reality, and it develops in a variety of ways.

---

11. Cf. Tertullian, *De praescriptione haereticorum*, XX: CCL I, 201f.

Among these ways, some have particular importance in the present situation of the Church and the world.

The First Form of Evangelization is Witness

42. People today put more trust in witnesses than in teachers (EN 41), in experience than in teaching, and in life and action than in theories. The witness of a Christian life is the first and irreplaceable form of mission: Christ, whose mission we continue, is the "witness" *par excellence* (Rev 1:5; 3:14) and the model of all Christian witness. The Holy Spirit accompanies the Church along her way and associates her with the witness he gives to Christ (cf. Jn 15:26-27).

The first form of witness *is the very life of the missionary, of the Christian family,* and *of the ecclesial community,* which reveal a new way of living. The missionary who, despite all his or her human limitations and defects, lives a simple life, taking Christ as the model, is a sign of God and of transcendent realities. But everyone in the Church, striving to imitate the Divine Master, can and must bear this kind of witness (LG 28, 35, 38; GS 43; AG 11-12); in many cases it is the only possible way of being a missionary.

The evangelical witness which the world finds most appealing is that of concern for people, and of charity toward the poor, the weak and those who suffer. The complete generosity underlying this attitude and these actions stands in marked contrast to human selfishness. It raises precise questions which lead to God and to the Gospel. A commitment to peace, justice, human rights and human promotion is also a witness to the Gospel when it is a sign of concern for persons and is directed toward integral human development (POP 21, 42).

43. Christians and Christian communities are very much a part of the life of their respective nations and can be a sign of the Gospel in their fidelity to their native land, people and national culture, while always preserving the freedom brought by Christ. Christianity is open to universal brotherhood, for all men and women are sons and daughters of the same Father and brothers and sisters in Christ.

The Church is called to bear witness to Christ by taking courageous and prophetic stands in the face of the corruption of political or economic power; by not seeking her own glory and material wealth; by using her resources to serve the poorest of the poor and by imitating Christ's own simplicity of life. The Church and her missionaries must also bear the witness of humility, above all with regard to themselves — a humility which allows them to make a personal and communal examination of conscience in order to correct in their behavior whatever is contrary to the Gospel and disfigures the face of Christ.

The Initial Proclamation of Christ the Savior

44. Proclamation is the permanent priority of mission. The Church cannot elude Christ's explicit mandate, nor deprive men and women of the "Good News" about their being loved and saved by God. "Evangelization will always contain — as the foundation, center and at the same time the summit of its dynamism — a clear proclamation that, in Jesus Christ . . . salvation is offered to all men, as a gift of God's grace and mercy" (EN 27). All forms of missionary activity are directed to this proclamation, which reveals and gives access to the mystery hidden for ages and made known in Christ (cf. Eph 3:3-9; Col 1:25-29), the mystery which lies at the heart of the Church's mission and life, as the hinge on which all evangelization turns.

In the complex reality of mission, initial proclamation has a central and irreplaceable role, since it introduces man "into the mystery of the love of God, who invites him to enter into a personal relationship with himself in Christ" (AG 13) and opens the way to conversion. Faith is born of preaching, and every ecclesial community draws its origin and life from the personal response of each believer to that preaching (EN 15; AG 13-14). Just as the whole economy of salvation has its center in Christ, so too all missionary activity is directed to the proclamation of his mystery.

The subject of proclamation is Christ who was crucified, died and is risen: through him is accomplished our full and authentic liberation from evil, sin and death; through him God bestows "new life" that is divine and eternal. This is the "Good News" which changes man and his history, and which all peoples have a right to hear. This proclamation is to be made within the context of the lives of the individuals and peoples who receive it. It is to be made with an attitude of love and esteem toward those who hear it, in language which is practical and adapted to the situation. In this proclamation the Spirit is at work and establishes a communion between the missionary and his hearers, a communion which is possible inasmuch as both enter into communion with God the Father through Christ (DEV 42, 64).

45. Proclamation, because it is made in union with the entire ecclesial community, is never a merely personal act. The missionary is present and carries out his work by virtue of a mandate he has received; even if he finds himself alone, he remains joined by invisible but profound bonds to the evangelizing activity of the whole Church (EN 60). Sooner or later, his hearers come to recognize in him the community which sent him and which supports him.

Proclamation is inspired by faith, which gives rise to enthusiasm and fervor in the missionary. As already mentioned, the Acts of the Apostles uses the word *parrhesia* to describe this attitude, a word which means to speak frankly and with courage. This term is found also in Saint Paul: "We had courage in our God to declare to you the Gospel of God in the face of great opposition" (1 Th 2:2); "Pray . . . also for me, that utterance may be given me in opening my mouth boldly to proclaim the mystery of the Gospel for which I am an ambassador in chains; that I may declare it boldly, as I ought to speak" (Eph 6:18-20).

In proclaiming Christ to non-Christians, the missionary is convinced that, through the working of the Spirit, there already exists in individuals and peoples an expectation, even if an unconscious one, of knowing the truth about God, about man, and about how we are to be set free from sin and death. The missionary's enthusiasm in proclaiming Christ comes from the conviction that he is responding to that expectation, and so he does not become discouraged or cease his witness even when he is called to manifest his faith in an environment that is hostile or indifferent. He knows that the Spirit of the Father is speaking through him (cf. Mt 10:17-20; Lk 12:11-12) and he can say with the Apostles: "We are witnesses to these things, and so is the Holy Spirit" (Acts 5:32). He knows that he is not proclaiming a human truth, but the "word of God," which has an intrinsic and mysterious power of its own (cf. Rom 1:16).

The supreme test is the giving of one's life, to the point of accepting death in order to bear witness to one's faith in Jesus Christ. Throughout Christian history, martyrs, that is, "witnesses," have always been numerous and indispensable to the spread of the Gospel. In our own age, there are many: Bishops, priests, men and women Religious, lay people — often unknown heroes who give their lives to bear witness to the faith. They are *par excellence* the heralds and witnesses of the faith.

Conversion and Baptism

46. The proclamation of the word of God has *Christian conversion* as its aim: a complete and sincere adherence to Christ and his Gospel through faith. Conversion

is a gift of God, a work of the Blessed Trinity. It is the Spirit who opens people's hearts so that they can believe in Christ and "confess him" (cf. 1 Cor 12:3); of those who draw near to him through faith Jesus says: "No one can come to me unless the Father who sent me draws him" (Jn 6:44).

From the outset, conversion is expressed in faith which is total and radical, and which neither limits nor hinders God's gift. At the same time, it gives rise to a dynamic and lifelong process which demands a continual turning away from "life according to the flesh" to "life according to the Spirit" (cf. Rom 8:3-13). Conversion means accepting, by a personal decision, the saving sovereignty of Christ and becoming his disciple.

The Church calls all people to this conversion, following the example of John the Baptist, who prepared the way for Christ by "preaching a baptism of repentance for the forgiveness of sins" (Mk 1:4), as well as the example of Christ himself, who "after John was arrested . . . came into Galilee preaching the Gospel of God and saying: 'The time is fulfilled, and the kingdom of God is at hand; repent and believe in the Gospel' " (Mk 1:14-15).

Nowadays the call to conversion which missionaries address to non-Christians is put into question or passed over in silence. It is seen as an act of "proselytizing"; it is claimed that it is enough to help people to become more human or more faithful to their own religion, that it is enough to build communities capable of working for justice, freedom, peace and solidarity. What is overlooked is that every person has the right to hear the "Good News" of the God who reveals and gives himself in Christ, so that each one can live out in its fullness his or her proper calling. This lofty reality is expressed in the words of Jesus to the Samaritan woman: "If you knew the gift of God," and in the unconscious but ardent desire of the woman: "Sir, give me this water, that I may not thirst" (Jn 4:10, 15).

47.   The Apostles, prompted by the Spirit, invited all to change their lives, to be converted and to be baptized. Immediately after the event of Pentecost, Peter spoke convincingly to the crowd: "When they heard this, they were cut to the heart, and said to Peter and the rest of the Apostles, 'Brethren, what shall we do?' And Peter said to them, 'Repent, and be baptized every one of you in the name of Jesus Christ for the forgiveness of your sins; and you shall receive the gift of the Holy Spirit' " (Acts 2:37-38). That very day some three thousand persons were baptized. And again, after the healing of the lame man, Peter spoke to the crowd and repeated: "Repent therefore, and turn again, that your sins may be blotted out!" (Acts 3:19).

Conversion to Christ is joined to Baptism not only because of the Church's practice, but also by the will of Christ himself, who sent the Apostles to make disciples of all nations and to baptize them (cf. Mt 28:19). Conversion is also joined to Baptism because of the intrinsic need to receive the fullness of new life in Christ. As Jesus says to Nicodemus: "Truly, truly, I say to you, unless one is born of water and the Spirit, he cannot enter the Kingdom of God" (Jn 3:5). In Baptism, in fact, we are born anew to the life of God's children, united to Jesus Christ and anointed in the Holy Spirit. Baptism is not simply a seal of conversion, a kind of external sign indicating conversion and attesting to it. Rather, it is the Sacrament which signifies and effects rebirth from the Spirit, establishes real and unbreakable bonds with the Blessed Trinity, and makes us members of the Body of Christ, which is the Church.

All this needs to be said, since not a few people, precisely in those areas involved in the mission *ad gentes,* tend to separate conversion to Christ from Baptism, regarding Baptism as unnecessary. It is true that in some places sociological considerations associated with Baptism obscure its genuine meaning as an act of faith. This is due to a variety of historical and cultural factors which must be removed where they still exist, so that the Sacrament of spiritual rebirth can be seen for what it truly is. Local ecclesial communities must devote themselves to this task. It is also true that many profess an interior commitment to Christ and his message yet do not wish to be committed sacramentally, since, owing to prejudice or because of the failings of Christians, they find it difficult to grasp the true nature of the Church as a mystery of faith and love (LG 6-9). I wish to encourage such people to be fully open to Christ, and to remind them that, if they feel drawn to Christ, it was he himself who desired that the Church should be the "place" where they would in fact find him. At the same time, I invite the Christian faithful, both individually and as communities, to bear authentic witness to Christ through the new life they have received.

Certainly, every convert is a gift to the Church and represents a serious responsibility for her, not only because converts have to be prepared for Baptism through the catechumenate and then be guided by religious instruction, but also because — especially in the case of adults — such converts bring with them a kind of new energy, an enthusiasm for the faith, and a desire to see the Gospel lived out in the Church. They would be greatly disappointed if, having entered the ecclesial community, they were to find a life lacking fervor and without signs of renewal! We cannot preach conversion unless we ourselves are converted anew every day.

Forming Local Churches

48. Conversion and Baptism give entry into a Church already in existence or require the establishment of new communities which confess Jesus as Savior and Lord. This is part of God's plan, for it pleases him "to call human beings to share in his own life not merely as individuals, without any unifying bond between them, but rather to make them into a people in which his children, who had been widely scattered, might be gathered together in unity" (AG 2; cf. LG 9).

The mission *ad gentes* has this objective: to found Christian communities and develop Churches to their full maturity. This is a central and determining goal of missionary activity, so much so that the mission is not completed until it succeeds in building a new particular Church which functions normally in its local setting. The Decree *Ad Gentes* deals with this subject at length (cf. AG chapter III, 19-22), and since the Council, a line of theological reflection has developed which emphasizes that the whole mystery of the Church is contained in each particular Church, provided it does not isolate itself but remains in communion with the universal Church and becomes missionary in its own turn. Here we are speaking of a great and lengthy process, in which it is hard to identify the precise stage at which missionary activity properly so-called comes to an end and is replaced by pastoral activity. Even so, certain points must remain clear.

49. It is necessary first and foremost to strive to establish Christian communities everywhere, communities which are "a sign of the presence of God in the world" (AG 15) and which grow until they become Churches. Notwithstanding the high number of dioceses, there are still very large areas where there are no local Churches or where their number is insufficient in relation to the vastness of the territory and the density of the population. There is still much to be done in implanting and developing the Church. This phase of ecclesial history, called the *plantatio Ecclesiae,* has not reached its end; indeed, for much of the human race it has yet to begin.

Responsibility for this task belongs to the universal Church and to the particular Churches, to the whole people of God and to all its missionary forces. Every Church, even one made up of recent converts, is missionary by its very nature, and is both evangelized and evangelizing. Faith must always be presented as a gift of God to be lived out in community (families, parishes, associations), and to be extended to others through witness in word and deed. The evangelizing activity of the Christian community, first in its own locality, and then elsewhere as part of the Church's universal mission, is the clearest sign of a mature faith. A radical conversion in thinking is required in order to become missionary, and this holds true both for individuals and entire communities. The Lord is always calling us to come out of ourselves and to share with others the goods we possess, starting with the most precious gift of all — our faith. The effectiveness of the Church's organizations, movements, parishes and apostolic works must be measured in the light of this missionary imperative. Only by becoming missionary will the Christian community be able to overcome its internal divisions and tensions, and rediscover its unity and its strength of faith.

Missionary personnel coming from other Churches and countries must work in communion with their local counterparts for the development of the Christian community. In particular, it falls to missionary personnel — in accordance with the directives of the Bishops and in cooperation with those responsible at the local level — to foster the spread of the faith and the expansion of the Church in non-Christian environments and among non-Christian groups, and to encourage a missionary sense within the particular Churches, so that pastoral concern will always be combined with concern for the mission *ad gentes.* In this way, every Church will make its own the solicitude of Christ the Good Shepherd, who fully devotes himself to his flock, but at the same time is mindful of the "other sheep, that are not of this fold" (Jn 10:16).

50. This solicitude will serve as a motivation and stimulus for a renewed commitment to ecumenism. The relationship between *ecumenical activity* and *missionary activity* makes it necessary to consider two closely associated factors. On the one hand, we must recognize that "the division among Christians damages the holy work of preaching the Gospel to every creature and is a barrier for many in their approach to the faith" (AG 6). The fact that the Good News of reconciliation is preached by Christians who are divided among themselves weakens their witness. It is thus urgent to work for the unity of Christians, so that missionary activity can be more effective. At the same time we must not forget that efforts toward unity are themselves a sign of the work of reconciliation which God is bringing about in our midst.

On the other hand, it is true that some kind of communion, though imperfect, exists among all those who have received Baptism in Christ. On this basis the Council established the principle that "while all appearance of indifferentism and confusion is ruled out, as well as any appearance of unhealthy rivalry, Catholics should collaborate in a spirit of fellowship with their separated brothers and sisters in accordance with the norms of the Decree on Ecumenism: by a common profession of faith in God and in Jesus Christ before the nations — to the extent that this is possible — and by their cooperation in social and technical as well as in cultural and religious matters" (AG 15; cf. UR 3).

Ecumenical activity and harmonious witness to Jesus Christ by Christians who belong to different Churches and Ecclesial Communities has already borne abundant fruit. But it is ever more urgent that they work and bear witness together at this time when Christian and para-Christian sects are sowing confusion by their activity. The expansion of these sects represents a threat for the Catholic Church and for all the Ecclesial Communities with which she is engaged in dialogue. Wherever possible, and in the light of local circumstances, the response of Christians can itself be an ecumenical one.

"Ecclesial Basic Communities" as a Force for Evangelization

51. A rapidly growing phenomenon in the young Churches — one sometimes fostered by the Bishops and their Conferences as a pastoral priority — is that of

"ecclesial basic communities" (also known by other names) which are proving to be good centers for Christian formation and missionary outreach. These are groups of Christians who, at the level of the family or in a similarly restricted setting, come together for prayer, Scripture reading, catechesis, and discussion on human and ecclesial problems with a view to a common commitment. These communities are a sign of vitality within the Church, an instrument of formation and evangelization, and a solid starting point for a new society based on a "civilization of love."

These communities decentralize and organize the parish community, to which they always remain united. They take root in less privileged and rural areas, and become a leaven of Christian life, of care for the poor and neglected, and of commitment to the transformation of society. Within them, the individual Christian experiences community and therefore senses that he or she is playing an active role and is encouraged to share in the common task. Thus, these communities become a means of evangelization and of the initial proclamation of the Gospel, and a source of new ministries. At the same time, by being imbued with Christ's love, they also show how divisions, tribalism and racism can be overcome.

Every community, if it is to be Christian, must be founded on Christ and live in him, as it listens to the word of God, focuses its prayer on the Eucharist, lives in a communion marked by oneness of heart and soul, and shares according to the needs of its members (cf. Acts 2:42-47). As Pope Paul VI recalled, every community must live in union with the particular and the universal Church, in heartfelt communion with the Church's Pastors and the Magisterium, with a commitment to missionary outreach and without yielding to isolationism or ideological exploitation (EN 58). And the Synod of Bishops stated: "Because the Church is communion, the new 'basic communities,' if they truly live in unity with the Church, are a true expression of communion and a means for the construction of a more profound communion. They are thus cause for great hope for the life of the Church." [12]

Incarnating the Gospel in Peoples' Cultures

52. As she carries out missionary activity among the nations, the Church encounters different cultures and becomes involved in the process of inculturation. The need for such involvement has marked the Church's pilgrimage throughout her history, but today it is particularly urgent.

The process of the Church's insertion into peoples' cultures is a lengthy one. It is not a matter of purely external adaptation, for inculturation "means the intimate transformation of authentic cultural values through their integration in Christianity and the insertion of Christianity in the various human cultures." [13] The process is thus a profound and all-embracing one, which involves the Christian message and also the Church's reflection and practice. But at the same time it is a difficult process, for it must in no way compromise the distinctiveness and integrity of the Christian faith.

Through inculturation the Church makes the Gospel incarnate in different cultures and at the same time introduces peoples, together with their cultures, into her own community (CT 53; SA 21). She transmits to them her own values, at the same time taking the good elements that already exist in them and renewing them from within (EN 20). Through inculturation the Church, for her part, becomes a more intelligible sign of what she is, and a more effective instrument of mission.

Thanks to this action within the local Churches, the universal Church herself is

---

12. Extraordinary Assembly of 1985, *Final Report*, II, C, 6.
13. Ibid., II, D, 4.

enriched with forms of expression and values in the various sectors of Christian life, such as evangelization, worship, theology and charitable works. She comes to know and to express better the mystery of Christ, all the while being motivated to continual renewal. During my Pastoral Visits to the young Churches I have repeatedly dealt with these themes, which are present in the Council and the subsequent Magisterium.[14]

Inculturation is a slow journey, which accompanies the whole of missionary life. It involves those working in the Church's mission *ad gentes,* the Christian communities as they develop, and the Bishops, who have the task of providing discernment and encouragement for its implementation (AG 22).

53. Missionaries, who come from other Churches and countries, must immerse themselves in the cultural milieu of those to whom they are sent, moving beyond their own cultural limitations. Hence they must learn the language of the place in which they work, become familiar with the most important expressions of the local culture, and discover its values through direct experience. Only if they have this kind of awareness will they be able to bring to people the knowledge of the hidden mystery (cf. Rom 16: 25-27; Eph 3:5) in a credible and fruitful way. It is not of course a matter of missionaries renouncing their own cultural identity, but of understanding, appreciating, fostering and evangelizing the culture of the environment in which they are working, and therefore of equipping themselves to communicate effectively with it, adopting a manner of living which is a sign of Gospel witness and of solidarity with the people.

Developing ecclesial communities, inspired by the Gospel, will gradually be able to express their Christian experience in original ways and forms that are consonant with their own cultural traditions, provided that those traditions are in harmony with the objective requirements of the faith itself. To this end, especially in the more delicate areas of inculturation, particular Churches of the same region should work in communion with each other (AG 22) and with the whole Church, convinced that only through attention both to the universal Church and to the particular Churches will they be capable of translating the treasure of faith into a legitimate variety of expressions (EN 64). Groups which have been evangelized will thus provide the elements for a "translation" of the Gospel message (EN 63),[15] keeping in mind the positive elements acquired down the centuries from Christianity's contact with different cultures and not forgetting the dangers of alterations which have sometimes occurred.[16]

54. In this regard, certain guidelines remain basic. Properly applied, inculturation must be guided by two principles: "compatibility with the Gospel and communion with the universal Church" (FC 10). Bishops, as guardians of the "deposit of faith," will take care to ensure fidelity and, in particular, to provide discernment (EN 63-65), for which a deeply balanced approach is required. In fact there is a risk of

---

14. Address to the Bishops of Zaire, Kinshasa (3 May 1980, 4-6); to the Bishops of Kenya, Nairobi (7 May 1980); to the Bishops of India, Delhi (1 February 1986); Homily at Cartagena, 6 July 1986; cf. also SA 21-22.

15. Particular Churches "have the task of assimilating the essence of the Gospel message and of transposing it, without the slightest betrayal of its essential truth, into the language that these people understand, then of proclaiming it in this language. . . . And the word 'language' should be understood here less in the semantic or literary sense than in the sense which one may call anthropological or cultural."

16. Cf. Address at the General Audience of 13 April 1988, *Insegnamenti* XI/1 (1988) 877-881.

passing uncritically from a form of alienation from culture to an overestimation of culture. Since culture is a human creation and is therefore marked by sin, it too needs to be "healed, ennobled and perfected" (LG 17).

This kind of process needs to take place gradually, in such a way that it really is an expression of the community's Christian experience. As Pope Paul VI said in Kampala: "It will require an incubation of the Christian 'mystery' in the genius of your people in order that its native voice, more clearly and frankly, may then be raised harmoniously in the chorus of other voices in the universal Church."[17] In effect, inculturation must involve the whole people of God, and not just a few experts, since the people reflect the authentic *sensus fidei* which must never be lost sight of. Inculturation needs to be guided and encouraged, but not forced, lest it give rise to negative reactions among Christians. It must be an expression of the community's life, one which must mature within the community itself, and not be exclusively the result of erudite research. The safeguarding of traditional values is the work of a mature faith.

Dialogue with our Brothers and Sisters of other Religions

55. Interreligious dialogue is a part of the Church's evangelizing mission. Understood as a method and means of mutual knowledge and enrichment, dialogue is not in opposition to the mission *ad gentes;* indeed, it has special links with that mission and is one of its expressions. This mission, in fact, is addressed to those who do not know Christ and his Gospel, and who belong for the most part to other religions. In Christ, God calls all peoples to himself and he wishes to share with them the fullness of his revelation and love. He does not fail to make himself present in many ways, not only to individuals but also to entire peoples through their spiritual riches, of which their religions are the main and essential expression, even when they contain "gaps, insufficiencies and errors."[18] All of this has been given ample emphasis by the Council and the subsequent Magisterium, without detracting in any way from the fact that *salvation comes from Christ and that dialogue does not dispense from evangelization.*[19]

In the light of the economy of salvation, the Church sees no conflict between proclaiming Christ and engaging in interreligious dialogue. Instead, she feels the need to link the two in the context of her mission *ad gentes.* These two elements must maintain both their intimate connection and their distinctiveness; therefore they should not be confused, manipulated or regarded as identical, as though they were interchangeable.

I recently wrote to the Bishops of Asia: "Although the Church gladly acknowledges whatever is true and holy in the religious traditions of Buddhism, Hinduism and Islam as a reflection of that truth which enlightens all men, this does not lessen her duty and resolve to proclaim without fail Jesus Christ who is 'the way, and the truth and the life.'. . . The fact that the followers of other religions can receive God's grace and be saved by Christ apart from the ordinary means which he has established

---

17. Address of Paul VI to those participating in the Symposium of African Bishops in Kampala (31 July 1969) 2.

18. Paul VI, Address at the opening of the Second Session of Vatican Council II (29 September 1963); cf. NA 2; LG 16; AG 9; EN 53).

19. Cf. ES; AG 11, 41; and Secretariat for Non-Christians, *L'atteggiamento della Chiesa di fronte ai seguaci di altre religioni: Riflessioni e orientamenti su dialogo e missione* (4 September 1984).

does not thereby cancel the call to faith and baptism which God wills for all people."[20] Indeed Christ himself "while expressly insisting on the need for faith and baptism, at the same time confirmed *the need for the Church,* into which people enter through Baptism as through a door" (LG 14; cf. AG 7). Dialogue should be conducted and implemented with the conviction that *the Church is the ordinary means of salvation* and that *she alone* possesses the fullness of the means of salvation (UR 3; AG 7).

56. Dialogue does not originate from tactical concerns or self-interest, but is an activity with its own guiding principles, requirements and dignity. It is demanded by deep respect for everything that has been brought about in human beings by the Spirit who blows where he wills (RH 12). Through dialogue, the Church seeks to uncover the "seeds of the Word," (AG 11, 15), a "ray of that truth which enlightens all men" (NA 2); these are found in individuals and in the religious traditions of mankind. Dialogue is based on hope and love, and will bear fruit in the Spirit. Other religions constitute a positive challenge for the Church: they stimulate her both to discover and acknowledge the signs of Christ's presence and of the working of the Spirit, as well as to examine more deeply her own identity and to bear witness to the fullness of Revelation which she has received for the good of all. This gives rise to the spirit which must enliven dialogue in the context of mission. Those engaged in this dialogue must be consistent with their own religious traditions and convictions, and be open to understanding those of the other party without pretense or closed-mindedness, but with truth, humility and frankness, knowing that dialogue can enrich each side. There must be no abandonment of principles nor false irenicism, but instead a witness given and received for mutual advancement on the road of religious inquiry and experience, and at the same time for the elimination of prejudice, intolerance and misunderstandings. Dialogue leads to inner purification and conversion which, if pursued with docility to the Holy Spirit, will be spiritually fruitful.

57. A vast field lies open to dialogue, which can assume many forms and expressions: from exchanges between experts in religious traditions or official representatives of those traditions to cooperation for integral development and the safeguarding of religious values; and from a sharing of their respective spiritual experiences to the so-called "dialogue of life," through which believers of different religions bear witness before each other in daily life to their own human and spiritual values, and help each other to live according to those values in order to build a more just and fraternal society.

Each member of the faithful and all Christian communities are called to practice dialogue, although not always to the same degree or in the same way. The contribution of the laity is indispensable in this area, for they "can favor the relations which ought to be established with the followers of various religions through their example in the situations in which they live and in their activities" (CL 35). Some of them also will be able to make a contribution through research and study (AG 41).

I am well aware that many missionaries and Christian communities find in the difficult and often misunderstood path of dialogue their only way of bearing sincere witness to Christ and offering generous service to others. I wish to encourage them to persevere with faith and love, even in places where their efforts are not well received. Dialogue is a path toward the Kingdom and will certainly bear fruit, even if the times and seasons are known only to the Father (cf. Acts 1:7).

---

20. Letter to the Fifth Plenary Assembly of Asian Bishops' Conferences (23 June 1990) 4.

Promoting Development by Forming Consciences

58. The mission *ad gentes* is still being carried out today, for the most part in the southern regions of the world, where action on behalf of integral development and liberation from all forms of oppression is most urgently needed. The Church has always been able to generate among the peoples she evangelizes a drive toward progress. Today, more than in the past, missionaries are being recognized as *promoters of development* by governments and international experts, who are impressed at the remarkable results achieved with scanty means.

In the Encyclical *Sollicitudo Rei Socialis*, I stated that "the Church does not have technical solutions to offer for the problem of underdevelopment as such," but "offers her first contribution to the solution of the urgent problem of development when she proclaims the truth about Christ, about herself and about man, applying this truth to a concrete situation" (SRC 41). The Conference of Latin American Bishops at Puebla stated that "the best service we can offer to our brother is evangelization, which helps him to live and act as a son of God, sets him free from injustices and assists his overall development." [21] It is not the Church's mission to work directly on the economic, technical or political levels, or to contribute materially to development. Rather, her mission consists essentially in offering people an opportunity not to "have more" but to "be more," by awakening their consciences through the Gospel. "Authentic human development must be rooted in an ever deeper evangelization." [22]

The Church and her missionaries also promote development through schools, hospitals, printing presses, universities and experimental farms. But a people's development does not derive primarily from money, material assistance or technological means, but from the formation of consciences and the gradual maturing of ways of thinking and patterns of behavior. *Man is the principal agent of development, not money or technology.* The Church forms consciences by revealing to peoples the God whom they seek and do not yet know, the grandeur of man created in God's image and loved by him, the equality of all men and women as God's sons and daughters, the mastery of man over nature created by God and placed at man's service, and the obligation to work for the development of the whole person and of all mankind.

59. Through the Gospel message, the Church offers a force for liberation which promotes development precisely because it leads to conversion of heart and of ways of thinking, fosters the recognition of each person's dignity, encourages solidarity, commitment and service of one's neighbor, and gives everyone a place in God's plan, which is the building of his Kingdom of peace and justice, beginning already in this life. This is the Biblical perspective of the "new heavens and a new earth" (cf. Is 65:17; 2 Pt 3:13; Rev 21:1), which has been the stimulus and goal for mankind's advancement in history. Man's development derives from God, from the model of Jesus — God and man — and must lead back to God (POP 14-21; SRC 27-41). That is why there is a close connection between the proclamation of the Gospel and human promotion.

The contribution of the Church and of evangelization to the development of peoples concerns not only the struggle against material poverty and underdevelopment in the South of the world, but also concerns the North, which is prone to a

---

21. Documents of the Third Conference of Latin American Bishops, no. 1145; cf. John Eagleson and Philip Scharper, eds., *Puebla and Beyond* (Maryknoll, NY: Orbis Books, 1979), p. 265.

22. Address to Clergy and Religious, Jakarta (10 October 1989).

moral and spiritual poverty caused by "overdevelopment" (SRC 28). A certain way of thinking, uninfluenced by a religious outlook and widespread in some parts of today's world, is based on the idea that increasing wealth and the promotion of economic and technical growth is enough for people to develop on the human level. But a soulless development cannot suffice for human beings, and an excess of affluence is as harmful as excessive poverty. This is a "development model" which the North has constructed and is now spreading to the South, where a sense of religion as well as human values are in danger of being overwhelmed by a wave of consumerism.

"Fight hunger by changing your lifestyle" is a motto which has appeared in Church circles and which shows the people of the rich nations how to become brothers and sisters of the poor. We need to turn to a more austere way of life which will favor a new model of development that gives attention to ethical and religious values. To the poor, *missionary activity* brings light and an impulse toward true development, while a new evangelization ought to create among the wealthy a realization that the time has arrived for them to become true brothers and sisters of the poor through the conversion of all to an "integral development" open to the Absolute (cf. SRC, chapter IV, 27-34; POP 19-21, 41-42).

Charity: Source and Criterion of Mission

60. As I said during my Pastoral Visit to Brazil: "The Church all over the world wishes to be the Church of the poor . . . she wishes to draw out all the truth contained in the Beatitudes of Christ, and especially in the first one: 'Blessed are the poor in spirit.'. . . She wishes to teach this truth and she wishes to put it into practice, just as Jesus came to do and to teach." [23]

The young Churches, which for the most part are to be found among peoples suffering from widespread poverty, often give voice to this concern as an integral part of their mission. The Conference of Latin American Bishops at Puebla, after recalling the example of Jesus, wrote that "the poor deserve preferential attention, whatever their moral or personal situation. They have been made in the image and likeness of God to be his children, but this image has been obscured and even violated. For this reason, God has become their defender and loves them. It follows that the poor are those to whom the mission is first addressed, and their evangelization is *par excellence* the sign and proof of the mission of Jesus." [24]

In fidelity to the spirit of the Beatitudes, the Church is called to be on the side of those who are poor and oppressed in any way. I therefore exhort the disciples of Christ and all Christian communities — from families to dioceses, from parishes to Religious Institutes — to carry out a sincere review of their lives regarding their solidarity with the poor. At the same time, I express gratitude to the missionaries who, by their loving presence and humble service to people, are working for the integral development of individuals and of society through schools, health-care centers, leprosaria, homes for the handicapped and the elderly, projects for the promotion of women, and other similar apostolates. I thank the priests, religious Brothers and Sisters, and members of the laity for their dedication, and I also encourage the volunteers from non-governmental organizations who in ever increasing numbers are devoting themselves to works of charity and human promotion.

It is in fact these "works of charity" that reveal the soul of all missionary activity: *love,* which has been and remains *the driving force of mission,* and is also "the sole

---

23. Address to the residents of Favela Vidigal in Rio de Janeiro (2 July 1980).
24. Puebla Documents, no. 1142.

criterion for judging what is to be done or not done, changed or not changed. It is the principle which must direct every action, and the end to which that action must be directed. When we act with a view to charity, or are inspired by charity, nothing is unseemly and everything is good." [25]

CHAPTER VI

LEADERS AND WORKERS
IN THE MISSIONARY APOSTOLATE

61. Without witnesses there can be no witness, just as without missionaries there can be no missionary activity. Jesus chooses and sends people forth to be his witnesses and apostles, so that they may share in his mission and continue his saving work: "You shall be my witnesses in Jerusalem and in all Judea and Samaria and to the end of the earth" (Acts 1:8).

The Twelve are the first to work in the Church's universal mission. They constitute a "collegial subject" of that mission, having been chosen by Jesus to be with him and to be sent forth "to the lost sheep of the house of Israel" (Mt 10:6). This collegiality does not prevent certain figures from assuming prominence within the group, such as James, John and above all Peter, who is so prominent as to justify the expression: "Peter and the other Apostles" (Acts 2:14, 37). It was thanks to Peter that the horizons of the Church's universal mission were expanded, and the way was prepared for the outstanding missionary work of Paul, who by God's will was called and sent forth to the nations (cf. Gal 1:15-16).

In the early Church's missionary expansion, we find, alongside the Apostles, other lesser figures who should not be overlooked. These include individuals, groups and communities. A typical example is the local Church at Antioch which, after being evangelized, becomes an evangelizing community which sends missionaries to others (cf. Acts 13:2-3). The early Church experiences her mission as a community task, while acknowledging in her midst certain "special envoys" or "missionaries devoted to the Gentiles," such as Paul and Barnabas.

62. What was done at the beginning of Christianity to further its universal mission remains valid and urgent today. *The Church is missionary by her very nature,* for Christ's mandate is not something contingent or external, but reaches the very heart of the Church. It follows that the universal Church and each individual Church is sent forth to the nations. Precisely "so that this missionary zeal may flourish among the people of their own country," it is highly appropriate that young Churches should "share as soon as possible in the universal missionary work of the Church. They should themselves send missionaries to proclaim the Gospel all over the world, even though they are suffering from a shortage of clergy" (AG 20). Many are already doing so, and I strongly encourage them to continue.

In this essential bond between the universal Church and the particular Churches the authentic and full missionary nature of the Church finds practical expression: "In a world where the lessening of distance makes the world increasingly smaller, the Church's communities ought to be connected with each other, exchange vital energies and resources, and commit themselves as a group to the one and common mission of proclaiming and living the Gospel. . . . So-called younger Churches have need of the strength of the older Churches and the older ones need the witness and the impulse of the younger, so that each Church can draw on the riches of the other Churches" (CL 35).

---

25. Isaac of Stella, *Sermon 31, PL* 194, 1793.

Those Primarily Responsible for Missionary Activity

63. Just as the Risen Lord gave the universal missionary mandate to the College of the Apostles with Peter as its head, so this same responsibility now rests primarily with the College of Bishops, headed by the Successor of Peter (AG 38). Conscious of this responsibility, I feel the duty to give expression to it in my meetings with the Bishops, both with regard to new evangelization and the universal mission. I have traveled all over the world in order "to proclaim the Gospel, to 'strengthen the brothers' in the faith, to console the Church, to meet people. They are journeys of faith . . . they are likewise opportunities for traveling catechesis, for evangelical proclamation in spreading the Gospel and the apostolic Magisterium to the full extent of the world." [26]

My brother Bishops are directly responsible, together with me, for the evangelization of the world, both as members of the College of Bishops and as Pastors of the particular Churches. In this regard the Council states: "The charge of announcing the Gospel throughout the world belongs to the body of shepherds, to all of whom in common Christ gave the command" (LG 23). It also stated that the Bishops "have been consecrated not only for a particular diocese but for the salvation of the entire world" (AG 38). This collegial responsibility has certain practical consequences. Thus, "the Synod of Bishops . . . should, among the concerns of general importance, pay special attention to missionary activity, the greatest and holiest duty of the Church" (AG 29). The same responsibility is reflected to varying degrees in Episcopal Conferences and their organisms at a continental level, which must make their own contribution to the missionary task (AG 38).

Each Bishop too, as the Pastor of a particular Church, has a wide-ranging missionary duty. It falls to him "as the ruler and center of unity in the diocesan apostolate, to promote missionary activity, to direct and coordinate it. . . . Let him also see to it that apostolic activity is not limited only to those who are already converted, but that a fair share both of personnel and funds be devoted to the evangelization of non-Christians" (AG 30).

64. Each particular Church must be generous and open to the needs of the other Churches. Cooperation between the Churches, in an authentic reciprocity that prepares them both to give and to receive, is a source of enrichment for all of them and touches the various spheres of ecclesial life. In this respect, the declaration of the Bishops at Puebla is exemplary: "The hour has finally come for Latin America . . . to be projected beyond her frontiers, *ad gentes.* Certainly we have need of missionaries ourselves, nevertheless we must give from our own poverty." [27]

In the same spirit, I exhort Bishops and Episcopal Conferences to act generously in implementing the provisions of the *Norms* which the Congregation for the Clergy issued regarding cooperation between particular Churches and especially regarding the better distribution of clergy in the world. [28]

The Church's mission is wider than the "communion among the Churches"; it ought to be directed not only to aiding re-evangelization but also and primarily to missionary activity as such. I appeal to all the Churches, young and old alike, to share in this concern of mine by seeking to overcome the various obstacles and increase missionary vocations.

---

26. Address to Cardinals and those associated in the work of the Roman Curia, Vatican City, and the Vicariate of Rome (28 June 1980) 10, *Insegnamenti* III/1 (1980), 1887.

27. Puebla no. 368, loc. cit., p. 174.

28. Cf. Norms for the Cooperation of the Local Churches among Themselves and especially for a Better Distribution of the Clergy in the World, *Postquam Apostoli* (25 March 1972), *AAS* 72 (1980) 343-363.

Missionaries and Religious Institutes Ad Gentes

65. Now, as in the past, among those involved in the missionary apostolate a place of fundamental importance is held by the persons and institutions to whom the Decree *Ad Gentes* devotes the special chapter entitled "Missionaries" (AG Chapter IV, 23-27). This requires careful reflection, especially on the part of missionaries themselves, who may be led, as a result of changes occurring within the missionary field, no longer to understand the meaning of their vocation and no longer to know exactly what the Church expects of them today.

The following words of the Council are a point of reference: "Although the task of spreading the faith, to the best of one's ability, falls to each disciple of Christ, the Lord always calls from the number of his disciples those whom he wishes, so that they may be with him and that he may send them to preach to the nations. Accordingly, through the Holy Spirit, who distributes his gifts as he wishes for the good of all, Christ stirs up a missionary vocation in the hearts of individuals, and at the same time raises up in the Church those Institutes which undertake the duty of evangelization, which is the responsibility of the whole Church, as their special task" (AG 23).

What is involved, therefore, is a "special vocation," patterned on that of the Apostles. It is manifested in a total commitment to evangelization, a commitment which involves the missionary's whole person and life, and demands a self-giving without limits of energy or time. Those who have received this vocation, "sent by legitimate authority, go out, in faith and obedience, to those who are far from Christ, set aside for the work to which they have been called as ministers of the Gospel" (AG 23). Missionaries must always meditate on the response demanded by the gift they have received, and continually keep their doctrinal and apostolic formation up to date.

66. Missionary Institutes, drawing from their experience and creativity while remaining faithful to their founding charism, must employ all means necessary to ensure the adequate preparation of candidates and the renewal of their members' spiritual, moral and physical energies (AG 23, 27). They should sense that they are a vital part of the ecclesial community and should carry out their work in communion with it. Indeed, "every Institute exists for the Church and must enrich her with its distinctive characteristics, according to a particular spirit and a specific mission"; the guardians of this fidelity to the founding charism are the Bishops themselves.[29]

In general, Missionary Institutes came into being in Churches located in traditionally Christian countries, and historically they have been the means employed by the Congregation of *Propaganda Fide* for the spread of the faith and the founding of new Churches. Today, these Institutes are receiving more and more candidates from the young Churches which they founded, while new Missionary Institutes have arisen in countries which previously only received missionaries, but are now also sending them. This is a praiseworthy trend which demonstrates the continuing validity and relevance of the specific missionary vocation of these Institutes. They remain "absolutely necessary" (AG 27), not only for missionary activity *ad gentes,* in keeping with their tradition, but also for stirring up missionary fervor both in the Churches of traditionally Christian countries and in the younger Churches.

The special vocation of missionaries *"for life"* retains all its validity: it is the model of the Church's missionary commitment, which always stands in need of radical and total self-giving, of new and bold endeavors. Therefore the men and women missionaries who have devoted their whole lives to bearing witness to the Risen Lord among the

---

29. Cf. Sacred Congregation for Religious and Secular Institutes and the Sacred Congregation for Bishops, Directives for Mutual Relations between Bishops and Religious in the Church, *Mutuae Relationes* (14 May 1978) 14b; *AAS* 70 (1978) 482. Cf. loc. cit., n. 28, p. 490.

nations must not allow themselves to be daunted by doubts, misunderstanding, rejection or persecution. They should revive the grace of their specific charism and courageously press on, preferring — in a spirit of faith, obedience and communion with their Pastors — to seek the lowliest and most demanding places.

Diocesan Priests for the Universal Mission

67. As co-workers of the Bishops, priests are called by virtue of the Sacrament of Orders to share in concern for the Church's mission: "The spiritual gift that priests have received in ordination prepares them, not for any narrow and limited mission, but for *the most universal and all-embracing mission of salvation* 'to the end of the earth.' For every priestly ministry shares in the universal scope of the mission that Christ entrusted to his Apostles' " (PO 10; cf. AG 39). For this reason, the formation of candidates to the priesthood must aim at giving them "*the true Catholic spirit,* whereby they will learn to transcend the bounds of their own diocese, country or rite, and come to the aid of the whole Church, in readiness to preach the Gospel anywhere."[30] All priests must have the mind and heart of missionaries — open to the needs of the Church and the world, with concern for those farthest away, and especially for the non-Christian groups in their own area. They should have at heart, in their prayers and particularly at the Eucharistic Sacrifice, the concern of the whole Church for all of humanity.

Especially in those areas where Christians are a minority, priests must be filled with special missionary zeal and commitment. The Lord entrusts to them not only the pastoral care of the Christian community, but also and above all the evangelization of those of their fellow-citizens who do not belong to Christ's flock. Priests will "not fail to make themselves readily available to the Holy Spirit and the Bishop, to be sent to preach the Gospel beyond the borders of their country. This will demand of them not only maturity in their vocation, but also an uncommon readiness to detach themselves from their own homeland, culture and family, and a special ability to adapt to other cultures, with understanding and respect for them."[31]

68. In his Encyclical *Fidei Donum,* Pope Pius XII, with prophetic insight, encouraged Bishops to offer some of their priests for temporary service in the Churches of Africa, and gave his approval to projects already existing for that purpose. Twenty-five years later, I pointed out the striking newness of that Encyclical, which "surmounted the territorial dimension of priestly service in order to direct it toward the entire Church."[32] Today it is clear how effective and fruitful this experience has been. Indeed, *Fidei Donum* priests are a unique sign of the bond of communion existing among the Churches. They make a valuable contribution to the growth of needy ecclesial communities, while drawing from them freshness and liveliness of faith. Of course, the missionary service of the diocesan priest must conform to certain criteria and conditions. The priests to be sent should be selected from among the most suitable candidates, and should be duly prepared for the particular work that awaits them (AG 38).[33] With an open and fraternal attitude, they should become part of the new setting of the Church which welcomes them, and form one presbyterate

---

30. Vatican Council II Decree on Priestly Formation, *Optatam Totius*, 20; cf. "Guide de la vie pastorale pour les prêtes diocésains des Eglise qui dependent de la Congrégation pour l'Evangélisation des Peuples" (Rome 1989).

31. Address to the Plenary Assembly of the Congregation for the Evangelization of Peoples (14 April 1989) 4; *AAS* 81 (1989) 1140.

32. Message for World Mission Day (1982); *Insegnamenti* V/2 (1982) 1979.

33. Sacred Congregation for the Clergy, Norms, *Postquam Apostoli* 24-25.

with the local priests, under the authority of the Bishop.[34] I hope that a spirit of service will increase among the priests of the long-established Churches, and that it will be fostered among priests of the Churches of more recent origin.

The Missionary Fruitfulness of Consecrated Life

69. From the inexhaustible and manifold richness of the Spirit come the vocations of the *Institutes of Consecrated Life,* whose members, "because of the dedication to the service of the Church deriving from their very consecration, have an obligation to play a special part in missionary activity, in a manner appropriate to their Institute" (CIC 783). History witnesses to the outstanding service rendered by Religious Families in the spread of the faith and the formation of new Churches: from the ancient monastic institutions, to the medieval Orders, up to the more recent Congregations.

(a) Echoing the Council, I invite *Institutes of Contemplative Life* to establish communities in the young Churches, so as to "bear glorious witness among non-Christians to the majesty and love of God, as well as to unity in Christ" (AG 40). This presence is beneficial throughout the non-Christian world, especially in those areas where religious traditions hold the contemplative life in great esteem for its asceticism and its search for the Absolute.

(b) To *Institutes of Active Life,* I would recommend the immense opportunities for works of charity, for the proclamation of the Gospel, for Christian education, cultural endeavors and solidarity with the poor and those suffering from discrimination, abandonment and oppression. Whether they pursue a strictly missionary goal or not, such Institutes should ask themselves how willing and able they are to broaden their action in order to extend God's Kingdom. In recent times many Institutes have responded to this request, which I hope will be given even greater consideration and implementation for a more authentic service. The Church needs to make known the great Gospel values of which she is the bearer. No one witnesses more effectively to these values than those who profess the consecrated life in chastity, poverty and obedience, in a total gift of self to God and in complete readiness to serve man and society after the example of Christ (EN 69).

70. I extend a special word of appreciation to the missionary Religious Sisters, in whom virginity for the sake of the Kingdom is transformed into a motherhood in the spirit that is rich and fruitful. It is precisely the mission *ad gentes* that offers them vast scope for "the gift of self with love in a total and undivided manner" (MD 20). The example and activity of women who through virginity are consecrated to love of God and neighbor, especially the very poor, are an indispensable evangelical sign among those peoples and cultures where women still have far to go on the way toward human promotion and liberation. It is my hope that many young Christian women will be attracted to giving themselves generously to Christ, and will draw strength and joy from their consecration in order to bear witness to him among the peoples who do not know him.

All the Laity are Missionaries by Baptism

71. Recent Popes have stressed the importance of the role of the laity in missionary activity (EP; FD; PP; EN 70-73). In the Exhortation *Christifideles Laici,* I spoke explicitly of the Church's "permanent mission of bringing the Gospel to the multitudes — the millions and millions of men and women — "who as yet do not know Christ the Redeemer of humanity" (CL 35), and of the responsibility of the lay faithful in this regard. The mission *ad gentes* is incumbent upon the entire People of

---

34. Ibid., 29; AG 20.

God. Whereas the foundation of a new Church requires the Eucharist and hence the priestly ministry, missionary activity, which is carried out in a wide variety of ways, is the task of all the Christian faithful.

It is clear that from the very origins of Christianity, the laity — as individuals, families, and entire communities — shared in spreading the faith. Pope Pius XII recalled this fact in his first Encyclical on the missions (EP), in which he pointed out some instances of lay missions. In modern times, this active participation of lay men and women missionaries has not been lacking. How can we forget the important role played by women: their work in the family, in schools, in political, social and cultural life, and especially their teaching of Christian doctrine? Indeed, it is necessary to recognize — and it is a title of honor — that some Churches owe their origins to the activity of lay men and women missionaries.

The Second Vatican Council confirmed this tradition in its description of the missionary character of the entire People of God and of the apostolate of the laity in particular (LG 17, 33ff.), emphasizing the specific contribution to missionary activity which they are called to make (AG 35-36, 41). The need for all the faithful to share in this responsibility is not merely a matter of making the apostolate more effective; it is a right and duty based on their baptismal dignity, whereby "the faithful participate, for their part, in the threefold mission of Christ as Priest, Prophet and King" (CL 14). Therefore, "they are bound by the general obligation and they have the right, whether as individuals or in associations, to strive so that the divine message of salvation may be known and accepted by all people throughout the world. This obligation is all the more insistent in circumstances in which only through them are people able to hear the Gospel and to know Christ" (CIC 225; AA 6, 13). Furthermore, because of their secular character, they especially are called "to seek the Kingdom of God by engaging in temporal affairs and ordering these in accordance with the will of God."

72. The sphere in which lay people are present and active as missionaries is very extensive. "Their own field . . . is the vast and complicated world of politics, society and economics" (EN 70) on the local, national and international levels. Within the Church, there are various types of services, functions, ministries and ways of promoting the Christian life. I call to mind, as a new development occurring in many Churches in recent times, the rapid growth of "ecclesial movements" filled with missionary dynamism. When these movements humbly seek to become part of the life of local Churches and are welcomed by Bishops and priests within diocesan and parish structures, they represent a true gift of God both for new evangelization and for missionary activity properly so-called. I therefore recommend that they be spread, and that they be used to give fresh energy, especially among young people, to the Christian life and to evangelization, within a pluralistic view of the ways in which Christians can associate and express themselves.

Within missionary activity, the different forms of the lay apostolate should be held in esteem, with respect for their nature and aims. Lay missionary associations, international Christian volunteer organizations, ecclesial movements, groups and sodalities of different kinds — all these should be involved in the mission *ad gentes* as cooperators with the local Churches. In this way the growth of a mature and responsible laity will be fostered, a laity whom the younger Churches are recognizing as "an essential and undeniable element in the *plantatio Ecclesiae*" (CL 35).

The Work of Catechists and the Variety of Ministries

73. Among the laity who become evangelizers, catechists have a place of honor. The Decree on the Missionary Activity of the Church speaks of them as "that army of catechists, both men and women, worthy of praise, to whom missionary work

among the nations owes so much. Imbued with the apostolic spirit, they make a singular and absolutely necessary contribution to the spread of the faith and of the Church by their strenuous efforts" (AG 17). It is with good reason that the older and established Churches, committed to a new evangelization, have increased the numbers of their catechists and intensified catechetical activity. But "the term 'catechists' belongs above all to the catechists in mission lands. . . . Churches that are flourishing today would not have been built up without them" (CT 66).

Even with the extension of the services rendered by lay people both within and outside the Church, there is always need for the ministry of catechists, a ministry with its own characteristics. Catechists are specialists, direct witnesses and irreplaceable evangelizers who, as I have often stated and experienced during my missionary journeys, represent the basic strength of Christian communities, especially in the young Churches. The new Code of Canon Law acknowledges the tasks, qualities and qualifications of catechists (CIC 785, 1).

However, it must not be forgotten that the work of catechists is becoming more and more difficult and demanding as a result of ecclesial and cultural changes. What the Council suggested is still valid today: a more careful doctrinal and pedagogical training, continuing spiritual and apostolic renewal, and the need to provide "a decent standard of living and social security" (AG 17). It is also important to make efforts to establish and support schools for catechists, which are to be approved by the Episcopal Conferences and confer diplomas officially recognized by the latter.[35]

74. Besides catechists, mention must also be made of other ways of serving the Church and her mission; namely, other Church personnel: leaders of prayer, song and liturgy; leaders of basic ecclesial communities and Bible study groups; those in charge of charitable works; administrators of Church resources; leaders in the various forms of the apostolate; religion teachers in schools. All the members of the laity ought to devote a part of their time to the Church, living their faith authentically.

The Congregation for the Evangelization of Peoples and Other Structures for Missionary Activity

75. Leaders and agents of missionary pastoral activity should sense their unity within the communion which characterizes the Mystical Body. Christ prayed for this at the Last Supper when he said: "Even as you, Father are in me, and I in you, that they also may be in us, so that the world may believe that you have sent me" (Jn 17:21). The fruitfulness of missionary activity is to be found in this communion. But since the Church is also a communion which is visible and organic, her mission requires an external and ordered union between the various responsibilities and functions involved, in such a way that all the members "may in harmony spend their energies for the building up of the Church" (AG 28).

To the Congregation responsible for missionary activity it falls to "direct and coordinate throughout the world the work of evangelizing peoples and of missionary cooperation, with due regard for the competence of the Congregation for the Oriental Churches."[36] Hence its task is to "recruit missionaries and distribute them in accordance with the more urgent needs of various regions . . . draw up an ordered plan of action, issue norms and directives, as well as principles which are appropriate for the

---

35. Plenary Assembly of the Sacred Congregation for the Evangelization of Peoples (1969), on catechists, and the related "Instruction" of April 1970; *Bibliographia Missionaria* 34 (1970) 197-212 and *S.C. de Propaganda Fide Memoria Rerum*, III/2 (1976) 821-831.

36. Apostolic Constitution *Pastor Bonus* (28 June 1988) 85; cf. AG 29.

work of evangelization, and assist in the initial stages of their work" (AG 29; cf. PB 86). I can only confirm these wise directives. In order to relaunch mission *ad gentes,* a center of outreach, direction and coordination is needed, namely the Congregation for the Evangelization of Peoples. I invite Episcopal Conferences and their various bodies, the Major Superiors of Orders, Congregations and Institutes, as well as lay organizations involved in missionary activity, to cooperate faithfully with this Dicastery, which has the authority necessary to plan and direct missionary activity and cooperation worldwide.

The same Congregation, which has behind it a long and illustrious history, is called to play a role of primary importance with regard to reflection and programs of action which the Church needs in order to be more decisively oriented toward the mission in its various forms. To this end, the Congregation should maintain close relations with the other Dicasteries of the Holy See, with the local Churches and various missionary forces. In an ecclesiology of communion in which the entire Church is missionary, but in which specific vocations and institutions for missionary work *ad gentes* remain indispensable, the guiding and coordinating role of the Congregation for the Evangelization of Peoples remains very important in order to ensure a united effort in confronting great questions of common concern, with due regard for the competence proper to each authority and structure.

76. Episcopal Conferences and their various groupings have great importance in directing and coordinating missionary activity on national and regional levels. The Council asks them to "confer together in dealing with more important questions and urgent problems, without, however, overlooking local differences" (AG 31), and to consider the complex issue of inculturation. In fact, large-scale and regular activity is already taking place in this area, with visible results. It is an activity which must be intensified and better coordinated with that of other bodies of the same Conferences so that missionary concern will not be left to the care of only one sector or body, but will be shared by all.

The bodies and institutions involved in missionary activity should join forces and initiatives as opportunity suggests. Conferences of Major Superiors should have this same concern in their own sphere, maintaining contact with Episcopal conferences in accordance with established directives and norms (AG 33), and also having recourse to mixed commissions.[37] Also desirable are meetings and other forms of cooperation between the various missionary institutions, both in formation and study,[38] as well as in the actual apostolate.

CHAPTER VII

COOPERATION IN MISSIONARY ACTIVITY

77. Since they are members of the Church by virtue of their Baptism, all Christians share responsibility for missionary activity. "Missionary cooperation" is the expression used to describe the sharing by communities and individual Christians in this right and duty.

Missionary cooperation is rooted and lived, above all, in personal union with Christ. Only if we are united to him as the branches to the vine (cf. Jn 15:5) can we produce good fruit. Through holiness of life every Christian can become a fruitful

---

37. Cf. Paul VI, Apostolic Letter Motu Proprio *Ecclesiae Sanctae* (6 August 1966) II, 43; *AAS* 58 (1966) 782.

38. Cf. AG 34; *Ecclesiae Sanctae*, III, 22.

part of the Church's mission. The Second Vatican Council invited all "to a profound interior renewal, so that having a lively awareness of their personal responsibility for the spreading of the Gospel, they may play their part in missionary work among the nations (AG 35; cf. CIC 211, 781).

Sharing in the universal mission therefore is not limited to certain specific activities, but is the sign of maturity in faith and of a Christian life that bears fruit. In this way, individual believers extend the reach of their charity and show concern for those both far and near. They pray for the missions and missionary vocations. They help missionaries and follow their work with interest. And when missionaries return, they welcome them with the same joy with which the first Christian communities heard from the Apostles the marvelous things which God had wrought through their preaching (cf. Acts 14:27).

Prayer and Sacrifice for Missionaries

78. Among the forms of sharing, first place goes to spiritual cooperation through prayer, sacrifice and the witness of Christian life. Prayer should accompany the journey of missionaries so that the proclamation of the word will be effective through God's grace. In his Letters, Saint Paul often asks the faithful to pray for him so that he might proclaim the Gospel with confidence and conviction. Prayer needs to be accompanied by sacrifice. The redemptive value of suffering, accepted and offered to God with love, derives from the sacrifice of Christ himself, who calls the members of his Mystical Body to share in his sufferings, to complete them in their own flesh (cf. Col 1:24). The sacrifice of missionaries should be shared and accompanied by the sacrifices of all the faithful. I therefore urge those engaged in the pastoral care of the sick to teach them about the efficacy of suffering, and to encourage them to offer their sufferings to God for missionaries. By making such an offering, the sick themselves become missionaries, as emphasized by a number of movements which have sprung up among them and for them. The Solemnity of Pentecost — the beginning of the Church's mission — is celebrated in some communities as a "Day of Suffering for the Missions."

"Here I am, Lord! I am Ready! Send Me!" (Is 6:8)

79. Cooperation is expressed above all by promoting missionary vocations. While acknowledging the validity of various ways of being involved in missionary activity, it is necessary at the same time to reaffirm that *a full and lifelong commitment to the work of the missions holds pride of place,* especially in missionary Institutes and Congregations. Promoting such vocations is at the heart of missionary cooperation. Preaching the Gospel requires preachers; the harvest needs laborers. The mission is carried out above all by men and women who are consecrated for life to the work of the Gospel and are prepared to go forth into the whole world to bring salvation.

I wish to call to mind and to recommend this *concern for missionary vocations.* Conscious of the overall responsibility of Christians to contribute to missionary activity and to the development of poorer peoples, we must ask ourselves how it is that in some countries, while monetary contributions are on the increase, missionary vocations, which are the real measure of self-giving to one's brothers and sisters, are in danger of disappearing. Vocations to the priesthood and the consecrated life are a sure sign of the vitality of a Church.

80. As I think of this serious problem, I appeal with great confidence and affection to families and to young people. Families, especially parents, should be conscious that they ought to "offer a special contribution to the missionary cause of the Church by fostering missionary vocations among their sons and daughters" (FC 54).

An intense prayer life, a genuine sense of service to one's neighbor and a generous participation in Church activities provide families with conditions that favor vocations among young people. When parents are ready to allow one of their children to leave for the missions, when they have sought this grace from the Lord, he will repay them, in joy, on the day that their son or daughter hears his call.

I ask young people themselves to listen to Christ's words as he says to them what he once said to Simon Peter and to Andrew at the lakeside: "Follow me, and I will make you fishers of men" (Mt 4:19). May they have the courage to reply as Isaiah did: "Here am I, Lord! I am ready! Send me!" (cf. Is 6:8). They will have a wonderful life ahead of them, and they will know the genuine joy of proclaiming the "Good News" to brothers and sisters whom they will lead on the way of salvation.

"It is More Blessed to Give than to Receive" (Acts 20:35)

81. The material and financial needs of the missions are many: not only to set up the Church with minimal structures (chapels, schools for catechists and seminarians, housing), but also to support works of charity, education and human promotion — a vast field of action especially in poor countries. The missionary Church gives what she receives, and distributes to the poor the material goods that her materially richer sons and daughters generously put at her disposal. Here I wish to thank all those who make sacrifices and contribute to the work of the missions. Their sacrifices and sharing are indispensable for building up the Church and for showing love.

In the matter of material help, it is important to consider the spirit in which donations are made. For this we should reassess our own way of living: the missions ask not only for a contribution but for a sharing in the work of preaching and charity toward the poor. All that we have received from God — life itself as well as material goods — does not belong to us but is given to us for our use. Generosity in giving must always be enlightened and inspired by faith: then we will truly be more blessed in giving than in receiving.

World Mission Day, which seeks to heighten awareness of the missions, as well as to collect funds for them, is an important date in the life of the Church, because it teaches how to give: as an offering made to God, *in* the Eucharistic celebration and *for all* the missions of the world.

New Forms of Missionary Cooperation

82. Today, cooperation includes new forms — not only economic assistance, but also direct participation. New situations connected with the phenomenon of mobility demand from Christians an authentic missionary spirit.

International tourism has now become a mass phenomenon. This is a positive development if tourists maintain an attitude of respect and a desire for mutual cultural enrichment, avoiding ostentation and waste, and seeking contact with other people. But Christians are expected above all to be aware of their obligation to bear witness always to their faith and love of Christ. Firsthand knowledge of the missionary life and of new Christian communities also can be an enriching experience and can strengthen one's faith. Visiting the missions is commendable, especially on the part of young people who go there to serve and to gain an intense experience of the Christian life.

Reasons of work nowadays bring many Christians from young communities to areas where Christianity is unknown and at times prohibited or persecuted. The same is true of members of the faithful from traditionally Christian countries who work for a time in non-Christian countries. These circumstances are certainly an opportunity to live the faith and to bear witness to it. In the early centuries, Christianity spread because Christians, traveling to or settling in regions where Christ had not yet been proclaimed, bore courageous witness to their faith and founded the first communities there.

More numerous are the citizens of mission countries and followers of non-Christian religions who settle in other nations for reasons of study or work, or are forced to do so because of the political or economic situations in their native lands. The presence of these brothers and sisters in traditionally Christian countries is a challenge for the ecclesial communities, and a stimulus to hospitality, dialogue, service, sharing, witness and direct proclamation. In Christian countries, communities and cultural groups are also forming which call for the mission *ad gentes,* and the local Churches, with the help of personnel from the immigrants' own countries and of returning missionaries, should respond generously to these situations.

Missionary cooperation can also involve leaders in politics, economics, culture and journalism, as well as experts of the various international bodies. In the modern world it is becoming increasingly difficult to determine geographical or cultural boundaries. There is an increasing interdependence between peoples, and this constitutes a stimulus for Christian witness and evangelization.

Missionary Promotion and Formation among the People of God

83. Missionary formation is the task of the local Church, assisted by missionaries and their Institutes, and by personnel from the young Churches. This work must be seen not as peripheral but as central to the Christian life. Even for the "new evangelization" of Christian countries the theme of the missions can prove very helpful: the witness of missionaries retains its appeal even for the non-practicing and non-believers, and it communicates Christian values. Particular Churches should therefore make the promotion of the missions a key element in the normal pastoral activity of parishes, associations and groups, especially youth groups.

With this end in view, it is necessary to spread information through missionary publications and audiovisual aids. These play an important role in making known the life of the universal Church and in voicing the experiences of missionaries and of the local Churches in which they work. In those younger Churches which are still not able to have a press and other means of their own, it is important that Missionary Institutes devote personnel and resources to these undertakings.

Such formation is entrusted to priests and their associates, to educators and teachers, and to theologians, particularly those who teach in seminaries and centers for the laity. Theological training cannot and should not ignore the Church's universal mission, ecumenism, the study of the great religions and missiology. I recommend that such studies be undertaken especially in seminaries and in houses of formation for men and women Religious, ensuring that some priests or other students specialize in the different fields of missiology.

Activities aimed at promoting interest in the missions must always be geared to these specific goals; namely, informing and forming the People of God to share in the Church's universal mission, promoting vocations *ad gentes* and encouraging cooperation in the work of evangelization. It is not right to give an incomplete picture of missionary activity, as if it consisted principally in helping the poor, contributing to the liberation of the oppressed, promoting development or defending human rights. The missionary Church is certainly involved on these fronts but her primary task lies elsewhere: the poor are hungry for God, not just for bread and freedom. Missionary activity must first of all bear witness to and proclaim salvation in Christ, and establish local Churches which then become means of liberation in every sense.

The Primary Responsibility of the Pontifical Mission Societies

84. The leading role in this work of promotion belongs to the *Pontifical Mission Societies,* as I have often pointed out in my Messages for World Mission Day. The four Societies — Propagation of the Faith, Saint Peter the Apostle, Holy Childhood and the Missionary Union — have the common purpose of fostering a universal missionary spirit among the People of God. The Missionary Union has as its immediate and specific purpose the promotion of missionary consciousness and formation among priests and men and women Religious, who in turn will provide this consciousness and formation within the Christian communities. In addition, the Missionary Union seeks to promote the other Societies, of which it is the "soul." [39] "This must be our motto: All the Churches united for the conversion of the whole world." [40]

Because they are under the auspices of the Pope and of the College of Bishops, these Societies, also within the boundaries of the particular Churches, rightly have "the first place . . . since they are the means by which Catholics from their very infancy are imbued with a genuinely universal and missionary spirit; they are also the means which ensure an effective collection of resources for the good of all the missions, in accordance with the needs of each one" (AG 38). Another purpose of the Missionary Societies is the fostering of lifelong vocations *ad gentes,* in both the older and younger Churches. I earnestly recommend that their promotional work be increasingly directed to this goal.

In their activities, these Societies depend at the worldwide level on the Congregation for the Evangelization of Peoples; at the local level they depend on the Episcopal Conferences and the Bishops of individual Churches, in collaboration with existing promotional centers. They bring to the Catholic world that spirit of universality and of service to the Church's mission, without which authentic cooperation does not exist.

Not only Giving to the Missions but Receiving from Them as Well

85. Cooperating in missionary activity means not just giving but also receiving. All the particular Churches, both young and old, are called to give and to receive in the context of the universal mission, and none should be closed to the needs of others. The Council states: "By virtue of . . . catholicity, the individual parts bring their own gifts to the other parts and to the whole Church, in such a way that the whole and individual parts grow greater through the mutual communication of all and their united efforts toward fullness in unity. . . . Between the different parts of the Church there are bonds of intimate communion with regard to spiritual riches, apostolic workers and temporal assistance" (LG 13).

I exhort all the Churches, and the Bishops, priests, religious and members of the laity, to *be open to the Church's universality,* and to avoid every form of provincialism or exclusiveness, or feelings of self-sufficiency. Local Churches, although rooted in their own people and their own culture, must always maintain an effective sense of the universality of the faith, giving and receiving spiritual gifts, experiences of pastoral work in evangelization and initial proclamation, as well as personnel for the apostolate and material resources.

The temptation to become isolated can be a strong one. The older Churches, involved in new evangelization, may think that their mission is now at home, and

---

39. Cf. Paul VI, Apostolic Epistle *Graves et Increscentes* (5 September 1966).

40. P. Manna, *Le nostre "Chiese" e la propagazione del Vangelo* (Trentola: Ducenta, 1952), p. 35.

thus they may risk slackening their drive toward the non-Christian world, begrudgingly conceding vocations to missionary Institutes, Religious Congregations or other particular Churches. But it is by giving generously of what we have that we will receive. Already the young Churches, many of which are blessed with an abundance of vocations, are in a position to send priests and men and women Religious to the older Churches.

On the other hand, the young Churches are concerned about their own identity, about inculturation, and about their freedom to grow independently of external influences, with the possible result that they close their doors to missionaries. To these Churches I say: Do not isolate yourselves; willingly accept missionaries and support from other Churches, and do likewise throughout the world. Precisely because of the problems that concern you, you need to be in continuous contact with your brothers and sisters in the faith. With every legitimate means, seek to ensure recognition of the freedom to which you have a right, remembering that Christ's disciples must "obey God rather than men" (Acts 5:29).

God is Preparing a New Springtime for the Gospel

86. If we look at today's world, we are struck by many negative factors that can lead to pessimism. But this feeling is unjustified: we have faith in God our Father and Lord, in his goodness and mercy. As the third millennium of the Redemption draws near, God is preparing a great springtime for Christianity, and we can already see its first signs. In fact, both in the non-Christian world and in the traditionally Christian world, people are gradually drawing closer to Gospel ideals and values, a development which the Church seeks to encourage. Today in fact there is a new consensus among peoples about these values: the rejection of violence and war; respect for the human person and for human rights; the desire for freedom, justice and brotherhood; the surmounting of different forms of racism and nationalism; the affirmation of the dignity and role of women.

Christian hope sustains us in committing ourselves fully to the new evangelization and to the worldwide mission, and leads us to pray as Jesus taught us: "Thy Kingdom come. Thy will be done, on earth as it is in heaven" (Mt 6:10).

The number of those awaiting Christ is still immense: the human and cultural groups not yet reached by the Gospel, or for whom the Church is scarcely present, are so widespread as to require the uniting of all the Church's resources. As she prepares to celebrate the Jubilee of the year 2000, the whole Church is even more committed to a new missionary advent. We must increase our apostolic zeal to pass on to others the light and joy of the faith, and to this high ideal the whole People of God must be educated.

We cannot be content when we consider the millions of our brothers and sisters, who like us have been redeemed by the blood of Christ but who live in ignorance of the love of God. For each believer, as for the entire Church, the missionary task must remain foremost, for it concerns the eternal destiny of humanity and corresponds to God's mysterious and merciful plan.

CHAPTER VIII

MISSIONARY SPIRITUALITY

87. Missionary activity demands a specific spirituality, which applies in particular to all those whom God has called to be missionaries.

Being Led by the Spirit

This spirituality is expressed first of all by a life of complete docility to the Spirit. It commits us to being molded from within by the Spirit, so that we may become ever more like Christ. It is not possible to bear witness to Christ without reflecting his image, which is made alive in us by grace and the power of the Spirit. This docility then commits us to receive the gifts of fortitude and discernment, which are essential elements of missionary spirituality.

An example of this is found with the Apostles during the Master's public life. Despite their love for him and their generous response to his call, they proved to be incapable of understanding his words and reluctant to follow him along the path of suffering and humiliation. The Spirit transformed them into courageous witnesses to Christ and enlightened heralds of his word. It was the Spirit himself who guided them along the difficult and new paths of mission.

Today, as in the past, that mission is difficult and complex, and demands the courage and light of the Spirit. We often experience the dramatic situation of the first Christian community, which witnessed unbelieving and hostile forces "gathered together against the Lord and his Anointed" (Acts 4:26). Now, as then, we must pray that God will grant us boldness in preaching the Gospel; we must ponder the mysterious ways of the Spirit and allow ourselves to be led by him into all the truth (cf. Jn 16:13).

Living the Mystery of Christ, "the One who was Sent"

88. An essential characteristic of missionary spirituality is intimate communion with Christ. We cannot understand or carry out the mission unless we refer it to Christ as the one who was sent to evangelize. Saint Paul describes Christ's attitude: "Have this mind among yourselves, which is yours in Christ Jesus, who, though he was in the form of God, did not count equality with God a thing to be grasped, but emptied himself, taking the form of a servant, being born in the likeness of men. And being found in human form he humbled himself and became obedient unto death, even death on a Cross" (Phil 2:5-8).

The mystery of the Incarnation and Redemption is thus described as a total self-emptying which leads Christ to experience fully the human condition and to accept totally the Father's plan. This is an emptying of self which is permeated by love and expresses love. The mission follows this same path and leads to the foot of the Cross.

The missionary is required to "renounce himself and everything that up to this point he considered as his own, and to make himself everything to everyone" (AG 24). This he does by a poverty which sets him free for the Gospel, overcoming attachment to the people and things about him, so that he may become a brother to those to whom he is sent and thus bring them Christ the Savior. This is the goal of missionary spirituality: "To the weak I became weak. . . . I have become all things to all men, that I might by all means save some. I do it all for the sake of the Gospel" (1 Cor 9:22-23).

It is precisely because he is "sent" that the missionary experiences the consoling presence of Christ, who is with him at every moment of life — "Do not be afraid . . . for I am with you" (Acts 18:9-10) — and who awaits him in the heart of every person.

Loving the Church and Humanity as Jesus Did

89. Missionary spirituality is also marked by apostolic charity, the charity of Christ who came "to gather into one the children of God who are scattered abroad" (Jn 11:52), of the Good Shepherd who knows his sheep, who searches them out and

offers his life for them (cf. Jn 10). Those who have the missionary spirit feel Christ's burning love for souls, and love the Church as Christ did.

The missionary is urged on by "zeal for souls," a zeal inspired by Christ's own charity, which takes the form of concern, tenderness, compassion, openness, availability and interest in people's problems. Jesus's love is very deep: he who "knew what was in man" (Jn 2:25) loved everyone by offering them redemption and suffered when it was rejected.

The missionary is a person of charity. In order to proclaim to all his brothers and sisters that they are loved by God and are capable of loving, he must show love toward all, giving his life for his neighbor. The missionary is the "universal brother," bearing in himself the Church's spirit, her openness to and interest in all peoples and individuals, especially the least and poorest of his brethren. As such, he overcomes barriers and divisions of race, caste, or ideology. He is a sign of God's love in the world — a love without exclusion or partiality.

Finally, like Christ he must love the Church: "Christ loved the Church and gave himself up for her" (Eph 5:25). This love, even to the point of giving one's life, is a focal point for him. Only profound love for the Church can sustain the missionary's zeal. His daily pressure, as Saint Paul says, is "anxiety for all the Churches" (2 Cor 11:28). For every missionary "fidelity to Christ cannot be separated from fidelity to the Church" (PO 14).

The True Missionary is the Saint

90. The call to mission derives, of its nature, from the call to holiness. A missionary is really such only if he commits himself to the way of holiness: "Holiness must be called a fundamental presupposition and an irreplaceable condition for everyone in fulfilling the mission of salvation in the Church" (CL 17).

The universal call to holiness is closely linked to the universal call to mission. Every member of the faithful is called to holiness and to mission. This was the earnest desire of the Council, which hoped to be able "to enlighten all people with the brightness of Christ, which gleams over the face of the Church, by preaching the Gospel to every creature" (LG 1). The Church's missionary spirituality is a journey toward holiness.

The renewed impulse to the mission *ad gentes* demands holy missionaries. It is not enough to update pastoral techniques, organize and coordinate ecclesial resources, or delve more deeply into the biblical and theological foundations of faith. What is needed is the encouragement of a new "ardor for holiness" among missionaries and throughout the Christian unity, especially among those who work most closely with missionaries.[41]

Dear Brothers and Sisters: let us remember the missionary enthusiasm of the first Christian communities. Despite the limited means of travel and communication in those times, the proclamation of the Gospel quickly reached the ends of the earth. And this was the religion of a man who had died on a cross, "a stumbling block to Jews and folly to Gentiles" (1 Cor 1:23)! Underlying this missionary dynamism was the holiness of the first Christians and the first communities.

91. I therefore address myself to the recently baptized members of the young communities and young Churches. Today, you are the hope of this two-thousand-

---

41. Cf. Address at CELAM (Conference of Latin American Bishops) Meeting, Port-au-Prince (9 March 1983); *AAS* 75 (1983) 771-779; *Homily* for the Opening of the "Novena of Years" promoted by CELAM, Santo Domingo (12 October 1984); *Insegnamenti* VII/2 (1984) 885-897.

year-old Church of ours: being young in faith, you must be like the first Christians and radiate enthusiasm and courage, in generous devotion to God and neighbor. In a word, you must set yourselves on the path of holiness. Only thus can you be a sign of God in the world and relive in your own countries the missionary epic of the early Church. You will also be a leaven of missionary spirit for the older Churches.

For their part, missionaries should reflect on the duty of holiness required of them by the gift of their vocation, renew themselves in spirit day by day, and strive to update their doctrinal and pastoral formation. The missionary must be a "contemplative in action." He finds answers to problems in the light of God's word and in personal and community prayer. My contact with representatives of the non-Christian spiritual traditions, particularly those of Asia, has confirmed me in the view that the future of mission depends to a great extent on contemplation. Unless the missionary is a contemplative he cannot proclaim Christ in a credible way. He is a witness to the experience of God, and must be able to say with the Apostles: "that which we have looked upon . . . concerning the word of life . . . we proclaim also to you" (1 Jn 1:1-3).

The missionary is a person of the Beatitudes. Before sending out the Twelve to evangelize, Jesus, in his "missionary discourse" (cf. Mt 10), teaches them the paths of mission: poverty, meekness, acceptance of suffering and persecution, the desire for justice and peace, charity — in other words, the Beatitudes, lived out in the apostolic life (cf. Mt 5:1-12). By living the Beatitudes, the missionary experiences and shows concretely that the Kingdom of God has already come, and that he has accepted it. The characteristic of every authentic missionary life is the inner joy that comes from faith. In a world tormented and oppressed by so many problems, a world tempted to pessimism, the one who proclaims the "Good News" must be a person who has found true hope in Christ.

CONCLUSION

92. Today, as never before, the Church has the opportunity of bringing the Gospel, by witness and word, to all people and nations. I see the dawning of a new missionary age, which will become a radiant day bearing an abundant harvest, if all Christians, and missionaries and young Churches in particular, respond with generosity and holiness to the calls and challenges of our time.

Like the Apostles after Christ's Ascension, the Church must gather in the Upper Room "together with Mary the Mother of Jesus" (Acts 1:14), in order to pray for the Spirit and to gain strength and courage to carry out the missionary mandate. We too, like the Apostles, need to be transformed and guided by the Spirit.

On the eve of the third Millennium the whole Church is invited to live more intensely the mystery of Christ by gratefully cooperating in the work of salvation. The Church does this together with Mary and following the example of Mary, the Church's Mother and model: Mary is the model of that maternal love which should inspire all who cooperate in the Church's apostolic mission for the rebirth of humanity. Therefore, "strengthened by the presence of Christ, the Church journeys through time toward the consummation of the ages and goes to meet the Lord who comes. But on this journey . . . she proceeds along *the path* already trodden by the Virgin Mary." [42]

To "Mary's mediation, wholly oriented toward Christ and tending to the revelation of his salvific power," [43] I entrust the Church and, in particular, those who

---

42. Encyclical Letter *Redemptoris Mater* (25 March 1987) 2; *AAS* 79 (1987), 362f.
43. Ibid., 22, p. 390.

commit themselves to carrying out the missionary mandate in today's world. As Christ sent forth his Apostles in the name of the Father and of the Son and of the Holy Spirit, so too, renewing that same mandate, I extend to all of you my Apostolic Blessing, in the name of the same Most Holy Trinity. Amen.

Given in Rome, at Saint Peter's, on 7 December, the Twenty-fifth Anniversary of the Conciliar Decree *Ad Gentes*, in the year 1990, the thirteenth of my Pontificate.

Pope John Paul II

Commentary on Redemptoris Missio

Marcello Zago, O.M.I.

Marcello Zago is Superior General of the Oblates of Mary Immaculate and a member of the Vatican Congregation for Consecrated Life, as well as Consultor to the Congregation for the Evangelization of Peoples and to the Pontifical Council for Interreligious Dialogue. Father Zago studied Buddhism in Laos and later did a doctoral dissertation on Buddhism at the Gregorian University. He has long been active in Buddhist–Christian dialogue.

Introduction

The encyclical letter *Redemptoris Missio** is central to the teaching of Pope John Paul II. From a missiological viewpoint it is certainly the most significant and authoritative document of his pontificate. An encyclical is the direct result of the Pope's own initiative and he is personally responsible for it.[1] The importance of this particular document also derives from the occasion of its publication, which is the twenty-fifth anniversary of the Council Decree *Ad Gentes* on missionary activity in the Church.[2] In

---

* References to paragraph (article) numbers in the text of *Redemptoris Missio* are made by giving the number of the paragraph in parentheses without the abbreviation "RM" unless this is needed to clear up ambiguity; references to other official documents will give the standard abbreviation. See the table of abbreviations for full names of cited documents.

1. It is important to note that there are various types of documents in the papal magisterium. Next to papal pronouncements *ex cathedra*, encyclicals are the most important and authoritative form of teaching. An encyclical is composed by the Pope or under his direct authority and supervision. Less importance is attached to apostolic exhortations. In recent times, postsynodal exhortations have been in this category; they are signed by the Pope but prepared by members of the Permanent Council of the Synod, who are elected by the previous synod. Documents issued by the Roman Curia have the authority of the office that issues them; normally they are approved at a plenary session of that office attended by its Cardinal and bishop members.

2. A commemorative date on a papal document may be very significant. A number of

fact, *Redemptoris Missio* is the principal papal document to commemorate and recall the greatest ecclesial event of this century, the Second Vatican Council.

Every document has its place in a given historical and ecclesial context. We shall consider four aspects of the context in which *Redemptoris Missio* is situated: the situation of missions in the world, continuity with other missionary encyclicals of this century and the features proper to this encyclical, its place in the pontificate of John Paul II, and its relationship to the outlook and dynamics of Vatican Council II. These four aspects are, in fact, mentioned in the encyclical itself. We shall then point out those to whom the encyclical is addressed and give an evaluation of it before concluding with a word about its structure and the language of the document itself.

1. Missionary Context

The Pope's intention is to situate the encyclical in the context of mission today. He is careful to deal with concrete situations, bringing to bear on them the light of evangelical discernment. He points out the phenomena that influence mission today.[3] He takes a careful look at the situation of humanity in relation to the faith and its transmission through evangelization. On this basis he points out the priorities that it is the church's duty to adopt (cf. 33f.). These new situations thus become the modern *areopagi* where the missionaries must be present to exercise their ministry (cf. 37f., 82).

The Pope is aware of the many developments of mission from the Second Vatican Council to the present time. Several times he recalls the positive aspects of this evolution (cf. 2). He also goes back to this positive evaluation when describing the present religious picture (cf. 32) when he observes:

The results of missionary activity in modern times are certainly positive. The Church has been established on every continent; indeed today the majority of believers and particular Churches is to be found no longer in Europe but on the continents which missionaries have opened up to the faith. (40)

For this reason the Pope is optimistic about the future (cf. 86). Several times he thanks missionaries for their dedication and creativity (cf. 2, 60, 66, 70). It is important to stress this positive attitude, which dominates the document and allows it to be understood correctly (cf. 2, 6, 32, 37, 38, 40, 51, 86).

However, the Pope is also aware of the negative aspects and of the difficulties that hinder mission. He points out these difficulties from the very beginning:

---

social and missionary encyclicals have been issued to commemorate previous documents on the same subject. They are not merely a celebration of the event but are also an occasion to apply the teachings of the original document to later situations. *Redemptoris Missio* bears the date 7 December 1990, the twenty-fifth anniversary of the Vatican Council II Decree on Missions, *Ad Gentes*. It was published on 22 January 1991, at the height of the Gulf War. The presentation to the press was made by Cardinal Jozef Tomko, Prefect of the Congregation for the Evangelization of Peoples, assisted by the author of this commentary, Marcello Zago, of the Oblates of Mary Immaculate.

3. The Pope mentions migration (32, 37, 40, 82); urbanization (32, 37); relativism (11, 36); the "horizontalization" and secularization of the concept of salvation (8, 11, 36); pluralism (11a, 32); and materialism and the quest for the sacred (32, 38, 50). Particular mention is made of the various factors affecting the proclamation of the Gospel and its realization (3, 30, 86, 92).

Nevertheless, in this "new springtime" of Christianity there is an undeniable negative tendency, and the present document is meant to help overcome it. Missionary activity specifically directed "to the nations" (*ad gentes*) appears to be waning, and this tendency is certainly not in line with the directives of the Council and of subsequent statements of the Magisterium. Difficulties both internal and external have weakened the Church's missionary thrust toward non-Christians, a fact which must arouse concern among all who believe in Christ. For in the Church's history, missionary drive has always been a sign of vitality, just as its lessening is a sign of a crisis of faith. (2)

In Chapter IV, which gives an overall picture of the missionary situation and needs, the Pope first recalls that the task of proclaiming Jesus Christ to all peoples, "appears immense and out of all proportion to the Church's human resources," and then goes on to mention the internal and external difficulties that tend to hinder and weaken the missionary commitment (cf. 35f.). With regard to internal difficulties there is a long list that develops those mentioned in the introduction. These reflect the withdrawal of people and communities into themselves; lack of fervor, of joy and hope; fatigue; divisions. He mentions in particular widespread indifferentism and relativism (36). Even the theological ambiguities mentioned in the first three chapters show the present context of missionary thought and practice. (See below, section 6, for more on this.)

The concept of mission *ad gentes* is analyzed in the present complex religious situation, which is ever changing (cf. 32-34, 37f.), without hiding the problems, widespread ideas and an "uneasiness" that "denotes a real change, one which has certain positive aspects" (32). Looking at today's world from the viewpoint of evangelization, we can distinguish three situations within the one mission of the church, which require three forms of ecclesial activity: specifically missionary activity among non-Christians, the pastoral care of Christians, and the new evangelization of those who are no longer Christians (cf. 33).

To explain the concept of mission and to show its necessities and channels, various spheres in which it is carried out are indicated: territorial context, new social phenomena, and cultural areas or the *areopagi*. The long number of fields for mission that he cites shows the complexity, the division, and the necessities of the scene in which mission *ad gentes* is exercised. Contextualization is also seen in the light of the new pastoral initiatives. In the postconciliar period missionary activity has undertaken and developed new ways, such as human promotion, inculturation, base communities, and new ministries (cf. 51-59, 74).

For the agents of the mission (cf. 61-76), there are also new suggestions that take account of the postconciliar progress and of new needs that have arisen in the meantime. With the emphasis given to missionary Institutes and missionaries "for life," two categories have quite rightly appeared on the scene: diocesan priests and the laity. They are present precisely because of their specific vocation. Although all the churches are invited to be open to the missionary dimension in order to be faithful to their universal calling and to find incentive for renewal, particular attention is given to the young churches, on which to a large extent the missionary thrust will depend in the various geographical areas of the world.

The various forms of cooperation also have new horizons (cf. 77-85). In the treatment of the traditional forms stress is laid on the inner incentive of holiness and the importance of promoting specific vocations, while new ways of cooperation are made possible or necessary because of human mobility and world interdependence, such as tourism, emigration, and international, political, and economic repercussions (cf. 82, 34). In this context mission is important everywhere, although there are well-defined areas of priority. It is the responsibility of all, even though it needs certain people who are totally devoted to it.

The contextualization of the encyclical is also evident from the fact that it takes on board the values that are dear to the hearts of the men and women of today. Commitment to and respect for liberty (cf. 8, 39, 11), for persons (cf. 42, 29, 58), for peoples (cf. 28f., 52f.), ecumenical and interreligious dialogue (20, 25, 29, 50, 55ff.), altruism and charity (14f., 20, 26, 42, 51, 58-60, 70, 72, 81, 82), the quality of being as superior to having (7, 13, 15, 31, 60, 89), and witness (13, 23, 42, 90f.) are all presented as characteristic of and required by mission. At a time when conflict and integralism seem so prevalent, the Pope's invitation to commitment to the mission is quite different from much of today's propaganda, even in the religious sphere, which so often is an invitation to holy war or at least to conquest. The mission must always be exercised in affective and effective charity toward all, in respect for persons and cultures, in promoting liberty of thought and choice for persons and peoples. These values, which are so precious to the people of today, are presented as being a natural part of the Christian message.

2. Context of the Missionary Magisterium

The encyclical is an integral part of the traditional papal magisterium. In the course of the present century the Popes have issued five missionary encyclicals. Benedict XV began immediately after the First World War with *Maximum Illud* dated 30 November 1919. Pius XI wrote *Rerum Ecclesiae* dated 28 February 1926. Pius XII published two missionary encyclicals: *Evangelii Praecones* on 2 June 1951 and *Fidei Donum* on 21 April 1957, commemorating the missionary encyclical of his predecessor. John XXIII concluded the preconciliar series with *Princeps Pastorum* dated 28 November 1959 and commemorating the fortieth anniversary of Benedict XV's encyclical.

The purpose of all these encyclicals, including that of Pope John Paul II, is to promote missions among non-Christian peoples, encouraging the missionaries and their work for the evangelization of non-Christians and the implantation of the church, and involving the whole church in missionary cooperation.

However, each one of these encyclicals is situated in a certain historical context and emphasizes aspects considered important at the time of publication. In *Maximum Illud* Benedict XV warns the missionaries of 1919 against nationalism and he invites them to promote local clergy. In 1926, Pius XI develops in *Rerum Ecclesiae* the theme of various native vocations, both clerical and religious, contemplative and catechist, and he promotes missionary cooperation under the direction of the Pontifical Missionary Societies. In his first missionary encyclical, Pius XII emphasizes the role of the laity, respect for cultural values and the importance of social action in the mission. The second encyclical, published in 1959, is devoted to the urgent needs of the African continent at the time of political independence and he invites diocesan priests to give a few years to serving in the missions. John XXIII's encyclical is devoted to the responsibilities and the formation of local clergy and laity.

As well as mentioning these encyclicals in the introduction, *Redemptoris Missio* refers to four of them more directly. Speaking of the need to overcome cultural and nationalistic barriers, in contrast to Benedict, who cautioned the foreign missionaries against a nationalism that could damage mission work, John Paul cautions the local churches whose nationalism could shut them off from the universal Church (39, cf. 85).

On the subject of the promotion of the laity, *Redemptoris Missio* refers to the first missionary encyclical of Pius XII and to that of John XXIII, which were largely devoted to this subject (cf. 71). Pope John Paul II reminds us that in the encyclical

Fidei Donum Pius XII "with prophetic insight, encouraged Bishops to offer some of their priests for temporary service in the Churches of Africa, and gave his approval to projects already existing for that purpose" (68). These references are not merely celebrating a memory. Together with the continuity they demonstrate, they also show the progress and novelty of certain themes, such as the role of native clergy and laity, respect for culture, commitment to human promotion, and motivation for the mission. Vatican Council II has evidently marked a turning point. Nevertheless, changes between the preconciliar and the postconciliar era are always characterized also by continuity. Papal magisterium has always been a guide for the progress of missionary activity by accepting the challenges and illuminating them with a wider outlook. In this way it has prepared the Council itself.

In relation to the preconciliar missionary encyclicals, it can be said that *Redemptoris Missio* is composed to respond to present-day problems but does not limit itself to a few special aspects. This is due to the fact that mission has been questioned or has undergone scrutiny in most aspects of its existence. *Redemptoris Missio* is a global document that looks afresh at all aspects of missionary activity. Though it has a consistent theological structure and the teaching is more developed that in the other encyclicals, it is mainly directed to practice. Its theological basis is mostly taken from the New Testament and it takes account of some present-day problems. Even the first part, which is doctrinal, takes account of such problems and, on the whole, is intended to provide missionary inspiration and animation and not only theological clarifications. The second part, which is more directly pastoral, is enriched with a theological outlook. It is only in this light, for instance, that we can understand the value of dialogue or of human promotion, as well as their relationship to explicit proclamation. The overall objective is pastoral: that is, it seeks to promote the missionary activity of the whole church but especially of the younger churches.

3. Within the Context of John Paul II's Pontificate

The missionary encyclical is not merely a fortuitous document in the pontificate of Pope John Paul II. It is an integral part of the Pope's missionary commitment, as expressed in his ordinary pastoral activity of meetings and teachings, as well as in the extraordinary ministry of traveling abroad and more solemn magisterium. In the realm of his ordinary pastoral ministry we may refer to his meetings with Bishops from all over the world on the occasion of their visits with him every five years. His addresses to them deal with the missionary needs and requirements of their particular churches. Other occasions are provided by recurring events such as world mission days and his meetings with the members of the plenary sessions of the Congregation for the Evangelization of Peoples in which he deals with missionary themes.

The Pope's journeys abroad may be considered as extraordinary pastoral ministry because of the importance attributed to them. During these journeys he meets with a wide variety of groups and gives numerous addresses, which constitute an anthology for the local church. There is an echo of these addresses in the encyclical as may be gathered from numerous footnotes.[4] On the subject of these journeys the Pope points out the personal choices made and the impressions received:

> From the beginning of my Pontificate I have chosen to travel to the ends of the earth in order to show this missionary concern. My direct contact with peoples who do not know Christ has convinced me even more of the *urgency of missionary activity*, a subject to which I am devoting the present encyclical (1, emphasis in original; cf. 63, 91).

---

4. Cf. notes in RM 4, 8, 10, 14, 20, 22, 23, 31, 32, 35, 41.

As regards the more solemn magisterium, it will be sufficient to deal with the encyclicals of Pope John Paul II. *Redemptoris Missio* is the eighth of the pontificate and it quotes six of the seven that went before. There is no explicit mention of *Laborem Exercens* (14 September 1981), the subject of which was taken up again in 1988.

The three trinitarian encyclicals[5] receive most mention in *Redemptoris Missio* and they provide the theme for the first three chapters, each of which begins with a quotation from one of them. They also provide inspiration for other parts of the document. For instance, flashes from *Redemptor Hominis* with its two key concepts concerning Christ and man can be found explicitly mentioned in sections dealing with liberty (cf. 39, 8, 11), dialogue (cf. 56), and humanity (cf. 2, 29, 39, 58); indirect mention is made in sections dealing with human promotion (cf. 58f.), proclamation and conversion (cf. 45, 47), and salvation (cf. 2, 4-7, 11f., 18, 23, 36, 39, 88).

The encyclical on the mercy of God not only provides the structure for the second chapter, on the Kingdom of God, but pervades the whole of mission theology. The merciful love of the Father is the beginning and end of the mission, which is therefore the expression of love and introduces the person to the love of God (cf. 7, 12, 13, 15, 20, 22f., 31, 44, 46, 60, 89). The love of God the Father embraces non-Christians (cf. 3, 11-13, 45, 55, 86).

The encyclical on the Holy Spirit provides the introduction to the theme of chapter three. In the two sections on the Spirit present and active at all times and in all places, it is quoted at length four times (cf. 28f.), and again in pointing out the dynamics of proclamation (cf. 44). It is evident however in all of the theology of the Holy Spirit, which pervades the document.[6]

Quotations and reflections from the other three encyclicals are more limited. *Slavorum Apostoli* (2 June 1895) is quoted in the context of incarnating the Gospel in the culture of the people (cf. 52); *Sollicitudo Rei Socialis* is quoted three times in the discussion of development (cf. 58f.) and *Redemptoris Mater* is quoted twice in the conclusion (cf. 92). The full missionary dimension of these encyclicals does not appear here, however, in all its richness. Thus the theme of *Slavorum Apostoli*, on the work of Saints Cyril and Methodius, contains significant elements that seem somewhat glossed over in *Redemptoris Missio*. Neither can the short references to *Redemptoris Mater* give all the missionary content of that document. The social encyclicals develop other points that are important for missionary activity.

Redemptoris Missio, however, not only synthesizes and reflects the missionary teaching of John Paul II but it also brings together in a form of "practical" harmony all his teaching. The document is concerned with overcoming the dichotomy that tends to appear in both missionary practice and reflection. It is by no means rare, for instance, to contrast dialogue and proclamation, human promotion and inculturation, witnessing presence and activity, justice and spirituality, social reality and religious reality, Christian renewal and universal salvation. *Redemptoris Missio*, on the other hand, offers a theological and practical pedagogy, which I am inclined to call an *integration* or, in the terminology of some Asiatic schools, *harmony*. At a time of change marked by lack of certainty and by novelty, it presents three important

---

5. *Redemptor Hominis* ("The Redeemer of Humanity," 4 March 1979), *AAS* 71 (1979), pp. 1277-1340; *Dives in Misericordia* ("Rich in Mercy," 30 November 1980), *AAS* 72 (1980), pp. 1174-1234; *Dominum et Vivificantem* ("Lord and Giver of Life," 18 May 1986), *AAS* 78 (1986), pp. 809-900.

6. In *Redemptoris Missio* the Holy Spirit is mentioned 98 times; 51 of them are in the third chapter; cf. 10, 21-25, 28-30, 44f., 56, 87, 92; see below, sections 9 and 10 of this commentary for reflections on this.

methodological principles. First, in times of uncertainty one must renew the central nucleus of one's faith. Thus, based on Sacred Scripture, which is the permanent model of the church's life, the need for and the nature of mission are measured up to Christ and his message (cf. 4-8, 10f.), to the reality of the Kingdom of God (cf. 12-20), and to the Spirit working in the church and in the world (cf. 21-30).

Second, faced with the emerging changes in the world, new discoveries are not contrasted with older values but rather integrated with them. Thus, dialogue is seen in relation to proclamation (cf. 55), human freedom in relation to conversion (cf. 7, 10, 39, 46), respect for religions in relation to the role of the church (cf. 5-11, 28f., 46, 55), salvation offered to all in relation to the newness of Christianity (cf. 7, 10f., 46-55), and respect for others in relation to a deeper awareness of one's own identity (cf. 7, 10f., 33). Life grows by absorbing new values without denying itself or the values that constitute it.

Third, the encyclical not only points out the values but also a methodology for absorbing them and integrating them in one's own life and activity. It provides a hierarchy of principles but without denying the need for realism in their application and respect for persons and for the hand of providence. Thus it states: "All forms of missionary activity are directed to this proclamation, which reveals and gives access to the mystery hidden for ages and made known in Christ" (44). All the diverse forms of missionary commitment, however different one from another, have a reciprocal harmony and an innate tendency toward direct proclamation, which is the very heart of the missionary mandate (cf. 2, 20, 23, 31, 34, 44f., 58f.). In practice, however, one must discern what is concretely opportune or possible. Thus we should recognize "that many missionaries and Christian communities find in the difficult and often misunderstood path of dialogue their only way of bearing sincere witness to Christ and offering generous service to others" (57).

4. Post-Vatican II Conciliar Context

The missionary encyclical was published to commemorate the missionary decree *Ad Gentes*, but it also reflects how Pope John Paul II relates to Vatican Council II. For him the Council is an important and decisive event, inserted however in the rich tradition of the church. Addressing the Roman Curia on 22 December 1992, the Pope called to mind the thirtieth anniversary of the Council's beginning: "A Council always takes place at a determined point in history, but it also springs up, as it were, from the subsoil of the Church's history, right from the beginning. . . . It is a major work of the Magisterium and, at the same time, a programming of the apostolic and pastoral mission of the Church."[7] The Council is a point of reference and communion for the whole People of God, as he writes in his first encyclical: "In fact, what the Spirit says to the Church through the Council of our time, what the Spirit says through that Church to other Churches, cannot — in spite of passing concerns — serve any other purpose than a greater solidarity among the People of God, fully aware of its saving mission" (RH 3).

The Council is for him a source of inspiration, as is obvious from the frequent quotations from it throughout his magisterium. The references are central to his thought and teaching. In this encyclical the most quoted document (cited about fifty times) is the Decree *Ad Gentes*. Next come the two Constitutions on the church in the modern world: *Lumen Gentium* is quoted about fifteen times and *Gaudium et Spes* about ten. There are two quotations each from the declaration on religious

---

7. John Paul II, "Address to the Roman Curia on Vatican Council II," *Osservatore Romano* (23 December 1992), p. 6.

liberty, ecumenism, interreligious dialogue, and *Presbyterorum Ordinis*. Comparisons are made with the major themes of the Council such as Christ and the church, the freedom and dignity of the human being, and the autonomy of culture and society. Pope John Paul II preserves the positive outlook of the Council on the world of today, on the Christian churches, on religions and cultures, and therefore major tendencies are interpreted positively or as challenges (2, 6, 30, 32, 37, 38, 40, 86).

On the lips of the Pope, an appeal to the Council is also an appeal for discernment and verification with regard to the present progress of the church. It achieves this aim through its purpose of being missionary and promoting renewal, as well as through its documents. The encyclical reminds us of this right from the Introduction by pointing out the positive and negative aspects of the mission:

> The Council has already borne much fruit. . . . Nevertheless . . . missionary activity specifically directed "to the nations" (*ad gentes*) appears to be waning, and this tendency is certainly not in line with the directives of the Council and of subsequent statements of the Magisterium. (2)

There is a return to the subject when dealing with the present difficulties of the universal mission. *Redemptoris Missio* also quotes Pope Paul VI's apostolic exhortation *Evangelii Nuntiandi* to make the point that it is wrong to appeal to the Council to support excuses not to evangelize (cf. 36).

The Council, for John Paul, is not an event sufficient unto itself but is the beginning of a process that is largely new and must be followed through with fidelity to its teachings and in response to new needs. In addressing the Roman Curia in 1992 on the thirtieth anniversary of the Council's beginning, the Pope said: "Our reflection on the past becomes all the more meaningful if we look at the Council through the experience of the postconciliar period. Although the church in every part of the earth is the same as that of yesterday, in Christ she lives and realizes the 'today' that began especially with Vatican II. This 'today' has also been given expression in the postconciliar documents of a universal nature."[8]

The postconciliar progress is apparent in the Magisterium it inspires, such as the postsynodal documents beginning especially with *Evangelii Nuntiandi* by Pope Paul VI, the new code of Canon Law, and the documents issued by some of the Roman Curia and the continental federations of episcopal conferences.

Evangelii Nuntiandi is the document most quoted (about twenty times) after the Decree *Ad Gentes*. In *Redemptoris Missio* we find a new reading and redefining of the concept of evangelization as compared with the Exhortation of Pope Paul VI. John Paul II prefers to use the term "mission" to indicate the worldwide activity of the church, while he reserves the term "evangelization" for the proclamation of the word in all its forms. He emphasizes the fact that missionary activity constitutes a reality distinct from the evangelization of Christians or of those who are no longer Christian.

The most quoted of the other postsynodal documents is *Christifideles Laici* to which there are eight references (cf. 9, 31, 34, 57, 62, 71f.). Of the documents from the continental conferences we find that of the Latin American episcopate meeting in Puebla quoted three times (cf. 58, 60, 64). Among the documents of the Roman Curia, one from the Secretariat for Non-Christians issued in 1984 merits special attention.[9] It is quoted in relation to dialogue with other religions (cf. 55f.). Its

---

8. Ibid.

9. Cf. Secretariat for Non-Christians, "Attitudes of the Catholic Church toward the Followers of other Religions," *Reflections and Directives on Dialogue and Mission, AAS*

directives, however, are reflected in other parts of *Redemptoris Missio*, for example in describing "mission as a single but complex reality which develops in many ways" (41; cf. 31; D&M 13), charity as the criterion for mission (cf. 60; D&M 9, 19), the role of the Spirit (cf. 28f.; D&M 24, 39), the promotion of the Kingdom as a purpose of the mission (cf. 19f.; D&M 25, 41) and respect for the patience of God (cf. 57; D&M 44).

A second document by this same curial office on the subject *Dialogue and Proclamation* was published after the encyclical but had been approved beforehand by the Plenary Council of 1990. Besides the use of some of its terminology this document is also reflected in *Redemptoris Missio*, as was pointed out by Cardinal Tomko in his presentation of the newly published encyclical at the press conference.[10]

Apart from reference to its documents, *Redemptoris Missio* acknowledges the Council especially by referring to the progress of the church. When it speaks of basic church communities, dialogue, inculturation, human promotion, option for the poor, contemplation, martyrdom, witness, and so forth, it acknowledges the missionary progress of the church in the postconciliar period. Every missionary can find a confirmation of his or her apostolic commitment, as a mirror reflecting the lived reality of the mission. Perhaps it is because of this that some have not seen anything new in it. However, the encyclical also challenges the missionaries and the special commitments because it reminds us that the commitment and experience of the individual missionary do not express the requirements of whole mission.[11]

It is precisely on this account that the French theologian, Claude Geffré, states:

> this great document has a special importance. It constitutes the mission *Manifesto* of Christ's Church on the eve of the third Millennium of our Redemption. Its doctrinal importance can escape nobody's attention. Twenty-five years after the decree *Ad Gentes*, it is a perfect illustration of what is achieved by an active acknowledgement of the Council in fidelity to its teachings and to the lessons to be learned from the present history of the Church.[12]

5. The Encyclical's Addressees

The encyclical is an appeal from the heart, indeed it is a cry of alarm as the Pope himself defines it (1, 11), addressed to certain people, so that they may receive it and respond accordingly. The initial greeting is addressed to: "Venerable Brothers, beloved Sons and Daughters." It is addressed, in other words, to the Bishops as Brothers and to all Catholics defined as sons and daughters,[13] therefore addressed to all the members of the Catholic Church, not just as a simple courtesy of information, but

---

84 (1984), pp. 816-828. The documents of the council for dialogue are the result of wide consultation among the bishop members of the council and specialist consultors. Both major documents of this office were examined and approved in detail and substance by the assemblies of its members. Cf. M. Zago, "Les documents du Conseil Pontifical pour le dialogue religieux," *Bulletin* (1989), pp. 362-376.

10. Josef Tomko, "Dialogue et annonce: le lien avec l'enciclique *Redemptoris Missio*," *Bulletin* 77 (1991); cf. M. Zago, "Dialogue and Proclamation: An Explanatory Document of Great Importance," *Omnis Terra* 224 (January 1992), pp. 20-26.

11. Cf. M. Zago, "Interreligious Dialogue and Experience of God," *Omnis Terra* (September/October 1992), pp. 388-392.

12. Claude Geffré, "Introduction préliminaire à *La Mission du Christ Rédempteur*" (Paris: Cerf, 1991), p. xii.

13. It is interesting to note that the words "brothers" and "brothers and sisters" are used

because, today more than ever, the mission *ad gentes* depends on all: "*Missionary activity is a matter for all Christians*, for all dioceses and parishes, Church institutions and associations" (2; emphasis in original).

The cry is directed first of all to the church as a whole (cf. 3), because, "The Church, and every individual Christian within her, may not keep hidden or monopolize this newness and richness which has been received from God's bounty in order to be communicated to all mankind" (11; cf. 27, 30, 39, 43). And, "Responsibility for this task belongs to the universal Church and to the particular Churches, to the whole People of God and to all its missionary forces. Every Church, even one made up of recent converts, is missionary by its very nature, and is both evangelized and evangelizing" (49; cf. 62, 77-80, 86).

Further, the cry is addressed to all the local churches and to the young churches. Attention to the young churches as the protagonists of mission in their own territory and in the world is original in this encyclical. From the Introduction on, the Pope stresses that one of the goals of the encyclical is "to give a fresh impulse to missionary activity by fostering the commitment of the particular Churches — especially those of recent origin — to send forth and receive missionaries" (2; cf. 39, 49, 85). This because,

The universal Church and each individual Church is sent forth to the nations. Precisely "so that this missionary zeal may flourish among the people of their own country," it is highly appropriate that young Churches "should share as soon as possible in the universal missionary work of the Church." (62; cf. 64)

Local churches, even though they are still young, are responsible for the missionary animation of their members (cf. 83; see also section 8 below).

With regard to persons, the Pope's appeal is addressed above all to bishops who are "responsible . . . for the evangelization of the world, both as members of the College of Bishops and as Pastors of the particular Churches" (63). The Congregation for Evangelization is responsible for the coordination, animation, and study of missionary tasks throughout the world (cf. 75). Episcopal conferences and conferences of the religious have a corresponding responsibility but with a universal extension. The Pontifical Societies are responsible for animation and cooperation (cf. 63, 76, 84).

The cry is addressed to all ecclesial groups, many of whom are mentioned directly. Missionaries, whose special vocation is modeled on that of the Apostles, are invited to be faithful and to renew themselves (cf. 27, 53, 57, 65-67, 91). Diocesan priests, especially in countries with a Christian minority, must be open to and available for the missions (cf. 67f.). The religious, both contemplative and active, are invited to a greater missionary commitment (cf. 69f., 76). Theologians are called upon to make a deeper study of the theological aspects of mission (cf. 2, 36). In addressing the laity, the appeal is frequently in general terms (cf. 40, 77-85), stating that all believers are invited to join in mission (cf. 58), but also that laity are particularly suited, in specialized forums, where they have expertise, to contribute to the improvement of the world (cf. 71-72, 77, 80). Laity are invited to make a special contribution to dialogue (cf. 58) and to the new forms of cooperation (cf. 82). The call to mission is also addressed to catechists and those who carry on new ministries (cf. 73f.), and also to ecclesial movements who are also expected to be available and willing to respond to that call (cf. 72, 79-80, 82f.).

The encyclical is also addressed to those who do not belong to the church, stating

---

to refer to members of other Christian confessions (50), to believers in other religious traditions (55), and even to all humanity (43).

that the Pope wishes "to assure non-Christians and particularly the authorities of countries to which missionary activity is being directed that all missionary work has but one purpose: to serve man by revealing to him the love of God made manifest in Jesus Christ" (2). It invites people to be open with confidence to the Gospel message. "Peoples everywhere, open the doors to Christ! His Gospel in no way detracts from man's freedom, from the respect that is owed to every culture and to whatever is good in each religion" (3). It invites those who are afraid to receive Baptism to accept Christ fully and completely by entering into his Church (47).

6. Aims and Objectives of the Encyclical

One of the questions asked when a document is issued by the Pope and becomes part of the papal magisterium regards the *real* reasons for its publication. Pope John Paul II clearly declares his motives for issuing this document at the very beginning when he states:

> The mission of Christ the Redeemer ... is still very far from completion ... we must commit ourselves wholeheartedly to its service. . . . I wish to invite the Church to a renewed missionary commitment ... to give fresh impulse to missionary activity. (1-2)

This invitation is based on his interpretation of certain facts and on personal conviction. The basic fact concerns the situation of humanity in relation to the Gospel:

> The number of those who do not know Christ and do not belong to the Church is constantly on the increase. . . . When we consider this immense portion of humanity which is loved by the Father and for whom he sent his Son, the urgency of the Church's mission is obvious.
>   On the other hand, our own times offer the Church new opportunities in this field. . . . God is opening before the Church the horizons of a humanity more fully prepared for the sowing of the Gospel. (3; cf. 10, 30, 40, 86, 92)

To the urgency of the mission are added new opportunities for its exercise (cf. 3, 86, 92).

The conviction comes from awareness that it is Spirit who provides the urge to proclaim the works of God (3), the Spirit who is "the principal agent of mission" (21), "the source of the drive to press on, not only geographically but also beyond the frontiers of race and religion, for a truly universal mission" (25). Under the influence of this interior driving force of the Spirit and faced with the urgent needs for missionary activity, which he himself has experienced personally (1, 91), the Pope feels it his duty to echo the call of the Apostle Paul: "It is not for me to boast about preaching the Gospel; it is my duty to do so, woe betide me if I do not preach the Gospel" (1 Cor 9:16). The aim of the encyclical is to echo that call, to verbalize it in the world of today.

In the Introduction the Pope develops other motivations for the encyclical that may often be identified with those of the church's mission to non-Christians. Ten are listed. Some of these are intermediary objectives that will help to achieve the main purpose of the encyclical, the renewal of missionary commitment. They show what the Pope's concerns are.

The first is a *commemorative reason* ("Twenty-five years after the conclusion of the Council and the publication of the Decree ... *Ad Gentes* ... I wish to invite the

Church *to renew her missionary commitment*" (2, emphasis in original; cf. 36) in the context of a negative tendency that the present document is meant to overcome. Missionary activity directed *ad gentes* "appears to be waning, and this tendency is certainly not in line with the directives of the Council and of subsequent statements of the Magisterium" (2). Therefore there must be a new drive to promote the missionary aims of the Council itself.

The present document has as an interior aim the renewal of faith and Christian life. For missionary activity renews the church, revitalizes faith and Christian identity, and offers fresh enthusiasm and a new incentive. Thus the Pope says: "in the Church's history, missionary drive has always been a sign of vitality, just as its lessening is a sign of the crisis of faith" (2). If the life of the church is to be renewed, a new drive must be given to the missions. Commitment to the missions renews the church and each individual Christian in two ways. First, *it renews Christian life* by strengthening the faith and consolidating the Christian identity (49; cf. 11, 42); for "evangelizing activity . . . is the clearest sign of mature faith," (49) and "Sharing in the universal mission . . . is not limited to certain specific activities, but is the sign of maturity in faith and of a Christian life that bears fruit" (77). Therefore there is a reciprocity between holiness and mission: "The *universal call to holiness* is closely linked to the *universal call to mission*. Every member of the faithful is called to holiness and to mission" (90, emphasis in original). Missionary commitment also gives rise to more authentic interecclesial relationships: "Only by becoming missionary will the Christian community be able to overcome its internal divisions and tensions, and rediscover its unity and its strength of faith" (49).

Second, missionary commitment also *renews the whole of church activity*. The pastoral care of Christians, new evangelization among those who used to be Christians, the evangelization of those who were never Christian are three interdependent activities. "It is in commitment to the Church's universal mission that the new evangelization of Christian peoples will find inspiration and support" (2). "Without the mission *ad gentes*, the Church's very missionary dimension would be deprived of its essential meaning and of the very activity that exemplifies it" (34). Universal missionary commitment, however, does not provide a legitimate substitute for apostolic and missionary work necessary in one's own milieu:

> The Churches in traditionally Christian countries, for example, involved as they are in the challenging task of new evangelization, are coming to understand more clearly that they cannot be missionaries to non-Christians in other countries and continents unless they are seriously concerned about the non-Christians at home. Hence missionary activity *ad intra* is a credible sign and a stimulus for missionary activity *ad extra*, and vice versa. (34)

Missionary evangelization is the most important contribution that the church can offer to each one and to humanity. "It is *the primary service which the Church can render to every individual and to all humanity*" because only Christ the Savior can fully reveal the individual to himself or herself (2, emphasis mine). Not only does mission open the person to God, but it helps the individual to understand his or her dignity. Repeating the words of the Latin American Bishops at Puebla, the Pope says that "the best service we can offer to our brother is evangelization, which helps him to live and act as a son of God . . . and assists his overall development" (58). To illustrate this he continues:

> Through the Gospel message, the Church offers a force for liberation which promotes development precisely because it leads to conversion of heart and of

ways of thinking, fosters the recognition of each person's dignity, encourages
solidarity, commitment and the service of one's neighbor, and gives everyone
a place in God's . . . Kingdom of peace and justice, beginning already in this
life. (59)

In so doing, mission does not impinge upon individual liberty or cultural richness.
Rather, of its very nature it promotes them (cf. 39, 7, 11, 35, 46f.).

For this reason also, knowledge of the Gospel message is *the right of every
person and of every people.* Drawing on insights of Pope Paul VI, John Paul states
that faith demands a free adherence on the part of the person, but at the same time
faith must also be offered to the person, because

the multitudes have the right to know the riches of the mystery of Christ —
riches in which we believe that the whole of humanity can find, in unsuspected fullness, everything that it is gropingly searching for concerning God,
man and his destiny, life and death, and truth. . . . This is why the Church
keeps her missionary spirit alive, and even wishes to intensify it in the moment of history in which we are living. (8; cf. 11, 46)

Another reason the encyclical was written was "*to respond to many requests* for a
document of this sort" (2, emphasis mine). For example, a request along these lines
was made directly to the Pope on the occasion of a missiological congress held in the
Urbaniana University in Rome during 1988 on the theme of salvation.[14] Similar
requests came from members of different missionary institutes especially after the
apostolic exhortation *Evangelii Nuntiandi*, which, in the opinion of some, seemed to
equate all apostolic endeavors as forms of "missionary" evangelization. A further
aim of the encyclical is clearly that of dissipating "doubts and ambiguities" concerning the validity and necessity of mission *ad gentes* (2; cf. 4, 7, 11 where they are
expressed as a series of questions).

The second chapter of *Redemptoris Missio* comes to grips with one of the most
important themes of postconciliar missiological reflection: *the nature and the requirements of the Kingdom of God.* Although the chapter is a reply to present research, the
whole problem is laid out in article 17. In reply to the positions of anthropo-, king-
dom- and theo-centric reductionism it is stated that the Kingdom cannot be separated
from Christ nor from the church. Here, too, what is new is firmly integrated with the
solid teachings of tradition, both as regards the purpose of mission and the different
ways in which the realization of the Kingdom is understood (cf. 18-20).

A series of doubts is taken up in chapter four in relation to the idea of the mission
ad gentes and the question of geographical and cultural frontiers. In this context, the
threefold activity of the church in evangelization is explained (cf. 32-34), following
which the encyclical takes up the question of the external difficulties, such as the
limits placed by authorities who will not allow evangelization (35). But the Pope
mentions also difficulties *within* the People of God that are especially painful to him,
among which special mention is made of the excuses for not engaging in mission for
which people "claim to find support for such and such a teaching of the Council" (36).

In the pastoral field too, doubts and difficulties are not lacking. For instance, "the
call to conversion missionaries address to non-Christians" is called an act of "proselytizing"; and it is claimed that it is enough to help people to become "more human

---

14. Martins J. Saraiva, "Conclusioni del Congresso Internazionale di Missiologia, 'La
salvezza oggi,' " *Studia Urbaniana* (Rome: Pontificia Universitas Urbaniana, 1989), p.
223.

or more faithful to their own religion," or that it is sufficient "to build communities capable of working for justice, freedom, peace and solidarity"; the response to which, he says, is in biblical sources which Christian communities are challenged to appropriate (46f.).

When speaking of the agents of mission, special mention is made of the missionaries and institutes specializing in mission *ad gentes*, lest they be led to misunderstand "the meaning of their vocation and no longer know exactly what the Church expects of them today" (65). This kind of questioning has been frequent and widespread in many missionary groups and has sometimes influenced statements coming from their meetings and assemblies and their actual operational policies.[15] Local needs, the Pope observes, make churches tend to close in upon themselves and respond in a circumscribed way to new calls made upon them. Instead they should be *"open to the Church's universality* and . . . avoid every form of provincialism or exclusiveness or feelings of self-sufficiency" (85, emphasis in original).

Accordingly, *Redemptoris Missio* can legitimately be seen as an answer to problems and doubts that disturb the minds not only of restless spirits but even of sincere Christians. Some are widespread errors, such as the secularization of salvation (cf. 11), a horizontal understanding of the Kingdom of God (cf. 17), the fear of proselytism (cf. 46) and interfering with the freedom of human beings (4). Others are more sophisticated, such as the distinction between the Christ of history and the Word of God (6), the separation between Kingdom, Christ and church, or between the earthly and the eschatological kingdom (cf. 17-19). Others still separate — even to the point of opposing — complementary activities, such as proclamation, dialogue, human promotion, inculturation, and so forth.

The encyclical provides responses to such problems and clarifies the ambiguities by reference to faith and to the data of revelation, thus confirming

- the universality of salvation in Christ and the fullness and completeness of God's revelation in Christ (5);
- the unity between the Word and Jesus Christ (6);
- the real possibility of salvation in Christ for all men and women and the need for the church in the order of this salvation (9);
- the necessary relationship between Kingdom, Christ and church and between the terrestrial and the eschatological kingdom (18-19);
- the need to promote the Kingdom of God in the pursuit of the different aims of mission (20);
- the harmony between the active guidance of the Spirit in the church and his operative presence in every time and place (24-29);
- how the different activities for promoting the mission in all its requirements are complementary to one another, although recognizing the priority to be given to explicit proclamation (41-60);
- respect for personal liberty and the intentional proclamation of the Gospel (8, 39, 46-47).

Doubts and ambiguities concerning mission, in the Pope's analysis, are seen to arise from changes taking place and from the complexity of certain situations. By noting that such things occur, he does not intend to reproach anyone but to state facts. Thus, in the Pope's mind, the encyclical is an instrument of clarification, a path toward solving these difficulties. Nevertheless, it does not aim to provide a

---

15. Cf. Hugh MacMahon, "If you are not asking the question. . . ," *Columban Intercom* (December 1992), pp. 249-252.

theological development of the different facets of the problems nor to explore in depth their solution. Accordingly, one of the aims of *Redemptoris Missio* is to "encourage theologians to explore and expound systematically the various aspects of missionary activity" (2).

Words of encouragement for theologians are repeated twice at important points in the document. Having spoken about the external and internal difficulties of the mission, which should not cause us "to be either pessimistic or inactive," John Paul states:

> In this regard, I earnestly ask theologians and professional Christian journalists to intensify the service they render to the Church's mission in order to discover the deep meaning of their work, along the sure path of "thinking with the Church" (*sentire cum Ecclesia*). (36)

Theologians have a specific service to give and an important work to do for the mission, and it must be done with a feeling for the church.

In the second place where the Pope addresses theologians, the missionary animation and formation of the People of God and especially of its pastors is of primary importance; contributing to this task are:

> theologians, particularly those who teach in seminaries and centers for the laity. Theological training cannot and should not ignore the Church's universal mission, ecumenism, the study of great religions and missiology. (83)[16]

Research in the field of mission theology is far from being exhausted. The missionary dimension must, besides, be integrated into the teaching in general courses of theology. If the whole church is to be missionary, then theology must become missionary. In fact theology must be missionary if it is to be at the service of the church.

Still another reason for the encyclical is "To confirm in their commitment those exemplary brothers and sisters dedicated to missionary activity and all those who assist them" (57). Encouragement is given to those missionaries who find that dialogue is the only means available to them to give sincere witness and to serve humanity generously. Again in the context of works of charity, the Pope assures his readers of his gratitude to missionaries — lay and clerical — who work for the integral development of individuals and of society through such projects as schools, health-care centers, and for the promotion of women and human promotion in general (60).

Speaking of the "missionary fecundity of consecration," a whole paragraph is devoted to an appreciation of women religious missionaries

> in whom virginity for the sake of the Kingdom is transformed into a motherhood in the spirit that is rich and fruitful. . . . The example and activity of women who through virginity are consecrated to love of God and neighbor, especially the very poor, are an indispensable evangelical sign among those peoples and cultures where women still have far to go on the way toward human promotion and liberation. (70)

---

16. The assignment of these duties is taken up also in John Paul II's apostolic exhortation on priestly formation, *Pastores dabo vobis*, art. 54f.; cf. M. Zago, "Priests for Mission," *Omnis Terra* (1992), pp. 230-233.

The encyclical confirms the special vocation of the missionary, which "is the model of the Church's missionary commitment" (66). It confirms also the role of the specifically missionary institutes, which remain necessary, not only for missionary activity *ad gentes*, but also for animating the missionary consciousness both of churches in traditionally Christian countries and in "younger Churches" (ibid.). Approval is also given to such groups "for receiving more and more candidates from the young Churches which they have founded," while new institutes that send out missionaries are coming into being in them (66).

The encyclical confirms the different missionary vocations (67-74),[17] and the cooperation of all in cooperating with missionary activity both according to the traditional means and according new ways suggested (77, 83). A special form of spirituality is required for those involved in missionary activity *ad gentes*. This spirituality is outlined not only in the wealth of material in the chapter that bears this heading (87-92) but also in many other parts of the document (for instance, 23, 43f., 65ff., 69, 77).

The promotion of missionary vocations still is another of the aims of *Redemptoris Missio*. One of the consequences of the encyclical's overall purpose is to promote commitment to the mission *ad gentes*.[18] Pope John Paul II points specifically to the lifetime calling of missionary vocations as a perennial need in the church (27, 32, 61, 65, 75, 79). Such vocations are the model of missionary commitment, a total and radical gift of self, and a sign of the vitality of each local church (66, 79, 49), which promotes communion among the churches (64, 75, 85), and, even more important, they promote a missionary mentality essential to being church (27, 61f.). Promoting vocations should indeed be the aim of every church (75) as it is of the Vatican Congregation for the Evangelization of Peoples (84); of the Pontifical Mission-Aid Societies (79); and is also a specific aim of missionary animation (83). In order to promote such vocations the Pope addresses the different categories within the church: bishops, priests, and religious, individual lay people and lay movements, families, and especially young people (64, 68-70, 80).

The corporate missionary duty of the church as a whole "does not preclude . . . that there be persons with a specific vocation to be 'life-long missionaries *ad gentes*'" (32). Notwithstanding the commitment of every church community to the non-Christians in their own milieu and notwithstanding the sending of members belonging to the different categories as missionaries, the encyclical emphasizes the present-day need for the specific charism of the missionary and devotes two numbers to this theme (65f.). It reserves for them the first place after the bishops in their responsibility for the mission and its accomplishment. It also reasserts the validity of lifetime commitment to missionary life, an idea about which doubts have been cast in recent decades (66). And the practice in the early church is held up as an example, citing the Acts of the Apostles (27; cf. 61, 66f.).

Redemptoris Missio reminds us of the characteristic features of this "special vocation" and "specific charism," recalling those pointed out by Vatican II (AG 23-27), and adds new features that are important, emphasizing the charismatic character of this vocation. Namely, that Christ the Lord calls missionaries by means of the Holy Spirit; it is he who kindles a missionary vocation in the heart of each one and who raises suitable missionary Institutes in the church — this is "a 'special vocation,' patterned on that of the Apostles" (65).

---

17. Cf. M Zago, "The 'Charismatics' of the Mission," *Omnis Terra* (1991), pp. 236-238.

18. See M. Zago, "Missionary Vocation according to *Redemptoris Missio*," *Omnis Terra* (1992), pp. 423-424.

This missionary vocation in *Redemptoris Missio* implies a total giving of self for the sake of commitment to evangelize those who are "far from Christ" (65):

> Promoting such vocations is at the heart of missionary cooperation. Preaching the Gospel requires preachers; the harvest needs laborers. The mission is carried out above all by men and women who are consecrated for life to the work of the Gospel and are prepared to go forth into the whole world to bring salvation. (79)

Accordingly the Pope is "solicitous for missionary vocations," including diocesan priests who give themselves to mission, religious and lay people, and especially for persons who join missionary institutes and congregations of men and women (79; cf. 66). Financial offerings for missions are not sufficient; rather, it is necessary to promote missionary vocations, the best yardstick of giving to others and a sure sign of the vitality of a church (73).

The two sections devoted specifically to the theme point out some guidelines for vocations promotion in pastoral work. Those specially addressed are Christian communities, on the one hand, and families and young people on the other. The elements to be stressed in that pastoral ministry are many, including the necessary willingness of parents and young people to allow and to respond to the call, prayer to obtain the missionary vocation, and witness concerning the beauty and joy of missionary life. These will instill a genuine sense of service to one's neighbor stemming from generous participation in church activities (80) rooted in knowledge of the universal Church and ongoing contact with missionaries and the local churches in which they work (83).

Addressing the Bishops, as those mainly responsible for missionary activity, the Pope reminds them that "each particular Church must be generous and open to the needs of other Churches . . . regarding cooperation between particular Churches and especially regarding the better distribution of the clergy in the world . . . primarily to missionary activity." Therefore the Pope appeals to all "the Churches, young and old alike, to share in this concern by seeking to . . . increase missionary vocations" (64; cf. 34, 39, 62, 77, 85).

Still another aim of the encyclical is *to encourage the commitment of the younger churches to send and receive missionaries.* The Pope expresses himself as seeing this necessary to "give a fresh impulse to missionary activity" (2). One should recall that since the beginning of the modern missionary movement in the sixteenth century, missionary activity was carried on by recognized missionary institutes under the guidance of the Congregation de Propaganda Fide. The rest of the church, especially during the past century, saw itself fulfilling its part when it cooperated with or sustained such missionary groups from the background. When the local hierarchies began to be established in the second quarter of the twentieth century, local clergy were entrusted with the more developed parts of these churches, while the more inaccessible and least evangelized areas continued to be entrusted to missionary institutes. Pope Pius XII involved older, established dioceses in missionary work by asking them to send (*Fidei Donum*) diocesan priests to the missions. In its drive to promote recognition of the intrinsically missionary character of the church and to emphasize the apostolic character of the episcopal and sacerdotal order, Vatican Council II called on everybody to be committed to the missions, even those churches which had been founded recently. Gradually local hierarchies were established widely and the rise in numbers of local vocations to ecclesial ministries made it possible for local personnel to cover wider areas. A new relationship, consequently, developed between dioceses and missionary institutes. Given this situation, the encyclical underlines the commitment of all churches not only to help one another mutually but to reach outward in the mission *ad gentes* (64; cf. 34, 36).

This invitation to send and receive missionaries, to evangelize non-Christians in one's own milieu and to be committed simultaneously to the evangelization of other peoples is addressed in particular to the churches of recent foundation. They, in fact, have abundant vocations at present and live in the midst of cultures that have never been evangelized. They will find their identity and their dynamism in the work of evangelization as did the church of the early centuries. Local churches, according to the Pope, should be missionary right from the beginning (49; cf. 39, 62, 66f.).

> Already the young Churches, many of which are blessed with an abundance of vocations, are in a position to send priests and men and women Religious to the older Churches.
>
> On the other hand, the young Churches are concerned about their own identity, about inculturation, and about their freedom to grow independently of external influences, with the possible result that they close their doors to missionaries. To these Churches I say: Do not isolate yourselves; willingly accept missionaries and support from other Churches, and do likewise throughout the world. Precisely because of the problems that concern you, you need to be in continuous contact with your brothers and sisters in the faith. With every legitimate means, seek to ensure recognition of the freedom to which you have a right, remembering that Christ's disciples must "obey God rather than men" (Acts 5:29). (85)

A final goal of the encyclical is to *reassure non-Christians and governments* in countries in which missionary activity is being carried on that evangelization has only one aim in view — "to serve humanity by revealing the love of God which is made manifest in Jesus Christ" (2). This section is added because the Pope realizes every encyclical is apt to be read and scrutinized in non-Christian milieux, even though it is not formally addressed to non-Christians. Awareness of this fact, which ensures that certain themes will be dealt with more respectfully by the church than might once have been the case, is certainly a positive feature brought about by social communications in today's world.

The authorities are reminded that missionary activity has only one aim — *to serve mankind*. But the horizon of this service is not limited to the realms discernible by the social sciences. Instead, the core of this service consists principally in revealing God's love manifested in Christ Jesus (cf. 29, 39, 58-59).

The attempt to address governments and civil authorities is important, since the Pope observes that "In certain countries missionaries are refused entry. In others not only is evangelization forbidden, but conversion as well, and even Christian worship" (35). In some countries, he notes that there is discrimination against both local and expatriate Christians. Such negative elements have been met not only in Muslim countries but also in Hindu and Buddhist countries, frequently marked by prohibitions on the admission of missionaries.

John Paul's appeal to non-Christians is encapsulated in a phrase that has become emblematic of his pontificate:

> *Peoples everywhere, open the doors to Christ!* His Gospel in no way detracts from man's freedom, from the respect that is owed to every culture and to whatever is good in each religion. (3, emphasis in original; cf. 39, 47, 85)

Far from uttering this in a triumphal way, the Pope sees in these words themes that are repeated throughout the document as intrinsic to Christian mission and the flowering of every human community — respect for basic human freedom, for culture, and for all religions.

7. Structure and Language

There are two parts to the encyclical. The first four chapters constitute the first part, clarifying the basis and concept of the mission *ad gentes*. The last four chapters constitute the pastoral and operational part of the document. Each chapter develops a major theme, in logical sequence. Their contents may be described as follows: (1) reasons rooted in faith for universal mission — *Jesus Christ, the only Savior*; (2) the integral nature of missionary activity and purpose — *the Kingdom of God*; (3) the dynamics of missionary activity according the New Testament — *the Holy Spirit: principal agent of mission*; (4) the areas in which the mission is to be exercised at the present time — *the vast horizons of the mission ad gentes*; (5) the principal expressions of missionary activity at the present time — *the paths of mission*; (6) those who cooperate in missionary activity — *leaders and workers in the missionary apostolate*; (7) forms of participation in universal mission — *cooperation in missionary activity*; (8) the quality of Christian life for the mission — *missionary spirituality*.

The method of organizing the material takes account of the content itself. This is obvious if we compare the encyclical with the Vatican Council II document on mission. Comparing the first four chapters of *Redemptoris Missio* with the first nine numbers of *Ad Gentes*, we can see, first, that the encyclical starts from the Vatican II rooting of mission in the Trinity and that it structures the first three chapters on this theme in order to present the reasons and the requirements of mission in the light of the contemporary problems. There are references to the Trinity throughout the document (cf. 1, 5, 10, 21f., 28f., 31-33, 36, 39, 44-46, 61, 87f.) emphasizing that the Trinity is both the ultimate source of Christian mission and its final aim, whether in the present time or in its eschatological realization (cf. 7, 190, 12, 14f., 20, 23, 31, 44, 47, 55).

In drawing comparisons with *Ad Gentes*, the second thing to note is that discourse on the church is made in relation to the theme of salvation (cf. 9f., 20, 31), to the Kingdom (cf. 17-20), to the aims of mission (cf. 48-50), and to missionary concern (cf. 22f., 26, 39, 49, 61f., 64, 77), while *Ad Gentes* tends to limit itself to missionary concern and to sending missionaries (cf. AG 5).

Thirdly, the purposes of mission are developed explicitly and broadly, in contradistinction to giving attention mainly to proclaiming the Gospel and planting the church in *Ad Gentes* (AG 6), *Redemptoris Missio* stresses the need to promote the Gospel and Kingdom values (cf. 20, 34, 48). Fourth, the concept of mission is developed in this same wide perspective. Still, there is only one source of mission, which is multifaceted because of diverse circumstances in which it is carried on in various social and cultural milieux (cf. 33f., 37f.). Fifth, *Redemptoris Missio* develops further the theological and doctrinal aspects of mission, taking account of conciliar and postconciliar documents and of the present-day situation, examining and extending conciliar teaching in the light of its reading of the recent situation.

A comparison of the second part of *Redemptoris Missio* with the last five chapters of *Ad Gentes* reveals that the encyclical is simpler and more meaningful. For instance, *Redemptoris Missio* does not follow the path of evolving from missionary presence to young church. Here dialogue, works of charity, and witness are not different steps towards proclamation — a sort of pre-evangelization — but integral aspects of mission in and of their very nature (cf. AG 10-13). And the concrete exercise of the various elements that comprise mission arise in love, the moving force and criterion of mission, which discerns the call of the Spirit in the concrete needs of human beings. The agents of mission, who in *Ad Gentes* are treated in five successive chapters, are dealt with in one chapter in *Redemptoris Missio*. This has the effect of emphasizing the fact that the mission of the church is an integral part of the church itself and is exercised everywhere, without, however, putting all situations on the same footing. The theme of cooperation or participation in mission is developed in manifestations both traditional and new (cf. AG 16f., 21, 23-28, 34, 38-41), rather than according to the specific tasks of individual persons (cf. AG 35-41). In *Redemptoris Missio* this is finally brought into relief in the chapter on missionary spirituality, which the Pope refuses to confine to missionaries alone, but extends "throughout the Christian unity, especially among those who work closely with missionaries" (90; cf. 26f., 77, 87-92; AG 24).

The repetitive style of the language of the encyclical carries with it a need to realize that a given theme may be dealt with in different places and from different points of view. Consequently, to see the full meaning of a particular theme, it must be studied in all parts of the document in which it is treated. This creates problems for interpreting correctly *Redemptoris Missio* but it also enriches it. In this connection, the exhortatory style is also repetitive but it also integrates different approaches and activities to problems and concerns of importance to the Pope. The running titles and subtitles in the text are also important, since many of them give the kernel of the theme dealt with in that section, often clarifying what the main point is.

Numerous interrogatory sentences that reflect peoples' questioning are intended to make the text more pliable and to attract attention, even though, admittedly, the replies sometimes do not seem to be satisfactory (cf. 4, 7f., 11). Similarly, the use of some terms is not as precise or uniform as one finds in other documents issued by offices of the Roman Curia, precisely because the text of an encyclical such as this one follows a different preparatory process. For example, the term "evangelization" is sometimes used as the equivalent of mission or missionary activity or even of proclamation and not in its precise meaning (cf. 2).

As with all church documents, translating of *Redemptoris Missio* into different languages sometimes results in limitations. Terms are inevitably understood according to the linguistic patterns and experience of readers in quite diverse circumstances. Thus "inclusive" or "generic" language has become widely accepted in some English-speaking milieux, while it seems strange in others. The official translators of the encyclical, however, had to make choices, knowing that not everyone would be happy, and they have not been.

Then, too, some terms, though apparently univocal across linguistic barriers, are understood differently because of the historical experiences and semantic traditions. Thus the term "mission" in some countries in the South conjures up distasteful memories of the colonial period. In other linguistic traditions, it refers primarily to non-religious, military and diplomatic activities. In French-speaking milieux the term "movement" tends to refer to some specialized forms of Catholic Action, while in Italian it denotes all overt forms of Catholic association. Latin languages distinguish between announcing and proclamation. Announcing can be familiar or personal, while proclamation is official and solemn. The term used in English is "proclamation" or "initial proclamation." Translation of official statements for the world Church is a difficult undertaking.

It is perhaps important, too, to observe that there are many quotations from the Bible and from council statements; these are not used simply a collection of texts but to show the continuity and foundations of Catholic. They are also useful as instruments that point to resources for a deeper study of the theme, which can allow the reader to compare present teaching with older sources. We should note that there are twice as many Biblical quotations within the text as there are texts of conciliar or papal origin. This shows the prevalence of the Biblical element in the doctrinal part of the encyclical.

8. *Nature and Context of Mission ad gentes*

In regard to the unity and diversity of mission activity, the Pope states that the diversity of activities in mission is not intrinsic to mission in itself, but arises in the variety of circumstances in which mission is carried out (33). It is the variety of circumstances which determines the diversity of the church's activities, as was already pointed out in the missionary decree of Vatican II (AG 6). The present encyclical states that we face today "a religious situation which is extremely varied and changing," one in which "religious and social upheaval makes it difficult to apply in practice certain ecclesial distinctions and categories to which we have become accustomed" (32).

In this regard, the encyclical distinguishes three situations in relation to the faith (33). First, there are groups and peoples who have received the Gospel and who participate in the life of the church. Then, there are other peoples and groups who have never received the Gospel and among whom the church has never taken root. Finally there are groups who, although once connected with the church, have now lost the faith and have ceased to belong to the church in any meaningful way. Among Christians who practice their faith, to a greater or lesser degree, the church exercises *ordinary pastoral care*. Among those who have never been Christians the church carries on *mission ad gentes*, in its most specific sense. Those who are no longer Christians require a *new evangelization*.[19]

The three activities have different aims, although the Pope regards them as "not clearly definable," and he also says that it is "unthinkable to create barriers between them or to put them into water-tight compartments" (34). Pastoral care, nevertheless, tends to deepen the Christian identity and the evangelical dynamism of persons and communities; new evangelization offers an occasion for a new discovery and acceptance of Christ and his church; and mission *ad gentes* "is characterized as the work of proclaiming Christ and his Gospel, building up the local church and promoting the Kingdom" (34; cf. 20, 46-48). The three activities are complementary to one another and are interdependent. As the Pope notes, "there is a real and growing interdependence between these various saving activities," such that each aspect of mission "influences, stimulates and assists the others" (34). The encyclical, accordingly, regards them not only as interdependent but as coalescing to give energy to one another (2, 32, 34, 41, 55f., 82f., 85, 89).

The variety of apostolic works comprising mission should tend toward the mission *ad gentes*; taken together, they tend toward explicit proclamation (3, 20, 23, 31, 34, 37, 40, 45. 55, 58f.):

> There must be no lessening of the impetus to preach the Gospel and to establish new Churches among peoples or communities where they do not yet exist, for this is the first task of the Church. . . . Without the mission *ad gentes*, the Church's very missionary dimension would be deprived of its essential meaning and of the very activity that exemplifies it. (34)

---

19. Cf. M. Zago, "New Evangelization and Religious Life according to Pope John Paul II," *Omnis Terra* (1991), pp. 283-293.

In defining the context of the mission *ad gentes*, the encyclical uses first and principally *ethnic and cultural criteria*. Thus, it does not speak of individuals who have never received the faith but of groups of people who are considered in relation to the faith and to the church's presence in their midst. Peculiar to the mission *ad gentes* is the fact that it is directed to non-Christians.

It is distinct from other ecclesiastical activities inasmuch as it is addressed to groups and settings which are non-Christian because the preaching of the Gospel and the presence of the Church are either absent or insufficient. (34)

Elsewhere the encyclical speaks of "human and cultural groups" (86), as well as mentioning groups and sociocultural contexts in which Christ and the Gospel are not known, or which "lack Christian communities sufficiently mature to be able to incarnate their faith in their own environment and proclaim it to other groups" (33).

The theme of the non-Christian peoples is repeated constantly throughout the encyclical (cf. 31-34, 37, 40, 45, 55, 66 and elsewhere). Even though they do not know Christ and are outside the church, when the church considers this immense portion of humanity, "which is loved by the Father and for whom he sent his Son, the urgency of the Church's mission is obvious" (3).[20] Non-Christians are considered collectively not only because human beings are social beings and because "the Spirit's presence and activity affect not only individuals but also society and history, peoples, cultures and religions" (28; cf. 10, 15, 20, 55). In turn, the traditional goal of planting of the church is an aim of the mission because the Lord does the work of salvation in a communitarian fashion, not just individually (cf. 20, 26, 34, 48f.; cf. AG 2, 5f.). Therefore the church must be incarnated in all cultural situations, must become native to them, since only thus can it be an integral sign of salvation in the midst of a people and in the culture in which they live (cf. 37, 48f.; AG 19, 22).

Having reminded his readers that non-Christian groups and peoples are the object of mission, the Pope uses three categories to determine *the context of mission ad gentes* "so as to have a real picture of the situation" (37). *Redemptoris Missio*, accordingly, points out the territorial, social, and cultural contexts of mission. First is the *geographical criterion*, described in the first part of art. 37; the use of this term is not restricted to a merely territorial meaning. Rather, the territorial context is used insofar as the territory in question is inhabited by non-Christian peoples. Terms such as "country," "nation," "cultural area," and "human and cultural area" indicate living, ethnically defined realities in many milieux. The ethnic aspect of mission is so important that even in traditionally Christian countries, "a special mission *ad gentes* status" should be assigned to regions where there are "groups or areas which have not been evangelized."[21]

There are two further supplementary but important principles made in the encyclical. The first is that it is not sufficient that the church merely be present in a

---

20. The idea that the love of God embraces non-Christians is mentioned repeatedly. See, for instance, art. 11-13, 44, 55, 86.

21. In the Vatican II Decree *Ad Gentes*, note 37 indicated that this was possible in Latin America. The present text refers to a wider possibility, as is clear from the note referring to the Pope's address to the members of the symposium of the European Bishops' Conference on 11 October 1985. In *Redemptoris Missio*'s chapter on cooperation, mention is made of the numerous immigrants who form human and cultural minority groups in Christian countries and who remind us of the need for mission *ad gentes*: "The presence of these brothers and sisters . . . is a challenge for the ecclesial communities and a stimulus to hospitality, dialogue, service, sharing, witness and direct proclamation" (82).

country or another geopolitical unit; it must also be present in the different ethnic components of that unit.

> The growth in the number of new churches in recent times should not deceive us. Within the territories entrusted to these churches — particularly in Asia, but also in Africa, Latin America, and Oceania — there remain vast regions still to be evangelized. In many nations entire peoples and cultural areas of great importance have not yet been reached by the proclamation of the Gospel and the presence of the local Church. (37)

One need only to think of countries such as Thailand or India. There the church has diocesan structures covering entire nations, while the dominant cultures of these regions have never been evangelized. In such nations, there are entire peoples and ethnic groups without any effective church presence.

A second principle regards the ecclesial communities whose life and activity affect the ability of the church to bear witness. Four elements are discussed. First, *the native character* of the church. The Pope notes that "there are countries and geographical and cultural areas where native Christian communities are not present." This is the case in the majority of the Muslim countries in North Africa; there are diocesan structures and Christian communities there, but membership in these communities is entirely foreign. Their presence is important, but their "foreignness" of origin has an effect on the meaningfulness and influence of that presence. Second, there is made mention of the *numerical size* of these communities, frequently "so small as not to be a clear sign of the Christian presence." The strength of a theological sign is not caused purely by numbers of adherents to the Christian faith, but quantity does have an importance. One can think of dioceses such as Varanasi, India. Catholics there number nearly twenty-two thousand in a population of fourteen million. In addition, many of these Catholics are immigrants from other areas and other cultures of the country, and the small number of believers does not necessarily indicate universal fervor among them. *Missionary dynamism* especially reveals the state of health of a community. The encyclical speaks of communities that lack the dynamism to evangelize their societies, thus reminding us of one of the limitations of the church in many places (2). The rationale for counting missionary dynamism as a sign of a church's health derives from the centrality of mission to the essential nature of church:

> The evangelizing activity of the Christian community, first in its own locality, and then elsewhere as part of the Church's universal mission, is the clearest sign of a mature faith. A radical conversion in thinking is required in order to become missionary, and this holds true both for individuals and entire communities. (49; cf. 39, 62, 64, 66f., 85, 91)

If there is no zeal to share faith outside the boundaries of the community, in other words, one can wonder about the depth of the community's appropriation of the Gospel.

The final element in this series of matters affecting the missionary impact of Christian communities is present when Christians form tiny, isolated minorities. Such Christian communities — Laos, Bangladesh, Pakistan, Thailand, and so forth spring to mind — may belong to minority groups that are alien to the dominant national culture. Such Christian communities are often comprised of persons from minority animist groups that are marginal to the national Buddhist or Muslim culture.

The geographical factor, while accidental to mission in one sense, is still useful for understanding the context of missionary activity. In this context, the Pope makes special mention of Asia where "there remain vast regions still to be evangelized" (37a; cf. 30, 40, 55, 69, 91).[22] Merely because groups to be evangelized are to be found everywhere, Christians should not forget that conditions affecting mission vary greatly from one place to another. The situation of those who are no longer Christians and have to be evangelized anew but who live in cultures permeated by the faith is not identical to that of peoples who need initial evangelization and whose cultures have never been influenced by Gospel values (37a).

Geographical criteria for mission, merely mentioned in passing by the mission decree of Vatican II, are, then, still valid. The many examples given in the encyclical have no sympathy with a widely-spread opinion, according to which Christians should speak of "*a single missionary situation,* with one single mission, the same everywhere" (32, emphasis in original). Instead, *Redemptoris Missio* states that "care must be taken to avoid the risk of putting very different situations on the same level and of reducing, or even eliminating, the Church's mission and missionaries *ad gentes*" (32).

A second set of criteria is *sociological.* They take into account the "rapid and profound transformations which characterize today's world, especially in the southern hemisphere" (37b). The encyclical mentions urbanization, youth, migration, poverty. The rapidly changing social context is considered as it has an impact on cultures and, consequently, how it represents both a challenge and an opportunity for mission.[23] In this light, *urbanization* is presented not merely as a demographic phenomenon but also as a cultural reality. The massive growth of city populations creates economic problems but also causes the emergence of "new customs and styles of living . . . new forms of culture and communication, which then influence the wider population." The Pope sees the spread of the church in important urban centers as occurring under the influence of the Spirit (25).

In this context, the encyclical formulates a very important principle for effective missionary activity and which now as in the past can easily be forgotten:

> It is true that the "option for the neediest" means that we should not overlook the most abandoned and isolated human groups, but it is also true that individuals or small groups cannot be evangelized if we neglect the centers where a new humanity, so to speak, is emerging and where new models of development are taking shape. (37b)

This is said in reference to the fact that in the past many missionaries, faced with the difficulty of penetrating and working successfully in all reaches of highly developed literate cultures, withdrew to work among ethnic minorities and receptive animist groups. This, however, had the effect of marginalizing the church in the Asian context. Here the encyclical invites missionaries to overcome a twofold modern tendency: (1) the neglect of centers and groups who will hold sway in now changing and emerging societies; and (2) the preference of missionaries for work in isolated areas. This guideline should guide the formulation and application of missionary strategy and the formation of those who will work as missionaries. It is only in this way that cultures will be evangelized.

The second social element referred to is *youth,* not only because they constitute

---

22. Cf. M. Zago, "*Redemptoris Missio*, an Encyclical for Asia," *Omnis Terra* (1991), pp. 423-427.

23. The decree *Ad Gentes* called attention to the social conditions (*condiciones et adiuncta*) of peoples, groups, and individuals in art. 6. The problem is discussed and developed in much greater detail in *Redemptoris Missio*.

the vast majority of the population in the southern hemisphere, but also because they represent the future and because the ordinary pastoral means for approaching them are totally inadequate. Young people are seen as a challenge to which we must respond generously and as potential agents to be invited to respond to the missionary vocation. The encyclical appeals to associations and institutions, special groups and centers, and social and cultural initiatives for young people to bring this invitation home. Contemporary initiatives focused on youth are in a special way invited to missionary commitment (72).

The third phenomenon characteristic of the contemporary world is that of *migration*, to which is added the phenomenon of refugees. Migration and population movements are seen as a missionary challenge "creating fresh opportunities for contacts and cultural exchanges, and calling the Church to hospitality, dialogue, service and, in a word, to fraternity" (37b). Migration as a missionary opportunity is considered in a dual way: non-Christians in Christian countries; and Catholics in mission territories. A further element to be added is *tourism* (82).

The fourth important social phenomenon affecting mission is *poverty:* "The proclamation of Christ and the Kingdom of God must become the means for restoring the human dignity of these people" (37b). Mission, says the Pope, is neither to be considered as activity *in* the Third World or *for* the Third World, as certain types of propaganda would have us believe, nor as an escape from the difficulties of evangelization. Neither is poverty to be seen as a factor to be exploited to make evangelization easier. Instead mission should assume the role of liberator which the Gospel portrays as integral in the church's relationship to the poor. The two sections on human promotion develop this aspect. First, evangelization disposes the person to see himself or herself as a child of God; it liberates the person from injustice and promotes him or her integrally. And second, man is seen as the principal agent of development, while in the Gospel message the Church offers a liberating force that leads to the conversion of heart and mind, acknowledges the dignity of each person, and makes that person open to solidarity, commitment, and service to one's fellow human being. Development integrates the person in God's plan, which is the building up of the Kingdom of peace and justice already in this life (58f.; cf. 14f., 20, 26, 42, 51, 69f., 72, 81f.).

The encyclical thus points out the specific contribution of mission without denying that there are other concrete helps to be provided as integral characteristics of missionary activity, the ultimate moving spirit of which is charity (cf. 60, 7, 13, 15, 31, 89).

The third context deals mainly with culture considered not in an anthropological sense but as intellectual, scientific, technical, and modern development (cf. 37f.). This frontier is not clearly distinguished or even separated from the social sphere mentioned above but does indicate culture in its more highly formalized, cultivated, and specialized sense. The term "Areopagus," taken from St. Paul's meeting with learned persons in Athens, is used with this meaning. It reminds us of Paul's efforts at inculturation and therefore of missionary activity (cf. 25, 43f., 52ff.). Three *Areopagi* are distinguished and they are dealt with in relation to evangelization. Says the Pope, "The first Areopagus of the modern age is *the world of communications,* which is unifying humanity and turning it into what is known as a 'global village'" (37c). In what has been called the most important text of the papal magisterium on social communications,[24] they are judged to be not only an instrument but to represent a veritable "new culture," which they "create" and which must be evangelized. For the Pope, "evangelization of modern culture depends to a great extent on the

24. Cf. P. Babin, "Communication," *CREC–AVEX* (Ecully, France: 1991), n. 15.

influence of the media. . . . It is also necessary to integrate that message into the 'new culture' created by communications" in order to overcome the discontinuity between Gospel and culture (ibid.).

The second Areopagus mentioned in this article is that of "culture, scientific research, and international relations." Here mission is involved in the promotion of dialogue and opening up new possibilities for improving the human lot. Here too *Redemptoris Missio* points to the impact these dynamic elements will have on peoples and cultures of the future: "That is why international organizations and meetings are proving increasingly important in many sectors of human life, from culture to politics, from the economy to research" (ibid.). The theme is taken up again in the section on the new forms of missionary cooperation where the Pope teaches that mission can also involve work with leaders in politics, economics, the arts, and journalism, as well as experts working for international bodies. One of the features of the contemporary world is the increasing difficulty one has in isolating important factors in social change within determinate geographical or cultural boundaries. The encyclical recognizes an increasing interdependence between peoples and how this constitutes a "stimulus for Christian witness and evangelization" (82).

These first two Areopagi show clearly that the possibilities of missionary activity are being broadened and may include a wider variety of agents, which it certainly needs. The third Areopagus in a pluralistic and mainly secularized and consumer world is that of the search for a life-giving spirituality, which the Pope sees manifested in "a desperate search for meaning, the need for an inner life, and a desire to learn new forms and methods of prayer." This "return to the sacred" is seen as an "antidote to dehumanization," which is "not without ambiguity, but it also represents an opportunity," an Areopagus to be evangelized (38).

By indicating the new social phenomena and modern Areopagi the encyclical defines the context of the mission *ad gentes,* "especially in the southern hemisphere" (37b). However, this also applies to the pastoral ministries of the church in all their forms and contexts, because these elements are characteristic of the "global village" (37c).

9. Motivation for Universal Mission

The first three chapters of *Redemptoris Missio* present motives and the nature of the mission *ad gentes* that Pope John Paul II holds to be a permanent and irreplaceable duty of the church. The first chapter deals with the problem of *salvation and its relation to the role of Christ and of the church.* The Pope emphasizes the fact that this can only be understood in the context of the faith. For, "It is only in faith that the Church's mission can be understood and only in faith that it finds its basis" (4). Furthermore, mission can be lived only in faith as the fruit of personal and communal faith. Therefore, commitment to universal mission is the yardstick of church vitality: "*Mission is an issue of faith,* an accurate indicator of our faith in Christ and his love for us" (11, emphasis in original); and, "In the Church's history, missionary drive has always been a sign of vitality, just as its lessening is a sign of a crisis of faith" (2).

Faith in this context is no mere generic religious faith or even faith in God. Rather, it is concretized faith in Christ as professed by the church. The quotation from the Creed of Nicea-Constantinople at the beginning of the chapter is significant for insight into the six christological reasons on which the missionary duty is based:

• "Christ is the one Savior of all" and therefore "salvation can only come from Jesus Christ" (5). Salvation is available to all human beings because of the grace that comes from Christ, which is the fruit of his sacrifice and is communicated through the Holy Spirit.

• "God's revelation becomes definitive and complete through his only-begotten Son. . . . This definitive word of his revelation is the fundamental reason why the Church is missionary by her very nature" (5).

• "Christ is the one mediator between God and humanity. . . . No one, therefore, can enter into communion with God except through Christ, by the working of the Holy Spirit" (5).

• Jesus may not be separated from Christ, nor Jesus Christ from the Word: "It is precisely this uniqueness of Christ which gives him absolute and universal significance" (6).

• In Christ there is a *"radical newness of life.* . . . This new life is a gift from God, and people are asked to accept and develop it, if they wish to realize the fullness of their vocation in conformity to Christ" (7, emphasis in original). Therefore, all human beings have the right to know the fullness of their vocation, which effectively is one and only one (10) and "all are called . . . and destined" to that vocation (11).

• The church, by divine will and in Christ, is the universal sacrament of salvation: "Salvation, which always remains a gift of the Spirit, requires man's cooperation, both to save himself and to save others. This is God's will, and this is why he established the Church and made her a part of his plan of salvation" (9). From this principle is derived the duty and necessity for the church and each of her members to witness "our faith in Christ, the one Savior of humanity" (11). "The Church cannot fail to proclaim that Jesus came to reveal the face of God and to merit salvation for all mankind by his Cross and Resurrection" (11). "The Church, and every individual Christian within her, may not keep hidden or monopolize this newness and richness which has been received from God's bounty in order to be communicated to all mankind" (11).

The second chapter draws out and explains motivation for mission. It does so in two ways. First, it presents the teaching and practice of Jesus in regard to *the Kingdom of God*. Chapter two presents the teaching of Jesus on the Kingdom of God (13-16), his way of acting, and dwells especially on the unity or

> identity between the message and the messenger, between saying, doing and being. His power, the secret of the effectiveness of his actions, lies in his total identification with the message he announces: he proclaims the "Good News" not just by what he says or does, but by what he is. (13)

The Pope notes that in the risen Jesus the Kingdom is inaugurated and proclaimed (16).

We have said that the Kingdom of God is the central theme of chapter two of the encyclical. It is useful to recall that the concept of the Kingdom, with all the wealth of missiological significance it contains, was brought to the fore in the post-Vatican Council II period. In many parts of the world, especially in Asia where the church operates in the midst of populations that are largely non-Christian, this is the favorite theme used in attempts to explain the scope and progress of mission. Basing themselves on interpretations of this concept, however, some have restricted motivation for the church's commitment to human promotion and peaceful coexistence to the "values" of the Kingdom without, however, stressing the need to propose conversion to Christ and to his church. A careful study of the teaching of Jesus and of the Apostles, as propounded in *Redemptoris Missio*, shows that the Kingdom of God cannot be reduced to a mere humanistic, anthropological, or theological level. The Kingdom, in the teaching of the encyclical, includes also, as an important component of its realization, the need to proclaim and accept the person of Christ, as well as to constitute concrete Christian communities as both a sign of the Kingdom and an instrument for radiating outward its effects.

The Kingdom of God, as it is outlined in *Redemptoris Missio* in keeping with both biblical and conciliar teaching, may be understood in five ways, all of which are interconnected and bear important consequences.

• The Kingdom of God means, first of all, God's salvific plan for humanity already "prepared for in the Old Testament, brought about by Christ and in Christ, and proclaimed to all peoples by the Church" (12). It is "God's plan" (13); "God's plan of salvation in all its fullness" (15); "God's plan" (20); "God's gift and work" (20). God reveals the reality, the characteristics and the requirements of this Kingdom (cf. 13-15).

• The Kingdom of God is also the eschatological realization of God's plan, "when Christ 'delivers the Kingdom to God the Father' and 'God will be everything to everyone' " (20), the "eschatological Kingdom" (20).

The Kingdom is activated by Christ and in Christ (12). "By raising Jesus from the dead, God has conquered death and he has definitively inaugurated his Kingdom in him" (16). "The Kingdom of God is not a concept, a doctrine, or a program subject to free interpretation, but it is before all else a *person* with the face and name of Jesus of Nazareth, the image of the invisible God" (18, emphasis in original). "The disciples recognize that the Kingdom is already present in the person of Jesus and is slowly being established within man and the world through a mysterious connection with him" (16).

• The church is "the seed, sign and instrument" of the Kingdom of God activated by Christ and in Christ, with the result being "a special relationship which, while not excluding the action of Christ and the Spirit outside the Church's visible boundaries, confers upon her a specific and necessary role; hence the Church's special connection with the Kingdom of God and of Christ, which she has 'the mission of announcing and inaugurating among peoples' " (18).

• "The inchoate reality of the Kingdom can also be found beyond the confines of the Church among peoples everywhere, to the extent that they live 'Gospel values' and are open to the working of the Spirit who breathes when and where he wills. . . . But it must be immediately added that this temporal dimension of the Kingdom remains incomplete unless it is related to the Kingdom of Christ present in the Church and straining toward eschatological fullness" (20).

All of these aspects or dimensions of the Kingdom are interconnected and all of them have important pastoral consequences in the realization of mission. Among the practical ramifications is one following from the design, plan and work of God. "We must ask for the Kingdom, welcome it and make it grow within us; but we must also work together so that it will be welcomed and will grow among all people" (20e). We must also discern the forms under which it is present and the ways in which it comes. The encyclical notes also that the Kingdom is not of concern only to Christians, for

The Kingdom is the concern of everyone: individuals, society, and the world. Working for the Kingdom means acknowledging and promoting God's activity, which is present in human history and transforms it. Building the Kingdom means working for liberation from evil in all its forms. In a word, the

Kingdom of God is the manifestation and the realization of God's plan of salvation in all its fullness. (15)

And because the Kingdom is an eschatological reality, the church must cooperate in "the eschatological salvation which is already begun in newness of life in Christ" (20). She does this mainly through proclaiming the need for conversion, founding new communities and establishing local churches. It must also be added that the church has a role in the eschatological salvation of every human being:

The Church is the sacrament of salvation for all mankind, and her activity is not limited only to those who accept her message. She is a dynamic force in humanity's journey toward the eschatological Kingdom. (20)

Because the Kingdom is accomplished and proclaimed in the risen Christ, "there is a need to unite *the proclamation of the Kingdom of God* (the content of Jesus's own 'kerygma') and *the proclamation of the Christ-event* (the 'kerygma' of the Apostles)" (16, emphasis in original). As a result, priority must be given to proclaiming Christ the Savior, to conversion and Baptism in order to share in the life transmitted by him (cf. 44-47, 7):

Preaching constitutes the Church's first and fundamental way of serving the coming of the Kingdom in individuals and in human society. Eschatological salvation begins even now in newness of life in Christ: "To all who believed in him, who believed in his name, he gave power to become children of God" (Jn 1:12). (20)

Because the church is the seed, sign and instrument of the Kingdom, indissolubly united with Christ and with the Kingdom itself, it has a specific and necessary role. According to Pope John Paul, "The Church serves the Kingdom by establishing communities and founding new particular Churches, and by guiding them to mature faith and charity in openness toward others, in service to individuals and society, and in understanding and esteem for human institutions" (20). From this it follows that, "It is necessary first and foremost to strive to establish Christian communities everywhere, communities which are a sign of the presence of God in the world and which will grow until they become Churches" (49). Because the Kingdom is an incipient reality outside the boundaries of the church, she serves the Kingdom by

spreading . . . the "Gospel values" which are an expression of the Kingdom and which help people to accept God's plan. . . . She is a dynamic force in mankind's journey toward the eschatological Kingdom, and is the sign and promoter of Gospel values (GS 39). The Church contributes to mankind's pilgrimage of conversion to God's plan through her witness and through such activities as dialogue, human promotion, commitment to justice and peace, education and care of the sick, and aid to the poor and to children. In carrying out these activities, however, she never loses sight of the priority of the transcendent and spiritual realities which are premises of eschatological salvation. (20)

In the light of all this, the Pope is convinced that correctly understanding the nature of Kingdom of God does not weaken the universal mission of Christ, but makes it more complete and more demanding (20). A full understanding of the theology of the Kingdom enables us to develop an outlook and practice of missionary activity that includes the various aspects of the church's mission in the world, according to all its phases in God's plan of salvation: "God, who is rich in mercy, he whom Jesus Christ has revealed to us" (12). Not only will it help us understand why the church must realize her worldwide mission but how she is to go about it, without reducing it in any way.

In order to cooperate with God's plan, the church must take lessons from and be in tune with the *Spirit, the principal agent of mission,* the one who guides the church. The way in which the Spirit acts, as we learn from the church of the early centuries, is the model to which we must always try to measure up (cf. 21, 62). The missionary mandate and the example of the church as portrayed in the New Testament and explicated in the third chapter of the encyclical, expand our understanding further concerning motivation for and many forms of the church's universal mission.

The missionary mandate entrusted by Christ to the church and enunciated in the four gospels, has always been understood by the church as the motive on which missionary activity is derived and from which it receives its thrust. The command given by Christ is not something extrinsic but expresses the dynamism of the divine presence in history and constitutes the very nature of the church. The encyclical recognizes, however, a plurality of motivations in the Scriptures, versions that, nevertheless "contain common elements as well as characteristics proper to each" (23), two of which are found in all the versions. First, "the universal dimension of the task entrusted to the Apostles," and then the assurance given to the Apostles that they "will receive the strength and the means necessary"; mission, accordingly, is not a result of mere human effort, but is based "on the power of the Risen Lord" (ibid.).

This mandate was initially and is still carried out under the guidance of the Spirit, "a powerful experience which completely transforms [the missionary] . . . the experience of Pentecost" (24) rendered by the Spirit, who will enable missionaries "to fulfill the mandate they have received" (22). Whatever may be the circumstances, mission can advance only with the assistance of the Spirit. And therefore the Pope notes that we must be available and docile to the Spirit (cf. 30, 87), as were the first Apostles during the public life of Jesus. Without the Spirit, they proved unable to understand his words and reluctant to follow him until:

> the Spirit transformed them into courageous witnesses to Christ and enlightened heralds of his word. It was the Spirit himself who guided them along the difficult and new paths of mission.
> Today, as in the past, that mission is difficult and complex, and demands the courage and light of the Spirit. (87)

Like the Apostles after Christ's Ascension, the church today "must gather in the Upper Room 'together with Mary the Mother of Jesus' (Acts 1:14), in order to pray for the Spirit and to gain strength and courage to carry out the missionary mandate" (92).

In the vision of the encyclical, mission is no mere human enterprise but one justified solely by faith and capable of being realized only by lively faith translated into prayer that disposes one to become available to do the work of God. Urged on by the Spirit, the Apostles went into the world, opening doors, not by preaching an abstract message but by

> taking into account people's hopes and expectations, their anguish and sufferings, as well as their culture, in order to proclaim to them salvation in Christ. . . .
> It is the Spirit who is the source of the drive to press on, not only geographically, but also beyond the frontiers of race and religion, for a truly universal mission. (25)

It is this same Spirit who constitutes the church, who transmits the multiplicity of charisms in the first Christian communities, making them dynamically "open and missionary" (26). It is the Spirit who chooses and sends missionaries toward "new frontiers" (27), and it is he who guides the process of inculturation, ensuring that the church opens her doors and becomes "the house which all may enter, and in which all can feel at home, while keeping their own culture and traditions, provided that these are not contrary to the Gospel" (24).

By being attentive to the Spirit, we are enabled not only to understand the reasons and ways of the universal mission, but the possibility for human beings in all times and places to be saved. The Pope notes that the Second Vatican Council teaches that the Spirit is at work

> in the heart of every person, through the "seeds of the Word," to be found in human initiatives — including religious ones — and in man's efforts to attain truth, goodness and God himself. . . . The Spirit's presence and activity affect not only individuals but also society and history, peoples, cultures and religions. (28; cf. 21, 29f., 44, 56, 87)

In these numerous quotations one finds a synthesis of the Council teaching concerning the action of the Spirit and the salvation worked by him. There are also significant expressions that better portray the universality of this action and which, together with the motivations for dialogue, are the basis of a theology of religions.

In regard to such contemporary questions as theology of religions, as is the case throughout the encyclical, the method demonstrated is one that integrates a variety of insights and images, bringing into harmony approaches, understandings, and activities that are sometimes interpreted as opposed to one another. In this vein, the Pope says that

> The universal activity of the Spirit is not to be separated from his particular activity within the Body of Christ, which is the Church. Indeed, it is always the Spirit who is at work, both when he gives life to the Church and impels her to proclaim Christ, and when he implants and develops his gifts in all individuals and peoples, guiding the Church to discover these gifts, to foster them and receive them through dialogue. (29)

10. The Future of Mission

Redemptoris Missio reaffirms the vision of the Second Vatican Council, harmonizing that with the New Testament's vision of mission. It also confirms and harmonizes important aspects of missionary experience of the past thirty years. In so doing, it also gives us an energetic thrust toward the future and has been called the *Magna Charta* of mission for the third millennium. The Pope is asking for a radical turn about, similar to other important historical transitions when the church set out for new frontiers (cf. 30).

The encyclical expresses the Pope's wish that the whole church be mobilized for mission, asking that there be greater awareness and more concrete commitment by the church in regard to missionary activity among non-Christian peoples who constitute two-thirds of humanity. All can and must collaborate in that effort (cf. 61f., 77-82, and above section 5), for this "is the primary service which the Church can render to every individual and to all humanity" (2; cf 31, 34, 44, 58f.). No part of the church can be missionary on its own: priests need the laity; natives need expatriates; religious need seculars. Mission is an activity of the whole church, and all its modes and charisms must be involved, as they were in the primitive church (cf. 26-27, 61-74, 77-83, 85). In summary, missionary cooperation cannot be limited to distant activities because mission is everywhere. Unevangelized groups are everywhere;

witness can be needed, given and received in any situation; and therefore there are infinite numbers of new possibilities and the responsibility to exploit them (cf. 3, 32ff., 82, 86, 92).

The encyclical envisages a *church that is entirely missionary everywhere,* a community committed to be missionary in a world that is not yet Christian and in which every local church must live the missionary calling proper to it. This is a program of action based on the immense needs to which the church must respond. Certainly there are ecclesiastical structures in almost every nation, but their incarnation of and ability to radiate the Gospel of the Kingdom are often minimal. Some churches are still made up of communities that are considered to be, or *are,* foreign; others consist of tiny segments of the population; others lack visibility and the capacity to engage in an outward-looking missionary stance (cf. 31, 33ff., 37, 40, 85f.; see above section 8). The location of unevangelized groups, furthermore, is not restricted to specific geographical areas, since migration is displacing and otherwise moving people around like wildfire (cf. 32, 37, 82). Thus there are new *areopagi* to be evangelized — the world and culture of communications, urban areas, youth, social strata, and people searching for an experience of the sacred. The church must, in the light of all this, promote renewal in its existing communities to make them living, witnessing realities; she must promote a "new" evangelization of persons and cultures that have ceased to be meaningfully Christian as well as to evangelize those who have never been Christian (cf. 33f., 85f.).

Pope John Paul seeks to *renew the church by mission.* Missionary commitment, in his view, promotes the renewal of pastoral ministries and also helps the spiritual renewal of the church as a whole: "*Faith is strengthened when it is given to others!* It is in commitment to the Church's universal mission that the new evangelization of Christian peoples will find inspiration and support" (2, emphasis in original; cf. 34, 49, 77, 90, and above section 6). The solidarity of humanity that will result from Christian mission, he says, will ensure the solution of social and economic problems in the Third World if rich nations will develop a new lifestyle, an adoption of which, one is permitted to hope, a new evangelization will assist (cf. 59, 81).

The encyclical proposes an *integral vision of mission,* one in which diverse missionary activities are both possible and realized — promoting human development, dialogue, commitment to justice, incarnation, and explicit witness with its natural tendency to proclamation (cf. 41-60; see above section 9). It is an aim whose achievement requires the promotion of all ecclesial charisms and communion among persons who have these gifts, which are given to build up the church. This must be done through the mission entrusted to all members, even though it is carried out diversely according to the variety of gifts and the requirements of the circumstances in which they are exercised. The integral nature of mission, as it is expounded in *Redemptoris Missio,* also necessitates both a greater number of missionary workers and a greater variety of them than was presumed true in the past (cf. 20, 61-74).

Integral missionary activity requires recognition that *proclamation* is to be given pride of place because of its nature at the center of mission, as is shown well in the following citations:

Just as the whole economy of salvation has its center in Christ, so too all missionary activity is directed to the proclamation of his mystery (44).

The Church is effectively and concretely at the service of the Kingdom. This is seen especially in her preaching, which is a call to conversion. Preaching constitutes the Church's first and fundamental way of serving the coming of the Kingdom in individuals and in human society (20; cf. 31, 34, 40, 44-47, 55, 58f, 83).

It is not right to give an incomplete picture of missionary activity, as if it consisted principally in helping the poor, contributing to the liberation of the oppressed, promoting development or defending human rights. The missionary Church is certainly involved on these fronts but her primary task lies elsewhere: the poor are hungry for God, not just for bread and freedom. Missionary activity must first of all bear witness to and proclaim salvation in Christ, and establish local Churches which then become means of liberation in every sense. (83)

While mission involves proclamation, it must also be carried on respectfully and in a spirit of dialogue. *Redemptoris Missio* proposes a missionary activity that respects freedom and the human person (cf. 7f., 35, 39, 46f.), cultures (cf. 24f., 34, 37, 52ff.), and religions (cf. 5f., 9-11, 28f., 46, 55ff., 91). Respect is based on intrinsic values with which these persons and things are endowed in the divine plan:

God calls all peoples to himself and he wishes to share with them the fullness of his revelation and love. He does not fail to make himself present in many ways, not only to individuals but also to entire peoples through their spiritual riches, of which their religions are the main and essential expression, even though they contain "gaps, insufficiencies and errors." (55; cf. 21, 88)

From this respect for others springs a dialogic relationship with them, one that constitutes both the spirit of mission and a specific activity within mission (cf. 55ff.). The presence of the "seeds of the Word" and the action of the spirit in these religious and cultural expressions of the peoples with whom one is in dialogue is also an incentive to ecclesial inculturation (cf. 52).

Another important aspect of the future of universal mission inculcated by *Redemptoris Missio* is that it is also to be *undertaken by "young churches"* that have been founded in recent centuries and that must become active both in their own milieux and in the world as a whole. Upon their missionary involvement the future of the church depends (cf. 2, 48f., 62, 64, 66f., 85, 92; see above sections 5 and 6). The churches are the concrete presence, the sign and sacrament of the Kingdom in their milieux, which in the main, especially in Asia, are not Christian. It is to them that the Lord is today sending vocations. The Pope calls upon them to help, saying among other things:

Do not isolate yourselves; willingly accept missionaries and support from other Churches, and do likewise throughout the world. (85)

Being young in faith, you must be like the first Christians and radiate enthusiasm and courage, in generous devotion to God and neighbor. In a word, you must set yourselves on the path of holiness. (91)

Mission still requires *special vocations*, even though the whole church must be missionary, including every community and individual member. Precisely to obtain this result, a special kind of missionary is needed — "missionaries 'for life,'" whose special vocation retains its validity. For the Pope, in fact, that vocation "is the model of the Church's missionary commitment, which always stands in need of radical and total self-giving, of new and bold endeavors" (66; cf. 32, 64-74, 79f., 84; see above section 6). The Pope makes an insistent call for promoting missionary vocations (cf. 79).

The renewal of mission must also be based on *sound theology*. Mission needs the contribution of theologians and their reflection in order to respond adequately to new challenges (cf. 2, 36, 83; see above, section 6). The encyclical is itself an example of the importance of theology to understand and relaunch mission. In addition, the present crisis in mission has theological roots, as the questions repeatedly asked by the Pope in the first three chapters make clear.

Mission is, above all, *cooperation with the Christ and his Spirit.* Stressing this point, the encyclical explicates the role of the mystery of the Trinity in mission. It follows, as is pointed out in the great missionary commission, that the mission of disciples is not dependent "on human abilities" but on the "power of the Risen Lord" (23; cf. 16, 36, 42, 88), with the Spirit the "principal agent of the whole of the Church's mission" as he was for the mission of the Apostles (21; cf. 24, 44f., 88). In the words of the Pope, this should give us great encouragement, and

> Internal and external difficulties must not make us pessimistic or inactive. What counts, here as in every area of Christian life, is the confidence that comes from faith, from the certainty that it is not we who are the principal agents of the Church's mission, but Jesus Christ and his Spirit. We are only co-workers, and when we have done all that we can, we must say: "We are unworthy servants, we have only done what was our duty" (Lk 17:10). (36)

Mission, as work accomplished mainly by Christ through the Spirit is, however, dependent on the spirituality of the church and the missionary, a spirituality "expressed first of all by a life of complete docility to the Spirit," a life that commits the believer to being renewed and molded from within by the Spirit, making the disciple ever more like Christ (87). This in turn consoles the missionary (cf. 88), who realizes ever more deeply that he or she has been sent by one who remains ever present (Acts 18:9-10). Charity is the ultimate criterion for evaluating the genuineness of that missionary life (cf. 15, 60, 89). Personal and community witness are a prerequisite for missionary life, and these require the consistent giving of one's whole life to the cause (cf. 13, 42f.). Holiness is the source of all fruitful cooperation in missionary activity (cf. 77), a principle that is linked closely to the vocation of all Christians to participate in mission:

> Every member of the faithful is called to holiness and to mission. . . . The renewed impulse to the mission *ad gentes* demands holy missionaries. It is not enough to update pastoral techniques, organize and coordinate ecclesial resources, or delve more deeply into the biblical and theological foundations of faith. What is needed is the encouragement of a "new ardor for holiness" among missionaries and throughout the Christian unity, especially among those who work most closely with the missionaries. (90)

Conclusion

The church today needs not only a new evangelization but a new sense of mission with which to respond to new needs and to a new understanding of herself and her activity. The horizons of Christian mission are limitless. The aims and activities of mission make necessary commitment on the part of all Christians, but also of persons who will specially devote themselves to the missionary vocation.

The horizons of mission are limitless, not only because of the many needs that exist, but especially because of the universal, salvific role of the Christ, the only perfect model of all humanity, great parts of which need to be vitally introduced to him, which is one of the chief tasks of mission (cf. 4-8). These horizons are also limitless because the church has been assigned a key role as the necessary instrument of salvation for the building up of the Kingdom of God, the Kingdom to which all men and women are called (cf. 9, 19f.). In the words of the Pope:

> The history of humanity has known many turning points which have encouraged missionary outreach. . . . Today the Church must face other challenges and push forward to new frontiers, both in the initial mission *ad gentes* and in the new evangelization of those peoples who have already heard Christ proclaimed. Today all Christians, the particular Churches and the universal Church, are called to have the same courage that inspired the missionaries of the past, and the same readiness to listen to the voice of the Spirit. (30)

Part Two

Dialogue and Proclamation

1

Dialogue and Proclamation

Reflections and Orientations on Interreligious Dialogue and the Proclamation of the Gospel of Jesus Christ

**Issued by the
Pontifical Council for Inter-Religious Dialogue
and the
Congregation for the Evangelization of Peoples**[*]

Outline of the Statement

---

*Reprinted from the *Bulletin of the Pontifical Council on Interreligious Dialogue*, vol. 26, no. 2, 1991 (Rome: Vatican Polyglot Press).

III. Interreligious Dialogue and Proclamation
    A. Interrelated yet not Interchangeable
    B. The Church and Religions
    C. Proclaiming Jesus Christ
    D. Commitment to the One Mission
    E. Jesus our Model

Conclusion

Text of the Statement

INTRODUCTION

1. It is twenty-five years since *Nostra Aetate*, the declaration of the Second Vatican Council on the Church's relationship to other religions, was promulgated. The document stressed the importance of interreligious dialogue. At the same time it recalled that the Church is in duty bound to proclaim without fail Christ, the Way, the Truth, and the Life, in whom all people find their fulfillment (cf. NA 2).

A document on dialogue and mission
2. To foster the work of dialogue, Pope Paul VI set up in 1964 the Secretariat for Non-Christians, recently renamed the Pontifical Council for Interreligious Dialogue. Following its Plenary Assembly of 1984, the Secretariat issued a document entitled "The Attitude of the Church toward the Followers of Other Religions: Reflections and Orientations on Dialogue and Mission." This document states that the evangelizing mission of the Church is a "single but complex and articulated reality." It indicates the principal elements of this mission: presence and witness; commitment to social development and human liberation; liturgical life, prayer and contemplation; interreligious dialogue; and finally, proclamation and catechesis.[1] Proclamation and dialogue are thus both viewed, each in its own place, as component elements and authentic forms of the one evangelizing mission of the Church. They are both oriented toward the communication of salvific truth.

is followed by one on dialogue and proclamation.
3. The present document gives further consideration to these two elements. It first puts forward the characteristics of each, and then studies their mutual relationship. If dialogue is treated first, this is not because it has any priority over proclamation. It is simply due to the fact that dialogue is the primary concern of the Pontifical Council for Interreligious Dialogue which initiated the preparation of the document. The document in fact was first discussed during the Plenary Assembly of the Secretariat in 1987. The observations made then, together with further consultation, have led to this text, which was finalized and adopted at the Plenary Assembly of the Pontifical Council for Interreligious Dialogue in April 1990. In the process there has been close collaboration between the Pontifical Council for Interreligious Dialogue

---

1. "The Attitude of the Church toward the Followers of Other Religions (Reflections and Orientations on Dialogue and Mission)," *AAS* 76 (1984), pp. 816-828; see also *Bulletin Secretariatus pro non Christianis*, 56 (1984/2), art. 13. (This document will be referred to henceforth as D&M for "Dialogue and Mission," the short title by which the statement is commonly known.)

and the Congregation for the Evangelization of Peoples. Both dicasteries are offering these reflections to the universal Church.

The theme is relevant

4. Among the reasons which make the relationship between dialogue and proclamation a relevant theme for study, the following may be mentioned:

in a pluralistic world

(a) In the world of today, characterized by rapid communications, mobility of peoples, and interdependence, there is a new awareness of the fact of religious plurality. Religions do not merely exist, or simply survive. In some cases they give clear evidence of a revival. They continue to inspire and influence the lives of millions of their adherents. In the present context of religious plurality, the important role played by religious traditions cannot be overlooked.

where there is hesitation about dialogue

(b) Interreligious dialogue between Christians and followers of other religious traditions, as envisaged by the Second Vatican Council, is only gradually coming to be understood. Its practice remains hesitant in some places. The situation differs from country to country. It can depend on the size of the Christian community, on which other religious traditions are present, and on various other cultural, social and political factors. A further examination of the question may help to stimulate dialogue.

and questions are raised.

(c) The practice of dialogue raises problems in the minds of many. There are those who would seem to think, erroneously, that in the Church's mission today dialogue should simply replace proclamation. At the other extreme, some fail to see the value of interreligious dialogue. Yet others are perplexed and ask: If interreligious dialogue has become so important, has the proclamation of the Gospel message lost its urgency? Has the effort to bring people into the community of the Church become secondary or even superfluous? There is a need therefore for doctrinal and pastoral guidance to which this document wishes to contribute, without pretending to answer fully the many and complex questions which arise in this connection.

As this text was in its final stages of preparation for publication, the Holy Father, Pope John Paul II, offered to the Church his Encyclical Letter *Redemptoris Missio*, in which he addressed these questions and many more. The present document spells out in greater detail the teaching of the Encyclical on dialogue and its relationship to proclamation (cf. RM 55-57). It is therefore to be read in the light of this Encyclical.

The World Day of Prayer for Peace in Assisi

5. The World Day of Prayer for Peace in Assisi, on 27 October 1986, held at the initiative of Pope John Paul II, provides another stimulus for reflection. Both on the day itself and after, especially in his address to the Cardinals and to the Roman Curia in December, 1986, the Holy Father explained the meaning of the Assisi celebration. He underlined the fundamental unity of the human race, in its origin and its destiny, and the role of the Church as an effective sign of this unity. He brought out forcibly the significance of interreligious dialogue, while at the same time affirming the Church's duty to announce Jesus Christ to the world.[2]

---

2. *Insegnamenti di Giovanni Paolo II*, vol. 9, 2 (1986), pp. 1249-1273; 2019-2029 (hereafter referred to as *Insegnamenti*). Cf. *Bulletin* 64 (1987/1), which contains all the Pope's discourses before, during, and after the day of prayer in Assisi.

and the encouragement given by Pope John Paul II

6. The following year, in his address to the members of the Plenary Assembly of the Pontifical Council for Interreligious Dialogue, Pope John Paul II declared: "Just as interreligious dialogue is one element in the mission of the Church, the proclamation of God's saving work in Our Lord Jesus Christ is another. . . . There can be no question of choosing one and ignoring or rejecting the other."[3] The lead given by the Pope encourages us to give further attention to the present theme.

are further stimuli in addressing the topic.

7. This document is addressed to all Catholics, particularly to all who have a leadership role in the community or are engaged in formation work. It is offered as well for the consideration of Christians belonging to other Churches or ecclesial communities who themselves have been reflecting on the questions it raises.[4] It is hoped that it will receive attention also from the followers of other religious traditions.

Terms are clarified:

Before proceeding it will be useful to clarify the terms being used in this document.

8. *Evangelizing mission*, or more simply, *evangelization*, refers to the mission of the Church in its totality. In the Apostolic Exhortation *Evangelii Nuntiandi*, the term evangelization is taken in different ways. It means "to bring the Good News into all areas of humanity, and through its impact, to transform that humanity from within, making it new" (EN 18). Thus, through evangelization the Church "seeks to convert solely through the divine power of the Message she proclaims, both the personal and collective consciences of people, the activities in which they engage, their ways of life, and the actual milieux in which they live" (EN 18). The Church accomplishes her evangelizing mission through a variety of activities. Hence there is a broad concept of evangelization. Yet in the same document, evangelization is also taken more specifically to mean "the clear and unambiguous proclamation of the Lord Jesus" (EN 22). The Exhortation states that "this proclamation — *kerygma*, preaching or catechesis — occupies such an important place in evangelization that it has often become synonymous with it; and yet it is only one aspect of evangelization" (EN 22). In this document the term *evangelizing mission* is used for evangelization in its broad sense, while the more specific understanding is expressed by the term *proclamation*.

dialogue,

9. *Dialogue* can be understood in different ways. Firstly, at the purely human level, it means reciprocal communication, leading to a common goal or, at a deeper level, to interpersonal communion. Secondly, dialogue can be taken as an attitude of respect and friendship, which permeates or should permeate all those activities constituting the evangelizing mission of the Church. This can appropriately be called "the spirit of dialogue." Thirdly, in the context of religious plurality, dialogue means "all positive and constructive interreligious relations with individuals and communities of other faiths which are directed at mutual understanding and enrichment" (D&M 3), in obedience to truth and respect for freedom. It includes both witness and the exploration of respective religious convictions. It is in this third sense that the present document uses the term dialogue for one of the integral elements of the Church's evangelizing mission.

3. *Insegnamenti*, vol. 10, 1 (1987) pp. 1449-52. Cf. *Bulletin* 66 (1987/3), pp. 223-225.

4. *Guidelines on Dialogue with People of Living Faiths and Ideologies*, World Council of Churches (Geneva: World Council of Churches, 1979); "Mission and Evangelism — an Ecumenical Affirmation," *International Review of Mission* 71 (1982), pp. 427-451.

proclamation,

10. *Proclamation* is the communication of the Gospel message, the mystery of salvation realized by God for all in Jesus Christ by the power of the Spirit. It is an invitation to a commitment of faith in Jesus Christ and to entry through baptism into the community of believers which is the Church. This proclamation can be solemn and public, as for instance on the day of Pentecost (cf. Acts 2:5-41), or in a simple private conversation (cf. Acts 8:30-38). It leads naturally to catechesis which aims at deepening this faith. Proclamation is the foundation, center, and summit of evangelization (cf. EN 27).

conversion,
11. Included in the idea of *conversion* there is always a general movement toward God, "the humble and penitent return of the heart to God in the desire to submit one's life more generously to him" (D&M 37). More specifically, conversion may refer to a change of religious adherence, and particularly to embracing the Christian faith. When the term conversion is used in this document, the context will show which sense is intended.

religions and religious traditions.
12. The terms *religions* or *religious traditions* are used here in a generic and analogical sense. They cover those religions which, with Christianity, are wont to refer back to the faith of Abraham,[5] as well as the religious traditions of Asia, Africa, and elsewhere.

13. Interreligious dialogue ought to extend to all religions and their followers. This document, however, will not treat of dialogue with the followers of "New Religious Movements" due to the diversity of situations which these movements present and the need for discernment on the human and religious values which each contains.[6]

I. INTERRELIGIOUS DIALOGUE

A. A Christian Approach to Religious Traditions

Religious traditions are viewed positively
14. A just appraisal of other religious traditions normally presupposes close contact with them. This implies, besides theoretical knowledge, practical experience of interreligious dialogue with the followers of these traditions. Nevertheless, it is also true that a correct theological evaluation of these traditions, at least in general terms, is a necessary presupposition for interreligious dialogue. These traditions are to be approached with great sensitivity, on account of the spiritual and human values enshrined in them. They command our respect because over the centuries they have

5. Because the spiritual patrimony common to Christians and Jews is so great (cf. NA 4), dialogue between Christians and Jews has its own special requirements. These are not dealt with in this document. For a full treatment, see "Commission on Religious Relations with Jews, Guidelines on Religious Relations with Jews," 1 December 1974, in Austin P. Flannery, ed., *Documents of Vatican II* (Grand Rapids: Eerdmans, 1984), pp. 743-749); see also "Notes for a Correct Presentation of Jews and Judaism in Catholic Preaching and Catechesis," 24 June 1985, *Origins*, 15 (No. 2, 4 July 1985), pp. 102-107.
6. The question of New Religious Movements has been treated in a recent document published in collaboration by the following Pontifical Councils: PC for Promoting Christian Unity, PC for Interreligious Dialogue, PC for Dialogue with Nonbelievers and PC for Culture. The complete text can be found in *Origins*, 16, 1 (22 May 1986).

borne witness to the efforts to find answers "to those profound mysteries of the human condition" (NA 1) and have given expression to the religious experience and the longings of millions of their adherents, and they continue to do so today.

by Vatican II

15. The Second Vatican Council has given the lead for such a positive assessment. The exact meaning of what the Council affirms needs to be carefully and accurately ascertained. The Council reaffirms the traditional doctrine, according to which salvation in Jesus Christ is, in a mysterious way, a reality open to all persons of good will. A clear enunciation of this basic conviction in Vatican II is found in the Constitution *Gaudium et Spes*. The Council teaches that Christ, the New Adam, through the mystery of his incarnation, death, and resurrection, is at work in each human person to bring about interior renewal:

> This holds true not for Christians only but also for all persons of good will in whose hearts grace is active invisibly. For since Christ died for all, and since all are in fact called to one and the same destiny, which is divine, we must hold that the Holy Spirit offers to all the possibility of being made partners, in a way known to God, in the Paschal mystery. (GS 22)

which finds in them the effects of God's grace,

16. The Council proceeds further. Making its own the vision and the terminology of some early Church Fathers, *Nostra Aetate* speaks of the presence in these traditions of "a ray of that Truth which enlightens all" (NA 2). *Ad Gentes* recognizes the presence of "seeds of the word," and points to "the riches which a generous God has distributed among the nations" (AG 11). Again, *Lumen Gentium* refers to the good which is "found sown" not only "in minds and hearts," but also "in the rites and customs of peoples" (LG 17).

sees the action of the Holy Spirit,

17. These few references suffice to show that the Council has openly acknowledged the presence of positive values not only in the religious life of individual believers of other religious traditions, but also in the religious traditions to which they belong. It attributed these values to the active presence of God through his Word, pointing also to the universal action of the Spirit: "Without doubt," *Ad Gentes* affirms, "the Holy Spirit was at work in the world before Christ was glorified" (AG 4). From this it can be seen that these elements, as a preparation for the Gospel (cf. LG 16), have played and do still play a providential role in the divine economy of salvation. This recognition impels the Church to enter into "dialogue and collaboration" (NA 2; cf. GS 92-93): "Let Christians, while witnessing to their own faith and way of life, acknowledge, preserve and encourage the spiritual and moral good found among non-Christians, as well as their social and cultural values" (NA 2).

yet stresses the role of the Church's activity.

18. The Council is not unaware of the necessity of the missionary activity of the Church in order to perfect in Christ these elements found in other religions. The Council states very clearly: "Whatever truth and grace are to be found among the nations, as a sort of secret presence of God, this activity frees from all taint of evil and restores to Christ its Maker, who overthrows the devil's domain and wards off the manifold malice of vice. And so, whatever good is found to be sown in the hearts and minds of men, or in the rites and cultures peculiar to various peoples, is not lost. More than that, it is healed, ennobled, and perfected for the glory of God, the shame of the demon, and the bliss of men" (AG 9).

The history of God's saving deeds

19. The Old Testament testifies that from the beginning of creation God made a Covenant with all peoples (Gen 1-11). This shows that there is but one history of salvation for the whole of humankind. The Covenant with Noah, the man who "walked with God" (Gen 6:9), is symbolic of the divine intervention in the history of the nations. Non-Israelite figures of the Old Testament are seen in the New Testament as belonging to this one history of salvation. Abel, Enoch and Noah are proposed as models of faith (cf. Heb 11:4-7). They knew, adored and believed in the one true God who is identical with the God who revealed himself to Abraham and Moses. The Gentile High Priest Melchisedek blesses Abraham, the father of all believers (cf. Heb 7:1-17). It is this history of salvation which sees its final fulfillment in Jesus Christ in whom is established the new and definitive Covenant for all peoples.

extends beyond the Chosen People to include all nations.

20. The religious consciousness of Israel is characterized by a deep awareness of its unique status as God's Chosen People. This election, accompanied by a process of formation and continuous exhortations to preserve the purity of monotheism, constitutes a mission. The prophets continually insist on loyalty and fidelity to the One True God and speak about the promised Messiah. And yet these prophets, particularly at the time of the Exile, bring a universal perspective, for God's salvation is understood to extend beyond and through Israel to the nations. Thus Isaiah foretells that in the final days the nations will stream to the house of the Lord, and they will say: "Come, let us go up to the mountain of the Lord, to the house of the God of Jacob; that he may teach us his ways and that we may walk in his paths" (Is 2:3). It is also said that "all the ends of the earth shall see the salvation of our God" (Is 52:10). In the Wisdom literature also, which bears witness to cultural exchanges between Israel and its neighbors, the action of God in the whole universe is clearly affirmed. It goes beyond the boundaries of the Chosen People to touch both the history of nations and the lives of individuals.

Jesus's universal mission

21. Turning to the New Testament, we see that Jesus professes to have come to gather the lost sheep of Israel (cf. Mt 15:24) and forbids his disciples for the moment to turn to the Gentiles (cf. Mt 10:5). He nevertheless displays an open attitude toward men and women who do not belong to the chosen people of Israel. He enters into dialogue with them and recognizes the good that is in them. He marvels at the centurion's readiness to believe, saying that he has found no such faith in Israel (cf. Mt 8:5-13). He performs miracles of healing for "foreigners" (cf. Mk 7:24-30; Mt 15:21-28), and these miracles are signs of the coming of the Kingdom. He converses with the Samaritan woman and speaks to her of a time when worship will not be restricted to any one particular place, but when true worshipers will "worship the Father in spirit and truth" (Jn 4:23). Jesus is thus opening up a new horizon, beyond the purely local, to a universality which is both Christological and Pneumatological in character. For the new sanctuary is now the body of the Lord Jesus (cf. Jn 2:21) whom the Father has raised up in the power of the Spirit.

announced God's reign

22. Jesus's message, then, proved by the witness of his life, is that in his own person the Kingdom of God is breaking through to the world. At the beginning of his public ministry, in Galilee of the nations, he can say: "The time has come, and the Kingdom of God is close at hand." He also indicates the conditions for entry into this Kingdom: "Repent, and believe the Good News" (Mk 1:15). This message is not

confined only to those who belong to the specially chosen people. Jesus in fact explicitly announces the entry of the Gentiles into the Kingdom of God (cf. Mt 8:10-11; Mt 11:20-24; Mt 25:31-32, 34), a Kingdom which is to be understood as being at one and the same time historical and eschatological. It is both the Father's Kingdom, for the coming of which it is necessary to pray (cf. Mt 6:10), and Jesus's own Kingdom, since Jesus openly declares himself to be king (cf. Jn 18:33-37). In fact in Jesus Christ, the Son of God made man, we have the fullness of revelation and salvation and the fulfillment of the desires of the nations.

reaching out to all peoples.

23. References in the New Testament to the religious life of the Gentiles and to their religious traditions may appear to be contrasting, but can be seen as complementary. There is, on the one hand, the negative verdict of the Letter to the Romans against those who have failed to recognize God in his creation and have fallen into idolatry and depravity (cf. Rom 1:18-32). On the other hand, the Acts testify to Paul's positive and open attitude toward the Gentiles, both in his discourse to the Lycaonians (cf. Acts 14:8-18) and in his Areopagus speech at Athens, in which he praised their religious spirit and announced to them the one whom unknowingly they revered as the "unknown God" (cf. Acts 17:22-34). Nor must it be forgotten that the Wisdom tradition is applied in the New Testament to Jesus Christ as the Wisdom of God, the Word of God that enlightens every man (cf. Jn 1:9) and who in his Incarnation pitches his tent among us (cf. Jn 1:14).

The early Fathers

24. The post-Biblical tradition also contains contrasting data. Negative judgments on the religious world of their time can easily be gleaned from the writings of the Fathers. Yet the early tradition shows remarkable openness. A number of Church Fathers take up the sapiential tradition reflected in the New Testament. In particular, writers of the second century and the first part of the third century such as Justin, Irenaeus and Clement of Alexandria, either explicitly or in an equivalent way, speak about the "seeds" sown by the Word of God in the nations.[7] Thus it can be said that for them, prior to and outside the Christian dispensation, God has already, in an incomplete way, manifested himself. This manifestation of the *Logos* is an adumbration of the full revelation in Jesus Christ to which it points.

offered a theology of history

25. In fact, these early Fathers offer what may be called a theology of history. History becomes salvation history, inasmuch as through it God progressively manifests himself and communicates with humankind. This process of divine manifestation and communication reaches its climax in the incarnation of the Son of God in Jesus Christ. For this reason, Irenaeus distinguishes four "covenants" given by God to the human race: in Adam, in Noah, in Moses, and in Jesus Christ.[8] The same

---

7. Justin speaks about the "seeds" sown by the *Logos* in the religious traditions. Through the Incarnation the manifestation of the *Logos* becomes complete (*1 Apol.* 46, 1-4; *2 Apol.* 8, 1; 10:1-3; 13:4-6). For Irenaeus, the Son, the visible manifestation of the Father, has revealed himself to mankind "from the beginning"; yet the Incarnation brings about something entirely new (*Adv. Haer.* 4, 6, 5-7; 4, 7, 2; 4, 20, 6-7). Clement of Alexandria explains that "philosophy" was given to the Greeks by God as a "covenant," as a "stepping stone to the philosophy which is according to Christ," as a "schoolmaster" bringing the Hellenistic mind to him (*Stromata*, 5; 6, 8; 7, 2).

8. *Adv. Haer.*, 3, 11, 8.

patristic current, whose importance is not to be underestimated, may be said to culminate in Augustine who in his later works stressed the universal presence and influence of the mystery of Christ even before the Incarnation. In fulfillment of his plan of salvation, God, in his Son, has reached out to the whole of humankind. Thus, in a certain sense, Christianity already existed "at the beginning of the human race." [9]

developed anew by the Magisterium.
26. It was to this early Christian vision of history that the Second Vatican Council made reference. After the Council, the Church's Magisterium, especially that of Pope John Paul II, has proceeded further in the same direction. First the Pope gives explicit recognition to the operative presence of the Holy Spirit in the life of the members of other religious traditions, as when in *Redemptor Hominis* he speaks of their "firm belief" as being "an effect of the Spirit of truth operating outside the visible confines of the Mystical Body" (RH 6). In *Dominum et Vivificantem*, he takes a further step, affirming the universal action of the Holy Spirit in the world before the Christian dispensation, to which it was ordained, and referring to the universal action of the same Spirit today, even outside the visible body of the Church (DEV 53).

Pope John Paul II
27. In his address to the Roman Curia after the World Day of Prayer for Peace in Assisi, Pope John Paul II stressed once more the universal presence of the Holy Spirit, stating that "every authentic prayer is called forth by the Holy Spirit, who is mysteriously present in the heart of every person," Christian or otherwise. But again, in the same discourse, the Pope, going beyond an individual perspective, articulated the main elements which together can be seen as constituting the theological basis for a positive approach to other religious traditions and the practice of interreligious dialogue.

teaches the mystery of the unity of humanity
28. First comes the fact that the whole of humankind forms one family, due to the common origin of all men and women, created by God in his own image. Correspondingly, all are called to a common destiny, the fullness of life in God. Moreover, there is but one plan of salvation for humankind, with its center in Jesus Christ, who in his incarnation "has united himself in a certain manner to every person" (RH 13; cf. GS 22.2). Finally there needs to be mentioned the active presence of the Holy Spirit in the religious life of the members of the other religious traditions. From all this the Pope concludes to a "mystery of unity" which was manifested clearly at Assisi, "in spite of the differences between religious professions." [10]

and the unity of salvation.
29. From this mystery of unity it follows that all men and women who are saved share, though differently, in the same mystery of salvation in Jesus Christ through his Spirit. Christians know this through their faith, while others remain unaware that Jesus Christ is the source of their salvation. The mystery of salvation reaches out to them, in a way known to God, through the invisible action of the Spirit of Christ. Concretely, it will be in the sincere practice of what is good in their own religious traditions and by following the dictates of their conscience that the members of other religions respond positively to God's invitation and receive salvation in Jesus Christ, even while they do not recognize or acknowledge him as their savior (cf. AG 3, 9, 11).

---

9. *Retract.*, 1, 13, 3; cf. *Enarr. in Ps. 118* (*Sermo* 29, 9), 142, 3.
10. *Insegnamenti*, vol. 9, 2 (1986), pp. 2019-2029; English text in *L'Osservatore Romano*, weekly edition in English, 5 January 1987, and *Bulletin* n. 64 (1987/1), pp. 54-62.

Discernment is needed

30. The fruits of the Spirit of God in the personal life of individuals, whether Christian or otherwise, are easily discernible (cf. Gal 5:22-23). To identify in other religious traditions elements of grace capable of sustaining the positive response of their members to God's invitation is much more difficult. It requires a discernment for which criteria have to be established. Sincere individuals marked by the Spirit of God have certainly put their imprint on the elaboration and the development of their respective religious traditions. It does not follow, however, that everything in them is good.

31. To say that the other religious traditions include elements of grace does not imply that everything in them is the result of grace. For sin has been at work in the world, and so religious traditions, notwithstanding their positive values, reflect the limitations of the human spirit, sometimes inclined to choose evil. An open and positive approach to other religious traditions cannot overlook the contradictions which may exist between them and Christian revelation. It must, where necessary, recognize that there is incompatibility between some fundamental elements of the Christian religion and some aspects of such traditions.

and in dialogue all are challenged.

32. This means that, while entering with an open mind into dialogue with the followers of other religious traditions, Christians may have also to challenge them in a peaceful spirit with regard to the content of their belief. But Christians, too, must allow themselves to be questioned. Notwithstanding the fullness of God's revelation in Jesus Christ, the way Christians sometimes understand their religion and practice it may be in need of purification.

B. The Place of Interreligious Dialogue
in the Evangelizing Mission of the Church

The Church is the universal sacrament of salvation,

33. The Church has been willed by God and instituted by Christ to be, in the fullness of time, the sign and instrument of the divine plan of salvation (cf. LG 1), the center of which is the mystery of Christ. She is the "universal sacrament of salvation" (LG 48)) and is "necessary for salvation" (LG 14). The Lord Jesus himself inaugurated her mission "by preaching the good news, that is, the coming of God's Kingdom" (LG 5).

the seed and the beginning of the Kingdom,

34. The relationship between the Church and the Kingdom is mysterious and complex. As Vatican II teaches, "principally the Kingdom is revealed in the person of Christ himself." Yet the Church, which has received from the Lord Jesus the mission of proclaiming the Kingdom "is, on earth, the seed and the beginning of that Kingdom." At the same time the Church "slowly grows to maturity (and) longs for the completed Kingdom" (LG 5). Thus "the Kingdom is inseparable from the Church, because both are inseparable from the person and work of Jesus himself. . . . It is therefore not possible to separate the Church from the Kingdom as if the first belonged exclusively to the imperfect realm of history, while the second would be the perfect eschatological fulfillment of the divine plan of salvation." [11]

11. John Paul II, "Discourse to Indian Bishops on 'ad limina' Visit," 14 April 1989 (*AAS*, vol. 81), p. 1126; *Bulletin*, n. 71 (1989/2), p. 149.

and to her all are related.

35. To the Church, as the sacrament in which the Kingdom of God is present "in mystery," are related or oriented (*ordinantur*; cf. LG 16) the members of other religious traditions who, inasmuch as they respond to God's calling as perceived by their conscience, are saved in Jesus Christ and thus already share in some way in the reality which is signified by the Kingdom. The Church's mission is to foster "the Kingdom of our Lord and his Christ" (Rev 11:15), at whose service she is placed. Part of her role consists in recognizing that the inchoate reality of this Kingdom can be found also beyond the confines of the Church, for example in the hearts of the followers of other religious traditions, insofar as they live evangelical values and are open to the action of the Spirit. It must be remembered nevertheless that this is indeed an inchoate reality, which needs to find completion through being related to the Kingdom of Christ already present in the Church yet realized fully only in the world to come.

The pilgrim Church

36. The Church on earth is always on pilgrimage. Although she is holy by divine institution, her members are not perfect; they bear the mark of their human limitations. Consequently, her transparency as sacrament of salvation is blurred. This is the reason why the Church herself, "insofar as she is an institution of men here on earth," and not only her members, is constantly in need of renewal and reform (UR 6).

advances toward the plenitude of divine truth

37. With regard to divine Revelation the Council taught that "the most intimate truth which this revelation gives us about God and the salvation of man shines forth in Christ, who is himself both the mediator and the sum total of revelation" (DV 2). Faithful to the command received from Christ himself, the apostles handed on this Revelation. Yet "the Tradition that comes from the apostles makes progress in the Church, with the help of the Holy Spirit. There is growth in insight into the realities and words that are being passed on" (DV 8). This happens through study and spiritual experience. It also comes about through the teaching of the bishops who have received a sure charism of truth. Thus the Church "is always advancing toward the plenitude of divine truth, until eventually the words of God are fulfilled in her" (DV 8). This in no way contradicts the Church's divine institution nor the fullness of God's Revelation in Jesus Christ which has been entrusted to her.

in a dialogue of salvation

38. Against this background it becomes easier to see why and in what sense interreligious dialogue is an integral element of the Church's evangelizing mission. The foundation of the Church's commitment to dialogue is not merely anthropological but primarily theological. God, in an age-long dialogue, has offered and continues to offer salvation to humankind. In faithfulness to the divine initiative, the Church too must enter into a dialogue of salvation with all men and women.

with people of other religions

39. Pope Paul VI taught this clearly in his first Encyclical *Ecclesiam Suam*. Pope John Paul II too has stressed the Church's call to interreligious dialogue and assigned to it the same foundation. Addressing the 1984 Plenary Assembly of the Pontifical Council for Interreligious Dialogue, the Pope declared: "[Interreligious] dialogue is fundamental to the Church, which is called to collaborate in God's plan with her methods of presence, respect and love toward all persons." He went on to call attention to a passage from *Ad Gentes*: "closely united to men in their life and work, Christ's disciples hope to render to others true witness of Christ and to work for this salvation, even where they are not able to proclaim Christ fully" (AG 12). He

prefaced this by saying: "dialogue finds its place within the Church's salvific mission; for this reason it is a dialogue of salvation." [12]

leading to deeper commitment

40. In this dialogue of salvation, Christians and others are called to collaborate with the Spirit of the Risen Lord who is universally present and active. Interreligious dialogue does not merely aim at mutual understanding and friendly relations. It reaches a much deeper level, that of the spirit, where exchange and sharing consist in a mutual witness to one's beliefs and a common exploration of one's respective religious convictions. In dialogue Christians and others are invited to deepen their religious commitment, to respond with increasing sincerity to God's personal call and gracious self-gift which, as our faith tells us, always passes through the mediation of Jesus Christ and the work of his Spirit.

and conversion to God.

41. Given this aim, a deeper conversion of all toward God, interreligious dialogue possesses its own validity. In this process of conversion "the decision may be made to leave one's previous spiritual or religious situation in order to direct oneself toward another" (D&M 37). Sincere dialogue implies, on the one hand, mutual acceptance of differences, or even of contradictions, and on the other, respect for the free decision of persons taken according to the dictates of their conscience (cf. DH 2). The teaching of the Council must nevertheless be borne in mind: "All men are bound to seek the truth, especially in what concerns God and his Church, and to embrace it and to hold on to it as they come to know it" (DH 1).

C. Forms of Dialogue

The forms of dialogue

42. There exist different forms of interreligious dialogue. It may be useful to recall those mentioned by the 1984 document of the Pontifical Council for Interreligious Dialogue (cf. D&M 28-35). It spoke of four forms, without claiming to establish among them any order of priority:

a.
The *dialogue of life*, where people strive to live in an open and neighborly spirit, sharing their joys and sorrows, their human problems and preoccupations.

b.   The *dialogue of action*, in which Christians and others collaborate for the integral development and liberation of people.

c.   The *dialogue of theological exchange*, where specialists seek to deepen their understanding of their respective religious heritages, and to appreciate each other's spiritual values.

d.
The *dialogue of religious experience*, where persons, rooted in their own religious traditions, share their spiritual riches, for instance with regard to prayer and contemplation, faith and ways of searching for God or the Absolute.

are interconnected,

43. One should not lose sight of this variety of forms of dialogue. Were it to be reduced to theological exchange, dialogue might easily be taken as a sort of luxury item in the Church's mission, a domain reserved for specialists. On the contrary,

---

12. *Insegnamenti*, vol. 7, 1 (1984), pp. 595-599; English text in *Bulletin*, no. 56 (1984/2), pp. 122-125.

guided by the Pope and their bishops, all local Churches, and all the members of these Churches, are called to dialogue, though not all in the same way. It can be seen, moreover, that the different forms are interconnected. Contacts in daily life and common commitment to action will normally open the door for cooperation in promoting human and spiritual values; they may also eventually lead to the dialogue of religious experience in response to the great questions which the circumstances of life do not fail to arouse in the minds of people (cf. NA 2). Exchanges at the level of religious experience can give more life to theological discussions. These in turn can enlighten experiences and encourage closer contacts.

touching human liberation

44. The importance of dialogue for integral development, social justice and human liberation needs to be stressed. Local Churches are called upon, as witnesses to Christ, to commit themselves in this respect in an unselfish and impartial manner. There is need to stand up for human rights, proclaim the demands of justice, and denounce injustice not only when their own members are victimized, but independently of the religious allegiance of the victims. There is need also to join together in trying to solve the great problems facing society and the world, as well as in education for justice and peace.

and culture.

45. Another context in which interreligious dialogue seems urgent today is that of culture. Culture is broader than religion. According to one concept, religion can be said to represent the transcendent dimension of culture and in a certain way its soul. Religions have certainly contributed to the progress of culture and the construction of a more humane society. Yet religious practices have sometimes had an alienating influence upon cultures. Today, an autonomous secular culture can play a critical role with regard to negative elements in particular religions. The question is complex, for several religious traditions may coexist within one and the same cultural framework while, conversely, the same religion may find expression in different cultural contexts. Again, religious differences may lead to distinct cultures in the same region.

46. The Christian message supports many values found and lived in the wisdom and the rich heritage of cultures, but it may also put in question culturally accepted values. Attentive dialogue implies recognizing and accepting cultural values which respect the human person's dignity and transcendent destiny. It may happen, nevertheless, that some aspects of traditional Christian cultures are challenged by the local cultures of other religious traditions (cf. EN 20). In these complex relationships between culture and religion, interreligious dialogue at the level of culture takes on considerable importance. Its aim is to eliminate tensions and conflicts, and potential confrontations by a better understanding among the various religious cultures of any given region. It may contribute to purifying cultures from any dehumanizing elements, and thus be an agent of transformation. It can also help to uphold certain traditional cultural values which are under threat from modernity and the leveling down which indiscriminate internationalization may bring with it.

D. Dispositions for Interreligious Dialogue and Its Fruits

Dialogue requires balance,

47. Dialogue requires, on the part of Christians as well as of the followers of other traditions, a balanced attitude. They should be neither ingenuous nor overly critical, but open and receptive. Unselfishness and impartiality, acceptance of differ-

ences and of possible contradictions, have already been mentioned. The will to engage together in commitment to the truth and the readiness to allow oneself to be transformed by the encounter are other dispositions required.

religious conviction,

48. This does not mean that in entering into dialogue the partners should lay aside their respective religious convictions. The opposite is true: the sincerity of interreligious dialogue requires that each enters into it with the integrity of his or her own faith. At the same time, while remaining firm in their belief that in Jesus Christ, the only mediator between God and man (cf. 1 Tim 2:4-6), the fullness of revelation has been given to them, Christians must remember that God has also manifested himself in some way to the followers of other religious traditions. Consequently, it is with receptive minds that they approach the convictions and values of others.

and openness to truth,

49. Moreover, the fullness of truth received in Jesus Christ does not give individual Christians the guarantee that they have grasped that truth fully. In the last analysis, truth is not a thing we possess, but a person by whom we must allow ourselves to be possessed. This is an unending process. While keeping their identity intact, Christians must be prepared to learn and to receive from and through others the positive values of their traditions. Through dialogue, they may be moved to give up ingrained prejudices, to revise preconceived ideas, and even sometimes to allow the understanding of their faith to be purified.

but promises rich rewards.

50. If Christians cultivate such openness and allow themselves to be tested, they will be able to gather the fruits of dialogue. They will discover with admiration all that God's action through Jesus Christ in his Spirit has accomplished and continues to accomplish in the world and in the whole of humankind. Far from weakening their own faith, true dialogue will deepen it. They will become increasingly aware of their Christian identity and perceive more clearly the distinctive elements of the Christian message. Their faith will gain new dimensions as they discover the active presence of the mystery of Jesus Christ beyond the visible boundaries of the Church and of the Christian fold.

E. Obstacles to Dialogue

Difficulties in dialogue can arise

51. Already on a purely human level it is not easy to practice dialogue. Interreligious dialogue is even more difficult. It is important to be aware of the obstacles which may arise. Some would apply equally to the members of all religious traditions and impede the success of dialogue. Others may affect some religious traditions more specifically and make it difficult for a process of dialogue to be initiated. Some of the more important obstacles will be mentioned here.

from various human factors

52.
a. Insufficient grounding in one's own faith.
b. Insufficient knowledge and understanding of the belief and practices of other religions, leading to a lack of appreciation for their significance and even at times to misrepresentation.
c. Cultural differences, arising from different levels of instruction, or from the use of different languages.

d. Sociopolitical factors or some burdens of the past.
e. Wrong understanding of the meaning of terms such as conversion, baptism, dialogue, etc.
f. Self-sufficiency, lack of openness leading to defensive or aggressive attitudes.
g. A lack of conviction with regard to the value of interreligious dialogue, which some may see as a task reserved to specialists, and others as a sign of weakness or even a betrayal of the faith.
h. Suspicion about the other's motives in dialogue.
i. A polemical spirit when expressing religious convictions.
j. Intolerance, which is often aggravated by association with political, economic, racial and ethnic factors, a lack of reciprocity in dialogue which can lead to frustration.
k. Certain features of the present religious climate, e.g., growing materialism, religious indifference, and the multiplication of religious sects, which creates confusion and raises new problems.

53. Many of these obstacles arise from a lack of understanding of the true nature and goal of interreligious dialogue. These need therefore to be constantly explained. Much patience is required. It must be remembered that the Church's commitment to dialogue is not dependent on success in achieving mutual understanding and enrichment; rather it flows from God's initiative in entering into a dialogue with humankind and from the example of Jesus Christ whose life, death and resurrection gave to that dialogue its ultimate expression.

which are never insurmountable.
54. Moreover, the obstacles, though real, should not lead us to underestimate the possibilities of dialogue or to overlook the results already achieved. There has been a growth in mutual understanding, and in active cooperation. Dialogue has had a positive impact on the Church herself. Other religions have also been led through dialogue to renewal and greater openness. Interreligious dialogue has made it possible for the Church to share Gospel values with others. So despite the difficulties, the Church's commitment to dialogue remains firm and irreversible.

II. PROCLAIMING JESUS CHRIST

A. The Mandate from the Risen Lord

Jesus sent his disciples to proclaim the Gospel
55. The Lord Jesus gave to his disciples a mandate to proclaim the Gospel. This fact is reported by all four Gospels and by the Acts of the Apostles. There are however certain nuances in the different versions. In Matthew Jesus says to his disciples: "All authority in heaven and earth has been given to me. Go therefore and make disciples of all nations, baptizing them in the name of the Father and of the Son and of the Holy Spirit, teaching them to observe all that I have commanded you; and lo, I am with you always, to the close of the age" (Mt 28:18-20).
In Mark the command is given more succinctly: "Go into all the world and preach the Gospel to the whole creation. He who believes and is baptized will be saved; but he who does not believe will be condemned" (Mk 16:15-16).
In Luke the expression is less direct: "Thus it is written that the Christ should suffer and on the third day rise from the dead, and that repentance and forgiveness of sins should be preached in his name to all the nations, beginning from Jerusalem. You are witnesses of these things" (Lk 24:46-48).

In Acts the extent of this witness is emphasized: "But you shall receive power when the Holy Spirit has come upon you; and you shall be my witnesses in Jerusalem and in all Judea and Samaria and to the end of the earth" (Acts 1:8).

In John again the mission is expressed differently: "As you sent me into the world, I have sent them into the world" (Jn 17:18); "As the Father sent me, so am I sending you" (Jn 20:21).

Announcing the Good News to all, witnessing, making disciples, baptizing, teaching, all these aspects enter into the Church's evangelizing mission, yet they need to be seen in the light of the mission accomplished by Jesus himself, the mission he received from the Father.

which he himself had proclaimed,

56. Jesus proclaimed the Gospel from God saying: "The time is fulfilled, and the Kingdom of God is at hand; repent and believe in the Gospel" (Mk 1:14-15). This passage sums up the ministry of Jesus. Jesus does not proclaim this Good News of the Kingdom by word alone, but also by his actions, attitudes and options, indeed by means of his whole life and finally through his death and resurrection. His parables, his miracles, the exorcisms he works, all are related to the Kingdom of God which he announces. This Kingdom moreover is not just something to be preached, quite unrelated to his own person. Jesus makes it clear that it is through him and in him that the Reign of God is breaking through into the world (cf. Lk 17:20-22), that in him the Kingdom has already come upon us, even though it still needs to grow to its fullness.[13]

and to which he had borne witness by his life.

57. His teaching is confirmed by his life. "Even if you refuse to believe in me, at least believe in the work I do" (Jn 10:38). Similarly, his deeds are explained by his words which spring from his awareness of being one with the Father. "I tell you most solemnly, the Son can do nothing by himself, he can only do what he sees the Father doing" (Jn 5:19). In the trial before Pilate, Jesus says that he has come into the world "to bear witness to the truth" (Jn 18:37). The Father also bears witness to him, both in words spoken from heaven and in the mighty works, the signs, which Jesus is enabled to perform. It is the Spirit who "seals" Jesus's witness, authenticating it as true (cf. Jn 3:32-35).

B. The Role of the Church

The Church's work of proclamation

58. It is against this background that the mandate given by the Risen Lord to the Apostolic Church needs to be understood. The Church's mission is to proclaim the Kingdom of God established on earth in Jesus Christ, through his life, death and resurrection, as God's decisive and universal offer of salvation to the world. For this reason "there is no true evangelization if the name, the teaching, the life, the promises, the Kingdom and the mystery of Jesus of Nazareth, the Son of God are not proclaimed" (EN 22). There is continuity between the Kingdom preached by Jesus and the mystery of Christ announced by the Church.

---

13. In the early Church the Kingdom of God is identified with the Reign of Christ (cf. Eph 5:5; Rev 11:15; 12:10). See also Origen, *In Mt 14:7; Hom.in Lc 36*, where he calls Christ *autobasileia*, and Tertullian, *Adv. Marc.* IV, 33, 8: "In evangelio est Dei Regnum, Christus ipse." On the correct understanding of the term "kingdom," see the report of the International Theological Commission (8 October 1985), *Selected Themes in Ecclesiology*, n. 10, 3.

continues that of Jesus.

59. Continuing the mission of Jesus, the Church is "the seed and beginning" of the kingdom (cf. LG 5). She is at the service of this Kingdom and "witnesses" to it. This includes witness to faith in Christ, the Savior, since this is the very heart of the Church's own faith and life. In the history of the Church, all the Apostles were "witnesses" to the life, death and resurrection of Christ.[14] Witness is given by words and deeds which are not to be set one against the other. The deed validates the word, but without the word the deed may be misinterpreted. The witness of the Apostles, both in words and signs, is subordinate to the Holy Spirit, sent by the Father to fulfill this talk of witness.[15]

C. The Content of Proclamation

Peter preached the risen Christ.

60. On the Day of Pentecost, in fulfillment of Christ's promise, the Holy Spirit came down on the Apostles. At that time "there were devout men living in Jerusalem from every nation under heaven" (Acts 2:5) — the list of people present, given in the book of Acts, serves to underline the universal import of this first ecclesial event. In the name of the Eleven Peter addressed those assembled, announcing Jesus, commended by God with miracles and portents, crucified by men but raised to life again by God. He concluded: "For this reason the whole house of Israel can be certain that God has made this Jesus, whom you crucified, both Lord and Christ" (Acts 2:36). This was followed by the invitation to his hearers to repent, to become disciples of Jesus by being baptized in his name for the forgiveness of sins, and thus to receive the gift of the Holy Spirit. A little later, before the Sanhedrin, Peter bore witness to his faith in the risen Christ, stating clearly: "Only in him is there salvation, for of all names in the world given to men this is the only one by which we can be saved" (Acts 4:11-12). The universal nature of the Christian message of salvation is brought out again in the account of the conversion of Cornelius. When Peter witnessed to the life and work of Jesus, from the beginning of his ministry in Galilee right up to his Resurrection, "the Holy Spirit came down on all the listeners" so that those who had accompanied Peter were astonished that the gift of the Holy Spirit should be poured out on gentiles too" (Acts 10:44-45).

Paul announced the mystery kept hidden through all the ages.

61. The Apostles therefore, following the Pentecost event, present themselves as witnesses to Christ's resurrection (cf. Acts 1:22; 4:33; 5:32-33), or, in a more concise formula, simply as witnesses to Christ (cf. Acts 3:15; 13:31). Nowhere is this clearer than in Paul, "called to be an apostle, set apart for the service of the Gospel" (Rom 1:1), who received from Jesus Christ the "apostolic mission of winning the obedience of faith among all the nations for the honor of his name" (Rom 1:5). Paul preaches "the Gospel that God promised long ago through his prophets in the holy scriptures" (Rom 1:2), the "Gospel of his Son" (Rom 1:9). He preaches a crucified Christ: "a stumbling block to Jews and folly to Gentiles" (1 Cor 1:23; cf. 2:2), "for no other foundation can any one lay than that which is laid" (1 Cor 3:11). The whole message of Paul is, as it were, summed up in his solemn declaration to the Ephesians: "I, who am less than the least of all God's holy people, have been entrusted with this special grace, of proclaiming to the gentiles this unfathomable treasure of Christ and of throwing light on the inner workings of the mystery kept hidden through all the ages in God, the Creator of everything," this many-sided

---

14. Cf. Acts 2:32; 3:15; 10:39; 13:31; 23:11.
15. Cf. Jn 15:26ff.; 1 Jn 5:7-10; Acts 5:32.

wisdom of God which he has now revealed through the Church, "according to the plan which he had formed from all eternity in Christ Jesus our Lord" (Eph 3:8-11).

The same message is found in the Pastoral Letters. God "desires all men to be saved and to come to the knowledge of the truth. For there is one God, and there is one mediator between God and men, the man Christ Jesus, who gave himself as a ransom for all" (1 Tim 2:4-6). This "mystery of our religion" which is "very deep" finds expression in a liturgical fragment: "He was manifested in the flesh, vindicated in the spirit, seen by angels, preached among the nations, believed on in the world, taken up in glory" (1 Tim 3:16).

John bore witness to the Word of Life.

62. Turning to the apostle John, we find that he presents himself above all as a witness, one who has seen Jesus and discovered his mystery (cf. Jn 13:23-25; 21:24). "We are declaring to you what we have seen and heard" — of the Word of life — "so that you too may share our life" (1 Jn 1:3). "We ourselves have seen and testify that the Father sent his Son as savior of the world" (1 Jn 4:14). Central to the message of John is the Incarnation: "The Word became flesh, he lived among us, and we saw his glory, the glory that he has from the Father as only Son of the Father, full of grace and truth" (Jn 1:14). Through Jesus, therefore, the Father can be seen (cf. Jn 14:9). He is the way to the Father (cf. Jn 14:6). Lifted up on the cross he draws all people to himself (cf. Jn 12:32). He is truly "the Savior of the World" (Jn 4:42).

The word, proclaimed by the Church, is full of power.

63. "Proclaim the word," Paul writes to Timothy (2 Tim 4:2). The content of this word is expressed in different ways: it is the Kingdom (cf. Acts 20:25), the Gospel of the Kingdom (cf. Mt 24:14), the Gospel of God (cf. Mk 1:14; 1 Thess 2:9). But these different formulations really mean the same thing: to preach Jesus (cf. Acts 9:20; 19:13), to preach Christ (cf. Acts 8:5). Just as Jesus spoke God's own words (cf. Jn 3:34), so the apostles preach the word of God, for Jesus whom they preach is the Word.

The Christian message therefore is a powerful one, to be welcomed for what it really is, "not the word of any human being, but God's sword" (1 Thess 2:13). Accepted in faith the word will be "alive and active," cutting "more incisively than any two-edged sword" (Heb 4:12). It will be a word which purifies (cf. Jn 15:3), it will be the source of the truth which brings freedom (cf. Jn 8:31-32). The word will become an interior presence: "Anyone who loves me will keep my word, and my Father will love him, and we shall come to him and make a home in him" (Jn 14:23). This is the word of God which is to be proclaimed by Christians.

D. *The Presence and Power of the Holy Spirit*

The Church relies on the presence

64. In proclaiming this word, the Church knows that she can rely on the Holy Spirit, who both prompts her proclamation and leads the hearers to obedience of faith.

It is the Holy Spirit who today, just as at the beginning of the Church, acts in every evangelizer who allows himself to be possessed and led by him. The Holy Spirit places on his lips the words which he could not find by himself, and at the same time the Holy Spirit predisposes the soul of the hearer to be open and receptive to the Good News and to the Kingdom being proclaimed (EN 75).

and the power of the Spirit

65. The force of the Spirit is attested by the fact that the most powerful witness is often given precisely at that point where the disciple is most helpless, incapable of word or deed, and yet remains faithful. As Paul says:

I will all the more gladly boast of my weaknesses, that the power of Christ may rest upon me. For the sake of Christ, then, I am content with weaknesses, insults, hardships, persecutions, and calamities; for when I am weak, then I am strong. (2 Cor 12:9-10)

The witness by which the Spirit brings men and women to know Jesus as Lord is no human achievement but God's own work.

E. The Urgency of Proclamation

to fulfill its obligation

66. Pope Paul VI said in his exhortation *Evangelii Nuntiandi*: "The presentation of the Gospel message is not optional for the Church. It is her duty, by command of the Lord Jesus, so that men may believe and be saved. This message is indeed a necessary one. It is unique and irreplaceable. It allows of neither indifference, syncretism, nor compromise, for it concerns the salvation of mankind" (EN 5). The urgency had been indicated by Paul.

How then are they to call upon him if they have not come to believe in him? And how can they believe in him if they have never heard of him? And how will they hear of him unless there is a preacher for them? . . . But it is in that way that faith comes, from hearing, and that means hearing the word of Christ. (Rom 10:14ff.)

"This law, set down one day by the Apostle Paul, maintains its full force today . . . it is through listening to the Word that one is led to believe" (EN 42). It is fitting to remember also that other word of Paul: "For if I preach the Gospel, that gives me no ground for boasting. For necessity is laid upon me. Woe to me if I do not preach the Gospel" (1 Cor 9:16).

to proclaim salvation in Christ.

67. Proclamation is a response to the human aspiration for salvation. Wherever God opens a door for the word in order to declare the mystery of Christ, then the living God and he whom he has sent for the salvation of all, Jesus Christ, are confidently and perseveringly proclaimed to all men. And this is in order that non-Christians, whose hearts are being opened by the Holy Spirit, might, while believing, freely turn to the Lord who, since he is "the Way, the Truth, and the Life" (Jn 14:6), will satisfy all their inner hopes, or rather infinitely surpass them (AG 13).

F. The Manner of Proclamation

The Church follows the lead of the Spirit

68. While proclaiming the message of God in Jesus Christ, the evangelizing Church must always remember that her task is not exercised in a complete void. For the Holy Spirit, the Spirit of Christ, is present and active among the hearers of the Good News even before the Church's missionary action comes into operation (cf. RH 12, DEV 53). They may in many cases have already responded implicitly to God's offer of salvation in Jesus Christ, a sign of this being the sincere practice of their own religious traditions, insofar as these contain authentic religious values. They may have already been touched by the Spirit and in some way associated unknowingly to the paschal mystery of Jesus Christ (cf. GS 22).

in learning how to proclaim,

69. Mindful of what God has already accomplished in those addressed, the Church seeks to discover the right way to announce the Good News. She takes her lead from divine pedagogy. This means learning from Jesus himself, and observing the times and seasons as prompted by the Spirit. Jesus only progressively revealed to his hearers the meaning of the Kingdom, God's plan of salvation realized in his own mystery. Only gradually, and with infinite care, did he unveil for them the implications of his message, his identity as the Son of God, the scandal of the Cross. Even his closest disciples, as the Gospels testify, reached full faith in their Master only through their Easter experience and the gift of the Spirit. Those who wish to become disciples of Jesus today will pass through the same process of discovery and commitment. Accordingly the Church's proclamation must be both progressive and patient, keeping pace with those who hear the message, respecting their freedom and even their "slowness to believe" (EN 79).

with qualities derived from the Gospel,

70. Other qualities must also characterize the Church's proclamation. It should be:

a.   Confident, in the power of the Spirit, and in obedience to the mandate received from the Lord.[16]

b.   Faithful, in the transmission of the teaching received from Christ and preserved in the Church, which is the depository of the Good News to be proclaimed (cf. EN 15). "Fidelity to the message whose servants we are . . . is a pivotal point of proclamation" (EN 4). "Evangelization is for no one an individual and isolated act; it is one that is deeply ecclesial" (EN 60).

c.   Humble, in the awareness that the fullness of revelation in Jesus Christ has been received as a free gift (Eph 3:2), and that the messengers of the Gospel do not always fully live up to its demands.

d.   Respectful, of the presence and action of the Spirit of God in the hearts of those who listen to the message, in the recognition that the Spirit is the "principal agent of evangelization" (EN 75).

e.   Dialogical, for in proclamation the hearer of the Word is not expected to be a passive receiver. There is progress from the "seeds of the Word" already present in the hearer to the full mystery of salvation in Jesus Christ. The Church must recognize a process of purification and enlightenment in which the Spirit of God opens the mind and heart of the hearer to the obedience of faith.

f.   Inculturated, incarnated in the culture and the spiritual tradition of those addressed, so that the message is not only intelligible to them, but is conceived as responding to their deepest aspirations, as truly the Good News they have been longing for (cf. EN 20, 62).

in close union with Christ.

71. To maintain these qualities the Church must not only bear in mind the circumstances of life and the religious experience of those addressed. She must also live in constant dialogue with her Lord and Master through prayer and penance, meditation and liturgical life, and above all in the celebration of the Eucharist. Only then will both proclamation and celebration of the Gospel message become fully alive.

---

16. Cf. 1 Thess 2:2; 2 Cor 3:12; 7:4; Phil 1:20; Eph 3:12; 6:19-20; Acts 4:13, 29, 31; 9:27, 28, etc.

G. Obstacles to Proclamation

Proclamation meets with difficulties,

72. The Church's proclamation of the Good News makes serious demands both on the evangelizing Church and her members engaged in evangelization and on those called by God to the obedience of Christian faith. It is no easy task. Some of the principal obstacles she can meet with are mentioned here.

on the part of Christians

73. Difficulties from within:

a.   It can happen that Christian witness does not correspond to belief; there is a gap between word and deed, between the Christian message and the way Christians live it.

b.   Christians may fail to proclaim the Gospel through negligence, human respect, or shame, which Saint Paul called "blushing for the Gospel," or because of false ideas about God's plan of salvation (cf. EN 80).

c.   Christians who lack appreciation and respect for other believers and their religious traditions are ill-prepared to proclaim the Gospel to them.

d.   In some Christians, an attitude of superiority, which can show itself at the cultural level, might give rise to the supposition that a particular culture is linked with the Christian message and is to be imposed on converts.

and from outside the Christian community.

74. Difficulties from outside:

a.   The weight of history makes proclamation more difficult, as certain methods of evangelization in the past have sometimes aroused fear and suspicion on the part of the followers of other religions.

b.   The members of other religions may fear that the Church's evangelizing mission will result in the destruction of their religion and culture.

c.   A different conception of human rights or a lack of respect for them in practice can result in a lack of religious freedom.

d.   Persecution can render the Church's proclamation especially difficult or well-nigh impossible. It must be remembered, however, that the cross is a source of life: "The blood of martyrs is the seed of Christians."

e.   The identification of a particular religion with the national culture or with a political system creates a climate of intolerance.

f.   In some places, conversion is forbidden by law or converts to Christianity meet with serious problems, such as ostracism by their religious community of origin, social milieu or cultural environment.

g.   In pluralistic contexts, the danger of indifferentism, relativism, or of religious syncretism creates obstacles to the proclamation of the Gospel.

H. Proclamation in the Evangelizing Mission of the Church

Within the evangelizing mission of the Church

75. The Church's evangelizing mission has sometimes been understood as consisting simply in inviting people to become disciples of Jesus in the Church. Gradually a broader understanding of evangelization has been developed, in which proclamation of the mystery of Christ nevertheless remains central. The Second Vatican Council's decree on the Missionary Activity of the Church, when dealing

with missionary work, mentions solidarity with mankind, dialogue and collaboration, before speaking about witness and the preaching of the Gospel (cf. AG 11-13).
The 1974 Synod of Bishops and the Apostolic Exhortation *Evangelii Nuntiandi*
which followed it have both taken evangelization in a broad sense. In evangelization,
the whole person of the evangelizer is involved: words, actions, witness of life (cf.
EN 21-22). Likewise its aim extends to all that is human, as it seeks to transform
human culture and cultures with the power of the Gospel (cf. EN 18-20). Yet Pope
Paul VI made it quite clear that evangelization will always entail as the simultaneous
foundation, core and summit of its dynamism a clear proclamation that in Jesus
Christ, the Son of God made man, who died and rose from the dead, salvation is
offered to all as a gift of God's kindness and mercy (EN 27). It is in this sense that
the 1984 document of the Pontifical Council for Interreligious Dialogue lists proclamation among the various elements which make up the Church's evangelizing mission (cf. D&M 13).

proclamation is a sacred duty.
  76. Still it is useful to point out once again that to proclaim the name of Jesus
and to invite people to become his disciples in the Church is a sacred and major duty
which the Church cannot neglect. Evangelization would be incomplete without it
(EN 22), for without this central element the others, though in themselves genuine
forms of the Church's mission, would lose their cohesion and vitality. It is clear
therefore that in situations where, for political or other reasons, proclamation as such
is practically impossible, the Church is already carrying out her evangelizing mission
not only through presence and witness but also through such activities as work for
integral human development and dialogue. On the other hand, in other situations
where people are disposed to hear the message of the Gospel and have the possibility
of responding to it, the Church is duty bound to meet their expectations.

III. INTERRELIGIOUS DIALOGUE AND PROCLAMATION

A. Interrelated yet not Interchangeable

The Church's mission
  77. Interreligious dialogue and proclamation, though not on the same level, are
both authentic elements of the Church's evangelizing mission. Both are legitimate
and necessary. They are intimately related, but not interchangeable: true interreligious dialogue on the part of the Christian supposes the desire to make Jesus Christ
better known, recognized and loved; proclaiming Jesus Christ is to be carried out in
the Gospel spirit of dialogue. The two activities remain distinct but, as experience
shows, one and the same local Church, one and the same person, can be diversely
engaged in both.

must be sensitive to circumstances.
  78. In actual fact the way of fulfilling the Church's mission depends upon the
particular circumstances of each local Church, of each Christian. It always implies a
certain sensitivity to the social, cultural, religious and political aspects of the situation, as also attentiveness to the "signs of the times" through which the Spirit of God
is speaking, teaching and guiding. Such sensitivity and attentiveness are developed
through a spirituality of dialogue. This requires a prayerful discernment and theological reflection on the significance in God's plan of the different religious traditions
and the experience of those who find in them their spiritual nourishment.

B. The Church and Religions

It extends to all

79. In fulfilling her mission, the Church comes into contact with people of other religious traditions. Some become disciples of Jesus Christ in his Church, as a result of a profound conversion and through a free decision of their own. Others are attracted by the person of Jesus and his message, but for various reasons do not enter the fold. Yet others seem to have but little or no interest in Jesus. Whatever the case may be, the Church's mission extends to all. Also in relation to the religions to which they belong, the Church in dialogue can be seen to have a prophetic role. In bearing witness to Gospel values, she raises questions for these religions. Similarly, the Church, insofar as she bears the mark of human limitations, may find herself challenged. So in promoting these values, in a spirit of emulation and of respect for the mystery of God, the members of the Church and the followers of other religions find themselves to be companions on the common path which humanity is called to tread. At the end of the day of prayer, fasting, and pilgrimage for peace in Assisi, Pope John Paul II said: "Let us see in it an anticipation of what God would like the developing history of humanity to be: a fraternal journey in which we accompany one another toward the transcendental goal which he sets for us." [17]

in dialogue

80. The Church encourages and fosters interreligious dialogue not only between herself and other religious traditions, but even among these religious traditions themselves. This is one way in which she fulfills her role as "sacrament, that is, a sign and instrument of communion with God and unity among all people" (LG 1). She is invited by the Spirit to encourage all religious institutions and movements to meet, to enter into collaboration, and to purify themselves in order to promote truth and life, holiness, justice, love and peace, dimensions of that Kingdom which, at the end of time, Christ will hand over to his Father (cf. 1 Cor 15:24). Thus, interreligious dialogue is truly part of the dialogue of salvation initiated by God. [18]

C. Proclaiming Jesus Christ

and proclamation

81. Proclamation, on the other hand, aims at guiding people to explicit knowledge of what God has done for all men and women in Jesus Christ, and at inviting them to become disciples of Jesus through becoming members of the Church. When, in obedience to the command of the risen Lord and the Spirit's promptings, the Church fulfills this task of proclamation, this will often need to be done in a progressive manner. A discernment is to be made concerning how God is present in each one's personal history. The followers of other religions may discover, as may Christians also, that they already share many values. This can lead to a challenge in the form of the witness of the Christian community or a personal profession of faith, in which the full identity of Jesus is humbly confessed. Then, when the time is right, Jesus's decisive question can be put: "Who do you say that I am?" The true answer to this question can come only through faith. The preaching and the confession,

---

17. *Insegnamenti*, vol. 9, 2 (1986) p. 1262; *Bulletin*, n. 64 (1987/1), p. 41.

18. *Ecclesiam Suam*, chapter 3; cf. also *Insegnamenti* 7, 1 (1984), p. 598; English text in *Bulletin*, n. 56 (1984/2).

under the movement of grace, that Jesus of Nazareth is the Son of God the Father, the Risen Lord and Savior, constitutes the final stage of proclamation. One who freely professes this faith is invited to become a disciple of Jesus in his Church and to take a responsible part in her mission.

D. Commitment to the One Mission

as two ways of the same mission.

82. All Christians are called to be personally involved in these two ways of carrying out the one mission of the Church, namely proclamation and dialogue. The manner in which they do this will depend on the circumstances and also on their degree of preparation. They must nevertheless always bear in mind that dialogue, as has already been said, does not constitute the whole mission of the Church, that it cannot simply replace proclamation, but remains oriented toward proclamation inso-far as the dynamic process of the Church's evangelizing mission reaches in it its climax and its fullness. As they engage in interreligious dialogue they will discover the "seeds of the Word" sown in people's hearts and in the religious traditions to which they belong. In deepening their appreciation of the mystery of Christ they will be able to discern the positive values in the human search for the unknown or incompletely known God. Throughout the various stages of dialogue, the partners will feel a great need both to impart and to receive information, to give and to receive explanations, to ask questions of each other. Christians in dialogue have the duty of responding to their partners' expectations regarding the contents of the Christian faith, of bearing witness to this faith when this is called for, of giving an account of the hope that is within them (1 Pet 3:15). In order to be able to do this, Christians should deepen their faith, purify their attitudes, clarify their language and render their worship more and more authentic.

Love wishes to share

83. In this dialogical approach, how could they not hope and desire to share with others their joy in knowing and following Jesus Christ, Lord and Savior? We are here at the heart of the mystery of love. Insofar as the Church and Christians have a deep love for the Lord Jesus, the desire to share him with others is motivated not merely by obedience to the Lord's command, but by this love itself. It should not be surprising, but quite normal, that the followers of other religions should also desire sincerely to share their faith. All dialogue implies reciprocity and aims at banishing fear and aggressiveness.

under the guidance of the Spirit

84. Christians must always be aware of the influence of the Holy Spirit and be prepared to follow wherever in God's providence and design the Spirit is leading them. It is the Spirit who is guiding the evangelizing mission of the Church. It belongs to the Spirit to inspire both the Church's proclamation and the obedience of faith. It is for us to be attentive to the promptings of the Spirit. Whether proclama-tion be possible or not, the Church pursues her mission in full respect for freedom, through interreligious dialogue, witnessing to and sharing Gospel values. In this way the partners in dialogue proceed in response to the divine call of which they are conscious. All, both Christians and the followers of other religious traditions, are invited by God himself to enter into the mystery of his patience, as human beings seek his light and truth. Only God knows the times and stages of the fulfillment of this long human quest.

E. Jesus our Model

and according to the example of Jesus,

85. It is in this climate of expectation and listening that the Church and Christians pursue proclamation and interreligious dialogue with a true Gospel spirit. They are aware that "all things work together for the good of those who love God" (Rom 8:28). By grace they have come to know that he is the Father of all, and that he has revealed himself in Jesus Christ. Is not Jesus their model and guide in the commitment to both proclamation and dialogue? Is he not the only one who even today can say to a sincere religious person: "You are not far from the Kingdom of God" (Mk 12:34).

who gave himself for all humankind.

86. Christians are not only to imitate Jesus, but to be closely united to him. He invited his disciples and friends to join him in his unique offering on behalf of the whole of humanity. The bread and wine for which he gave thanks symbolized the entire creation. They became his body "given" and his blood "poured out for the forgiveness of sins." Through the ministry of the Church, the one Eucharist is offered by Jesus in every age and place, since the time of his passion, death and resurrection in Jerusalem. It is here that Christians unite themselves to Christ in his offering which "brings salvation to the whole world" (Eucharistic Prayer IV). Such a prayer is pleasing to God who "desires all men to be saved and to come to the knowledge of the truth" (1 Tim 2:4). Thus they offer thanks for "everything that is true, everything that is honorable, everything that is upright and pure, everything that we love and admire, whatever is good and praiseworthy" (Phil 4:8). Here they draw the grace of discernment, to be able to read the signs of the Spirit's presence and to recognize the favorable time and right manner of proclaiming Jesus Christ.

CONCLUSION

Special attention to each religion

87. The aim of these reflections on interreligious dialogue and proclamation has been to provide some basic clarifications. However, it is important to remember that the various religions differ from one another. Special attention should therefore be given to relations with the followers of each religion.

demands study

88. It is also important that specific studies on the relationship between dialogue and proclamation be undertaken, taking into account each religion within its geographical area and its sociocultural context. Episcopal Conferences could entrust such studies to the appropriate commissions and theological and pastoral institutes. In the light of the results of these studies, these institutes could also organize special courses and study sessions in order to train people for both dialogue and proclamation. Special attention is to be given to young people living in a pluralistic environment, who meet the followers of other religions at school, at work, in youth movements and other associations and even within their own families.

and prayer.

89. Dialogue and proclamation are difficult tasks, and yet absolutely necessary. All Christians, according to their situations, should be encouraged to equip themselves so that they may better fulfill this twofold commitment. Yet more than tasks

to be accomplished, dialogue and proclamation are graces to be sought in prayer. May all continually implore the help of the Holy Spirit so that he may be "the divine inspirer of their plans, their initiatives and their evangelizing activity" (EN 75).

Pentecost, 19 May 1991

Francis Cardinal Arinze
President, Pontifical Council for
Inter-Religious Dialogue

Josef Cardinal Tomko
Prefect, Congregation for the
Evangelization of Peoples

2

A Theological Commentary: Dialogue and Proclamation

Jacques Dupuis, S.J.

Jacques Dupuis, S.J., is a native of Belgium and professor of theology at the Gregorian University. He taught for many years in India and was the founding editor of the Indian theological journal *Vidyajyoti*. Author of the much-acclaimed Orbis books *Jesus Christ at the Encounter of World Religions* (1991), and *Who Do You Say I Am? Introduction to Christology* (1994), Father Dupuis is currently at work on historical and theological aspects of encounters between Christianity and other religious traditions. Approaching *emeritus* status at the Gregorian, Father Dupuis is a consultor for the Pontifical Council on Inter-Religious Dialogue.

INTRODUCTION

On the occasion of the twenty-fifth anniversary of Vatican II's Decree *Ad Gentes* (AG) (1965), Pope John Paul II published the Encyclical Letter *Redemptoris Missio* "on the permanent validity of the Church's missionary mandate" (hereafter RM). It is signed 7 December 1990, but was made public in January 1991.[1] A few months later, on the occasion of the twenty-fifth anniversary of Vatican II's Declaration *Nostra Aetate* (NA) (1965), another document, dated May 1991, was published under the title "Dialogue and Proclamation: Reflections and Orientations on Inter-religious Dialogue and the Proclamation of the Gospel of Jesus Christ" (hereafter DP). This document is jointly signed by Cardinal Francis Arinze, President of the Pontifical Council for Interreligious Dialogue (PCDI) and Cardinal Jozef Tomko, Prefect of the Congregation for the Evangelization of Peoples (CEP); it was made public on 20 June of the same year.[2]

---

1. Original Italian text in *Civiltà Cattolica* 143 (1991), pp. 255-284; 369-404. English translation in *Origins* 20 (1991), pp. 541-568.
2. Original English text in *Origins* 21 (1991), pp. 121-135; also in *Bulletin. Pontificium Consilium pro dialogo inter religiones*, 77: 26 (1991/2), pp. 210-250. The official text, however, is the Italian. It was first published in *Osservatore Romano* and, subsequently, in *AAS* 75 (1992/5), pp. 414-446.

The purpose of the two documents differs vastly. The scope of the Pope's encyclical is much broader: it is a question, in the Pope's own words, of showing the "urgency of missionary evangelization" or of "missionary activity *ad gentes*" (RM 2) in the world of today. The intent of the other document is much more restricted: building upon a previous document of the Secretariat for Non-Christians[3] which stated that interreligious dialogue and the proclamation of the Gospel are two distinct elements of the Church's evangelizing mission, it means to elaborate further on these two components of mission and to show how they are related to each other (DP 3).

Our intention here is to provide a theological commentary of the document of the two Vatican dicasteries which may help for its correct interpretation. To this end we will recall briefly the genesis and process of composition of the document. More importantly we will situate it in relation to the doctrine of Vatican II and the post-conciliar teaching on religions and interreligious dialogue. We will then expose the document's understanding of dialogue and proclamation as well as of their place and mutual relationship within the evangelizing mission of the Church. A rapid comparison will follow on the same subject between the papal encyclical and the dicasterial document. Finally, a general assessment of DP will be attempted.

For a correct interpretation it seems important to take into account the relationship between the papal encyclical and the dicasterial document, regarding the time of composition and the possible influence of one on the other. DP informs us that the encyclical RM was published as this document — which "was first discussed during the Plenary Assembly of the Secretariat in 1987" (DP 3) — "was in its final stages of preparation for publication" and that, while it "spells out in greater detail the teaching of the encyclical on dialogue and its relationship to proclamation," it is "to be read in the light of this Encyclical" (DP 4c). This reference to RM — the only one to be found in the entire text of DP — is in fact a late addition, introduced right before the document's publication. This circumstance goes to show that DP was composed independently of RM and without reference to it; however, as will appear hereafter, corrections have been introduced in DP at an advanced stage which are not without relation to RM.

It is clear that by its very nature the encyclical has greater authority than the document of the two dicasteries; but this does not exclude the possibility of the latter going beyond what is taught in the former, or even having partly influenced its doctrine. A close analysis of the encyclical's section on "Dialogue with Our Brothers and Sisters of Other Religions" would show that its relatively brief treatment of interreligious dialogue is inspired and influenced by the more elaborate exposition given it in the dicasterial document. If then the dicasterial document must be interpreted in relation to the encyclical, it may in turn throw further light on what the encyclical treats succinctly. Nor does it necessarily follow that both documents share exactly the same view; in fact, there exist between them — as will be seen later — distinct approaches and nuances. One of the tasks of this commentary will consist in bringing to light the commonalities and divergences of both documents concerning the relationship between dialogue and proclamation.

As mentioned above and as explicitly stated in the text (DP 1), DP was published on the occasion of the twenty-fifth anniversary of the Declaration *Nostra Aetate*. This suffices to show the document's intention to link with the Council's call for interreligious dialogue. Its more immediate formal link, however, is with the Secre-

---

3. See "The Attitude of the Church toward the Followers of Other Religions: Reflections and Orientations on Dialogue and Mission" (henceforth D&M), *Bulletin. Secretariatus pro non christianis*, 56: 19 (1984/2), pp. 126-141.

tariat for Non-Christians' 1984 document, also referred to above (2).[4] This document stated that the evangelizing mission of the Church is a "single but complex and articulated reality" (D&M 13), of which it spelled out the "principal elements" as being: "presence and witness; commitment to social development and human liberation; liturgical life, prayer and contemplation; interreligious dialogue; and finally, proclamation and catechesis" (DP 2). Dialogue and proclamation were viewed as "component elements and authentic forms of the one evangelizing mission of the Church" (2). To give further consideration to these two elements and to clarify their "mutual relationship" is stated to be the formal intent of DP (3). The document hoped to strengthen NA's call for interreligious dialogue (NA 2) and to elucidate D&M's affirmation that it belongs to the Church's evangelizing mission; it would thus contribute to corroborate the pastoral commitment of local Churches to dialogue and establish its practice on a broader theological foundation.

The introduction of the document makes a brief reference to its genesis and process of composition, in which something transpires of its eventful and somewhat tormented history. Alluding to the title "Dialogue and Proclamation," the text in its late form observes that "if dialogue is treated first, this is not because it has any priority over proclamation. It is simply due to the fact that dialogue is the primary concern of the Pontifical Council for Interreligious Dialogue which initiated the preparation of the document" (DP 3). It then notes that "the document was first discussed during the Plenary Assembly of the Secretariat in 1987," after which a further process of consultation led to the finalization and adoption of the text at the Plenary Assembly of the Pontifical Council for Interreligious Dialogue, in April 1990. "In the process," it is said, "there has been close collaboration between the Pontifical Council for Interreligious Dialogue and the Congregation for the Evangelization of Peoples. Both dicasteries are now offering these reflections to the universal Church" (DP 3).

The real story is, however, somewhat more complex. The project of a document on "Dialogue and Proclamation" by the Secretariat for Non-Christians goes back to December 1986. Following a meeting of the Secretariat on 9 January 1987, at which suggestions for such a document were formulated, a draft was composed for a presentation of the topic at the Secretariat's forthcoming Plenary Assembly. Consultation within the Secretariat led to amendments of the draft presentation which, once amended, became the First Draft and was presented at the Plenary Assembly held 27 April–2 May 1987; it bore the title "Dialogue and Proclamation."

This First Draft was generally well received by the members of the Plenary Assembly as a working document and the plan for a formal document by the Secretariat on the same topic accepted. Numerous suggestions were, however, made for the redaction of the document. In the light of these, a Second Draft of the proposed document was composed which was ready in June 1987. This draft was circulated for comments and suggestions among consultors of the Secretariat. A Third Draft followed in November 1987 as a result of this first consultation. This new text became the object of a much broader process of consultation. It was circulated to episcopal conferences, individual bishops, consultors of the Secretariat in various countries, theological faculties and individual experts — a process which took a considerable amount of time. A large amount of material was received from all parts of the world, comprising reactions, observations, positive and negative, and suggestions — sometimes contradictory — for improving the draft.

An important procedural and structural change intervened, however, in the composition of the drafting committee. The Secretariat for Non-Christians had first taken

4. See note 3.

the initiative of the preparation of the document; the First and Second Draft had been its exclusive responsibility. However, on a request made by Cardinal Jozef Tomko, Prefect of the Congregation for the Evangelization of Peoples at the 1987 Plenary Assembly of the Secretariat for Non-Christians, a new, "mixed," drafting committee was composed, which would represent the two dicasteries. This, it was felt, would give the document a better balance as the legitimate concerns of the Congregation for Evangelization would be better attended to. Moreover, the subject matter of the proposed document was such by nature ("Dialogue and Proclamation") that it required the active involvement of both dicasteries in its composition as well as in its eventual publication.

It fell to the new drafting committee, first to produce the Third Draft and, thereafter, to sort and discuss the material which came from the broad consultation on it mentioned above, keeping for integration into a further draft whatever appeared useful and deserving of being retained. More importantly, the composition of the new draft was now entrusted to members of the committee representing respectively each of the two dicasteries: the first part on "Dialogue" going to the Secretariat for Non-Christians, the second on "Proclamation" to the Congregation for the Evangelization of Peoples. As this complex procedure required time, the joint committee could get the proposed document's Fourth Draft ready by the end of 1988 only.

At this stage a consultation on the Fourth Draft was initiated by way of a discussion of the joint committee together with the heads of the two dicasteries, Cardinals F. Arinze and J. Tomko, in February 1989. This consultation led to the introduction of new amendments as well as of additions and cancellations. It is this Draft — now the Fifth — which was circulated to the bishop-members of the Council for Interreligious Dialogue in view of the Plenary Assembly to be held 23–28 April, 1990.

As would be expected, the Plenary Assembly spent considerable time studying the proposed document. Lively discussion took place and new amendments, omissions, and additions — some lengthy ones — were made before a consensus was reached. Once amended by the Assembly itself, this Fifth Draft was adopted by the Plenary Assembly of the Council for Interreligious Dialogue, with virtually a unanimous vote (with one vote *juxta modum*, and Cardinal Tomko being absent at the voting session). It still bore the title "Dialogue and Proclamation."

There still remained, however, to ensure the *placet* of the Congregation for the Doctrine of the Faith, which at an earlier stage had already made observations on the draft of the document. In view of this, a meeting took place between the heads and secretaries of the three Vatican dicasteries, with few consultors, on 20 September 1990. This meeting led to some new amendments at the hands, this time, of a trilateral *ad hoc* committee appointed for the purpose. The Final Text, approved by the heads of the three dicasteries and signed by Cardinals Arinze and Tomko, was now ready to be sent to the Secretariat of State for approval of its publication. This, as mentioned above, took place on 19 May 1991. The document now bore the title: "Dialogue and Proclamation: Reflections and Orientations on Interreligious Dialogue and the Proclamation of the Gospel of Jesus Christ."

The long process of composition of the document can thus be divided into three stages, though of considerably different lengths of time, with reference to the three successive committees — unilateral, bilateral, and trilateral — to which composition and revision were entrusted.

It was necessary to explain, at least in its main lines, the long-protracted composition of the document; the vicissitudes it has known are an element which needs to be kept in mind for its correct interpretation. Speaking in general terms, some important observations may be made. On the one hand, the structural change that intervened with the formation of a mixed drafting committee ensured that equal attention would be given to proclamation as to dialogue, in terms of space allotted to each. It further secured a better balance as to their mutual relation in the evangelizing mission of the Church. On the other hand, however, assigning the draft of the different parts to members of the committee representing the two distinct dicasteries ran the risk of a juxtaposition of the two parts without a perfect integration of both, the third part on the relationship between dialogue and proclamation notwithstanding. Tensions could thus be created between the various parts of the document that would eventually remain unresolved and harm its overall unity. In fact, the vicissitudes the document has known over a period of five years have left their mark on its final redaction. Amendments had to be made to accommodate distinct tendencies, sometimes opposed to each other; compromise formulations were resorted to in search of a consensus, which, however, more often than not, resulted in a loss of vigor, of meaning and clarity. These fluctuations account for the final state of the document as it stands; they will need to be kept in mind in assessing it. The question will have to be asked, whether, in what way and to what extent, DP contributes something new to the Church's doctrine on dialogue and proclamation and their respective place in the Church's evangelizing mission.

I. THE ANTECEDENTS OF *DIALOGUE AND PROCLAMATION*

It is necessary to recall in its main lines the Church's recent doctrine on religions, interreligious dialogue, proclamation and evangelization, which forms the doctrinal background of our document. With no claim to being exhaustive, this may be done by reviewing summarily the teaching of Vatican II, as well as some salient documents of Popes Paul VI and John Paul II; the 1984 document of the Secretariat for Non-Christians on "Dialogue and Mission," which is the direct antecedent to our document, will also be considered.

The Teaching of Vatican II

While speaking of the Council's doctrine on the other religions, two things must be clearly distinguished: one is the unequivocal conciliar declaration that salvation in Jesus Christ is possible for the members of the other religions and outside the Church; the other is the Council's evaluation of the religious traditions themselves.

That salvation in Jesus Christ is possible for all people had long been the Church's traditional teaching. It is implicitly contained in the doctrine of the Council of Trent on baptism of desire (*in voto*) and explicitly affirmed by Pius XII's encyclical *Mystici Corporis* — to mention but two documents of the teaching office. If Vatican II strikes a specific note while resuming this traditional teaching, this needs to be seen in what may be called the optimistic vision of the Council: what in the past has often been proposed as a mere possibility left to God's inscrutable design, is affirmed by Vatican II as concrete reality beyond discussion. The Constitution *Lumen Gentium* already teaches that "those who through no fault of their own do not know the Gospel of Christ and his Church, but who nevertheless seek God with a sincere heart and, moved by grace, try in their actions to do his will as they know it through the dictates of their conscience, may achieve eternal salvation" (LG 16). The same teaching is resumed in the Constitution *Gaudium et Spes* where, however, it assumes a more concrete form. Having shown that Christians come in contact with the paschal mystery of the death and resurrection of Christ, the Constitution goes on to affirm that the same obtains with all persons of good will, for God's Spirit is universally present and active:

All this holds true not for Christians only but also for all men of good will in whose hearts grace is active invisibly. For since Christ died for all, and since all men are in fact called to one and the same destiny, which is divine, we must hold that the Holy Spirit offers to all the possibility of being made partners, in a way known to God, in the paschal mystery. (GS 22)

It needs to be underlined that Vatican II is the first council in the conciliar history of the Church to speak positively of the other religions. The relevant documents on the matter are LG, NA, AG, and GS. The Council sees in the religious traditions "a preparation for the Gospel," "seeds of the Word," "rays of that Truth which enlightens all human beings," "elements of truth and of grace" — to quote but the most salient expressions of the Council, some of which are borrowed from the early Church Fathers and applied by the Council to the religious traditions. Rather than examining each conciliar document in particular, we may, for brevity's sake, refer to the summary of the Council's teaching presented by the Secretariat for Non-Christians' 1984 document. Having referred to the Council's vision of the growth of the Kingdom of God in history, D&M adds:

> This vision induced the fathers of the Second Vatican Council to affirm that in the religious traditions of non-Christians there exist "elements which are true and good" (OT 16), "precious things, both religious and human" (GS 92), "seeds of contemplation" (AG 18), "elements of truth and grace" (AG 9), "seeds of the Word" (AG 11, 15), and "rays of that Truth which enlightens all human beings" (NA 2). According to explicit conciliar indications, these values are found preserved in the great religious traditions of humankind. Therefore, they merit the attention and esteem of Christians, and their spiritual patrimony is a genuine invitation to dialogue (cf. NA 2, 3; AG 11), not only in those things which unite us, but also in our differences. (D&M 26)

But does the Council consider the other religious traditions as "means" or "ways" of salvation for their members? To give a positive answer to this question would mean going beyond the explicit teaching of the Council. All that can be said is that the Council's positive approach and its explicit recognition of "elements of grace" in those traditions goes in that direction, opening the way for theological elaborations which would further develop such a view.

The Council's call for dialogue with the other religious traditions is found in NA 2. The Church "urges her sons to enter with prudence and charity into dialogue (*colloquia*) and collaboration with members of other religions. Let Christians, while witnessing to their own faith and way of life, acknowledge, preserve and encourage the spiritual and moral good found among non-Christians, as well as their social and cultural values" (NA 2). The same call is repeated in AG 11 which incites Christians through a "sincere and patient dialogue" (*dialogo*) to "learn of the riches which a generous God has distributed among the nations." It is found once more and further developed in GS 92 where, as will be seen hereafter, it is taken over from Paul VI's encyclical letter *Ecclesiam Suam*. For all this insistence, however, nowhere has the Council affirmed that interreligious dialogue is an integral part of the Church's evangelizing mission. In the conciliar documents "evangelization" remains identified with the proclamation of Jesus Christ to those who do not know him and the invitation which the Church extends to them of becoming his disciples in the Christian community (cf. LG 17; AG 6). A broader concept of the Church's evangelizing mission, comprising, besides the proclamation of the Gospel, other elements such as human promotion and liberation and interreligious dialogue, will be a postconciliar development.

The Teaching of Paul VI

To review Paul VI's teaching on religions, dialogue, proclamation and evangelization, two important documents must be principally considered: Paul VI's first programmatic encyclical, *Ecclesiam Suam* (1964), published during the Council, and the apostolic exhortation *Evangelii Nuntiandi* (1975), published by the Pope as a sequel to the Synod of Bishops in Rome on "The Evangelization of the Modern World" (1974).

Paul VI became the "Pope of dialogue" with the publication of ES, which undoubtedly influenced deeply the Council's positive attitude toward the world as well as members of other religious traditions. The Pope saw the entire history of salvation as made up of an unceasing dialogue of salvation between God and humankind; he also visualized the Church as holding a privileged position for entering into dialogue with the entire world. In this context the Pope drew four "concentric circles," with the Church at the center, which represented four distinct spheres at which she must enter into dialogue. Starting from the most remote and moving toward the closest, the four circles were: humankind and the world; the world religions; the other Christian Churches and communities; and, finally, dialogue within the Church herself. This universal call for dialogue has been resumed by Vatican II in GS 92 where Paul VI's four circles of dialogue are explicitly developed, even though in the reverse order.

It must, however, be noted that the "Pope of dialogue" does not yet assign to interreligious dialogue a place in the Church's evangelizing mission, as constituting an integral part of that mission. More importantly still, attention must be drawn to the Pope's evaluation of the other religious traditions. In line with what the Council will say thereafter, Paul VI states the respect that the Church nourishes toward the "moral and spiritual values" contained in the other religions and expresses her desire to "join with them in promoting and defending common ideals of religious liberty, human brotherhood, good culture, social welfare and civil order." However, says the Pope, "honesty compels us to declare openly our conviction that there is but one true religion, the religion of Christianity" (*AAS* 56 [1964], 655).

This clear opposition between Christianity, defined as the only true religion, and the other religions of the world becomes even clearer and is further elaborated upon in the apostolic exhortation EN. This document's negative stand toward those religions is all the more striking because it contrasts with the conviction expressed at the synod by a sizable number of bishops, mostly Asian, that the Holy Spirit is present and active in the life of people belonging to those religious traditions and in the traditions themselves.[5]

Paul VI reaffirms the respect and esteem of the Church for those religions which "carry with them the echo of thousands of years of searching for God, a quest which is incomplete but often made with great sincerity and righteousness of heart. They possess an impressive patrimony of deeply religious texts. They have taught generations of people how to pray. They are impregnated with innumerable 'seeds of the

---

5. Cf. the interventions of Indian bishops in D. S. Amalorpavadass (ed.), *Evangelization of the Modern World* (Bangalore: NBCLC, 1975), pp. 124-138; G. Caprile, *Il sinodo dei vescovi: Terza assemblea generale* (Rome: Ed. Civiltà Cattolica, 1975). The Communication of the Federation of Asian Bishops' Conferences (FABC) to the 1974 synod deserves special attention. The other religious traditions are viewed in it as "positive elements in the economy of God's design of salvation." "How then," the bishops ask, "can we not give them reverence and honour? And how can we not acknowledge that God has drawn our peoples to Himself through them?" (14-15). Text in G. B. Rosales and C. G. Arevalo (eds.), *For All the Peoples of Asia. Federation of Asian Bishops' Conferences. Documents from 1970 to 1991* (Maryknoll, N.Y.: Orbis Books, 1992), p. 14.

Word' (AG 11) and can constitute a 'preparation for the Gospel' (LG 16)" (EN 53). However, he adds:

> Even in the face of natural religious expressions most worthy of esteem, the Church finds support in the fact that the religion of Jesus, which she proclaims through evangelization, objectively places man in relation with the plan of God, with his living presence and with his action; she thus causes an encounter with the mystery of divine paternity that bends over toward humanity. In other words, our religion effectively establishes with God an authentic and living relationship which the other religions do not succeed in doing, even though they have, as it were, their arms stretched out toward heaven. (EN 53)

This text leaves no room for equivocation. Christianity is distinct from the other religions as the one supernatural religion in relation to the others which are "natural": while those are various expressions of the human aspiration toward God, Christianity is the one God-given answer to this aspiration and, hence, the only religion capable of "effectively establish[ing] with God an authentic and living relationship." It must furthermore be noted that EN no longer speaks of dialogue with the members of other religions; these are only considered as the "beneficiaries" of the proclamation by the Church of the Good News of Jesus Christ (EN 53), while the Holy Spirit is only mentioned as He who inspires the Church's evangelizing action and is indeed "the principal agent of evangelization" (EN 75).

Does EN then propose a broad or a narrow notion of evangelization? Paul VI's view of evangelization is a broad one in more than one sense. First, insofar as the whole person of the evangelizer is involved in it: the witness of his life, his actions as much as his words (EN 21-22). Second, it embraces all that is human, its scope being the renewal of humankind and the transformation of human culture and cultures with the power of the Gospel (EN 18-20). Third, speaking of "human liberation" the Pope explicitly states that "the Church . . . has the duty to proclaim the liberation of millions of human beings, many of whom are her own children, the duty of assisting the birth of this liberation, of giving witness to it, of ensuring that it is complete" (EN 30). And he adds: "This is not foreign to evangelization" (EN 30).[6]

Human liberation belongs somehow to the Church's evangelizing mission; as noted above, nothing similar is said in EN on interreligious dialogue. Indeed, while the notion of evangelization proposed by EN is a broad one in more than one sense, passages of the apostolic exhortation are not wanting where it is nearly reduced to and identified with the proclamation of the Gospel. Thus the Pope affirms that the Church "exists in order to evangelize, that is to say in order to preach and teach, to be the channel of the gift of grace, to reconcile sinners with God and to perpetuate Christ's sacrifice in the mass, which is the memorial of his death and glorious resurrection" (EN 14). And again: "The Good News proclaimed by the witness of life sooner or later has to be proclaimed by the word of life. There is no true evangelization if the name, the teaching, the life, the promises, the Kingdom and the

---

6. Nevertheless, this somewhat restrictive view on human liberation stands in contrast with the much more positive assertion of the 1971 Synod of Bishops, which in its document *De Iustitia in Mundo* had declared it to be a "constitutive dimension of the preaching of the Gospel." This often quoted text reads as follows: "Action on behalf of justice and participation in the transformation of the world fully appear to us as a constitutive dimension (*ratio constitutiva*) of the preaching of the Gospel, or, in other words, of the Church's mission for the redemption of the human race and its liberation from every oppressive situation" (*AAS* 63 [1971], 924).

mystery of Jesus of Nazareth, the Son of God, are not proclaimed. . . . This proclamation — 'kerygma,' preaching or catechesis — occupies such an important place in
evangelization that it has often become synonymous with it; and yet it is only one
aspect of evangelization" (EN 22). But this last sentence is further explained as
follows: "Evangelization . . . is a complex process made up of varied elements: the
renewal of humanity, witness, explicit proclamation, inner adherence, entry into the
community, acceptance of signs, apostolic initiative" (EN 24) — all activities, it
must be noted, which have to do with announcing Jesus Christ to those who do not
know him, and sacramentalizing their conversion to Christianity.

Summarily and in the Pope's own words, while evangelization is seen in EN as a
"rich, complex and dynamic reality" (EN 17), it "will always entail as the simultaneous foundation, core and summit of its dynamism a clear proclamation that in
Jesus Christ, the Son of God made man, who died and rose from the dead, salvation
is offered to all as a gift of God's kindness and mercy" (EN 27). The question,
however, arises whether this papal teaching leaves room for interreligious dialogue
to be viewed as in its own right a genuine expression of the Church's evangelizing
mission. It will be necessary to return to this later.

The Teaching of John Paul II

Our survey will be limited here to some salient documents directly relevant to the
theme of religions and to the foundation of interreligious dialogue. The encyclical
letter RM will be further examined later, where a comparison between RM and DP
will be established concerning the manner in which both documents respectively
conceive of the mutual relationship between dialogue and proclamation and the
place of each in the Church's evangelizing mission.

One idea that Pope John Paul II has expressed from the beginning of his pontificate, and which progressively he has affirmed with increasing vigor and firmness, is
the universal presence and action of the Holy Spirit in the members of the other
religious traditions and in the traditions themselves. Already the first encyclical
Redemptor Hominis (1979) viewed the "firm belief of the followers of the non-
Christian religions" as "an effect of the Spirit of truth operating outside the visible
confines of the Mystical Body" (RH 6). The Pope exhorted the Church's mission to
an attitude of esteem and respect for all that has been brought about by the Spirit
which "blows where it wills" (Jn 3:8) in the members of the other religious faiths
(RH 12). Similarly, John Paul II has repeatedly affirmed that "every authentic prayer
is prompted by the Holy Spirit who is mysteriously present in every human heart." [7]

The most explicit text, however, concerning the economy of the Holy Spirit is
found in the encyclical *Dominum et Vivificantem* (1986), formally devoted to the
Holy Spirit. Here the Pope develops explicitly the universal action of the Holy Spirit
before the Christian economy as well as today "outside the visible body of the
Church." Before the Christian economy, the action of the Spirit was ordained toward
Christ in accordance with the divine plan of salvation; today, outside the Church it
results from the salvific event accomplished in him. The Pope thus explains what he
calls "the Christological content and the pneumatological dimension" (DEV 53) of
the salvific event. He goes on to say in DEV 53 that:

---

7. Cf. for instance the Pope's discourse to the members of the Roman Curia (22
December 1986), devoted to the event of the World Day of Prayer for Peace in Assisi (27
October 1986), in *Osservatore Romano* (English edition), 5 January 1987; also in *Bulle-
tin. Secretariatus pro non chistianis,* 64: 22 (1987/1), pp.54-62.

We cannot limit ourselves to the two thousand years which have passed since the birth of Christ. We need to go further back, to embrace the whole of the action of the Holy Spirit even before Christ — from the beginning, throughout the world, and especially in the economy of the Old Covenant. For this action has been exercised, in every place and at every time, indeed in every individual, according to the eternal plan of salvation, whereby this action was to be closely linked with the mystery of the Incarnation and Redemption, which in its turn exercised its influence on those who believed in the future coming of Christ. . . .

But . . . we need to look further and go further afield, knowing that "the wind blows where it wills.". . . The Second Vatican Council . . . reminds us of the Holy Spirit's activity also "outside the visible body of the Church." The Council speaks precisely of "all people of good will in whose hearts grace works in an unseen way." For, "since Christ died for all," and since the ultimate vocation of man is in fact one, and divine, we ought to believe that the Holy Spirit, in a manner known to God, offers to every man the possibility of being associated with this paschal mystery (GS 22).

The universal presence and action of the Holy Spirit is further reaffirmed in the recent encyclical RM. It manifests itself without limits of space or time, not only in the persons but in the traditions as well to which they belong. Its presence and action "affect not only individuals but also society and history, peoples, cultures and religions" (RM 28). It is the Spirit who "sows the seeds of the Word" present in various rites (*ritibus*) and cultures, "preparing them for full maturity in Christ" (DP 28). The Spirit "was already at work in the world before Christ was glorified (cf. AG 4)"; the Spirit remains operative today "in human hearts and in the history of peoples, in cultures and religions." This action must be understood "in reference to Christ" (RM 29); "moreover, the universal activity of the Spirit is not to be separated from his particular activity within the Body of Christ, the Church to whom he gives life and whom he impels to proclaim Christ" (RM 29).

The universal presence of the Spirit of which Pope John Paul II speaks is an important element in establishing the foundation for the Church's practice of inter-religious dialogue. Thus he wrote in RM 29 that the interreligious meeting in Assisi was meant to confirm his conviction that every authentic prayer is prompted by the Holy Spirit who is mysteriously present in every heart. In his discourse to the members of the Roman Curia in December 1986, after the Assisi event, the Pope further elaborated on the basis of interreligious dialogue. He made explicit reference in RM to three elements which together may be viewed as constituting its theological foundation. First is the "mystery of divine creation" and "the unity of the divine origin of the entire human family, of every man and woman, which is reflected in the unity of the divine image which each bears in himself/herself" (3). Accordingly, "there is only one divine plan for every human being who comes into the world, one single origin and goal" (3). Second, "the divine plan, unique and definitive, has its center in Jesus Christ" in whom all have been saved (4). Third, there is the "mysterious presence" of the Holy Spirit in the heart of every person by which every authentic prayer is prompted (11). Summing it all up, the Pope spoke of a "mystery of unity" that transcends "the differences of every type, and first of all the religious differences, (which) belong to another order" (5).

The Pope's discourse to the Curia thus established forcibly the foundation of interreligious dialogue; it brought out its significance in the life of the Church by recalling that the Church is in history the effective sign of the "mystery of unity" that is universally present in the world. At the same time, the Pope reaffirmed in unambiguous terms the Church's duty to announce Jesus Christ to the world. Some months later, in his address to the members of the Secretariat for Non-Christians, assembled in Plenary Assembly to discuss the First Draft of the projected document on "Dialogue and Proclamation" (April 1987), John Paul II made clear reference to dialogue and proclamation as complementary aspects of the Church's mission. He said: "Just as interreligious dialogue is one element in the mission of the Church, the proclamation of God's saving work in Our Lord Jesus Christ is another"; and he added: "There can be no question of choosing one and ignoring and rejecting the other."[8] It is this complementarity between dialogue and proclamation that the document under study here was intended to spell out. However, some clarifications in this direction had already been made by the 1984 document of the Secretariat for Non-Christians, to which we must now turn.

The Secretariat for Non-Christians' 1984 Document

The direct aim of D&M was to show the place which interreligious dialogue occupies in the overall evangelizing mission of the Church, thereby stating explicitly what other documents so far had left unsaid. The document leaves it to theologians to develop a theology of religions on which to base the practice of dialogue (D&M 6). Drawing rather from the ongoing practice of dialogue, its reflections are mainly pastoral in character (ibid.).

D&M gives interreligious dialogue a broad definition: "It means not only discussion, but also includes all positive and constructive interreligious relations with individuals and communities of other faiths which are directed at mutual understanding and enrichment" (3). D&M's main concern is "the relationship which exists between dialogue and mission" (5). It must be noted — and regretted — that in the introductory section of the document, this relationship seems to be conceived of in terms of a dichotomy between evangelization and dialogue: mention is made of the "duties of evangelization and dialogue which are found together in the mission of the Church," and of the difficulties that can arise between them (D&M 7). This impression of a dichotomy is, however, soon dissipated. For, in the first part on mission, the document explains that the mission of the Church "is one but comes to be exercised in different ways according to the conditions in which mission unfolds" (D&M 11). It recalls that RH 15, echoing the 1971 Synod of Bishops, considered "the commitment to humankind, to social justice, to liberty and the rights of man, and the reform of unjust social structures" "an essential element of the mission of the Church, and indissolubly connected with it" (D&M 12). Promotion of justice, however, is but one aspect, while the intention of the document is to put together the "different aspects and manners of mission" (ibid.). It does so in a text that, without pretending to be exhaustive, enumerates five "principal elements" of the "single but complex and articulated reality" of the Church's evangelizing mission. This important text has to be quoted at length:

> Mission is already constituted by the simple presence and living witness of the Christian life (cf. EN 21), although it must be recognized that we bear this treasure in "earthly vessels" (2 Cor 4:7). Thus the difference between the way the Christian appears existentially and that which he declares himself to be is never fully overcome.
>
> There is also the concrete commitment to the service of humankind and all the forms of activity for social development and for the struggle against poverty and the structures which produce it.

---

8. Cf. *Bulletin. Secretariatus pro non Christianis*, 66: 22 (1987/3), pp. 223-225.

Also, there is liturgical life and that of prayer and contemplation, eloquent testimonies to a living and liberating relationship with the active and true God who calls us to his Kingdom and to his glory (cf. Acts 2:42).

There is, as well, the dialogue in which Christians meet the followers of other religious traditions in order to walk together toward truth and to work together in projects of common concern.

Finally, there is announcement and catechesis in which the Good News of the Gospel is proclaimed and its consequences for life and culture are analyzed.

The totality of Christian mission embraces all these elements. (D&M 13)

"The totality of Christian mission embraces all these elements"; nor is the list complete. Some observations may be made. The proclamation of the Gospel through announcement and catechesis comes at the end, intentionally as it seems;[9] for mission and evangelization must be thought of as a dynamic reality or a process. This process culminates in fact in the proclamation of Jesus Christ through announcement (*kèrygma*) and catechesis (*didachè*). By the same token, however, the "liturgical life and that of prayer and contemplation" would better have come later, following after the proclamation of Jesus Christ with which it is directly connected — as in Acts 2:42 to which reference is made — and of which it is the natural outcome. The order would then have been as follows: presence, service, dialogue, proclamation, sacramentalization — the last two corresponding to those Church activities which in the more narrow but not untraditional view made up evangelization. In the broad perspective adopted by the document, the "single reality" of evangelization is said to be at once "complex and articulated"; it is a process. This means that, while all the elements making up the process are authentic forms of evangelization, not all have either the same place or the same value in the mission of the Church. Thus, for instance, interreligious dialogue precedes proclamation. It may or may not be followed by it; but only if it is, will the process of evangelization come to completion. For proclamation and sacramentalization are the climax of the Church's evangelizing mission.

The first part of the document ends by stressing once more "the place" of dialogue within the mission (D&M 19). Though our analysis of the document could end here, let us take note rapidly of some observations made in the second part, where dialogue is studied more closely. According to our document, dialogue is not only in itself a distinct aspect of evangelization; it is also an "attitude and a spirit" and, as such, "the norm and necessary manner of every form of Christian mission, as well as of every aspect of it, whether one speaks of simple presence and witness, service, or direct proclamation." All the forms of mission enumerated earlier must be "permeated by . . . a dialogical spirit" (D&M 29).

As for interreligious dialogue as a specific task of evangelization, which — it is said once more — "finds its place in the great dynamism of the Church's mission" (D&M 30), it itself can take on different forms: there is the dialogue of life, open and available to all (29-30); there is dialogue through a common commitment to deeds of justice and human liberation (31-32); there is intellectual dialogue in which specialists exchange on the level of their respective religious heritages, to promote commu-

---

9. The term "finally," found in the English, French, and German translations, is missing in the Italian text, which is the original text. However, the last place given to proclamation in the order of elements composing the "articulated" reality of evangelization appears even so quite intentional. The Italian original text is found in *Bulletin. Secretariatus pro non christianis*, 56: 19 (1984/2), pp. 166-180.

nion and fellowship (33-34); there is, finally, at the deepest level, the sharing of religious experiences, of prayer and contemplation, in a common search for the Absolute (35). All these forms of dialogue, it may be said, are on the part of the Christian partner, ways of working toward the "evangelical transformation of cultures" (34), and opportunities of sharing with the others in an existential way the values of the Gospel (35).

The document remains silent on the mutual relationship between dialogue and proclamation within the Church's evangelizing mission. This issue would, however, have to be treated, as it raised different questions, both theological and pastoral. It is this gap which the recent document, as its title "Dialogue and Proclamation" indicates, is intended to fill.

II. AN ANALYSIS OF *DIALOGUE AND PROCLAMATION*

From the outset DP defines clearly the key terms to which reference will have to be made throughout: evangelization, dialogue, proclamation, conversion, and religions or religious traditions. *"Evangelizing mission*, or more simply *evangelization*, refers to the mission of the Church in its totality." Thus, it is understood in the broad sense described earlier in D&M 13: "In this document the term *evangelizing mission* is used for evangelization in its broad sense, while the more specific understanding [which identified it with proclamation] is expressed by the term *proclamation*" (DP 8). *Dialogue* is taken in a specific meaning, as distinct from "the spirit of dialogue" which should permeate all the activities constituting the evangelizing mission of the Church. In this specific sense, as D&M 3 has explained, dialogue refers to "all positive and constructive interreligious relations with individuals and communities of other faiths which are directed to mutual understanding and enrichment" (D&M 9); as such it "constitutes one of the integral elements of the Church's evangelizing mission" (ibid.). *Proclamation*, on the other hand,

is the communication of the Gospel message, the mystery of salvation realized by God for all in Jesus Christ by the power of the Spirit. It is an invitation to a commitment of faith in Jesus Christ and to entry through baptism into the community of believers which is the Church. (DP 10)

Dialogue, therefore, is distinct from proclamation, each having its specific finality, though the witness of life is presupposed in both. The "single but complex and articulated reality" (DP 2; cf. D&M 13) of evangelization comprises both.

As for *conversion*, it is used in the document with two distinct meanings, which the context must each time clarify: there is conversion as "the humble and penitent return of the heart to God . . ." (DP 37) or *metanoia*; "more specifically, conversion may refer to a change of religious adherence, and particularly to embracing the Christian faith" (DP 11). Finally, "the terms *religions* or *religious traditions* are used here in a generic and analogical sense. They cover those religions which, with Christianity, are wont to refer back to the faith of Abraham, as well as the religious traditions of Asia, Africa, and elsewhere" (DP 12).

The special bond that exists between Christianity and the other "monotheistic" religions — a term that, however, is intentionally avoided here — because of their common reference to Abraham's faith, and even more specifically between Christianity and Judaism, explains why the term "religious traditions" is considered analogical: not all religions have the same relationship to Christianity. But this does not imply any limits to dialogue: "Interreligious dialogue ought to extend to all religions and their followers" (DP 13). Included here are not only the great world religions but also the traditional religions present in various continents. On the other hand, the "New Religious Movements" are left out of consideration because of the diverse situations they represent (ibid.). This restriction being made, the document considers it legitimate, the vast differences between the various religious traditions notwithstanding, to speak of interreligious dialogue in generic terms. It intends to show the foundation on which interreligious dialogue as a universal practice can be based, and to provide basic clarifications on the relationship between dialogue and proclamation. This being done, the document will be careful to note in conclusion that "it is important to remember that the various religions differ from one another" (DP 87). Special attention needs therefore to be given, and special studies to be undertaken, concerning relations to the followers of each particular religion (DP 87-88).

The general structure of the document is made up of three parts: Interreligious Dialogue (DP 14-54); Proclaiming Jesus Christ (DP 55-76); and Interreligious Dialogue and Proclamation (DP 77-86). The two sections of the first part bear the following titles: 1. A Christian Approach to Religious Traditions; 2. The Place of Interreligious Dialogue in the Evangelizing Mission of the Church. Other sections of the first part treat successively: 3. Forms of Dialogue; 4. Dispositions for Interreligious Dialogue and Its Fruits; 5. Obstacles to Dialogue. However, due to the emphasis it receives in the document itself, the first section, dedicated to "A Christian Approach to Religious Traditions," is treated here under a distinct heading, while the other sections are grouped together.

A Christian Approach to Religious Traditions

DP believes that the attitude of Christians toward the members of other religious traditions will depend on their appraisal of those traditions. An open attitude in interreligious dialogue can only be based on a positive evaluation of the religions themselves. This is why DP devotes a large section to the subject (14-32). By doing so, it in fact innovates, for no official Church document before it contained such a formal theological treatment of religious traditions. DP's approach to the subject is at once broad in its scope and balanced in its assessment.

The document notes from the outset that "these traditions are to be approached with great sensitivity, on account of the spiritual and human values enshrined in them. They command our respect because over the centuries they have borne witness to the efforts to find answers " 'to (the) profound mysteries of the human condition' (NA 1), and have given expression to the religious experience and the longings of millions of their adherents, and they continue to do so" (DP 14). DP then recalls that Vatican II has given a positive assessment of those traditions, affirming not only that salvation in Jesus Christ is open to all persons of good will (15; with the above-mentioned quotation from GS 22), but also the presence in the traditions themselves of "positive values": "rays of that Truth which enlightens all" (NA 2), "seeds of the Word" (AG 11), "elements of truth and grace" (AG 9), which are "found sown" not only "in the minds and hearts," but also "in the rites and customs of peoples" (LG 17) (DP 16). "These few references," the document says, "suffice to show that the Council has openly acknowledged the presence of positive values not only in the religious life of individual believers of other religious traditions, but also in the religious traditions to which they belong" (DP 17).

The Council attributed these values "to the active presence of God through his Word, pointing also to the universal action of the Spirit" who, as AG 4 states, without doubt "was at work in the world before Christ was glorified." The positive elements found present in the religious traditions go to show that these traditions have played a role as "a preparation for the Gospel (LG 16)" and keep even today a "providential role in the divine economy of salvation" (DP 17), while at the same time they need to be perfected through the missionary activity of the Church. Through it, as AG 9 states, "whatever good is found to be sown in the hearts and minds of men, or in the rites and cultures peculiar to various peoples, is not lost. More than that, it is healed, ennobled, and perfected" (DP 18).

Having recalled and commented upon the conciliar doctrine, DP turns to Sacred Scripture for a biblical foundation of the council's positive approach; and first to the Old Testament. The important affirmation is made from the outset that "there is but one history of salvation for the whole of humankind" (DP 19). Salvation history cannot, therefore, be said to begin — as has often been the case — with the history of Israel; it embraces the entire history of the human race, starting from creation. This is shown by the fact that "from the beginning of creation God made a covenant with all peoples" (DP 19). The covenant with Noah is a further indication of the same. Quite symptomatic is the fact that this covenant is not understood as a mere divine manifestation through the phenomena of nature; it is seen as "symbolic of the divine intervention in the history of the nations" (DP 19). The non-Israelite "saints" of the Old Testament are characteristically seen in the New Testament as "belonging to this one history of salvation" (DP 19). The text mentions Abel, Enoch, and Noah, to whom Melchisedek is added (cf. Heb 7:1-17). Their God is identical to that of Abraham and Moses. The history of salvation to which they belong is the one salvation history that will culminate in Jesus Christ (DP 19).

The universal character of the history of salvation does not contradict the "unique status" of Israel as God's chosen people. But the election of Israel constitutes a "mission." In fact, Israel grew in the awareness of her mission, and it is particularly at the time of the Exile that the prophets brought her to the realization of the "universal perspective" according to which "God's salvation extends beyond and through Israel to the nations" (DP 20). In the Wisdom literature too, "the action of God in the whole universe is clearly affirmed," touching both "the history of nations and the lives of individuals" (DP 20).

Turning to Jesus, in spite of the limitations of his own mission and of that of the disciples during his earthly life (cf. Mt 15:24 and 10:5), the Gospels show his open attitude toward and his entering into dialogue with persons who do not belong to the chosen people of Israel. The text mentions the centurion (Mt 8:5-13), and the Samaritan woman (Jn 4:23). Jesus is also shown working miracles for "foreigners" (cf. Mk 7:24-30; Mt 15:21-28). The text explains that "these miracles are signs of the coming of the Kingdom" (DP 21). It could have said more pointedly that those miracles showed the universality of the Kingdom, which was already breaking through and of which they were part. However, the text does state explicitly that in the person of Jesus the Kingdom of God was actually "breaking through to the world" (DP 22) and that it is "not confined only to those who belong to the specially chosen people" (ibid.). This is shown by Jesus's announcement of the entry of the Gentiles into the Kingdom (cf. Mt 8:10-11; 11:22-24; 25:31-34), which, as the text observes pointedly, "is to be understood as being at one and the same time historical and eschatological" (DP 22). This amounts to saying that the Kingdom of God is universally present in the world, while it must grow through history toward its eschatological fullness.

Turning from Jesus to the theology of the New Testament, and specifically to New Testament references to the religious traditions of the Gentiles, DP observes that these "may appear to be contrasting, but can be seen as complementary" (DP 23). This, however, is shown only in the case of Paul "whose negative verdict" about the Gentiles in Rom 1:18-32 is balanced by a "positive and open attitude" toward them in his discourse to the Lycaonians (cf. Acts 14:8-18) and his Areopagus speech at Athens (Acts 17:22-34) — both related by Luke in Acts (DP 23). Let us note that among many diverse interpretations of the Areopagus speech, DP opts for the more positive one, which understands Paul as praising the "religious spirit" of the Greeks and sees them "unknowingly" revering in their "unknown God" Jesus Christ whom he announces (DP 23). This interpretation, which, the term apart, comes close to making Paul's interlocutors "anonymous Christians" is not without theological implications, as will be seen below. For the rest, the text limits itself to pointing out the application New Testament theology makes to Jesus Christ of the Wisdom of God of Old Testament Wisdom literature. According to John's Prologue the Word of God, who was present and operative throughout salvation history (cf. Jn 1:1-5), enlightened every human being coming into the world (cf. Jn 1:9), even before he became incarnate in Jesus Christ (cf. Jn 1:14).

Passing over from Sacred Scripture to the post-biblical tradition, the document notes that here too "contrasting data" are found. "Negative judgments" on the religious world of the time of the Fathers can easily be gleaned from their writings. If this had been further elaborated, DP could have made explicit reference to the unanimous condemnation on the part of the Church Fathers of polytheism and idolatry wherever they found them present in the surrounding cultures and religions, as well as to their severe judgment on "mysteric religions" and some devious practices associated with them. Rather than spelling this out — though without ignoring it — DP prefers to note that, negative elements notwithstanding, there exists a current of "remarkable openness" in the early tradition, linked for the most part with the sapiential tradition as applied by John's Prologue to the Word of God before and in his incarnation.

The document refers explicitly to Justin's doctrine of the "seeds" sown by the divine *Logos* among the nations, to Irenaeus's vision of God's self-manifestation through the Son throughout history, even before the incarnation, and to Clement of Alexandria's view of God's covenant with Greek "philosophy" as a stepping stone to the philosophy that is according to Christ. Lack of space forbad long developments or citations; only some essential references are given in a footnote (DP 24). What matters, however, is that the document adopts once more an open interpretation of the texts concerned: the *Logos* is understood to refer, not to Philo's "reason," but to the divine "Word" of John's Prologue; similarly, the "philosophy" of the Greeks with which God has entered into a covenant relationship has more to do with divine "Wisdom" than with human reasoning.[10] The document can conclude by saying: "Thus it can be said that for [those writers], prior to and outside the Christian dispensation, God has already, in an incomplete way, manifested himself. This manifestation of the *Logos* is an adumbration of the full revelation in Jesus Christ to which it points" (DP 24). It proceeds further to the affirmation that the early Fathers "offer what may be called a theology of history" (DP 25). While the term is modern, its use here need not appear anachronistic for, as DP notes, "history becomes salvation history, inasmuch as through it God progressively manifests himself and communicates with humankind" (ibid.). This process of divine manifestation and communication, which begins with creation itself (DP 19), "reaches its climax in the incarnation of the Son of God in Jesus Christ" (DP 25). The four covenants given by God to the human race — in Adam, in Noah, in Moses, and in Jesus Christ — to

---

10. For a longer presentation and analysis of the patristic current under consideration, which corroborates the document's interpretation, cf. J. Fédou, "Les Pères de l'Eglise face aux religions de leur temps," *Bulletin. Consilium pro dialogo inter religiones*, 80: 27 (1992/2), pp. 173-185. Also J. Dupuis, *Jesus Christ and His Spirit* (Bangalore: Theological Publications in India, 1977), pp. 3-19.

which Irenaeus makes explicit reference, thus constitute the basic framework for a theology of salvation history. Irenaeus's text, which in DP is only referred to, is worth quoting here:

> Four covenants were bestowed upon humanity: the first, before the Deluge, in the time of Adam; the second, after the Deluge, in the time of Noah; the third, which is the gift of the Law, in the time of Moses; finally, the fourth, which renews the human being and recapitulates all things in itself — the one which, by the Gospel, exalts human beings and sends them soaring for the heavenly Reign. (*Adv. Haer.*, 3, 11, 8)

DP notes that the patristic current toward a universal approach to salvation history "may be said to culminate in Augustine" (DP 25). Here again, DP could have noted that Augustine's view of history is less optimistic than that of Irenaeus, markedly so in his *De Civitate Dei* where history is presented as a dramatic struggle between two cities, "the City of God" and "the terrestrial city." [11] Yet, the document is satisfied — rightly or wrongly — to refer to Augustine's affirmation that Christianity already existed "at the beginning of the human race" (*Enarr. in Ps.* 118) and that the "City of God" began with Abel: *Ecclesia ab Abel* (*Enarr. in Ps.* 142, 2). The main reference is to *Retract.*, 1, 13, 3, a text where Augustine, returning to his own writing, introduces in it some corrections. This text shows that, in virtue of the divine economy, God has encountered human beings in the Son since the very creation of the universe. Christianity has somehow existed since the inception of the human race. Augustine writes:

> The raw reality of what is called the Christian religion existed among the ancients. Nor was it absent from the inception of the human race to the coming of Christ in the flesh at the moment when the true religion, which had pre-existed, began to be called Christian. If, then, I have written: "Behold the religion that exists in our days, it is the Christian religion," this means not that it had never existed before, but that it only later acquired the name "Christian."

From the Fathers of the Church, DP turns to the recent teaching authority of the Church, which through Vatican II links with the "early Christian vision of history" (DP 26). It surveys rapidly the important documents of Pope John Paul II, previously analyzed here, where explicit reference is made to the universal presence and action of the Spirit in persons in the world at large, and to the "mystery of unity," which in its various elements can be seen as constituting the theological basis for a positive approach to the other religious traditions and the practice of interreligious dialogue" (27-28).

Building upon this foundation, DP arrives at a theological statement concerning the salvation in Jesus Christ of the members of other religious traditions and the role played in it by the traditions to which they belong. This text needs to be quoted extensively as it reflects a theological vision that goes beyond what Vatican II and the Church's central authority had yet expressly affirmed.

> From this mystery of unity it follows that all men and women who are saved share, though differently, in the same mystery of salvation in Jesus Christ through his Spirit. Christians know this through their faith, while others re-

---

11. See J. Fédou, loc. cit., pp. 181-182.

main unaware that Jesus Christ is the source of their salvation. The mystery of salvation reaches out to them, in a way known to God, through the invisible action of the Spirit of Christ. Concretely, it will be in the sincere practice of what is good in their own religious traditions and by following the dictates of their conscience that the members of other religions respond positively to God's invitation and receive salvation in Jesus Christ, even while they do not recognize or acknowledge him as their savior (cf. AG 3, 9, 11). (DP 29)

This text contains several important affirmations: 1. Christians and others who are saved share, "though differently," in the same mystery of salvation; 2. This is salvation in Jesus Christ through the Spirit; 3. Christians know this through their faith while others are unaware of it; 4. The mystery of salvation reaches out to them through the invisible action of the Spirit; 5. It is in the sincere practice of what is good in their tradition and following the dictates of their conscience that they reach salvation in Jesus Christ, even though they do not recognize him as their Savior; 6. For such is the concrete manner in which they respond positively to God's invitation of grace in Jesus Christ.

Not surprisingly, this text gave rise to much discussion before it reached its final form. Proposition 5 was especially contested and passed through several amendments. In the Fifth Draft proposed for discussion at the 1990 Plenary Assembly of the Pontifical Council for Interreligious Dialogue the text read more straightforwardly: "Concretely, and in normal circumstances, it will be in the sincere practice of what is good in their own traditions that the members of other religions who are saved respond positively to God's will and receive salvation in his Son, even while they remain unable to identify their Savior and to name him." This sentence was meant, moreover, to answer a straight question, which was stated as follows:

> The question . . . arises whether the sincere practice of their [i.e., others'] religious tradition plays any part in the mystery of their salvation. In attempting to answer this question it may first be noted that the religious life of individual persons cannot in reality be separated from their practice of the religious tradition to which they belong. There is no religious life which is not expressed in a tradition; nor does a religious tradition exist outside the persons and the community that uphold it and practice it.

This entire statement of the question and of the perspective in which an answer could be given to it had to be canceled, as some feared that it would be entering into theological considerations open to discussion and to which not all would assent. In the sentence that followed, an important amendment of the draft was proposed to the effect that for the words "in the sincere practice of what is good in their own tradition" the following be substituted: "by following the dictates of their conscience." If accepted as such, this amendment would have meant a simple return to the traditional doctrine reflected in LG 16. The final solution that was retained consisted in combining both phrases, to read as in the final text: "in the sincere practice of what is good in their own religious traditions *and* by following the dictates of their conscience" (DP 29, emphasis mine). Another amendment consists in the omission of the words "in normal circumstances." This, some feared, could be understood to make salvation outside Christianity the "normal way," even if not "normative."

As can be seen, the discussion to which the text gave rise and the amendments introduced in it testify to a certain fear on the part of some to concede too much to other religions as constituting ways of salvation, even though in relation to Jesus

Christ and his Spirit. In its final form the text has undoubtedly lost some of its previous incisiveness. However, the final text continues to affirm that the members of other religions are saved by Jesus Christ "in the sincere practice of what is good in their religious traditions." This is, even in its present form, a weighty statement, not found before in official documents of the central teaching authority, and whose theological import must not be underestimated. It means, in effect, that the members of other religions are not saved by Christ in spite of, or beside, their own tradition, but in it and in some mysterious way, "known to God," through it. If further elaborated theologically, this statement would be seen to imply some hidden presence — no matter how imperfect — of the mystery of Jesus Christ in these religious traditions in which salvation reaches their adherents.

This, DP goes on the explain, does not mean that "everything in them is good" in the other traditions. To identify in them the "elements of grace capable of sustaining the positive response of their members to God's invitation" is much more difficult than to recognize the fruits of the Spirit of God present in the life of individuals (cf. Gal 5:22-23) (DP 30). It requires a discernment, "for which criteria have to be established" (DP 30) — though the document does not proceed further with establishing such criteria. Rather, it gives reasons why "to say that other religious traditions include elements of grace does not imply that everything in them is the result of grace" (DP 31). For sin has been at work in the world and the religious traditions, "notwithstanding their positive values, reflect the limitations of the human spirit, sometimes inclined to choose evil" (ibid.). Account must also be taken of the "contradictions" that may exist between them and the Christian revelation, and, where necessary, of the "incompatibility" between some aspects of such traditions with fundamental elements of Christianity (ibid.). This goes to show that in dialogue Christians may have to challenge the members of other religious traditions "in a peaceful spirit with regard to the content of their belief" (DP 32). But "Christians, too, must allow themselves to be questioned. Notwithstanding the fullness of God's revelation in Jesus Christ, the way Christians sometimes understand their religion and practice it may be in need of purification" (ibid.). The Fourth Draft was here more forceful, and added: "Nor does all that emerged in the Christian tradition by way of accretions unequivocally bear the mark of the Gospel spirit." This sentence, however, disappeared in the Fifth Draft!

The Place of Interreligious Dialogue in the Evangelizing Mission of the Church

The section of DP under this title begins by recalling Vatican II's sacramental ecclesiology: the Church has been willed by God and instituted by Christ to be, in the fullness of time, the "sign and instrument" (cf. LG 1), the "universal sacrament of salvation" (cf. LG 48). As such, she is "necessary for salvation" (cf. LG 14) (DP 33).

There follow two paragraphs (DP 34-35) that intend to describe the relationship between the Church and the Kingdom of God, on the one hand, and, on the other, the relation to both of the members of the other religious traditions who are saved in Jesus Christ. The text begins by recognizing that "the relationship between the Church and the Kingdom is mysterious and complex" (DP 34). The distinction between the Church on earth and the eschatological Kingdom appears clearly, as in LG 5 to which reference is made (DP 34). However, the text is somehow ambiguous concerning the relationship between the Church on earth and the Kingdom already present in history. On the one hand, they seem to be identified, as in LG 5 and 3 to which reference is made explicitly or implicitly (DP 34-35). This impression is corroborated by the addition made to the text, after its approval by the Plenary

Assembly of the Pontifical Council for Inter-Religious Dialogue (PCID), of a long quotation from a discourse of John Paul II to the Indian bishops to the effect that "the Kingdom is inseparable from the Church, because both are inseparable from the person and work of Jesus himself" (DP 34). On the other hand, it is recognized that "the Church's mission is to 'foster the Kingdom . . .' at whose service she is placed" (DP 35); to which an important statement is added to the effect that:

> Part of her role consists in recognizing that the inchoate reality of this King-
> dom can be found also beyond the confines of the Church, for example in the
> hearts of the followers of other religious traditions, insofar as they live evan-
> gelical values and are open to the action of the Spirit. (DP 35)

But, again, a cautionary statement has been added at a late stage: "It must be remembered nevertheless that this is indeed an inchoate reality, which needs to find completion through being related to the Kingdom of Christ already present in the Church yet realized fully only in the world to come" (DP 35).

The somewhat involved redaction of this text leads to the conclusion that, while the Kingdom in its historical becoming is in some way present beyond the bound-aries of the Church, it is nevertheless already present in the Church in a distinct and privileged manner. Even in this subdued last form, this affirmation, it may be noted, is somewhat novel in official Church documents, while, as will be shown later, it constitutes an important point of contact between DP and RM.[12]

What then is the relationship of the members of the other religious traditions to the Kingdom and to the Church? Those among them who, responding positively to God's calling, are saved in Jesus Christ, "already share in some way in the reality which is signified by the Kingdom" (DP 35). As for their relationship to the Church, DP is satisfied to repeat the sober affirmation of Vatican II according to which they are "oriented" to the Church (LG 16) (DP 35). It is well known that the Council abstained intentionally from affirming that they are in some way members of the Church as pre-conciliar ecclesiology often explained by having recourse to various distinctions — some more felicitous, some less — such as: membership *in voto*, dis-tinct from *in re*; membership of the soul of the Church, not of her body; invisible membership, distinct from visible, etc. The conciliar notion of the Church as "one complex reality, made up of a double element, human and divine" — "in virtue of an analogy which is not without merit with the mystery of the Word incarnate" in whom the human is indissolubly united to the divine (LG 8) — prompted sobriety where the relation of the members of other religions to the Church is concerned. DP keeps the same sobriety. Those saved by Christ outside the Church do not belong to her as members, even while they are "oriented" toward her. It is clear that in this perspective, the traditional axiom "Outside the Church there is no salvation" — no matter how intelligible it may have been in the historical context in which it has been formulated[13] — has become misleading and can best be dropped. The "orientation" of the others to the Church, of which DP 35 speaks, is to be understood in terms of the "completion" which their real but incomplete belonging to the Kingdom of God may receive in the Church where the Kingdom is already present in a privileged manner. We may note, however, that, while affirming after Vatican II (LG 14) the

---

12. For an analysis of previous documents in Vatican II and after, on the relationship between the Church on earth and the Kingdom of God in history, cf. J. Dupuis, "L'Eglise, le Règne de Dieu et les 'autres' " (to be published).

13. See F. A. Sullivan, *Salvation outside the Church? Tracing the History of the Catholic Response* (New York and Mahwah: Paulist Press, 1992).

necessity of the Church as universal, DP enters no further into the question *how* this necessity applies, and how the Church is operative, in the salvation of people outside.

The two following paragraphs (DP 36-37) have to do with the pilgrim Church. Though holy by divine institution, it is recognized that her members "bear the mark of their human limitations" (DP 36) and, as Vatican II admitted, that not only her members but the Church herself, "insofar as she is an institution of men on earth" (UR 6), "is constantly in need of renewal and reform" (DP 36). Where revelation is concerned, while the fullness of revelation is contained in Jesus Christ, as the Council teaches (DEV 2), there is "growth in insight into the realities and words that are being passed on" through tradition, as Vatican II also recognized (DEV 8), stating that the Church "is always advancing toward the plenitude of divine truth, until eventually the words of God are fulfilled in her" (DEV 8). DP says as much (37), quoting from the Council. The text approved by the 1990 Plenary Assembly of the PCID concluded: "Therefore, it can be said that Christians and the members of other religious traditions are, though in different senses and in different ways, pilgrims toward the fullness of truth and life." With this conclusion the text meant to link with what the 1984 document of the Secretariat for Non-Christians had said when it spoke of interreligious dialogue "in which Christians meet the followers of other religious traditions in order to walk together toward truth" (D&M 13). As may be noted, the projected text of DP was more restrained in its wording; even so, the sentence approved by the vote of the PCID has gone by the wayside thereafter: that Christians and others are copilgrims toward the fullness of truth — even though in different ways — is no longer said!

What precedes, namely the Church's pilgrim status and the sharing of the others in the Kingdom of God, makes it easier — the document thinks — to see why and in what sense interreligious dialogue is an integral element of the Church's evangelizing mission (30). The foundation of her commitment to dialogue is "not merely anthropological but primarily theological" (DP 38). For it is found in the "age-long dialogue" through which God has offered and continues to offer salvation to humankind (DP 38), as Paul VI taught in ES. That dialogue belongs to evangelization has been stated explicitly by John Paul II when, addressing the 1984 Plenary Assembly of the Secretariat for Non-Christians, he said: "[Interreligious] dialogue is fundamental for the Church. . . . [It] finds its place within the Church's salvific mission; for this reason it is a dialogue of salvation" (DP 39). In such dialogue, Christians and others are called to collaborate with "the Spirit of the Risen Lord who is universally present and active" (DP 40). The aim of dialogue does not stop at mutual understanding and friendly relations; "it reaches a much deeper level, that of the spirit, where exchange and sharing consist in a mutual witness to one's beliefs and a common exploration of one's respective religious convictions" (ibid.). More deeply still, "in dialogue Christians and others are invited to deepen their religious commitment, to respond with increasing sincerity to God's personal call and gracious self-gift which, as our faith tells us, always passes through the mediation of Jesus Christ and the work of his Spirit" (ibid.). The aim of dialogue is, therefore, "a deeper conversion of all toward God" (DP 41), and as such it "possesses its own validity" (DP 41).

These important statements imply: 1. that the conversion aimed at in dialogue is not the conversion of the partner to one's own religious tradition, but a common deepening of both partners' conversion to God; 2. that dialogue has no need for further justification and cannot be considered a means for proclamation. More clearly, though these expressions are not found in the text: Dialogue is an authentic expression of the Church's evangelizing mission in its own right; it is, in a sense, mutual evangelization between Christians and others, through each other. Cautions are, however, once more added to the effect that in the process of conversion to God "the decision may be made to leave one's previous spiritual or religious situation in order to direct oneself toward another" (DP 41, quoting D&M 37). Sincere dialogue, then, implies "on the one hand, mutual acceptance of differences, or even of contradictions, and on the other, respect for the free decision of persons taken according to the dictates of their conscience (cf. DH 2)" (DP 41).

The section on the "Forms of Dialogue" briefly recalls the four forms mentioned and developed by D&M 28-35: the dialogue of life, of action, of theological exchange, and of religious experience (DP 42); sending back to the previous document may suffice by way of commentary. But DP goes on to insist that "all local Churches, and all the members of these Churches, are called to dialogue, though not all in the same way" (DP 43); it is therefore important not to reduce dialogue to theological exchange, lest it should appear as "a sort of luxury item in the Church's mission, a domain reserved for specialists" (DP 43). Moreover, the different forms of dialogue are interconnected, with one influencing the other (DP 43). Stress is placed on the "importance of dialogue for integral development, social justice and human liberation" to which local Churches should "commit themselves in an unselfish and impartial manner," standing up for human rights, proclaiming the demands of justice, and denouncing injustice "independently of the religious allegiance of the victims" (DP 44).

But the novelty in DP with regard to the forms of interreligious dialogue is the addition of a long text on dialogue in the context of culture. This came as a result of suggestions made by various correspondents during the large consultation that took place on the proposed document. The final text is, with the exception of inconsequential details, that of the draft proposed to the 1990 Plenary Assembly of the PCID; it was preferred to and received the upper hand over "an alternative text" proposed during the assembly itself. After noting that a "context in which interreligious dialogue seems urgent today is that of culture," the text analyzes in some detail the complex relationship and manifold mutual influence, sometimes beneficial, sometimes detrimental, that culture and religion exercise on each other (DP 45). It points out that "the Christian message supports many values found and lived in the wisdom and the rich heritage of cultures, but it may also put in question culturally accepted values"; on the other hand, "some aspects of traditional Christian cultures are challenged by the local cultures of other religious traditions" (DP 46). The aim of interreligious dialogue at the level of culture is to eliminate tensions and conflicts, and potential confrontations by a better understanding among the various religious cultures of a given region. It can help to uphold traditional cultural values that are threatened and contribute to purifying cultures from dehumanizing elements (ibid.).

The following section treats the "dispositions for interreligious dialogue and its fruits." These include openness and receptivity, acceptance of differences, and the "will to engage together in commitment to the truth and the readiness to allow oneself to be transformed" (DP 47). None of these, however, implies on the part of the partners "lay[ing] aside their respective religious convictions." For, "the opposite is true: the sincerity of interreligious dialogue requires that each enters into it with the integrity of his or her own faith" (DP 48). This important statement lays to rest the contention made by some in recent years that putting aside — at least provisionally — faith in Jesus Christ the universal Savior is, on the Christian side, a prerequired condition for entering into dialogue, and indeed the test of the sincerity of the dialogue itself. However, the text explains, while remaining firm in their belief in Jesus Christ as the only mediator and fullness of divine revelation, "Christians must remember that God has also manifested himself in some way to the followers of other religious traditions" (ibid.). They must therefore approach the convictions of others "with receptive minds" (ibid.) and be "prepared to learn and to receive from and through others the positive values of their traditions" (DP 49).

In other words, though this is not said explicitly in the text, interreligious dialogue is a two-way traffic that consists in giving and receiving, in listening and sharing. Nor does the fullness of truth in Jesus Christ contradict this; for, as the text explains, individual Christians have no guarantee that "they have grasped that truth fully" and "in the last analysis, truth is not a thing we possess, but a person by whom we must allow ourselves to be possessed" (DP 49). Indeed, through dialogue Christians "may be moved to give up ingrained prejudices, to revise preconceived ideas, and even sometimes to allow the understanding of their faith to be purified" (ibid.).

As for the fruits that Christians may gather from the sincere practice of dialogue, they are expressed as follows:

> They will discover with admiration all that God's action through Jesus Christ in his Spirit has accomplished and continues to accomplish in the world and in the whole of humankind. Far from weakening their own faith, true dialogue will deepen it. They will become increasingly aware of their Christian identity and perceive more clearly the distinctive elements of the Christian message. Their faith will gain new dimensions as they discover the active presence of the mystery of Jesus Christ beyond the visible boundaries of the Church and of the Christian fold. (DP 50)

The last section of DP's first part is devoted to "Obstacles to Dialogue." A long list of such obstacles is established (DP 52), some of which, it is said, would apply equally to members of all religious traditions while others would affect some traditions more specifically (DP 51). There is no need to spell them out here. The text observes, however, that "many of these obstacles arise from a lack of understanding of the true nature and goal of interreligious dialogue" (DP 53). It also reminds us that "the Church's commitment to dialogue is not dependent on success . . . rather it flows from God's initiative in entering into a dialogue with humankind and from the example of Jesus Christ whose life, death and resurrection gave to that dialogue its ultimate expression" (ibid.). Moreover, obstacles notwithstanding, the practice of interreligious dialogue has already yielded positive results, both on the Christian side and the other. And so, "despite the difficulties, the Church's commitment to dialogue remains firm and irreversible" (DP 54). The entire first part of DP ends with this declaration.

Proclaiming Jesus Christ

The second part of the document, entitled "Proclaiming Jesus Christ," is made up of eight short sections: 1. The Mandate from the Risen Lord; 2. The Role of the Church; 3. The Content of Proclamation; 4. The Presence and Power of the Holy Spirit; 5. The Urgency of Proclamation; 6. The Manner of Proclamation; 7. Obstacles to Proclamation; 8. Proclamation in the Evangelizing Mission of the Church. It will immediately be noticed that this structure does not entirely coincide with that of the first part. Such was not the case with the First Draft of the document where the structure of the first and second parts were closely similar. The second part was divided as follows: 1. The Church Commissioned by the Risen Lord to Announce the Good News; 2. Proclamation — Announcing in the Evangelizing Mission of the Church; 3. Forms and Ways of Proclamation; 4. The Goal of Proclamation; 5. Obstacles to Proclamation. This by itself goes to show that the second part of DP has undergone important changes in the course of composition, principally during its second stage under the mixed redaction committee. We follow here the final, official text, limiting ourselves to comments and critical observations that appear to be of some importance.

The first section begins by recalling the mandate given by the Risen Lord to the disciples to proclaim the Good News (DP 55). The first four drafts of the document were satisfied to note the different nuances that are found in the different versions of the Lord's mandate (Mt 28:18-20; Mk 16:15-16; Lk 24:46-48; Acts 1:8; Jn 20:21): "Matthew speaks of making disciples, baptizing, teaching; Mark of announcing the Good News to all creatures; Luke uses the term witnessing and Acts adds that the witness must reach to the ends of the world; John, for his part, speaks of being sent as Jesus himself was sent by the Father." The final text quotes in full each of the five versions, to reach the same conclusion: "Announcing the Good News to all, witnessing, making disciples, baptizing, teaching, all these aspects enter into the Church's evangelizing mission, yet they need to be seen in the light of the mission accomplished by Jesus himself" (DP 55).

This return to Jesus's own practice to perceive the full extent of the Church's mission is important, for failure to do this has often resulted in reducing evangelization to proclamation and the sacramentalization of conversion to Christianity. We have seen how the first part of the document sought a biblical foundation for dialogue as constituting part of evangelization in the practice of Jesus during his earthly life (DP 21-22); the same would apply even more clearly where involvement for justice and human liberation is concerned.

Where proclamation is concerned, return to the Jesus of history consists in recalling Jesus's own proclamation of the Gospel. The text does it by calling to mind Mark's programmatic summary of Jesus's ministry, at the beginning of his Gospel: "The time is fulfilled, and the Kingdom of God is at hand; repent and believe in the Gospel (Mk 1:15)" (DP 56). The Kingdom of God is thus, from the beginning, and will remain throughout, at the center of Jesus's entire ministry. DP expresses it well in a text that is worth quoting:

> Jesus does not proclaim this Good News of the Kingdom by word alone, but also by his actions, attitudes and options, indeed by means of his whole life and finally through his death and resurrection. His parables, his miracles, the exorcisms he works, all are related to the Kingdom of God which he announces. This Kingdom moreover is not just something to be preached, quite unrelated to his own person. Jesus makes it clear that it is through him and in him that the Reign of God is breaking through into the world (cf. Lk 17:20-21), that in him the Kingdom has already come upon us, even though it still needs to grow to its fullness. (DP 56)

DP specifies further that Jesus's teaching is confirmed by his life, and reciprocally his deeds explained by his words; and again, that while Jesus bears witness to the truth, God his Father bears witness to him (DP 57).

A second brief section, devoted to "The Role of the Church," states that "it is against this background that the mandate given by the Risen Lord to the Apostolic Church needs to be understood" (DP 58). The Kingdom of God must be at the center of the Church's proclamation as it was at the center of Jesus's own proclamation: "The Church's mission is to proclaim the Kingdom of God established on earth in Jesus Christ, through his life, death and resurrection, as God's decisive and universal offer of salvation to the world. . . . There is continuity between the Kingdom preached by Jesus and the mystery of Christ announced by the Church" (DP 58).

The Christocentric character of the Church's proclamation is thus forcibly expressed: the Church announces the Kingdom realized by God in Jesus Christ, not herself. The same is further stressed where DP adds that the Church "is at the service of this Kingdom and 'witnesses' to it." This includes "witness to faith in Christ, the Savior, since this is the very heart of the Church's own faith and life" (DP 59). The final version of the text introduces here a quotation from LG 5 to the effect that the Church is "the seed and beginning" of the Kingdom. This quotation was absent in the Fourth Draft of the document and the appropriateness of adding it here may be questioned. The reason is that this text (as also LG 3) seems to identify the Kingdom present in history with the Church, while the document meant to emphasize the Kingdom-centeredness of the Church's proclamation as opposed to a self-proclamation. We have already noted earlier, in relation to part I, that a tension remains in DP between two tendencies regarding the relationship between the Kingdom and the Church in history: that which distinguishes them and that which tends to identify them. The first tendency was clear in the early redaction of DP; the second has been reintroduced in the document at a late stage.

The next section is devoted to the "content of proclamation." This section — now the longest of the second part — was entirely missing in the Fifth Draft presented to the 1990 Assembly of the PCID. The request for such a section was made by the Assembly itself. A draft was thus prepared during the assembly and submitted for its approval. This text, voted by the assembly, limited itself to exposing the content of proclamation in terms of the early "kerygma," specifically of Peter's speech on the day of Pentecost as reported by Acts (Acts 2:22-36) and followed by the "invitation made by Peter to his hearers to repent, to become disciples of Jesus Christ by being baptized in his name for the forgiveness of sins, and thus to receive the gift of the Holy Spirit (Acts 2:37-38)." In the final document, however, the text approved by the assembly for this section is much abridged (DP 60); but a long development is added, comprising not only Peter's speech before the Sanhedrin (Acts 4) and the Cornelius episode (Acts 10) (DP 60), but also a long development on Paul (DP 61) and on John (DP 62). "The universal nature of the Christian message of salvation" is now being stressed everywhere, as expressed in Acts 4:11-12; 10:44-45; Eph 3:8-11; 1 Tim 2:4-6; Jn 4:42; 1 Jn 4:14.

This much-amplified development of the content of proclamation ends up with one more paragraph where Jesus Christ is shown once again to be the center of the Church's proclamation of the word — a word full of power:

> The content of [the word] is expressed in different ways: it is the Kingdom (cf. Acts 20:25), the Gospel of the Kingdom (cf. Mt 24:14), the Gospel of God (cf. Mk 1:14; 1 Th 2:9). But these different formulations really mean the same thing: to preach Jesus (cf. Acts 9:20; 19:13), to preach Christ (cf. Acts 8:5). Just as Jesus spoke God's own words (cf. Jn 3:34), so the apostles preach the word of God, for Jesus whom they preach is the Word. . . . This is the word of God which is to be proclaimed by Christians. (DP 63)

The power of the word that the Church proclaims, the next section explains, comes from the Holy Spirit, who "both prompts her proclamation and leads the hearers to obedience of faith" (DP 64). This is explained with a long quotation from EN 75, where Paul VI concluded — but this is not quoted here — that the Holy Spirit is the "principal agent of evangelization" (EN 75). Instead, DP concludes equivalently that "the witness by which the Spirit brings men and women to know Jesus as Lord is no human achievement but God's own work" (DP 65).

In order to establish in the next section "the urgency of proclamation," DP has recourse to Paul's sense of urgency in Rom 10:14-17: "faith comes from hearing," and 1 Cor 9:16: "necessity is laid upon me" — a sense of urgency that Paul VI echoes in EN: "The presentation of the Gospel message is not optional for the Church. It is her duty, by command of the Lord Jesus, so that men may believe and be saved. This message is indeed a necessary one. It is unique and irreplaceable. It allows of neither indifference, syncretism, nor compromise, for it concerns the salvation of mankind" (EN 5; cf. 42) (DP 66). Another lengthy quotation, this time from AG 13, establishes that "proclamation is a response to the human aspiration for salvation" (DP 67).

Explaining "the manner of proclamation," the next section first explains that the Church's task is not exercised in a complete void. "For the Holy Spirit, the Spirit of Christ, is present and active among the hearers of the Good News even before the Church's missionary action comes into operation (cf. RH 12; DEV 53)" (DP 68). Linking here with what was stated in the first part, the text adds:

> They [the hearers of the Good News] may in many cases have already responded implicitly to God's offer of salvation in Jesus Christ, *a sign of this being the sincere practice of their own religious traditions*, insofar as these contain authentic religious values. They may have already been touched by the Spirit and in some way associated unknowingly to the paschal mystery of Jesus Christ (cf. GS 22). (DP 68, emphasis mine)

The words italicized by us in this quotation link with what DP 29 had said earlier, to the effect that the mystery of salvation of members of other religious traditions in Jesus Christ, through their unconscious association with his paschal mystery, passes through the sincere practice of their religious tradition. This important link between DP's first and second part goes back to the document's first stage of composition, being already present — in a more direct form — in the First Draft of the document.

The same is true where the next paragraph (DP 69) is concerned. It further explains that in her way of proclamation the Church ought to be "mindful of what God has already accomplished" in those she addresses. This must mean "learning from Jesus himself," from the "divine pedagogy" with which he "progressively revealed to his hearers the meaning of the Kingdom, God's plan of salvation realized in his own mystery" (ibid.). Only gradually did Jesus unveil to them the implications of his message, his identity as the Son of God, the scandal of his cross. Even his closest disciples reached full faith in him only through their Easter experience. "Those who wish to become disciples of Jesus today will pass through the same process of discovery and commitment" (ibid.). Hence the Church's proclamation must be "both progressive and patient, keeping pace with those who hear the message" (ibid.). It must also be confident, faithful, humble, respectful, and, finally, dialogical and inculturated (DP 70). Dialogical, for "the hearer of the Word is not expected to be a passive receiver"; proclamation must build on the "seeds of the Word" to lead to the full mystery of Jesus Christ (ibid.). Inculturated, that is, "incarnated in the culture and the spiritual tradition of those addressed," so that the message be perceived by the hearers as responding to their deepest aspirations, as truly the Good News they have been longing for (ibid.). To maintain these qualities in her proclamation, the Church must "live in constant dialogue with her Lord and Master" (DP 71).

The "obstacles to proclamation" are dealt with in the next section. DP mentions "some of the principal" ones, under two headings: those arising on the part of the evangelizing Church and her members ("difficulties from within") (DP 73); those affecting the hearers of the Word who would be called by God to the obedience of Christian faith ("difficulties from outside") (DP 74).

The section on "Proclamation in the Evangelizing Mission of the Church," which in the First Draft came in second place in keeping with the structure of the first part of the document, has during the second stage of composition been transposed to the end of the second part. Its content has, moreover, been considerably amended to reinforce the place of proclamation in the overall mission. This is done partly by having recourse to some passages from EN that overwhelmingly — and somewhat one-sidedly — emphasize proclamation, coming close to identifying it with evangelization and the Church activities deriving from it.[14]

In its final form, this section of DP recalls that, while the Church's evangelizing mission has "sometimes" been reduced to proclamation, "gradually a broader understanding of evangelization has developed, in which proclamation of the mystery of Christ nevertheless remains central" (DP 75). Admittedly, Vatican II, when dealing with the Church's missionary activity in AG 11-13, mentions solidarity with humankind, dialogue and collaboration, before speaking about the preaching of the Gospel. Yet, notwithstanding the "broad sense" of evangelization put forward by Paul VI in EN (18-20; 21-22),[15] the same pope teaches nevertheless that "evangelization will *always* entail, as the *simultaneous foundation*, core and summit of its dynamism a clear proclamation" of Jesus Christ (EN 27) (DP 75, emphasis mine), and that "*there is no true evangelization*, if the name, the teaching, the life, the promises, the Kingdom and the mystery of Jesus of Nazareth, the Son of God, are not proclaimed" (EN 22; emphasis in original). This last text of Paul VI is not explicitly quoted in DP 75, but referred to, with the comment: "Evangelization would be incomplete without it [proclamation] (EN 22)" (DP 76); which in turn is further explained, saying: "Without this central element the others, though in themselves genuine forms of the Church's mission, would lose their cohesion and vitality" (ibid.).

In its final form the document immediately goes on to say:

It is clear therefore that in situations where, for political or other reasons, proclamation as such is practically impossible, the Church is already carrying out her evangelizing mission not only through presence and witness but also through such activities as work for integral development and dialogue. (DP 76; emphasis mine)

It may not be out of place to point out the lack of logic that is apparent here: the "centrality" of proclamation without which other forms of evangelization "would lose their cohesion and vitality" is understood to explain ("therefore") that through those other activities "the Church is already carrying out her evangelizing mission." The puzzle is solved by turning to Draft Four from which one sentence preceding: "It is clear, therefore," has been omitted during the 1990 Plenary Assembly. It read: "This should not be taken to mean that these other activities are ordained only to proclamation, as a preparation for it. They are in themselves genuine forms of the Church's mission. It is clear, therefore, ..." The restitution of the lost sentence would reestablish the logic and the sequence of the passage. Its suppression, on the contrary, is quite symptomatic.

For this, together with the immediately preceding observations, goes to show that a certain tension remains in the text between, on the one hand, the recognition of dialogue and other activities of the Church as "genuine forms of the Church's mission" and, on the other, the "centrality," even the necessity of proclamation, as "simultaneous foundation" "always" required in evangelization, professed by EN

---

14. See the analysis of the relevant passages of EN, here above.
15. See the analysis of these texts, here above.

and resumed from it by DP at the second stage of composition. The question must be asked how interreligious dialogue can *by itself*, prior to, and eventually in the absence of proclamation, be a genuine form of evangelization, if proclamation needs to be present *always*, as its *simultaneous foundation* without which "there is no true evangelization," as the quotations from EN supposes to which recourse is being had. Clearly, the relationship between dialogue and proclamation is not perfectly sorted out here, and some ambiguity has been introduced in the text. It remains to be seen whether the ambiguity is lifted up in the document's third part where the relationship between the two elements is treated more explicitly.

Interreligious Dialogue and Proclamation

The third part of DP contains five brief sections: 1. Interrelated yet not Interchangeable; 2. The Church and Religions; 3. Proclaiming Jesus Christ; 4. Commitment to the One Mission; 5. Jesus our Model. These titles suffice by themselves to indicate that this third part, perhaps unavoidably, partly repeats things already said. In our commentary we attempt to bring out what is new, and specifically to show more accurately than has yet been done, the precise relationship between dialogue and proclamation.

The first section states, from the outset, that

> Interreligious dialogue and proclamation, though not on the same level, are both authentic elements of the Church's evangelizing mission. Both are legitimate and necessary. They are intimately related, but not interchangeable. . . . The two activities remain distinct, but . . . one and the same local Church, one and the same person, can be diversely engaged in both. (DP 77)

It goes on to say that in actual fact "the way of fulfilling the Church's mission depends upon the particular circumstances." This supposes sensitivity to the situation and attentiveness to the "signs of the times," a true "spirituality of dialogue" (DP 78).

The second section returns to dialogue. It shows that, independently of people's response to Jesus, whether this be positive or negative, "the Church's mission extends to all"; indeed it extends to the religions themselves inasmuch as the witness to Gospel values given by the Church in dialogue may exercise a "prophetic role" in raising questions for the other religions; but in the process the Church "may find herself challenged" by the others. Thus, "the members of the Church and the followers of other religions find themselves to be companions on the common path which humanity is called to tread" (DP 79). The Fourth Draft was here more straightforward; it had: "find themselves to be companions on the way to the Kingdom," which corresponded better to the quotation from John Paul II speaking of "a fraternal journey in which we accompany one another toward the transcendental goal which he [God] sets for us" (ibid.).

Besides fostering dialogue between herself and the other religious traditions, the Church encourages it "even among these religious traditions themselves" (DP 80). The Spirit invites her to encourage all religious institutions and movements to collaboration in the promotion of the values of the Kingdom. In this manner, "interreligious dialogue is truly part of the dialogue of salvation initiated by God" (ibid.).

The third section returns again to proclamation. It recalls that proclamation "aims at guiding people to explicit knowledge of what God has done for all men and women in Jesus Christ, and at inviting them to be disciples of Jesus through becoming members of the Church" (DP 81). It also recalls that proclamation "will often need to be done in a progressive manner," keeping pace with the growth of the hearers in the obedience of faith. It calls for discernment "concerning how God is present in each one's personal history" (ibid.). The witness of the Christian community or a personal profession of faith in Jesus's true identity may become a challenge for the others, to whom, eventually, Jesus's decisive question can be asked: "Who do you say that I am?" "The true answer to this question can come only through faith." In fact, the "preaching and the confession, under the movement of grace, that Jesus of Nazareth is the Son of God the Father, the Risen Lord and Savior, constitutes the final stage of proclamation. One who freely professes this faith is invited to become a disciple of Jesus in his Church and to take a responsible part in her mission" (ibid.).

At this stage DP returns to the relationship between dialogue and proclamation as two ways of the same mission: "All Christians are called to be personally involved in these two ways of carrying out the one mission of the Church, namely proclamation and dialogue" (DP 82). Incidentally, it may be noted that the order between both has been surreptitiously inverted here; the text approved by the 1990 PCID had "dialogue and proclamation." The concrete way of involvement, it is said once more, will depend on circumstances. However, the text goes on to explain, Christians must always bear in mind that

> dialogue . . . does not constitute the whole mission of the Church, that it cannot simply replace proclamation, but remains oriented toward proclamation insofar as the dynamic process of the Church's evangelizing mission reaches in it its climax and its fullness. (DP 82)

This statement — which in substance is resumed from the First Draft, though it was strangely omitted in the Fourth Draft as also in the text approved by the 1990 Plenary Assembly — expresses more clearly than any other the relationship between dialogue and proclamation, and allows us to clear up the ambiguity that remained hitherto present. For clarity's sake, four distinct ways of conceiving of the relationship may be distinguished: 1. Dialogue is but a "means" for proclamation, not in itself an "authentic form" of evangelization; 2. Dialogue is part of evangelization but needs at all times and in any circumstances to be accompanied by proclamation, without which "there is no true evangelization"; 3. Dialogue is in itself an authentic form of evangelization, yet remains "oriented" toward proclamation without which evangelization remains incomplete and in which its dynamic process reaches its "climax and fullness"; 4. Dialogue and proclamation are "interchangeable" and therefore simply objects of free choice on the part of the evangelizers. Of these four views, DP had thus far successfully excluded 1 and 4. However, ambiguity remained as to the way in which to conceive that dialogue and proclamation are "not on the same level." The recourse made in part two of DP to EN 22 and 27 seemed to pull strongly toward 2; here, on the contrary, 3 is unambiguously stated. By doing so, DP links with D&M where the evangelizing mission had been stated to be a "single but complex and articulated reality," that is, a dynamic process that culminates in proclamation (D&M 13).

DP goes on to show the way in which from dialogue the Church's mission will, eventually, take on the form of proclamation. Having discovered the "seeds of the Word" sown in people's hearts and in their religious traditions, having further discerned "the positive values in the human search for the unknown or the incompletely known God," Christians in dialogue will find themselves involved with their partners in a process of asking questions and receiving explanations from each other. In such situations, Christians "have the duty of responding to their partners' expectations regarding the contents of the Christian faith, of bearing witness to this faith when this is called for, of giving an account of the hope that is within them (1 Pet 3:15)" (DP 82). Indeed, in such "dialogical approach" they will "hope and desire to share with others their joy in knowing and following Jesus Christ, Lord and Savior" (DP 83). In the last analysis, "we are here at the heart of the mystery of love." As the document says beautifully:

> Insofar as the Church and Christians have a deep love for the Lord Jesus, the desire to share him with others is motivated not merely by obedience to the Lord's command, but by this love itself. (DP 83)

But it goes on to note: "It should not be surprising, but quite normal, that the followers of other religions should also desire sincerely to share their faith" (DP 83). As Christians we must make space for them to do so; for "all dialogue implies reciprocity and aims at banishing fear and aggressiveness" (ibid.). The section ends appropriately by noting the need for Christians to "be prepared to follow wherever in God's providence and design the Spirit is leading them"; for to him it belongs "to inspire both the Church's proclamation and the obedience of faith," while "it is for us to be attentive to [his] promptings" (DP 84).

In every event, "whether proclamation be possible or not, the Church pursues her mission in full respect for freedom, through interreligious dialogue, witnessing to and sharing the Gospel values." This conclusion confirms once more that dialogue — informed by witness, as it must be in all circumstances — is by itself a form of evangelization, even in the absence of proclamation. In it, Christians and others respond to the call of God inviting them "to enter into the mystery of his patience," who alone knows the "times and stages" of the long human quest for light and truth (ibid.).

The last section turns to Jesus, our "model and guide in the commitment to both proclamation and dialogue," who alone can say to a sincere religious person: "You are not far from the Kingdom of God" (Mk 12:34) (DP 85). Christians must not only imitate Jesus, but "join him in his unique offering on behalf of the whole of humanity" (DP 86). The bread and wine for which he gave thanks "symbolized the entire creation." As through the ministry of the Church Jesus goes on to offer sacramentally his one sacrifice, Christians are united with him, offering thanks to God for "whatever is good and praiseworthy" (Ph 4:8) and on behalf of the whole world. Here too "they draw the grace of discernment, to be able to read the signs of the Spirit's presence and to recognize the favorable time and right manner of proclaiming Jesus Christ" (DP 86).

As was noted earlier, the conclusion of the document stresses the need to give "special attention" to relations with the followers of each religion in particular (DP 87). For which, "specific studies on the relationship between dialogue and proclamation [should] be undertaken, taking into account each religion within its geographical area and its sociocultural context" (DP 88). DP ends on a prayerful note: "Dialogue and proclamation are difficult tasks, and yet absolutely necessary. . . . Yet more than tasks to be accomplished, [they] are graces to be sought in prayer. May all continually implore the help of the Holy Spirit so that he may be 'the divine inspirer of their plans, their initiatives and their evangelizing activity' (EN 75)" (DP 89).

III. A COMPARISON OF DP AND RM
ON DIALOGUE AND PROCLAMATION

The introduction to this study has already explained that the purpose of RM and DP differs vastly, the intent of RM being much broader, that of DP more restricted. It has also shown the relationship that exists between the papal encyclical and the dicasterial document, taking into account the time of composition and the possible reciprocal influence that results. These factors must be kept in mind, as a brief comparison is here established between the two documents, and more pointedly between the section that RM dedicates to "Dialogue with our Brothers and Sisters of Other Religions" (55-57), among other "paths of mission," and the doctrine developed in DP on the same subject. Our introduction has already noted that distinct approaches and nuances are noticeable between the two documents. Our aim here is to bring to light the commonalities and divergences between them on some salient points concerning the other religious traditions, dialogue and proclamation, and the interrelationship between both.

1. RM does not devote a section to a Christian evaluation of the other religious traditions as a premise for its treatment of interreligious dialogue. This does not, however, mean that it contains no elements for such an evaluation on which to base the practice of dialogue. But, rather than being systematically organized, these elements are spread over the first, more doctrinal chapters of the encyclical. Especially worthy of note in this regard is RM's insistence on the universal, operative presence of the Holy Spirit, without limits of space and time, not only in persons, but also in the religious traditions to which they belong. The main texts have already been mentioned earlier. The presence and activity of the Spirit "affect not only individuals but also society and history, peoples, cultures, and religions" (RM 28). "It is the Spirit who sows the 'seeds of the Word' present in various customs (*ritibus*) and cultures, preparing them for full maturity in Christ" (ibid.). He was active before Christ was glorified, even as he works today outside the boundaries of the Church — though never without reference to Christ (RM 29).

DP believes that the attitude of Christians toward the members of other religious traditions will depend on their appraisal of those traditions. An open attitude in inter religious dialogue can only be based on a positive evaluation of the religions themselves. This is why DP devotes a large section to this subject (DP 14-32). It recalls that Vatican II has given the lead for such a positive assessment, affirming not only that salvation in Jesus Christ is open to all persons of good will (DP 15), but also the presence in the traditions themselves of "positive values" — rays of the truth and "seeds of the Word" (DP 16) — which the Council attributed to the active presence of God through his Word, pointing also to the universal action of the Spirit (DP 17). In an important text that bears being quoted a second time, DP itself affirms that

> all men and women who are saved share, though differently, in the same mystery of salvation in Jesus Christ through his Spirit. Christians know this through their faith, while others remain unaware that Jesus Christ is the source of their salvation. The mystery of salvation reaches out to them, in a way known to God, through the invisible action of the Spirit of God. (DP 29)

2. Another point of contact between RM and DP, besides the universal action of the Spirit, has to do with the relation between the Church and the Reign of God, and the implications of this for a theology of religions. A close analysis of the relevant passages of *Lumen Gentium* (3, 5, 9, 48) of Vatican II would show, as has been suggested earlier, that, while the Council distinguished clearly the Church and the Reign of God present in history from their full realization in the end of time, it continued to identify the Reign of God with the Church, whether in their historical reality or their eschatological fulfillment. The same would be true also of the document of the International Theological Commission on "Select Themes on Ecclesiology on the Occasion of the Twentieth Anniversary of the Conclusion of the Second

Vatican Council" in its chapter X entitled "The Eschatological Character of the Church: Kingdom and Church."[16] RM and DP appear to be the first two documents of the recent central doctrinal authority to distinguish the pilgrim Church from the reality of the Reign of God in history; both documents profess that the Reign of God is a broader reality than the Church, which is present and operative beyond her boundaries among the members of other religious traditions.

According to RM the specific role of the Church at the service of the Reign of God consists primarily and fundamentally in the proclamation of the Gospel by which people are called to conversion; secondly in the foundation of new particular Churches; she also serves the Kingdom by "spreading throughout the world the 'Gospel values' " (RM 20). In this context, RM notes:

> The inchoate reality of the Kingdom can also be found beyond the confines of the Church among peoples everywhere, to the extent that they live "Gospel values" and are open to the working of the Spirit who breathes when and where he wills (cf. Jn 3:8). But it must immediately be added that this temporal dimension of the Kingdom remains incomplete unless it is related to the Kingdom of Christ present in the Church and straining toward eschatological fullness. (RM 20)

In fact, the Church is sacrament of salvation for all humankind and her activity is not restricted to those who accept her message (ibid.). For those outside she is sacrament, insofar as she promotes the Gospel values through dialogue, human promotion, and so on; finally she serves the Kingdom by her intercession (ibid.).

It is in connection with the place of interreligious dialogue in the mission of the Church that DP explains the relationship between the Church and the Kingdom. It first resumes the teaching of Vatican II on the Church as the universal sacrament, that is, sign and instrument, of salvation (LG 1, 48) (DP 33). Having noted that the relationship between the Church and the Kingdom is "mysterious and complex," it quotes John Paul II to the effect that "the Kingdom is inseparable from the Church, because both are inseparable from the person and work of Jesus himself" (DP 34). The members of other religious traditions are "oriented" (*ordinantur*) (cf. LG 16) to the Church, as to the sacrament in which the Kingdom of God is already present "in mystery" (LG 3); but they already share in some way in "the reality which is signified by the Kingdom" (DP 35). In fact, DP goes on to say, part of the Church's role at the service of the Kingdom

> consists in recognizing that the inchoate reality of this Kingdom can be found also beyond the confines of the Church, for example in the hearts of the followers of other religious traditions, insofar as they live evangelical values and are open to the action of the Spirit. (35)

The Kingdom of God is thus recognized to be, in history, a wider reality than the Church, even though the following caution is added:

> It must be remembered nevertheless that this is indeed an inchoate reality, which needs to find completion through being related to the Kingdom of Christ already present in the Church yet realized fully only in the world to come. (35)

16. See M. Sharkey (ed.), *International Theological Commission, Texts and Documents 1969-1985* (San Francisco: Ignatius Press, 1989), pp. 267-304, and the study entitled "L'Eglise, le Règne et les 'autres,' " mentioned in note 12.

It was necessary here to quote extensively to allow the close similarity between RM and DP to stand out, both as regards the affirmation of the presence of the Kingdom outside the Church, and the added caution that relates this "inchoate reality" to her. Between RM and DP there is here more than a fortuitous point of contact, a clear dependence. In what direction? If it be remembered, as has been indicated earlier, that in DP the caution of the last sentence is a last-moment addition, the direction in which dependence must be seen, as far as that last sentence is concerned, is clear by itself.

3. Yet another point of contact worth noting is that both RM and DP develop a broad concept of the evangelizing mission of the Church, according to which evangelization is not reduced to proclamation and the Church activities deriving from it, but comprises as integral parts other activities, such as interreligious dialogue and others. Dialogue and proclamation are two distinct elements or expressions of the same evangelizing mission.

Interreligious dialogue, RM states, "is a part of the Church's evangelizing mission" (RM 55); it is "one of its expressions" (ibid.); and, moreover, "a path toward the Kingdom" (RM 57). These affirmations imply a broad view of the concept of evangelization. Interreligious dialogue and proclamation appear as "two elements" or distinct expressions of evangelization. Between both forms there is no opposition, but, at once, a close link and distinction. This is explained as follows:

> These two elements must maintain both their intimate connection and their distinctiveness; therefore, they should not be confused, manipulated [*strumentalizzati*], or regarded as identical, as though they were interchangeable. (RM 55)

That dialogue cannot be "manipulated" means that it cannot be reduced to being a means for proclamation, but must be viewed as a form of evangelization in its own right. That the two elements are not "interchangeable" or "identical" means that the practice of one or the other is not simply a matter of choice on the part of the evangelizer. However, while the two elements are said to be "distinct" forms of evangelization, it is also said, on the other hand, that "dialogue does not dispense from evangelization" (RM 55). We have observed, in passing, that in this passage evangelization is again, surreptitiously and implicitly, identified with proclamation. A certain ambiguity thus remains in the terminology used by RM, which here falls back on a narrow view of evangelization.

DP, on the contrary, began by providing clear definitions of the terms of evangelization (DP 8), dialogue (DP 9) and proclamation (DP 10), where the broad concept of evangelization stands out clearly as comprising dialogue as well as proclamation — a usage from which DP never departs.

That dialogue and proclamation are distinct, but related, expressions of the Church's evangelizing mission is clearly expressed in DP's following passage:

> Interreligious dialogue and proclamation, though not on the same level, are both authentic elements of the Church's evangelizing mission. Both are legitimate and necessary. They are intimately related, but not interchangeable. . . . The two activities remain distinct, but as experience shows, one and the same local Church, one and the same person, can be diversely engaged in both. (DP 77)

The point of contact with RM is once more clearly apparent. The same terminology is partly used to show the "distinction" between the two forms of evangelization and their "non-interchangeability."

4. Among the differences worth registering because of their theological implications, one regards the role played by the other religious traditions in the mystery of the salvation of their members in Jesus Christ. RM says nothing explicit on the subject, while stressing (as mentioned above) that the Holy Spirit is at work not only in the persons, but in the religious traditions to which they belong (RM 28, quoted above).

DP, on the contrary, goes beyond the affirmation of Vatican II according to which salvation in Jesus Christ reaches out to the others through their obedience to the dictates of their conscience (LG 16). It notes, in agreement with RM, that the mystery of salvation reaches them "through the invisible action of the Spirit of God" (DP 29). But it also indicates the role that their religious tradition plays in the mystery of their salvation in Jesus Christ:

> Concretely, it will be in the sincere practice of what is good in their own religious traditions and by following the dictates of their conscience that the members of other religions respond positively to God's invitation and receive salvation in Jesus Christ, even while they do not recognize or acknowledge him as their savior. (DP 29)

The members of other religions, then, are not saved by Christ in spite of, or beside, their own tradition, but in the sincere practice of it, and, in some mysterious way, through it. This does not, however, mean that everything in the other traditions can be conducive to the salvation of their members. In fact, to identify in them the "elements of grace capable of sustaining the positive response of their members to God's invitation" is a difficult task, requiring discernment (DP 30). Not everything in them is the result of grace, nor do they contain only positive values; "for sin has been at work in the world" and the traditions "reflect the limitations of the human spirit, sometimes inclined to choose evil" (DP 31).

5. Another significant difference consists in the distinct emphasis given in the two documents to interreligious dialogue. In RM dialogue is mentioned late in the chapter on "The Paths of Mission" (or forms of evangelization), after witness, proclamation, conversion, and baptism, forming local Churches, even after ecclesial basic communities and inculturation — though before promoting human development. The emphasis remains overwhelmingly on proclamation, which is what "missionary activity proper," that is, mission to the nations, is about (RM 34), and has the "permanent priority" (RM 44). In comparison, DP places more emphasis on interreligious dialogue. Where RM's main intention is to reaffirm strongly the relevance and urgency of proclamation, the primary concern of DP is that the significance of dialogue be not undervalued.

Moreover, the perspective of RM appears more ecclesiocentric in comparison with that of DP, which is more Christocentric. According to RM, "missionary activity proper" can "be characterized as the work of proclaiming Christ and his Gospel, building up the local Church and promoting the values of the Kingdom" (34); "the mission *ad gentes* has this objective: to found Christian communities and develop Churches to their full maturity" (RM 48). Emphasis is thus placed, in an ecclesiocentric perspective, on the building up of the Church. By contrast, DP's perspective is more Christocentric; linking with its predecessor of 1984 (D&M 13), it defines the mission of the Church simply in terms of evangelization (DP 8), and the "single but complex and articulated reality" of evangelization as comprising, among other elements, interreligious dialogue and proclamation (DP 2, 8, 82, referred to above).

6. Coming to the relation between dialogue and proclamation: It has already been seen that both RM and DP state clearly that they constitute distinct elements in the evangelizing mission of the Church, not to be confused nor separated (cf. RM 55 and DP 77, quoted above). RM states that they cannot be "manipulated," by which is implicitly meant that dialogue cannot be reduced to a "means" for proclamation. DP affirms equivalently that dialogue "possesses its own validity" (DP 41). As for their interrelationship, in the Church's mission, RM states the "permanent priority" of proclamation in virtue of which "all forms of missionary activity are directed to this proclamation" (RM 44). This priority must not be understood as temporal, as if proclamation had in all circumstances to precede other forms of evangelization, for it will be said thereafter that interreligious dialogue is often the "only way of bearing sincere witness to Christ and offering generous service to others" (RM 57). The "permanent priority" is of a logical and ideal order of importance: proclamation has a "central and irreplaceable role" (RM 44). DP, on its part, affirms unambiguously that "interreligious dialogue and proclamation . . . (are) not on the same level," but their relation is explained more theologically, saying that dialogue "remains oriented toward proclamation insofar as the dynamic process of the Church's evangelizing mission reaches in it its climax and its fullness" (DP 82).

7. Finally, the question may be asked whether and to what extent RM and DP have gone beyond what was previously affirmed by the central teaching authority with regard to the topics under consideration. Two main points may be made.

The positive attitude of Vatican II toward the other religious traditions is well known (cf. LG 16-17; NA; AG 3, 7-9, 11; GS 22). However, the Council, while recognizing positive values and "elements of truth and grace" (AG 9) in those traditions, did not assign them a role in the salvation of their members through Jesus Christ. DP, if not RM, represents a positive step in that direction. On the other hand, both RM and DP, as noted above, go beyond the Council in recognizing the operative presence of the Reign of God beyond the boundaries of the Church, in the other religious traditions.

Secondly, Vatican II recommended dialogue with the other religious traditions (NA 2; GS 92), but without stating that it is an integral part of the evangelizing mission of the Church. This is clearly affirmed both by RM and DP, following the lead of D&M. Furthermore, some ambiguity in RM's terminology notwithstanding, both RM and DP develop a broad concept of evangelization, which was not yet found in Vatican II; both assert, though in different ways, that dialogue cannot be reduced to a "means" for proclamation, but has value in itself. In these and other ways RM and DP, with their distinct emphases and nuances, constitute a step forward in the Church's doctrine on religions, evangelization, dialogue, and proclamation.

CONCLUSION

The Introduction of DP explained the reasons why it seemed important to clarify the relationship between interreligious dialogue and proclamation (DP 4). It mentioned in the first place the "new awareness of the fact of religious plurality" in today's world: "In the present context of religious plurality, the important role played by religious traditions cannot be overlooked" (DP 4a). Second, interreligious dialogue as envisaged by Vatican II "is only gradually coming to be understood";

further examination of the question may help to stimulate dialogue (DP 4b). Thirdly, "the practice of dialogue raises problems in the minds of many." Some of the questions raised were explicitly mentioned:

> There are those who would seem to think, erroneously, that in the Church's mission today dialogue should simply replace proclamation. At the other extreme, some fail to see the value of interreligious dialogue. Yet others are perplexed and ask: If interreligious dialogue has become so important, has the proclamation of the Gospel message lost its urgency? Has the effort to bring people into the community of the Church become secondary or even superfluous? (DP 4c)

In view of these questions, there is need for "doctrinal and pastoral guidance," to which DP hoped "to contribute, without pretending to answer fully the many and complex questions which arise in this connection" (DP 4c).

In conclusion to this study we may ask whether and to what extent DP has fulfilled its task in answering the questions it raised explicitly. It may be said that it has to a great extent. It has shown that interreligious dialogue and proclamation are both "distinct" and "necessary," that dialogue is "important," yet without proclamation having thereby become "secondary or even superfluous." It has further shown the "value" of dialogue while stating clearly that it cannot "simply replace" proclamation. It has elaborated their respective role and mutual relationship in the "single but complex and articulated reality" (DP 2) of the Church's evangelizing mission (DP 77): evangelization is a "dynamic process" that reaches "its climax and its fullness" in proclamation (DP 82).

However, our analysis of the document has shown that a certain tension remains in it between different tendencies, as the document was subject to two distinct influences. Compromise formulations have had to be sought, not without introducing some ambiguity. Thus, while, on the one hand, interreligious dialogue is said to be in itself an authentic form of evangelization (DP 77), even, if circumstances are such, in the absence of proclamation (DP 76), on the other hand, following EN 27 and 22, evangelization is said "always to entail as simultaneous foundation" a clear proclamation of Jesus Christ, which is the "central element" without which the others, "though in themselves genuine forms of the Church's mission, would lose their cohesion and vitality" (DP 76). If proclamation needs to be present always, is dialogue *in itself* a genuine form of evangelization? And can it be maintained that *both* are "absolutely necessary" (DP 89)?

This ambiguity has not escaped the attention of a commentator, who wrote:

> The overall impression one gets from the document is that it makes proclamation more important and makes dialogue subordinate to proclamation although it also states that both dialogue and proclamation are absolutely necessary. Here arises a question: Can we make dialogue subsidiary to proclamation and yet carry it out really as absolutely necessary?
>
> If one is really subsidiary to the other, can they *both be absolutely* necessary? Or to put it in another way: if both are really taken to be absolutely necessary, can one of them be considered to be subsidiary to the other? Thus there is some lack of clarity regarding the proper relationship between the two "absolutely necessary activities." This calls for further theologizing.[17]

---

17. A. Pushparajan, "Whither Interreligious Dialogue? A Reflective Response to the

Perhaps the different tendencies to which the document has been subject and which have left their trace in its final form, can be identified in terms of the distinction sometimes made between "integral" and/or "essential" elements of evangelization. The First Draft of the document had it that "both interreligious dialogue and proclamation are authentic forms and expressions, indeed *integral* elements of the Church's evangelizing mission." No distinction was made here — intentionally — between integral and essential elements. Another tendency, however, set in later, which advocated considering interreligious dialogue as an integral element of evangelization while proclamation is essential to it; thus it would be shown that both are "not on the same level" (DP 77). The tendency represented in the First Draft's formulation refused to distinguish dialogue and proclamation as being integral and essential to evangelization, respectively. The reasons put forward were that making such distinctions would mean introducing in the document theological niceties that in other contexts have only led to unhelpful discussion; moreover, the distinction would undermine the importance of dialogue. The compromise arrived at in the final text is the following: dialogue continues to be said, as in the First Draft, "an integral element" of evangelization (DP 9, 38); proclamation, though not being called "essential," is said to be the "foundation, core and summit" without which other elements would lose "their cohesion and vitality" (75-76; 10). The same, it would seem, is what is meant in RM by the "permanent priority" of proclamation (RM 44). The same is also the reason why in the Introduction of DP a sentence was added during the 1990 Plenary Assembly of PCID, to the effect that "If dialogue is treated first, this is not because it has any *priority* over proclamation. It is simply due to the fact that dialogue is the primary concern of the Pontifical Council for Interreligious Dialogue which initiated the preparation of the document" (DP 3, emphasis mine).

However this may be, and apart from some ambiguity that the document does not succeed in avoiding, it must be recognized that a certain tension remains and must remain, in the reality of the Church's evangelizing mission, between dialogue and proclamation. It has been suggested that this tension is between the "not yet" of the Church who, together with the "others" is in history a pilgrim toward the fullness of the Kingdom, and the "already" of the Church who is in time and in the world the sacrament of the Kingdom. The tension between the "already" and the "not yet" of the Reign of God is at the center of New Testament eschatology: already established by God in Jesus Christ, the Kingdom must grow through history toward its fullness in the end of times. The present time, often called the "time of the Church," is in reality that of the growth of the Reign of God toward its eschatological fullness. The tension between the "already" and the "not yet" is reflected in the Church's evangelizing mission and, markedly so, in the interrelationship within it between interreligious dialogue and proclamation: Insofar as the Church remains on her pilgrimage, together with the "others," toward the fullness of the Kingdom, she engages with them in dialogue; insofar as she is the sacrament of the reality of the Kingdom already present and operative in history, she proclaims to them Jesus Christ in whom the Kingdom of God has been established by God.

The tension between the "already" and the "not yet" as foundation for the complementarity and interrelationship between interreligious dialogue and proclamation, has been suggested by the "Guidelines for Interreligious Dialogue," published by the Commission for Dialogue and Ecumenism of the Catholic Bishops' Conference of India (CBCI), in which we read:

Vatican Document on 'Dialogue and Proclamation,' " *Vidyajyoti Journal of Theological Reflection* 56 (1992), pp. 224-232; see 231-232.

There is a tension in the Church, and in every Christian, between the two activities [dialogue and proclamation]. This tension has to be lived through life itself and is at the source of diversified vocations and charisms in the Church. It is a tension that corresponds to the tension between the two poles of the Church's existence: "not yet" and "already." Ours is a pilgrim Church, on the way to the Father and therefore imperfect; "not yet." At the same time, she is somehow an anticipation "already" now of the eschatological renewal by the power of the Spirit (LG 48). In the former aspect of her existence it is always her duty, as it is that of all other groups and of every person, to seek from within the human community an understanding and the accomplishment of God's design for humanity. This is the basis of our dialogue. On the other hand, as the anticipation of the eschatological renewal of all things and as the sign of God's Kingdom, it would be the Church's duty to invite people to conversion through the proclamation of the eschatological event of the resurrection of Jesus Christ, a proclamation done with the authority of the Risen Lord who lives in her (Mt 28:18-20) (AG 9). (DP 36)[18]

In every event, and whichever be the way in which the articulation of dialogue and proclamation is attempted, the perspective should be that of the Kingdom of God universally present in the world, of which the Church is the sacrament and at the service of which she is placed, till it will reach in God its eschatological fullness. Such a perspective is developed in the Conclusions of a Theological Consultation organized by the Office of Evangelization of the Federation of Asian Bishops' Conferences (FABC) (10 November 1991), from which it is worthwhile quoting at length:

The Kingdom of God (established by God in Jesus Christ) is . . . universally present and at work. Wherever men and women open themselves to the transcendent divine mystery which impinges upon them and go out of themselves in love and service of fellow humans, there the Reign of God is at work. As BIRA IV/2[19] puts it: "Where God is accepted, where Gospel values are lived, where man is respected . . . , there is the Kingdom" (II,1).[20] In all such cases people respond to God's offer of grace through Christ in the Spirit and enter into the Kingdom through an act of faith. . . . Thus they become sharers of the Kingdom of God in Jesus Christ unknowingly (29).

This goes to show that the Reign of God is a universal reality, extending far beyond the boundaries of the Church. It is the reality of salvation in Jesus Christ, in which Christians and others share together; it is the fundamental "mystery of unity" which unites us more deeply than differences in religious allegiance are able to keep us apart. Seen in this manner, a "Regnocentric" approach to mission theology does not in any way threaten the Christocentric perspective of our faith; on the contrary, "Regnocentrism" calls for "Christocentrism," and vice versa, for it is in Jesus Christ and through the Christ-event

---

18. CBCI Commission for Dialogue and Ecumenism, *Guidelines for Interreligious Dialogue*, second revised edition (New Delhi: CBCI Centre, 1989), pp. 40-41.

19. Bishops' Institute for Interreligious Affairs IV/2 on "Theology of Dialogue," held at Pattaya, Thailand (17 November 1985).

20. G. B. Rosales and C. G. Arevalo (eds.), *For All the Peoples of Asia. Federation of Asian Bishops' Conferences. Documents from 1970 to 1991* (Maryknoll, N.Y.: 1992), p. 252.

that God has established his Kingdom upon the earth and in human history (cf. RM 17-18) (30).

In this universal reality of the Reign of God the Church has a unique and irreplaceable role to play. . . . "The focus of the Church's mission of evangelization is building up the Kingdom of God and building up the Church to be at the service of the Kingdom. The Kingdom is therefore wider than the Church. The Church is the sacrament of the Kingdom, making it visible, ordained to it, promoting it, but not equating itself with it" (31). . . .[21]

. . . If the Church is the sacrament of the Kingdom, the reason is that she is the sacrament of Jesus Christ himself who is the mystery of salvation, to whom she is called to bear witness and whom she is called to announce. To be at the service of the Kingdom means for the Church to announce Jesus Christ. For this task she is endowed with special gifts and charisms and guided by the Spirit (33).[22]

The document goes on to show that in the Asian context the Church must be committed to dialogue in a special way (39-46). Through dialogue Christians and others "are called to promote together" "the universal reality of the Kingdom of God in which [they] belong" (47). It then asks: "Why then does the proclamation of Jesus Christ remain necessary and urgent?" (47), and answers:

The Holy Spirit, in ways known to God, gives to all human persons the opportunity of coming into contact with the paschal mystery of Jesus Christ, and thus to obtain salvation (cf. GS 22). The Church, as the visible sign and sacrament of the mystery of salvation, is in a unique position to offer them the opportunity of sharing in this mystery in a fully human way. She alone can convey to them the explicit knowledge of Jesus Christ their Saviour and Lord and invite them to celebrate in joy and thanksgiving the mystery of his Passover at her eucharistic table. Only in the life of the Church is found the full visibility of the mystery of salvation. Only there do the children of God come to the full realization of what it means to share in the Sonship of the Son. Thereby the Church's proclamation meets the deepest longings and aspirations of the human heart for liberation and wholeness of life. There the seeds of the Word contained in the religious traditions of the world grow to maturity and come to fulfillment. In this manner the Church shares with others "the fullness of the means of salvation" (RM 18) which she has received from her Lord and Master (49).[23]

This lengthy quotation will have shown that the Kingdom of God perspective is able to overcome the dichotomy and to relax the tension between dialogue and proclamation. It allows overcoming a narrow ecclesiocentrism according to which mission would be intended for increasing Church membership and to dispense salvation where without it it would remain beyond reach. As Claude Geffré aptly observes:

---

21. The cited text is from the "Theses on Interreligious Dialogue" (1987) of the FABC Theological Advisory Commission (6, 3), *FABC Papers*, n. 48, p. 16.

22. The Conclusions of the FABC Consultation are published as "Some Theological Reflections on the Asian Context of Evangelisation," in *Sedos Bulletin* (15 February 1992), pp. 50-55.

23. Ibid.

The Church is not placed at her own service: she is entirely oriented towards the Kingdom of God that is coming. For only the Kingdom, as the fullness of God's manifestation, is absolute. . . . The abiding vocation of the Church does not consist in the quantitative increase of her members; in dialogue and collaboration with all people of good will (who may belong to other religions and spiritual families), she is called to manifest and foster the Reign of God which . . . keeps happening through the religious history of humankind, well beyond the visible boundaries of the "People of God." [24]

---

24. Claude Geffré, "La mission comme dialogue de salut," *Lumière et vie*, 205 (1992/5), pp. 33-46; see 42.

Part Three

Views from the Field

1

Mission between Dialogue and Proclamation[1]

Eric J. Sharpe

Eric J. Sharpe was born in the north of England and was educated at the Universities of Manchester and Uppsala, where he completed his doctorate in missiology in 1965. Since 1977, Sharpe has been Professor of Religious Studies at the University of Sydney, Australia. His books include *Not to Destroy but to Fulfill, Comparative Religion: A History, Faith Meets Faith: The Universal Gita,* and, most recently, *Nathan Söderblom and the Study of Religion.*

ANOMALIES IN ASPIRING
TO DIALOGUE OR TO EVANGELIZE TODAY

Pope John Paul II's encyclical letter *Redemptoris Missio* (RM) has been called "the most important official Catholic statement on the world mission of the church since the Second Vatican Council," and a "landmark document."[2] Shortly after its promulgation early in 1991 it was supplemented by *Dialogue and Proclamation* (DP), a document prepared by the Pontifical Council for Inter-Religious Dialogue and the Congregation for the Evangelization of Peoples, which set out to expand on one of the themes of RM, namely, the relationship between the proclamation of the Gospel and the practice of "interreligious dialogue." Where RM is concise and sometimes cryptic, DP at least tries to be inclusive. RM, with or without DP in tow, has already generated a considerable literature, much of it centered on whether or not it actually has contributed to a renewal of the Church's missionary commitment, and to a new springtime for missiology (RM 2).

---

1. An earlier and shorter version of this essay appeared as a review in the *South Pacific Journal of Missionary Studies* 2/1 (November 1991), pp. 19-21. Since this journal still enjoys only a very limited circulation, I have taken the liberty of reusing the title I used then, together with a phrase or two I wrote at that time. I should like to acknowledge the help of Rev. Dr. Donald M. Wodarz, S.S.C., of the Pacific Mission Institute, North Turramurra, N.S.W., in keeping me supplied with material that otherwise I should certainly have missed.
2. See *International Bulletin of Missionary Research* 15 (April 1991), p. 49 (Editorial).

Curiously, though, the greater part of that literature seems more explanatory than critical. The critical function is always a hard one to sustain, without leaving an impression of hostility. Those who have had their books or their performances reviewed by an unsympathetic reviewer know, like Kipling's toad beneath the harrow, "exactly where each tooth-point goes." [3] Conversely, the writing of reviews can be an exercise in diplomacy as much as candor, once the purely descriptive mode has been left behind. Either that, or an opportunity to demonstrate the superiority of one approach, insight, or authority over its competitors. The academic critic, however, generally knows the author whose work is being examined, and can make adjustments and allowances. That is hardly possible in this present case. I do not mean any disrespect when I say that the documents under consideration, like those of Vatican II upon which they so largely rely, are so impersonal as to be almost abstract. At the same time they aim at being comprehensive.

The church, Emil Brunner said many years ago, exists by mission as fire exists by burning. If this is so, then what the church thinks of evangelization and mission at any given time is a vital clue to that church's self-understanding. Clearly, therefore, these documents deserve careful and critical attention, not on account of who compiled them, but solely for what they say. Merely to recapitulate their arguments is not enough.

The focal point of RM and DP together — the nature of the Christian mission in the modern world and especially the appropriate attitude for Christians to adopt when approaching followers of other Ways — may be styled "theological." But it is not only theological. It is practical, and therefore open to discussion on historical and social-scientific lines. It is not only a matter of the theoretical relationship in which "Christianity" stands to other so-called "world religions," singly or collectively. It is a matter of what actually happens on the human level when men and women who confess and call themselves Christians meet other men and women who do not. That is why the historian/phenomenologist might be able to contribute to the discussion. [4]

No one who comes, like the celebrated world traveler of the Book of Job, "from going to and fro on the earth, and from walking up and down in it" (1:7) can fail to be struck by the anomaly that while ours is (or claims to be) an age of dialogue, its level of open or latent conflict, much of it having a religious dimension, remains as high as it ever was. Certainly the frontiers between the squabbling parties have shifted somewhat: in religion, we have for instance less of denominational conflict than once was common; but we have instead bitter faction-fighting, often within the same commonwealth of faith. Once, rational debate was possible on all save a narrow range of subjects. Today, almost every issue seems capable of polarizing opinion and generating bad feeling.

Ironically, the dialogue issue is one of these. [5] The conflicting, contrasting or

---

3. Rudyard Kipling, *Pagett, M.P.:* "The toad beneath the harrow knows / Exactly where each tooth-point goes. / The butterfly upon the road / Preaches contentment to that toad."

4. Since attending my first "dialogue conference" in Bombay in 1969 I have made a number of attempts at a phenomenological approach to the dialogue question, notably "The Goals of Inter-Religious Dialogue," in J. Hick (ed.), *Truth and Dialogue in World Religions* (Philadelphia: The Westminster Press, 1974), pp. 77-95; *Faith Meets Faith* (London: SCM Press, 1977), passim; "Dialogue of Religions," in M. Eliade, ed., *The Encyclopedia of Religion* 4 (New York: Macmillan, 1987), pp. 344-348; and "The Limits of Inter-Religious Dialogue," in *Mission Studies* 18 (1992), pp. 228-235.

5. Cf. Robert B. Sheard, *Interreligious Dialogue in the Catholic Church since Vatican II* (Lewiston/Queenston: The Edwin Mellen Press, 1987); Fu and Spiegler (eds.), *Religious Issues and Interreligious Dialogue* (New York: Greenwood Press, 1989), Part II.

complementary positions we characterize as "dialogue" and "proclamation" (or "evangelization") are themselves the products of two separate lines of theological development. The cardinal issue may be seen as theological, ideological, or a mixture of both. It has to do with how far one is prepared to go along the path of radical egalitarianism that took political form in the eighteenth century, inspired Christian and other socialist experiments in the nineteenth, and has dominated the thinking of the so-called "Christian left" for most of the twentieth century.

Even to state the alternative without denunciation is almost tantamount to proclaiming oneself a dangerous reactionary. It relates to that bundle of ideas incorporating hierarchy, degree, rank, class, caste, and (in German terms) *Amt und Stand*; it involves the giving and obeying of orders and the exchange, in both directions, of the appropriate courtesies and acknowledgments; its motto (that of my old school, as it happens) was *praesis ut prosis*, more familiarly *noblesse oblige*. (There is a barbed variant in the Gospel of Luke, 12:41-48, of which the sharp point is in v. 48: "Everyone to whom much is given, of him will much be required.") Its conditions have been well described by C. S. Lewis in 1942: "According to this [hierarchical] conception degrees of value are objectively present in the universe. Everything except God has some natural superior; everything except God has some natural inferior."[6] This is not to say that between those occupying different rungs on the hierarchical ladder there could be no communication. It was on the other hand communication under constraints and limitations — which the dialogue movement would like to think the post-Hiroshima age has found ways to minimize, if not to eliminate altogether. It has done so only in part, and at considerable cost.

Etymologically, a "dialogue" (Gk. *dialogos*) is simply a conversation, irrespective of the number of participants, the spirit in which it proceeds, or the final outcome. (It is surprising how often the Greek *dia* "across" is confused with the Latin *duo* "two." A dialogue is not, therefore, a verbal exchange involving only two people, and there is, I am sorry to say, no such word as "trialogue.") Theologically, on the other hand, it has come to be assumed that dialogue is an exchange involving partners belonging to different traditions, but equal in status and prepared for mutual enrichment. Dialogue in this special sense presupposes the acknowledgment by each partner of the bonafides and integrity of the other(s); and is at its best when the partners are equally well informed, equally committed, and equally articulate. Should one partner assume an attitude of superiority over another, then, on these assumptions, the dialogue would be at an end. Ideally, no one participant should be better informed, more articulate, more intensely committed, than another; there must be no unfair advantage taken and no point-scoring. Self-criticism is entirely in order, but since to criticize another is to assume an attitude of superiority over that person, such criticism tends to be ruled out a priori.

How often (or rather, how seldom) this range of ideals is capable of being realized in practice may remain an open question. It is of more immediate interest, perhaps, to point out that from the point of view of the history of religions, dialogue resting on this set of egalitarian assumptions is strictly modern, and largely secular Christian. Elsewhere, while dialogues are common, they are almost always didactic, that is, slanted downward from the teacher, who possesses insight and authority, to the disciple, who does not, and whose active role is generally limited to the asking of respectful questions.[7] Respect is of the essence. In the Hindu tradition, for instance, the first condition for the making of spiritual progress is *sraddha*, the disciple's trust

---

6. C. S. Lewis, *A Preface to Paradise Lost* (Oxford University Press, 1960 ed.), p. 73.

7. See my article in *The Encyclopedia of Religion*, op. cit.

in and submission to the credentials, experience, and power of the *guru*. In the Buddhist world, the members of the *sangha* [monastic community] receive unqualified reverence from the laity, as does the *pir* among Sufi Muslims, while the role of prophetic or charismatic leadership is acknowledged worldwide. So while there may well be a high degree of democratic egalitarianism among rank-and-file disciples belonging to any given tradition, this does not extend to those whose special function it is to mediate between the seen and unseen worlds, and to interpret the needs and requirements of the one to the other. This of itself places certain limitations on the notion of dialogue as an instrument of heightened religious awareness *between* and *across* traditions.

It is a curiosity of *guru*dom (of all traditions: the Hindu *guru* is not a special case) that having attained a certain eminence, the instructor is reluctant to accept further instruction other than *in extremis*. As with individuals, so with institutions. It is not many years since the very idea of the Roman Catholic Church entering into respectful dialogue with any other religious tradition, let alone advocating dialogue as an overall policy, would have been laughed out of court. It was simply not part of the Vatican's style either to be overly egalitarian or to defer to the opinions of others. Here, though, we have a paradox.

It is this: that despite all the sonorous words contained in these documents about the need for dialogue with the followers of other traditions, there is no evidence in them of any input from beyond the Vatican walls. It would seem that councils and assemblies and conferences aside, mission in the 1990s has a communication problem hardly less serious than the denominational problems of the past. Today the factions function as the denominations once did. Still each does not as a rule read what the others write. In this present case, although I was not really expecting Vatican documents actually to quote non-Vatican material, it came as a disappointment that there is not the slightest hint in them that Christians outside the Roman fold might have ideas of their own about these issues, or that they might be able to contribute to the ongoing discussion. Out in the missions, not to mention the conferences, things work differently. Why then not a little more ecumenical generosity from the side of the hierarchy? Particularly since there was a period of something like sixty years during which Rome, having turned its back in 1907 on "Modernism," lost touch also with comparative religion and the encounters on which sound dialogue rests. The liberal wing of Protestantism did all the work between 1910 and World War II, before being undermined (or at least intimidated) by the neo-orthodox. In effect, the Vatican remained (with a few notable exceptions, of whom Baron Friedrich von Hügel was undoubtedly the greatest) out of touch with developments in the cross-cultural study of religion for something like three generations. The trouble with gaps of this magnitude is that they cannot easily be made up; habits of decades (perhaps centuries) cannot easily be changed.

I fully understand and accept that RM and DP are for the most part "in-house" documents, the object of which is to reinvigorate a church with respect to its missionary obligation. To the non-Catholic reader, despite the mildly radical language that is used from time to time, both documents sound (dare one say?) positively old-fashioned — at least compared with some of the wilder things one has read in recent years. The impression conveyed could not be more impersonal. This places the critic at an immediate disadvantage: how can one sum up a work for the precise wording of which no one in particular (not even the Holy Father, it seems) can be held finally responsible?

The argument of these statements circles around the meaning and present-day implications of a number of key words, notably "mission," "dialogue," and "proclamation" (or "evangelization") as modes of communication. Another key term is "culture." Needless to say, none has a self-evidently narrow range of meanings to begin with. Here I shall concentrate (space being limited) on "culture" and "dialogue." First, though, an outsider's observation of a more general nature.

My Catholic friends must forgive me, but I am unhappy at the frequent use in these documents of phrases like "as Vatican II teaches," "the Council taught," and "the teaching of the Council." A little more than a decade ago, an observer at Vatican II lamented that after fifteen or so years, a situation had arisen in which there were "more references to the documents than the continuation of the council's special charisma."[8]

The phenomenon as such is almost a commonplace in the history of religions: after an upheaval, councils will meet and confessions of faith will be formulated (the Westminster Confession, the Augsburg Confession, and the like), whereupon human nature takes over, the statements become to all intents and purposes supplementary scriptures, having in extreme cases unquestioned authority, such as that of the Qur'an over Old and New Testaments alike. It is slightly depressing to see this process repeating itself — not just that these documents fail (as we have noted) to quote from non-canonical sources, but that they leave the outsider with the impression of what almost amounts to a postconciliar fundamentalism. I mean no disrespect, but "the Bible says" and "the Council teaches" have a similar sound, and similar implications: that in point of fact, all the really serious questions have already been settled, canonically if not apostolically, the answers needing only to be understood to be accepted. DP 4(b) states, for instance, that interreligious dialogue, "as envisaged by the Second Vatican Council, is only gradually coming to be understood," while its practice remains "hesitant in some places." But is it not a little naive to suggest that Vatican II had the whole of the dialogical panorama clearly in its sights in the 1960s? Or that all we need to do in the 1990s is to "understand" what it had in mind? What else in the 1990s is what it was thirty years ago — except perhaps human nature?

Of course, in matters of missiology, Vatican II (especially *Ad Gentes*) required the follow-up documents we have before us; this is at least a sign that the hermeneutical process still has some way to go before finding its *télos*.

THE QUESTION OF CULTURE

Despite all that is still being written about interreligious dialogue, the favored term these days is "culture," with its derivatives "cultural" and "multicultural." Apparently, people feel freer speaking in cultural rather than in religious terms. But when it comes to the question of how what we call "culture" is related to what we call "religion" — both of them being in some measure terms we have pressed into service to account for the machinery of human diversity — we are still left floundering. Is religion, for instance, part of culture, a process parallel to culture or culture's transcendental dimension? We barely know. What we do know, on the other hand, is that for decades there has been a missiological problem having to do with the relationship between the Christian message in its essence, and the cultural manifestations in which it has expressed itself in the past, and continues to express itself in the present. We may insist that, in the title of Garry Trompf's book, "The Gospel Is Not Western." How far we have been able to persuade the non-Western world of that fact is another matter entirely.[9]

RM 35 touches on this question, noting among the difficulties facing the mission

8. Albert Outler, *NCP Newsletter* (December 1982), p. 30.
9. G. W. Trompf, *The Gospel Is Not Western* (Maryknoll: Orbis Books, 1987).

ad gentes, that some countries will not allow missionaries access, while others forbid conversion. And then: "Elsewhere the obstacles are of a cultural nature: passing on the Gospel message seems irrelevant or incomprehensible, and conversion is seen as a rejection of one's own people and culture." But having picked up the cultural hot potato, RM immediately drops it again, complaining about Christians' "widespread indifferentism," associated with the mistaken belief that "one religion is as good as another."

Conversion as "a rejection of one's own people and culture" has followed Christianity almost from the first. Examples are legion. Today the popular images are everywhere, decreeing that once Christianity allowed itself to be compromised by its association with temporal power at the time of Constantine, its spiritual integrity had been lost. Since then its agents have been, whether consciously or not, tools of political oppression and cultural vandalism. Therefore (so the story goes) to exchange one's ancestral religion for Christianity is to sell one's cultural birthright and to exchange the spontaneous for the mechanical, nature for artificiality. Every missiologist has heard and read these accusations *ad nauseam*. Mission historians know that some of them are true, many of them are false, and practically all of them are oversimplified. But because they express what the alienated and the disillusioned *want* to believe about the Christian mission, they continue to circulate.

Catholics are no less troubled than others by this cluster of ideas and impressions. Very likely they suffer more from them (as the Columbus celebrations in 1992 drove home). Why then should RM have shied away from the "cultural vandalism" issue? It is all very well to say that "the Gospel spirit must lead us to overcome cultural and nationalistic barriers, avoiding all isolationism" (RM 39). The problems arise when it comes to translating these sonorous generalizations into local terms, and persuading Christians in some hard-pressed cultural enclave to rethink their allegiances. Similarly, mention is made in RM 47 of the tension existing here and there between conversion and baptism, in which connection (it says) "sociological considerations" obscure baptism's "genuine meaning as an act of faith." These sociological considerations, however, must be taken with the utmost seriousness; baptism as an act of initiation is theologically central: that is not in question. But it may also be a political statement, an acceptance of a new identity, membership in a new community, access to a new support network and address list, and much more besides. The sacrament of spiritual rebirth "must be seen for what it truly is," we are urged. Indeed: it must be seen for *everything* it truly is, sacramentally, spiritually — and sociologically.[10]

The cultural theme emerges again in RM 52-56, where mention is made of the urgency of "inculturation," or the process of "the Church's insertion [one hopes that this sounds better in Latin] into peoples' cultures" (RM 52).

This, of course, has been happening throughout Christian history to a greater or lesser extent. We have various words to label the process: adaptation, indigenization, contextualization, inculturation, and perhaps others. To the historian of religions, this is a normal and natural process, brought about just as soon as people begin to express the Christian faith in their own languages and symbol systems and start to celebrate the Eucharist with the bread and wine of the country. Although the taproot will always be one and the same, the outermost branches may seem to have little enough to do with one another. The Gospel "incarnate in different cultures," each

---

10. To treat the baptism question in exclusively sociological terms does not on the other hand improve matters. The opposite of an error in this, as in so many cases, is merely an opposite error. However, the sociological dimension, especially where the consequences of baptism are concerned, can be evaluated, as the spiritual dimension often cannot.

with its own *Heimat* and history, language and traditions, signs and symbols, may be barely recognizable as the same Gospel, except by careful observation.

The term in RM is "inculturation." This would seem to involve a mixture of fairly common-sense processes — translation, adaptation, and cultural accommodation stopping somewhat short of "going native." One cannot help wondering whether missionaries still need to be exhorted, for instance, to learn local languages, and to "immerse themselves in the cultural milieu of those to whom they are sent." One would have thought that these lessons had been learned long ago — or is one being too optimistic? Language, of course, is the key; that, and a thorough knowledge of the various uses to which language can be put.[11] There is a serious practical point here, since these days, with language teaching in many cases being favored more for commercial than cultural purposes (I speak here with Australia in mind), and knowledge of the structure and functions of language at an all-time low, one wonders how realistic the language requirement is. Much again will depend on the individual missionary's aptitude for languages and length of service, though neither is open to generalization. All honor to the Bible translators, but there is rather more to it than that. Language school is the needle's eye through which the missionary (like the scholar) must still pass on the way to cultural understanding — though one suspects that the missionary has far more opportunities in a year to inflict lasting damage on a culture than the average academic in a lifetime.

No one would pretend that inculturation is an easy process, especially when one is not quite sure which aspects of the transmitted message are "cultural" and which supra-cultural. So while it is an objective of the Christian mission to transform "authentic cultural values" by integrating them into Christianity, it is another not to compromise "the distinctiveness and integrity of the Christian faith" (RM 52). When, to vary the language slightly, does inculturation become syncretism — a word not mentioned here, though the phrase "dangers of alterations" appears in RM 53. It is doubtful whether anyone at this present time could give a satisfactory blanket answer to this question. What happens is obvious enough: the followers of one Way meet the followers of another; they observe, talk, trade, fight, make peace, intermarry. Some of what the one learns from the other will be absorbed, whether consciously or not, while other elements will be firmly rejected. Others again will be adapted to fit the needs of the receiving community. The possibility of this process taking place beyond acceptable limits clearly alarms a certain theological and ecclesiastical mind; the historian of religions can merely observe that it happens, and describe under what conditions. I am disposed to add, however, that there is a normal and natural inculturation process, which can be neither programmed in advance nor directed toward temporarily fashionable goals. To attempt to do either is to fail in courtesy and respect, perhaps because one has forgotten (or never learned) to listen. This leads on naturally to the dialogue question.

THE QUESTION OF DIALOGUE

As we have seen, the dialogue issue is divisive, not necessarily because people do not want to talk together ("talking together" being strictly the only meaning of the word), but because of the ideological assumptions it makes. It presupposes, for instance, equality of status between individuals, and also implicitly between religious traditions and, therefore, what they contain by way of prophets, teachers,

---

11. See Bengt Sundkler, *The World of Mission* (London: Lutterworth, 1963), pp. 56ff.: "Mission is translation. Translation is a risk, but a risk which must be taken. Otherwise there can be no communication."

saviors, and ways of salvation. Some will contest this, on the grounds that dialogue in the world of religion is more a matter of an intelligence-gathering preliminary to "mission proper," or perhaps the equivalent of a peace conference between traditional enemies, at which, though the exchanges are civil, full trust is still some way off. Others again will have nothing to do with interreligious dialogue on any pretext whatever, for reasons too well known to require explanation.

Reading these documents, one is left with the distinct impression that in the end, the dialogical attitude might turn out to be largely an attitude of courtesy and sympathy on the Christian's part vis-à-vis other people's religious convictions and cultural expressions. They do not suggest in neo-Hindu fashion that one religious tradition is much the same as another where ultimate questions are concerned, though DP 79 comes close when it quotes John Paul II's Assisi-inspired words about human history being a "fraternal journey" toward a "transcendental goal" — an expression of which Sri Ramakrishna is unlikely to have disapproved! They do on the other hand make it clear that whatever the Christian may observe or feel instinctively about "the others," the Christian point of view must be expressed non-aggressively and nonjudgmentally. Therefore, the critical faculty must be, if not uncoupled, at least toned down. There is something of a resemblance here to that academic semi-discipline, "the phenomenology of religion," which similarly insists on the sympathetically intuitive approach to the religious beliefs and practices of others as the greatest of all academic virtues.[12] Here, too, negative criticism is ruled out as "arrogance" — except where Christianity is its target, though that is by the way.

The section of RM dealing with "Dialogue with our brothers and sisters of other religions" (RM 55-57) is too short for its purpose. It does, however, announce forcefully the *leitmotif* of these documents, that dialogue and evangelization are complementary, if not actually identical, as missionary approaches: "the Church sees no conflict between proclaiming Christ and engaging in interreligious dialogue" (RM 55). However, should there still be a question in anyone's mind about dialogue containing a tacit acknowledgment of the soteriological claims of other religious traditions, "Dialogue should be conducted and implemented with the conviction that *the Church is the ordinary means of salvation* and that *she alone* possesses the fullness of the means of salvation" (RM 55; emphasis in original). This at least is unambiguous, if to the non-Catholic gloomily familiar.

If the other religious traditions do not possess the fullness of the means of salvation, what *do* they possess? The answer is that they possess what the whole of humanity has always possessed, namely, the possibility of knowing God as Creator through the contemplation of that which God has created ("The heavens are telling the glory of God; and the firmament proclaims his handiwork," Ps. 19:1). All well and good: this is neither irrational nor unbiblical, and early in Christian history it was linked, through the celebrated *logos spermatikos* doctrine, with the more elaborate notion of a "creative word" inspiring not only Hebrew prophets, but equally Greek philosophers.[13] But it is easy to be carried away. However theoretically applicable to the world of Plato and Aristotle, there was never the slightest suggestion in the early Church that the doctrine should also apply to the world of "alternative religion" — to the mysteries of Isis, Serapis, Mithras, Orpheus, and the remainder of what I once heard the great T. W. Manson call "the *religions-geschichtliche* me-

---

12. On the phenomenology of religion, see my *Comparative Religion: A History*, second ed. (La Salle: Open Court, 1991), pp. 220ff., 294ff.; *Understanding Religion* (London: Duckworth, 1983), chapter 2.

13. There is a good account in A. C. Bouquet, *The Christian Faith and Non-Christian Religions* (London: Nisbet, 1958), pp. 137-165.

nagerie." And why not? Simply because they were *alternative soteriologies*, and in the eyes of the Church, therefore, idolatrous, demonic, and fraudulent. This is to say nothing about the religious plurality of our day: too much water has flowed under too many bridges in the meantime. But seemingly we must have precedents. This is understandable enough. But this being so, we have to take care that our precedents actually are precedents, and not flags of convenience under which missionary historiography has been sometimes known to sail.

Of course, there are pressing strategic reasons for Christians in these days not to be seen as perpetuating the intransigent attitudes of the past, where their relations with other religious traditions are concerned. The historian of religions is forced to point out all the same that the Bible offers only limited support, by way of the theology of natural revelation, to the kind of position some of the more advanced dialogicians seem to want to accept as normative. One does not have to be a conservative evangelical to recognize that the phrase "interreligious dialogue" is in biblical terms practically meaningless. The biblical record does not speak of "religion" and "the religions" in our sense. It speaks unequivocally of God and the gods (and goddesses), and of the folly of those who "exchanged the glory of the immortal God for images resembling mortal man or birds or animals or reptiles" (Rom. 1:23). Much has been made of late of the "no other name" text in Acts 4:12. But in biblical terms, it all begins with "no other gods" in Exodus 20:3 and no graven images in the following verse.

To be fair, Romans 1 is referred to in DP 23, but is immediately countered by an "on the other hand" clause, the main point of which is to stress that Paul, according to Acts 14:8 and 17:22-34 actually held a "positive and open attitude" toward the Gentiles. So, indeed, he did. It is, however, necessary to emphasize, since the subject after all has to do with inter*religious* dialogue, that Paul's attitude to the Gentiles' religious beliefs and practices was conventionally Jewish, especially where image-worship was concerned. There was, though, a loophole in his otherwise compact opposition to idolatry and its consequences, namely, the fact that Gentiles, too, live in a world created by God, even if they draw the wrong consequences from their observations.

In Acts 14:14f. Paul is driven to distraction by what the people of Lystra propose to do in his and Barnabas's honor. In Acts 17:16 "his spirit was provoked within him [= he was deeply offended] as he saw that the city was full of idols." What then is the significance of the Areopagus speech in Acts 17:22-31?[14] According to DP 23, Paul "praised" the "religious spirit" of the Athenians (v. 22). It does not seem to me that he was doing anything of the kind. He was saying that the people of Athens were, as we might say, "interested in religion" — but he was not paying them a compliment. The Greek word *deisdaimonostérous* is translated in the King James Version as "too superstitious," in the Revised Standard Version as "very religious," and in the Jerusalem Bible as "extremely scrupulous in all religious matters." Paul's precise shade of meaning is hard and perhaps impossible to recover. It is hardly likely, though, that a word containing the element *daimon* (from which we have our "demon," see Matt. 8:31) could have been used by a Jew in anything but a pejorative sense. The one thing that saved the situation was that Paul's attention had been caught by an altar bearing an inscription, in this case apparently a dedication to no god in particular. And an altar was at least not an idol.

It is characteristic of RM and DP that they are reluctant to give equal weight to

---

14. The classical study, which deserves to be far better known than it is, is Bertil Gartner, *The Areopagus Speech and Natural Revelation* (Uppsala: Acta Seminarii Neo-testamentici Upsaliensis XXI, 1955).

strong elements in the Christian tradition that not only question, but flatly contradict, what the dialogue movement since the 1960s has wanted its platform to contain. Mention has been made of their tendency to appeal to the documents of Vatican II, as though these already constituted holy writ, as well as being the repository of the ultimate dialogical wisdom. This surely is to do everyone concerned a disservice. Dare one say that many of the Council Fathers who were based in Europe and North America were the merest amateurs where the theory and practice of interreligious dialogue was concerned? But precedents could be found when external pressures required a change of position, if not in every case a change of heart. Precedents, however, need to be taken in context — which was not done in respect of Acts 17. As with Paul, so it is with the Early Church Fathers. With one voice, practically, they condemn other gods and other ways of salvation, though, of course, some of them (as DP duly notes) leave open a door to some of the philosophers. But is this to be taken to mean that because Justin, Irenaeus, and Clement (among others) were prepared to grant, say, Plato and Aristotle a place in the academy of truth, Jupiter, Mars and Quirinius, Isis and Osiris, Mithras and Serapis would be allowed in under the same cause?

There is nothing in DP to suggest that there might have been a difference in the early Christian centuries between high philosophers and low performers, between cults and the cultivated, between metaphysics and the mysteries. There is no mention of Paul's solemn warnings to the Corinthians, "shun the worship of idols . . . I do not want you to be partners with demons. . . . Shall we provoke the Lord to jealousy?" (1 Cor. 10:14, 20, 22). Failing to acknowledge the difference between ontology (God is) and soteriology (God saves), it is made to seem as though the first Christian generations were as ill-informed as ours, where the relationship between God and the gods was concerned. This may be the greatest underlying weakness of these documents: it is often unclear whether they are speaking in ontological or soteriological terms.

Concerning the *forms* of interreligious dialogue, DP 42-43 takes up a fourfold classification that was first, apparently, launched by the Pontifical Council for Interreligious Dialogue in 1984. One wonders what the members of this council had been reading. As far back as 1967 the late Richard W. Taylor proposed his fourfold scheme — Socratic, Buberian, Discursive, and Pedagogic dialogue, respectively.[15] In April 1970 at a conference in Birmingham, England, I launched a slightly different, though still fourfold, scheme, the corners of which I labeled Discursive, Human, Secular, and Interior Dialogue, the nature of each depending on the goal(s) to which it happened to be directed — Discursive aimed at intellectual grasp, Human at personal communication, Secular at a job to be done, Interior at the spiritual quest.[16] It is strange to find the Vatican in 1984 and 1991 taking up what is to all intents and purposes the same pattern, though in a different order. DP 42 lists "the dialogue of life" (= human dialogue), "the dialogue of action" (= secular dialogue), "the dialogue of theological exchange" (more or less = discursive dialogue, although the exchange is about much more than theology), and "the dialogue of religious experi-

---

15. Richard W. Taylor, "The Meaning of Dialogue," in Herbert Jai Singh, ed., *Inter-Religious Dialogue* (Bangalore: CISRS, 1967), pp. 55-64.

16. Sharpe, "The Goals of Inter-Religious Dialogue." I ought perhaps to add that I was virtually driven to propose some distinction between modes of dialogue by the sheer terminological confusion of those immediate postconciliar years where dialogue was concerned. My paper was delivered in the spring of 1970, and published, together with a rejoinder by Wilfred Cantwell Smith, in the journal *Religion* 3 (1973), pp. 89-105, under the title "Dialogue and Faith." The version in the Hick volume did not appear until 1974, a full four years after the conference at which it was delivered.

ence" (= interior dialogue), which is singled out as in a sense the culmination of the process (DP 43).

All this still seems to me workable for purposes of classification. It was, however, never meant to be rigid, and it is vitally necessary to bear in mind that the partner's response may well turn a dialogue abruptly from one mode into another. It is also worth remembering that to speak of dialogue as a single undifferentiated Christian approach to the world of religion in all its vast variety, as RM and DP seem to want to do, can only be sustained for as long as one is prepared to avoid concrete cases altogether. It is all very well to state that "the Church's commitment to dialogue [is] firm and irreversible" (DP 54), but should this be taken to mean "in every conceivable situation?" Presumably not: there must be some religious tradition, somewhere, with which no Christian could enter into dialogue with a clear conscience, and prophecy and politeness do not always coexist comfortably.

Actually, the "firm and irreversible" declaration has been preceded in DP 51-53 by a list of eleven "human factors" that are capable of hindering the free flow of dialogue. Here one suddenly finds oneself sliding off the mountain of harmonious idealized encounter into a briar patch of very real objections. A brief word about one or two of them may not be out of place, by way of conclusion.

First, there is "insufficient grounding in one's own faith," and secondly, "insufficient knowledge and understanding of the belief [sic] and practices of other religions." An educator might be tempted to stress the second of these factors above the first, the theologian perhaps vice versa. Speaking on this occasion as an educator, the historian of religions aims to know the world of religion, the phenomenologist to "understand" it. However, while knowledge can be communicated, understanding is an elusive quality. One has not understood someone else's religious tradition merely by being dissatisfied with one's own. Nor by attending a first-year course in World Religions and reading a couple of randomly acquired paperbacks. This all save the incurably romantic know well enough. Yet there is a somewhat romantic attitude abroad these days, decreeing that imaginative sympathy is to be preferred over actual knowledge, where the Christian encounter with other religious traditions is concerned. And in a sense, so it is. It is particularly useless for a Christian who has no Jewish, or Muslim, or Hindu acquaintances with whom to coexist on the level of old-fashioned friendship, to pontificate about the "relationship" between the traditions concerned. But not everything that is imaginative is necessarily sympathetic.

There is a diseased, as well as a dialogical, imagination, based not on trust and friendship and understanding, but on distrust and fear, and emptying into the swamps of paranoia. The paranoid imagination peoples the world with enemies and evil spirits, grotesques and gargoyles, conspiracies, secret societies and unclean beasts — but who dares deny that often it has flourished in the borderland where faith meets faith? I happen, in addition, seriously to doubt the extent to which one person can enter into the spiritual experience, or, indeed, share any of the memories, of another, except by special invitation.[17] I am entirely sure that it cannot be done to order. One may, of course, read the other people's holy scriptures, attend their rituals and admire their art, eat their food, and assume their dress; but while access to the outer courts may be freely granted — to the tourist as well as to the pilgrim — entry to the holy of holies is by initiation, and is not granted to the casual visitor.

DP 52 (d) lists as a further "human factor" standing in the way of ideal dialogue, "some burdens of the past." I have come to feel more and more strongly of late that

17. See my most recent essay on the subject, "The Limits of Inter-Religious Dialogue," a paper presented to the 1991 Conference of the International Association of Mission Studies in Hawaii.

the dialogue movement in conciliar Christianity pays far too little attention to the fact that partners in dialogue actually *have* a remembered past, as well as a wide-awake present. There is much in the past of interreligious encounter of which no one is likely to feel particularly proud. How many feuds have been kept alive, generation after generation, by the memory of atrocities, injustices, and misunderstandings of the past, no one can possibly know. It is, I think, neither cynical nor defeatist to admit that simply to proclaim a unilateral change of heart is not going to obliterate (nor should it) the memory of everything that preceded the 1960s.

DP 51 (h) admits that partners in dialogue may be suspicious of one another's motives. Sometimes they have reason to be, as an ideal dialogue drifts into the regions of apologetics and self-justification. RM 56, however, insists that dialogue "does not originate from tactical concerns," although how far the world's other communities of faith will be prepared to accept that must remain an open question, at least for the time being.

As a final point: one wonders, reading these documents over and over again, whether they are quite as open as they profess to be. Every religious tradition coming into contact with others will self-evidently form a theory of some kind to account for them, and to incorporate them into its own scale of values. At no point in either RM or DP do their compilers question the right of the Catholic Church to select from among the beliefs and practices of other traditions "what is good" in them (DP 29), though it is acknowledged that "criteria" for identifying in them "elements of grace capable of sustaining the positive response of their members to God's invitation" (DP 30) have to be found. That these have to be *Christian* criteria goes without saying. So, too, does the extreme difficulty in finding any set of criteria capable of being accepted, in the present fragmented state of Christian theology, by more than a segment or two of the larger Christian community. Meanwhile, one cannot help wondering how those who have framed these statements of faith and policy react to the criteria question in reverse, so to speak — Buddhist criteria for assessing Christianity in Korea, for instance, though here the permutations and combinations are legion.

There is a paragraph, DP 78, which speaks of a "spirituality of dialogue" — not to my mind the happiest of phrases — but also of the need for "a certain sensitivity to the social, cultural, religious and political aspects of the situation." Indeed. But why only "a certain sensitivity?" The dialogue issue must not be pursued on too narrow a front, or other than in the fullest possible awareness of the range of issues involved — religious, theological, social, political, and (in the most general sense) cultural. Sometimes I feel that the theological community has barely begun to scratch the surface of the question of the encounter of religious traditions, perhaps because of its paradoxical lack of confidence in dealing with religion multi-dimensionally.

All honor to those who have produced RM and DP, but these documents are more pointers to, than programs for, the future. One might perhaps be permitted to express a hope that the next item on the agenda might be a fuller recovery of past scholarly and practical achievements. For only when we know where we have been can we begin to sense where we might be going — "we" in this case being the Christian community as a whole.

2

Toward a Spirit Ecclesiology

Laurenti Magesa

Laurenti Magesa is a Tanzanian diocesan priest who has studied theology in Rome and has taught at the Catholic Higher Institute of East Africa. He has lectured at the Maryknoll School of Theology and has written widely on questions of inculturation of the Gospel for Africa, as well as on ethical issues in the areas of sexuality.

The encyclical *Redemptoris Missio* and the statement of the Council for Dialogue and the Congregation for Evangelization, *Dialogue and Proclamation*, deal with the question of Christian mission, interreligious dialogue, and the proclamation of the Gospel to non-Christians. In addition to discussing briefly and in general terms some of the major points they raise, I wish to situate these documents in the context of the African continent. Given the continent's history and its current sociocultural, economic, and religious situation, what message do the documents convey to Africa? In other words, what is their view of the religious substrata of the continent?

THE BASIC CONCERNS OF THE TWO ROMAN STATEMENTS

In the first chapter of RM, Pope John Paul underlines the theme of the permanent validity of the "Church's universal mission" (RM 4). Apparently because he is aware that questions are now being raised about this validity, the Pope has written this encyclical. Placed in the context of Africa, one may divide the Pope's concerns into three areas without doing violence to the integrity of their internal meaning. One concerns mission in the sense of announcing the Christian gospel, which for the two documents means the proclamation of the name of Jesus as universal savior. DP 4 describes it as "the effort to bring people into the community of the Church." Since the encyclical reflects on mission *ad gentes* [to the nations], with particular reference to the peoples of the Southern Hemisphere, of which Africa forms an important part, it has been much discussed here.

A second concern pertains to the attitude of Christianity with regard to non-Christian religious beliefs. What regulates the Christian Church's approach to them? As the Pope puts it, "Does not respect for conscience and for freedom exclude all efforts at conversion?" (RM 4). Further in the same article, the Pope asks a question that borrows from a commonly expressed belief, "Is it not possible to attain salvation in any religion?" For us in Africa, the question becomes, Do African religions contain anything worthwhile with reference to divine revelation and human salvation? Should Christianity be engaged in dialogue with them? Or does a vigorous and authentic Christian position entail not recognizing value in them and encouraging vigorous proselytism?

Finally, both RM and DP express the conviction that Christian missionary activity is as imperative now as it ever was (see RM 13 and *passim*; see also DP 14-32). If this is so, what motivates it? The phraseology of the Pope is much more stark. People are asking, he says, *"Why then should there be missionary activity"* (RM 4, emphasis in original) given positive appreciation of the salvific value of other religions? In our own context, is the missionary enterprise to Africa still valid?

With reference to the issue of Christian mission and interreligious dialogue in the African context, the Pope's questions are most apropos. Let me use them to guide this reflection. Since it is central to everything else, I will discuss the persistence of Christianity's negative attitude toward Africa and African religions first. It will be seen that practical non-recognition of the latter constitutes part of the environment of global Christianity that is not easily amenable to change. The condition of proclamation of the name of Jesus as savior and of interreligious dialogue in Africa is dependent upon this attitude.

ATTITUDE TOWARD AFRICAN RELIGIONS

Historical realities influence the attitudes of the church toward African religions. What has been the doctrinal and pastoral behavior of the Christian churches toward them? Because it provides a sense of the reality of mission in Africa today, the answer to this question is critical.

Evidence exists from very early on of the church's appreciation of culture as the privileged locus of God's self-disclosure to humankind. In Africa, however, this theoretical appreciation never really seeped to the level of practical evangelization. In fact, Africa was essentially denied of culture in the view of early Christian evangelizers. Christian mission in Africa, as Jean-Marc Ela has remarked, has been a process initiated and nurtured almost totally in the context both of the enslavement and colonization of the African peoples. "Western penetration of the lands across the sea is the event that sets the Church's [Western] 'captivity' in relief." [1] Christianization in Africa, he maintains, was used to justify the domination of a people. As Ela further observes, it was unfortunate that mission in Africa "became identified with a struggle against sorcery and polygamy," as if these constituted the entire domain of the religious beliefs of the people. These "typical traits of inferior, pagan societies," as they were perceived, almost exclusively determined the nature of the presence of the church in Africa and its pastoral activity. Characteristic of missionary activity in Africa was its crusade mentality against most manifestations of African religiosity.

If what I have just said indicates the attitude of the church toward African culture in general and African religions in particular in the past, the missionary paradigm has still not changed very significantly today. The outward signs of slavery and colonization have of course altered, but not the reality. Christian mission may therefore be operating today from the same presuppositions unawares. More to the point, RM and DP have, to my mind, been born in the context formed by what Ela characterizes as the "collusion" of the faith with the dominant culture of the Western world.

We live in the age of the so-called "New World Order." However, it is becoming

1. Jean-Marc Ela, *African Cry* (Maryknoll: Orbis, 1986), p. 43.

apparent that what this means is that the poor Southern Hemisphere of our world is virtually a vassal of the economically wealthy North. Despite all contrary noble intentions, the thrust of RM and DP is influenced by this situation. According to RM 3, for example, Christ's Gospel "in no way detracts from man's freedom, from the respect that is owed to every culture and to whatever is good in each religion." We read in DP 13 that "Interreligious dialogue ought to extend to all religions and their followers." Nevertheless, one wonders whether the encyclical, as a whole and in its basic presuppositions, is infused by such respect or whether it is primarily negative. Also, does DP consider African religions realities worthy of dialoguing with?

GENUINE RESPECT AS THE ISSUE

Respect for the integrity of peoples of other faiths in the real issue that must be grappled with. Both RM and DP broach this issue. DP notes that other religious traditions

> command our respect because over the centuries they have borne witness to the efforts to find answers "to those profound mysteries of the human condition" . . . and have given expression to the religious experience and the longings of millions of their adherents, and they continue to do so today. (DP 14)

This text echoes what Pope John Paul II affirms even more concisely and forcefully in RM. In the mission of the Church to proclaim Jesus, he declares, sight must not be lost of "Respect for man in his quest for answers to the deepest questions of his life" (RM 29). But what, concretely, does genuine respect involve? Do our two documents clearly inspire it?

J. Andrew Kirk has said something on this question that deserves consideration. He suggests that "we truly respect people when we allow them the integrity of actually believing what they profess to believe." According to Kirk, if respect has any meaning, no one has the right to tell others in categorical terms that what they believe "is not what they really believe."[2]

The documents under discussion seem reluctant to offer this level of respect. One wonders why. The fear of relativism? I suspect that the atmosphere in which the documents were written has conditioned their tone and orientation. Although it may seem too harsh to say this about an enterprise in which so many work so heroically, many Africans identify this atmosphere as one of pervasive, persistent attempts to dominate and control global Christian missionary activity, but especially so when Africa is concerned.

If respect for what and how others "profess to believe" is the point, what is one to make of the assertion in RM, for instance, that "No one . . . can enter into communion with God except through Christ" (RM 5)? Or that those who do not know Christ can enjoy "participated forms of mediation of different kinds and degrees" in the divine plan via non-Christian religious traditions, and that they acquire ultimate "meaning and value *only* from Christ's own mediation" (ibid.; emphasis in original)?

These and many other similar statements in the two documents under discussion obviously undermine the sense that one finds in them of genuine respect for other people's religious beliefs and convictions. They make missionary activity dogmatic and fundamentally destructive of people's self-worth. As for dialogue, it becomes a prejudiced or predetermined exercise with regard to its consequences from the start. This is what has and is happening in Africa under that rubric.

---

2. J. Andrew Kirk, *Loosing the Chains: Religion as Opium and Liberation* (London: Hodder & Stoughton, 1992), p. 159.

RM and DP offer Scriptural texts and theological rationales to justify these assertions. However, they sound close to telling people that what they believe "is not what they really believe" (the point of Kirk, whom I cited above). More concretely, the official position of the church as represented in these two documents seems to many to express the position that traditional (non-Christian) religions people belong to, and the faith they profess and live by, have in themselves no salvific value. To illustrate I cite RM article 10:

> For such people [as do not know or acknowledge Christ or belong to the Church] salvation in Christ is accessible by virtue of a grace which, while having a mysterious relationship to the Church, does not make them formally part of the Church but enlightens them in a way which is accommodated to their spiritual and material situation. This grace comes from Christ; it is the result of his Sacrifice and is communicated by the Holy Spirit. It enables each person to attain salvation through his or her free cooperation.

What statements of this kind are actually implying is that everyone who loves and does justice is "anonymously" Christian. The implication is that whether an individual professes to be non-Christian or explicitly rejects the Christian Church is inconsequential — such a person *nolens vel volens* does his or her righteous actions out of what the Pope terms "a mysterious relationship to the Church."

To the sensibilities of many Africans today, this theory of "Anonymous Christians," first explicated by Karl Rahner,[3] is not only condescending but offensive. What it does in practice is to make exclusive divine revelation claims for Christianity. It contradicts whatever respect for other people's beliefs that is called for in the Christian theory of mission. Once again, it makes the practice of dialogue unauthentic.

THE SUBJECTIVE NATURE OF RELIGIOUS BELIEF

Genuine respect for different cultures and religious orientations, which ought to characterize Christian mission *ad gentes* as well as interreligious dialogue, lies in the recognition of the subjective nature of all religious belief — the acceptance of things not seen but hoped for (Heb 11:1).To their credit, RM and DP contain the seeds of this recognition. However, they are overshadowed and almost eclipsed by overwhelming Christian dogmatic framework of the documents. The intention is to posit Jesus as the one and only "mediator" between God and all humanity (RM 5). In the same way, the documents postulate the Christian, or more precisely the Catholic, Church, not merely as the "universal sacrament of salvation" but also as "necessary for salvation" (DP 33). How does such a view end up treating those millions of African peoples who do not know the Christian Church? And those who have consciously rejected the church in favor of their own African ancestral beliefs?

---

3. For Karl Rahner, "The exclusive claims of Christianity operate only where Christianity is known; non-Christian faiths, which are the combined products of grace and sin, function as 'legitimate' and saving religions where Christianity is absent. Their adherents, in this view, should be classed as 'Anonymous Christians' having 'implicit' faith (that is, a disposition to believe what the Church believes). And the Church's missionary task is to make explicitly Christian the faith of the anonymously Christian world, as Paul did in Athens by introducing the God who was already being worshipped, though in ignorance." Quoted in Tokunboh Adeyemo, *Salvation in African Tradition* (Nairobi: Evangel Publishing House, 1979), p. 12.

There is one crucial question here, one that every Christian ought to answer honestly and without ambiguity in relation to African religious beliefs — Am I not morally obliged to uphold the right that I claim for myself as part and parcel of my existence as a person to those differently persuaded on matters religious? If I am not to depersonalize and violate the integrity and humanity of those others in the name of Christ, it seems obvious that I must.

This kind of respect for others demands that dialogue be not only the paradigm of fruitful interreligious intercourse but also of humane Christian missionary activity. It will situate "credal" propositions into the perspective of the subjectivity of religious belief.

A trait of confessional statements, it should be noted, is that they are addressed to and intended for those who already profess a degree of belief in a particular religious persuasion. Given certain central substitutes, they are also substantially religiously universalistic. Which is to say that confessional statements are uniquely capable of capturing what might be called the "essence" or central core of most religious ideals.

I do not wish to seem flippant when I note that if the reader of RM supplies Allah for God, Mohammed for Jesus, Muslim for Christian or Catholic, the Qur'an for the Old and New Testaments, and Islam for Christianity, and so on, RM is capable of being accepted by the devout Muslim. *Mutatis mutandis*, the same is true as well for DP.

The point is simple but crucial. It concerns the Christian approach to mission, to interreligious dialogue, and ultimately to the proclamation of the name of Jesus as universal savior, the activity central to RM and DP. There is a danger, I fear, in translating one's particular creed into an absolute and using it to make judgments over the truth value of other faiths. Religious absolutism inevitably contains intolerance with all of its ugly results. This is a point not to lose sight of.

History is full of crimes committed as a result of intolerance that is born of religious absolutism. The wholesale denigration of the religions of Africa at the dawn of Christian missionary activity in Africa is one tragic modern example. The contemporary rise of Christian and Islamic fundamentalism, with their bigotry and incitement to violence against those differently convinced in matters religious, are a vivid reminder of the danger of religious absolutism.

Since most religions make more or less similar claims with regard to the truth-value or truth-content of their doctrines and beliefs about the final destiny of humankind, "objective" evaluation of their purely religious orientation is practically impossible. What may, can, and, indeed, at times, must be objectively evaluated — with great delicacy — are the ethical claims that the particular religions espouse and the behavior they inspire and foster. To be sure, ethical claims and behavior do not comprise all the aspects of religious faith. Yet they do touch a central aspect of religion. They respond to the question of relationships. How does a particular religion regulate the exigencies of human relationships? Including those between humankind and the Divine?

THE "NAME ABOVE EVERY NAME"

It follows that the proclamation of Jesus Christ as "the only savior" must proceed also with care and discretion (cf. RM 4-10). I will underline from an African perspective what DP describes as the qualities that should characterize the Church's proclamation of the name of Jesus (DP 70). Among the most crucial are humility, respect, and cultural sensitivity (cf. DP 70f. and RM 56). Indeed "Christians who lack appreciation and respect for other believers and their religious traditions are ill prepared to proclaim the Gospel to them" (DP 73). In the African situation one cannot emphasize this enough.

Equally to be avoided, according to DP, is cultural imperialism in the name of religion. Addressing this issue as an "obstacle to proclamation," DP says:

In some Christians, an attitude of superiority, which can show itself at the cultural level, might give rise to the supposition that a particular culture is linked with the Christian message and is to be imposed on converts. (DP 73d)

It is curious that DP should state the fact so boldly. Does one perceive expressed here the lived experience of the African Cardinal Francis Arinze, President of the Pontifical Council for Interreligious Dialogue? The cultural arrogance DP points to in the above quotation, however, continues to be the daily experience of life in the church of African Christians. Christian mission in Africa remains to a large extent a "culture-mission." Deny it as they might — and sincere though they be in this denial — Western Christian missionaries identify their culture as having a special link with the Christian message. It is a matter of course to them to therefore impose it on African converts, seminarians, priests, and laity, indeed, on the whole life of the church in the continent, with no qualms of conscience at all about the harm this causes to people.

Proclamation of whatever is regarded by a given group of people as the "Name above every name" requires sensitivity, not least because it pertains to the sphere of religious hope. On whose or on what authority are "things not seen" believed and hoped for? This basic question concerns Christian mission and interreligious dialogue. It pertains to the issue of the source of human "knowledge" of the Divine and of divine will. In short, it is the question of revelation.

How is divine revelation mediated? Does it flow from humankind's desire to know the Creator (from "below") or by Divine initiative (from "above")? Is it rather a meeting of the two movements? Most importantly, how much revelation suffices, so to speak, for salvation? Is this available in African religions?

Though important, these are questions beyond the scope of this essay. Suffice it to say here that, concretely, in many (including African) religions revelation involves a savior or perhaps even several savior figures. It is this figure who (or what) is usually described by the faithful as the "Name above every name." The savior's exact name, of course, varies from place to place. This being the case, there is much logical sense in what missiologist Eugene Hillman has observed when expressing the opinion that "the question remains open whether this name 'above every name' . . . might also be predicated of such realities as Hkambageyo, or Krishna, or Purusha, or Isvara, or even Humanity."[4] Hillman cites Karl Rahner, saying:

there is no reason [for Christians] to exclude such discoveries (of extra-biblical savior figures) from the outset, or to write them off contemptuously, as if they stood in such contrast to faith in Jesus, as the eschatological and unsupersedable savior, that they can only be judged negatively.[5]

Such a theological stance is plausible (for reasons that we will offer below), and its implications for missionary activity and interreligious dialogue in Africa cannot be ignored. RM and DP, being documents intended for the universal Church, and written from a European (or Northern) perspective, fail to pay adequate attention to

---

4. Eugene Hillman, *Many Paths: A Catholic Approach to Religious Pluralism* (Maryknoll: Orbis, 1989), p. 56. According to Hillman, "Hkambageyo is a Christ-like historical figure who is central to the traditional religion of the Batem people (also called Sonjo) of Northern Tanzania" (p. 82, note 3).
    5. Ibid.

them. They fail to pay enough attention to the fact that the message of Jesus of love of God and neighbor is really not quite unique to him. Countless (and mostly re-membered only in folklore) African prophets, "priests," diviners, and teachers preached the same message long before the Christian religion touched the shores of the continent. They were the continent's "illuminati." Results of their revelations were ambiguous, to be sure. But so are those of Christianity. Consider the practical results of Christian evangelization throughout the world — among the worst of which the Holocaust takes on unique dimensions. Pope John Paul II himself de-scribes areas where Christianity has been for a long time to be now "in need of re-evangelization" (RM 32). Yet Africa, because of the work of its prophets, suc-ceeded in getting societies organized around the principle of radical communal love, cooperation, and sharing. In any respectful mission work and meaningful interreli-gious dialogue, these persons must be given due recognition.

TOWARD A "SPIRIT ECCLESIOLOGY"

Christ-like sacred historical figures such as Hkambageyo in African religions (and others in other faith-traditions) imply that the action of the Spirit of God in humankind is not necessarily tied to the missionary activity of the Christian Church. In regard to the theological and/or pneumatalogical significance of historico-mythic figures, who bear resemblances to the Christ-figure, there are also contradictory tendencies in the two Roman documents. On the one hand, they affirm the preemi-nence of what I should like to call a "Spirit ecclesiology." On the other hand, they seem to be ambivalent about it.

In RM, Pope John Paul II reminds his readers of what he said at Assisi in the presence of leaders of other religions and faiths. He was convinced, he said, that "every authentic prayer is prompted by the Holy Spirit, who is mysteriously present in every human heart" (RM 29). The most normal interpretation of this statement is as an affirmation of the universal work of the Spirit. But what is this affirmation if it is not also an implicit admission of the possibility of the existence of other Spirit-in-spired savior-figures and other divine witness-oriented ecclesial bodies outside Jesus and Christianity? RM and DP do not make explicit this logical consequence of their argumentation. Again, they are tied up by cultural constraints and their dogmatic commitment to Christ as the only universal savior.

Both RM and DP indicate that the work of the Spirit of God has priority, in time and space, over and beyond any ecclesiastical activity (see RM 28f.; DP 14-32). Recognition of this is what I wish to call a veritable appreciation of a "Spirit ecclesi-ology," by which I mean that it recognizes the possibility of salvific work of God through the Holy Spirit, which is owed deference in discussing the world's religions and cultures. There well may be many stories of salvation, for all we know. Ethi-cally, there exist many variations or, one might even say, "degrees of perfection" among them. But no tradition is complete and perfect in itself. It is for this reason that conversation among representatives of the many traditions is so important.

Africa's story of salvation is embodied in Africa's history and cultures. Obvi-ously, these do not begin with the advent of Christianity on the continent. Consistent with the thrust of a Spirit ecclesiology, one should anticipate that the Spirit's pres-ence and saving activity in and through African religious traditions and cultures precede the advent of Christianity and continue as an integral part of ongoing Afri-can religious history. It is nothing less than tragic, in my opinion, for Christianity to relegate African religions to the theological status of realities incapable of being the vehicles of God's self-revelation. Being the religion of the dominant politico-cultural powers, Christianity has historically done this.

African theology of inculturation has made significant strides in recent years in the effort to rehabilitate African religions as important and effective stories of God's saving activities. Following this, there has been some movement from the Christian "center" to dialogue with them. Still, the churches' basic attitude of not recognizing African religions as embodying valid ecclesial qualities, through the power of the Spirit of God, has not been relinquished altogether. By and large, Christian mission stands accused even now of being in the business of trying "to remake the black [person] in the image of the white."[6]

Do our two documents escape this accusation? Are they, even if only in spite of themselves, party to the cultural/religious "leveling down" and "indiscriminate internationalization" in the name of "modernity" that DP itself, for example, warns against (DP 46)? Complicity in this process, I wish to suggest, is a "sin" against the Spirit, specifically against Spirit ecclesiology. Neither the "uniqueness" of Jesus Christ nor that of the Christian Church demands it.

What Paul F. Knitter has argued about "relational uniqueness" in regard to the uniqueness of Jesus, may apply also to the uniqueness of the Church. If so, it clarifies a great deal about what I am calling Spirit ecclesiology, mission *ad gentes*, and dialogue among religious traditions. With regard to the assertion that Jesus is unique, Knitter writes that this should be seen "relationally," affirming:

> that Jesus *is* unique, but with a uniqueness defined by its ability to relate to — that is, to include and be included by — other unique religious figures. Such understanding of Jesus views him not as exclusive or even as normative but as *theocentric*, as a universally relevant manifestation (sacrament, incarnation) of divine revelation and salvation.[7]

The Christian/Catholic Church can be seen as "unique" in this same sense. Indeed, any ecclesial body, from the perspective of a Spirit ecclesiology, is distinctive because it embodies and mirrors the "fruits" or "gifts of the Spirit" spoken of in Galatians 5:22, gifts praised and desired by most religions and the great majority of humankind. Merely to claim for itself a monopoly of truth or divine inspiration is not enough. The test for attention to the Spirit's work is how the ecclesial body reflects concretely what other traditions, indeed, the whole of humankind, see and desire in themselves. In other words, what do they appreciate as "salvific" moments? It is uniqueness, as Knitter has put it, by inclusion, not by exclusion.

It is clear that the purpose of RM and DP is to assert the uniqueness of Jesus and the Christian Church. Their shortcoming, I suggest, lies in doing so chiefly by exclusion. African religions suffer particularly because, in Western scholarship, where RM and DP have their setting, they count as "tribal," not "world" religions. If by "tribal" religions is meant that they do not embody and reflect God's revelation, or that they invariably do so only to a lesser extent than those with scriptures, the basis of such claims should be shown. If they are not or cannot be shown, then one can only suspect that the assertion is gratuitous, chiefly a profession of faith, a subjective confession. In which case, as I indicated above, "other people's beliefs" should be accorded identical epistemological status and respect. Professions of faith, however, be they in savior figures or by warranting that one's revelations are of divine origin, are not, to use Walbert Bühlmann's apt way of putting it, a "point of departure." They can only be a "point of arrival."[8]

---

6. Ela, *African Cry*, p. 21.

7. Paul F. Knitter, *No Other Name: A Critical Survey of Christian Attitudes toward the World Religions* (Maryknoll: Orbis, 1985), pp. 171f.

8. Walbert Bühlmann, *God's Chosen Peoples* (Maryknoll: Orbis, 1982), p. 221.

Christians tend to make their claim that Jesus is the summit of divine revelation and that the history of Israel constitutes the history of human salvation a point of departure in relations with other traditions instead of a point at which one hopes the human community might someday arrive. To restrict divine revelation "to one people alone, to the Jesus," implies, according to Bühlmann, that "non-Jews and non-Christians, who have constituted the major portion of humanity from the very beginning" are ignored and despised by God, and he asks, "Is that really something to expect from God?"[9]

To be concrete, are we to judge that values of community, participation, and sharing, so central to African religions and social structures in general, are worthless? But this is what the concentration of divine inspiration and salvation in the Hebrew religious story implies. Both RM and DP do so to a certain extent. To such an extent they are alienating to African religious sensitivities.

WHY MISSION?

If divine inspiration and revelation are to be found also in non-Christian traditions — including the African — the question of the motivation for mission and missionary activity urgently requires consideration, which is what Pope John Paul II does when he asks, "Why then should there be missionary activity?" (RM 4). In fact, *Redemptoris Missio* may be considered in its entirety as an attempt to provide justification for missionary activity *ad gentes*. The Pope focuses principally on those regions of the world — mostly in Africa and Asia — where the great majority of the people have not heard or have decided not to accept the Christian understanding of God.

As an extended commentary on an important section of RM, *Dialogue and Proclamation* deals with the issue of the legitimacy of mission as well. DP approaches the question from the angle of methodology. How is interreligious dialogue an instrument of evangelization? In the end, the aims of RM and DP are identical — to posit Jesus as the summit of divine revelation and Christianity as the complete embodiment of divine inspiration, the guardian and exemplar of the "deposit of the truth of God," to use familiar Catholic language.

Here in a nutshell is Pope John Paul's rationale for Christian missionary activity, of which interreligious dialogue forms a part, in current circumstance:

Activities aimed at promoting interest in the missions must always be geared to these specific goals: namely, informing and forming the People of God to share in the Church's universal mission, promoting vocations *ad gentes* and encouraging cooperation in the work of evangelization. It is not right to give an incomplete picture of missionary activity, as if it consisted principally in helping the poor, contributing to the liberation of the oppressed, promoting development or defending human rights. The missionary Church is certainly involved on these fronts but her primary task lies elsewhere: the poor are hungry for God, not just for bread and freedom. Missionary activity must first of all bear witness to and proclaim salvation in Christ, and establish local Churches which then become means of liberation in every sense. (RM 83)

The Pope's distinction of missionary activity into primary and secondary responsibilities is questionable to many, but his point is clear. The proclamation of salvation in Christ and the promotion of social liberation are the essential functions of

9. Ibid., pp. 208f.

missionary work. One has to wonder, however, whether both of these motivations are not, in the final analysis, statements and positions of religious belief. They are valid not only for Christianity, but, *mutatis mutandis*, for every respectable religion.

If African religions do not entertain, and actually eschew, proselytizing efforts, this is not necessarily because they do not have an understanding of the Divine that is deep and reverent. Neither does it mean that they are not concerned with the questions of human freedom. On the contrary, these interlinked realities form the very lives of the majority of believers in African religions. Their choice not to proselytize reflects, rather, a profound trust in the work of God among all peoples. This does not indicate religious relativism either. It only indicates that, while rooted firmly in my own belief, I do not thereby exhaust the richness and extensiveness of the Divine. Others too possess God's light, and in dialogue we can gain greater and greater truth together — the truth that leads us to the fullness of God and sets us free (John 8:32).

CONCLUSION

In religious terms, the motivation for mission and missionary activity is nothing other than a faith imperative with ethical implications. Once again, just like religious persuasion itself, it is highly subjective. As a Catholic, I am constrained psychologically and spiritually to proclaim my belief in Christ as savior of the universe to all who care to listen. However, I must not forget that other people may be similarly compelled as regards their own savior figures. On this basis of mission and proclamation genuine dialogue ensues.

To use a metaphor suggested by Bishop Patrick Kalilombe from Malawi, mission means "building . . . bridges of interaction" across differences of religion, culture, and color.[10] And the task, insofar as it pertains to Christians, demands that Christians relate to other bridge builders as worthy partners in a common enterprise. Among these bridge builders are followers of African religious traditions. The proclamation of the salvation fostered by Jesus must not be absolutist. It must be done in intimate dialogue or conversation with Africa. Here lies the realization of the saving presence of the Holy Spirit among humankind, the beginning of an appreciation for a Spirit ecclesiology.

---

10. Patrick Kalilombe, "Reviving Mission *Ad Gentes*," *Catholic International* 2 (No. 6, 1992), p. 296.

3

Observations of an Evangelical
Protestant Missionary in Latin America

Jack Voelkel

Jack Voelkel, an ordained Presbyterian, was born in Korea of missionary parents and holds degrees from Wheaton College, Princeton Seminary, and Fuller Theological Seminary. He and his wife serve in the Seminario Biblico de Colombia in Medellín, where he teaches courses in missiology and his wife in counseling and adult education.

It is a singular privilege for me as an evangelical Protestant missionary in Latin America to share my perspectives on Pope John Paul II's encyclical on missions, *Redemptoris Missio*. However, I hasten to add the disclaimer that I do not pretend to speak as an official representative of Protestant missionaries nor much less for the Latin American national evangelical denominations[1] in general.

APPRECIATION

In a day when interest in mission is waning not only in some sectors of the Roman Catholic Church but also among many historic Protestant denominations, it is refreshing to read the Pope saying that "missionary activity still represents the greatest challenge for the Church" (RM 40). He notes rightly that this activity is itself a source of renewal,

> [for it] revitalizes faith and Christian identity, and offers fresh enthusiasm and new incentive. *Faith is strengthened when it is given to others!* It is in commitment to the Church's universal mission that the new evangelization of Christian peoples will find inspiration and support. (RM 2; emphasis in original)

We feel his passion as he summarizes:

---

1. In Latin America, the term "evangelical" (*evangélico*) is used to refer to the Protestant Churches in general, though some of them may not espouse necessarily what we would normally call a conservative evangelical position.

God is opening before the Church the horizons of a humanity more fully prepared for the sowing of the Gospel. I sense that the moment has come to commit all of the Church's energies to a *new evangelization* and to the *mission ad gentes*. No believer in Christ, no institution of the Church can avoid this supreme duty: to proclaim Christ to all peoples. (RM 3; emphasis mine)

To which we can only give a hearty, "Amen!"

In the quotation above, we note that the Pope is concerned about two areas of mission responsibility: "new evangelization" and "mission *ad gentes*." These will form the two major sections of my observations.

MISSION *"AD GENTES"* (MISSION *"AD EXTRA"*)

Catholic writers repeatedly refer to the Second Vatican Council as marking a "watershed" in their Church's appreciation for other religions (Wright 1991, 153). *Lumen Gentium* mentioned three degrees of participation of the People of God: the Catholic Faithful ("fully incorporated"), other baptized Christians ("linked"), and sincere members of other religions ("related in various ways"), specifically mentioning Jews and Moslems (LG 14-16). Quoting Paul F. Knitter, David Wright underscores that in Vatican II, for the first time in the history of the Church, "a magisterial statement recognized the value and validity not just of non-Christians but of non-Christian religions" (1991, 153). The publication of Knitter's work, *No Other Name?*, in 1985 pushed out the frontiers of salvation even more in what he refers to as "unitive pluralism," that is, religious plurality, but without either mutually exclusive claims or indifference (1985, 207), since the religions are more complementary than contradictory (220), based on his doubts about the reliability of much of the Christian tradition.[2]

As an illustration, we note that Latin American theologian Segundo Galilea, making reference to the teaching of Vatican II, made a revealing statement concerning the shift in goals with regard to the missionary responsibility of Latin America *ad gentes*: "Today there is agreement that mission and the faith it generates is not necessarily a question of salvation or condemnation, of life or death, but more of fullness, grace and humanization" (1981, 14).

The Theological Imperative: "Clear up Doubts"

One of the goals of the Pope in publishing *Redemptoris Missio* was to "clear up doubts and ambiguities regarding the missionary activity *ad gentes*" (RM 2). His problem was to balance two crucial Divine concerns. The first, God's salvific design for all people in all ages and times, is expressed in 1 Tim 2:3, 4: "God our Savior, who wants all men to be saved and come to a knowledge of the truth." The second, Jesus Christ is the only source of salvation, which Paul underscores in the following verse (1 Tim 2:5): "For there is one God and one mediator between God and men, the man Christ Jesus, who gave himself as a ransom for all men." How, then, can these two emphases be reconciled, since obviously great proportions of the human race have never and may never be within the sound of the gospel? The Pope seeks to reconcile these by first emphasizing Jesus Christ as being the only Savior, and then exploring the universal work of the Holy Spirit.

---

2. See David Bosch's discussion of Knitter, whose position he sees to be a "rehash of what Swami Vivekananda said at the World's Parliament of Religions a century ago" (1991, 482).

In dealing with the issue of salvation, the Pope comes down strongly on the unique role and ministry of Jesus Christ whom he calls "the one Savior of all, the only one able to reveal God and lead to God" (5). He quotes Peter's reply to the Jewish religious authorities: "there is salvation in no one else, for there is no other name under heaven given among men by which we must be saved (Acts 4:10)" (5). By stressing this verse, which Knitter uses in the title of his book (*No Other Name?*), he seems to indicate that Knitter had gone too far in his pluralism. He adds, "Although participated forms of mediation of different kinds and degrees are not excluded, they acquire meaning and values *only* from Christ's own mediation, and they cannot be understood as parallel or complementary to his" since Jesus Christ is the one mediator between God and mankind (5; emphasis in original).

The Pope also deals with another theological issue, what he has considered to be the exclusively horizontal approach of liberation theology. Fully aware of the social sensitivity of this school and the response it has enjoyed particularly among Latin American theologians, the Pope emphasizes his support of a gospel that is holistic. He speaks of the importance of "Gospel values" (3, 20), "peace, development and liberation of peoples," "the option for the neediest" (37, 60), and the prophetic responsibility to promote peace, justice, and human rights for the poor and the weak (42), and those who suffer discrimination, abandonment, and oppression (83).

However, he criticizes those who promote an "anthropocentric" gospel, in the "reductive sense of the word, inasmuch as they are focused on man's earthly needs . . . within a horizon that is closed to the transcendent" (17). He stresses that evangelism is the best service (58) and that the gospel message is a force for liberation (60). The spiritual task is the primary one, to proclaim salvation in Christ (83). Jesus Christ is the only Savior; social programs, as important as they are, cannot save.

Having firmly established the only basis of salvation being in Christ and his redemptive work, the Pope then emphasizes God's concern for the whole world and the universal operation of His Spirit. The Pope notes Vatican II's teaching that "the Spirit is at work in the heart of every person, through the 'seeds of the Word,' to be found in human initiatives — including religious ones — and in man's efforts to attain truth, goodness, and God himself" (28). He makes reference to the interreligious meeting held in Assisi where he sought to confirm his conviction that "every authentic prayer is prompted by the Holy Spirit, who is mysteriously present in every human heart" (29). He speaks of the "universality of salvation." Quoting *Gaudium et Spes*, he describes the following logical progression:

[Salvation] applies not only to Christians but to all people of good will in whose hearts grace is secretly at work. Since Christ died for everyone, and since the ultimate calling of each of us comes from God and is therefore a universal one, we are obliged to hold that the Holy Spirit offers everyone the possibility of sharing in this Paschal Mystery in a manner known to God. (10)

He speaks of millions of "our brothers and sisters who like us have been redeemed by the blood of Christ but who live in ignorance of the love of God" (86). Through these statements he appears to be espousing Karl Rahner's position of *anonymous Christianity*, which Bosch sees as "a shift from an ecclesiocentric to a christocentric approach to the theology of religions . . . [the] dominant current Catholic perspective on the theology of religions" (1991, 481).[3] No longer is "Christ against

---

3. Knitter agrees, describing Rahner's theology as "embodying the mainline Catholic view." See his "Catholic Theology of Religions at a Crossroads," cited by Wright (1991, 163).

the religions"; now we have "Christ within the religions" (Wright 1991, 163). Therefore, while on the one hand the Pope stresses the uniqueness of salvation in Christ, he indicates a wide open door for salvation of those who have never heard the gospel, of people he calls "brothers and sisters" yet who have never heard the gospel.[4]

An Evangelical Response

As an evangelical, I identify with the concern of our Catholic brethren who are struggling to reconcile the love of God for the world and His desire for all to be saved, with the uniqueness of Christ's mediatorial work. I am aware that this issue goes back to the earliest Church Fathers, such as Justin Martyr, who was one of the first to use the phrase "the seed of the Word" sown in the hearts of non-Christians, a phrase that appears often both in the Vatican II documents as well as in *Redemptoris Missio.*[5]

In dealing with a Christian approach to other religions, in the words of Charles Van Engen, "Our affirmation of Christian truth is based on our experience of Jesus Christ and grounded on the revelation of God as found in Scripture" (1991, 187). We cannot allow our theological speculation to go beyond these boundaries.

The fate of those who have not heard of Christ undoubtedly will always include an element of mystery. The Spirit does blow where he will. God is just and his ways are beyond our understanding. However, it seems to me that Paul gives us basic guidelines to orient our theology in his opening chapters of Romans. He speaks of the gospel as being the power of salvation for those who *believe* (Rom 1:16). He speaks of God's revelation, both natural (through creation) (1:20-23) and supernatural (the Law) (2:1-6). He notes that the central issue is neither ignorance of the truth or overtly rejecting Christ, but *sin* (2:9-12) of which all are guilty, either by going against their own conscience (2:5) or by consciously breaking God's law (2:17-27).

He concludes that all fall under God's judgment (3:9) because all have sinned (3:10, 23), the wages of which are death (5:23). The application of God's grace and justification comes by faith (3:30) for all who believe. These facts are what give Paul his tremendous sense of obligation to all people (1:14) and push him to minister in ever more remote geographical locations (cf. 15:24). He reiterates his convictions near the end of his Epistle:

> Everyone who calls on the name of the Lord will be saved. How, then, can they call on the one they have not believed in? And how can they believe in the one of whom they have not heard? And how can they hear without someone preaching to them? . . . Consequently, faith comes from hearing the message, and the message is heard through the word of Christ. (Rom 10:13-15, 17)

---

4. In *Redemptor Hominis*, the Pope spelled out even more radically this theme. "We are dealing with 'each' man, for each one is included in the mystery of the Redemption and with each one Christ has united himself forever through this mystery . . . the mystery in which each one of the four thousand million human beings living on our planet has become a sharer from the moment he is conceived beneath the heart of his mother . . . man—*every man without any exception whatever—has been redeemed by Christ*, and . . . with man—with each man without any exception whatever—Christ is in a way united, even when man is unaware of it" (Wright 1991, 157, 158; emphasis mine).

5. See Justin, *Apology II*. The only copy to which I have access is in Spanish: Daniel Ruiz Bueno (ed.), *Padres Apologetas Griegos*. Madrid: Biblioteca de Autores Cristianos, 1979. Evangelicals have also historically been concerned with this crucial issue, and recently a number of scholars explored this and related problems under three topics: Theological Questions, Biblical Exegesis, and Missiological Issues. See Crockett and Sigounto (1991).

I do not find in these passages hints of open doors through other faiths, as noble as they may be. Rather, I discover Paul's deep awareness of the terrible reality of sin[6] and its consequences, the great mercy of God through the gift of His Son, and the urgency for all everywhere to learn of the salvation that is available to them through repentance and faith in the name of Jesus.[7]

The Lausanne Covenant[8] recognizes "some knowledge of God through his general revelation" but denies that this can save, "for people suppress the truth by their unrighteousness" (Rom 1:18-32) (1992, 255). It continues,

> To proclaim Jesus as "the Savior of the world" (Jn 4:42) is not to affirm that all people are either automatically or ultimately saved, still less to affirm that all religions offer salvation in Christ. Rather it is to proclaim God's love for a world of sinners and to invite everyone to respond to him (Mt 11:28). (Ibid., 255)

The note of urgency has historically characterized evangelical mission leaders from Hudson Taylor's heart cry in the last century of "A million a month in China are dying without Christ," to the present, including this statement from the Lausanne Covenant:

> We have become freshly burdened by the vast numbers who have never heard the good news of Christ and are lost without him. . . . He has commanded us to proclaim his good news . . . to summon them to repent, to believe, and follow him. This mandate is urgent, for there is no other Savior but Jesus Christ. (Ibid., 275)

Evangelicals also emphasize the importance of personal and individual response to the gospel. This is part of our heritage rediscovered during the Reformation, renewed during the flowering of Pietism, and then bursting forth during the Great Awakening under John and Charles Wesley in eighteenth-century Britain. During his years of seeking spiritual assurance and peace, John Wesley was confronted by the Moravian missionary pietist, August Gottlieb Spangenberg. He notes in his Journal:

---

6. After reading *Through No Fault of Their Own? The Fate of Those Who Have Never Heard* (Crockett and Sigounto 1991), Kenneth S. Kantzer expressed the following thoughts in his Preface to the same book (14): "We need a deep sense of the awfulness of sin. . . . the awful ugliness and repulsiveness of sin did not seem to me to shine through with a crystal brilliance characteristic of the writings of Moses and Isaiah and Paul and John. Could it be that the church is facing this issue of lostness of humankind in acute form today because as a people we have lost a biblical sense of the awfulness of sin?" I would ask the same question of RM.

7. Note Douglas Moo's chapter, "Romans 2: Saved Apart from the Gospel?" (1991:137-145). He concludes, "Paul never says that Gentiles apart from the gospel can be saved by meeting the demands of the law, or by doing good works. The texts could mean this only if they are ripped out of context. Once the context is recognized, Paul's purposes understood, and his theology of justification taken into account, we quickly see that Gentiles cannot be saved apart from the gospel" (145).

8. The Lausanne Covenant is the legacy of the International Congress on World Evangelization (ICOWE) which met in Lausanne, Switzerland, from 16-25 July 1974. It brought together 2,700 participants from 150 countries—half of them from the non-western world. The Lausanne Covenant can be called the classic statement of contemporary evangelicalism.

[Spangenberg asked me] "Do you know Jesus Christ?" I paused and said, "I know He is the Saviour of the world." "True," replied he; "but do you know He has saved you?" I answered, "I hope He has died to save me." He only added. "Do you know yourself?" I said, "I do." But I fear they were vain words. (Parker n.d., 36-37)

Later, Wesley came to full assurance, the climax being when his heart was "strangely warmed" during the society meeting in Aldersgate Street, London, and his message to England was that all should find what he sought so long to discover (ibid., 64).[9]

How then do we deal with the subject of dialogue? The four forms of dialogue mentioned in DP 42 are helpful, though I would have problems with the fourth, the dialogue of religious experience. I do not find this pattern of dialogue in the New Testament, as we saw in Paul's experience in Acts 17. DP 81 presents Jesus as the model and guide, with reference to Mark 12:34, "You are not far from the Kingdom of God." However, this statement hardly illustrates, "sharing . . . spiritual riches" (DP 42d). Rather, Jesus is helping a true seeker from a position of superiority, affirming the truth that the seeker has already found, and encouraging him onward.

The Pope has little to say about evil or sin and does not mention Satan. In contrast, I discover that when Jesus prepared for his mission, he had two significant encounters. First he was filled with the Holy Spirit, then he faced the Devil. With reference to "all the kingdoms of the world" the Devil offers, "I will give you all their authority and splendor, it has been given to me" (Lk 4:5, 6). Jesus did not challenge this claim. Rather, when the Lord later appeared to Paul he commissioned him to open the eyes of the Gentiles and "turn them from darkness to light, and from the power of Satan to God" (Acts 26:17).

Paul writes to the Corinthians of how "the god of this age has blinded the minds of unbelievers, so that they cannot see the light of the gospel of the glory of Christ" (2 Cor 4:4). He describes our struggle as being against "the spiritual forces of evil" and specifically mentions the devil (Eph 6:11-12). John concludes his first epistle with several things he knows, one of them being that "the world is under the control of the evil one" (1 Jn 5:19). Thus, it would seem relevant for a statement on *Redemptoris Missio*, to underscore with greater clarity what we are being redeemed from, particularly when the Pope is exploring the universal work of the Holy Spirit.

The Lausanne Covenant, in its paragraph on Spiritual Conflict, states: "We believe that we are engaged in constant spiritual warfare with the principalities and powers of evil (Eph 6:12) who are seeking to overthrow the Church and frustrate its task of world evangelization" (1992, 258).

Semmia Busab, a member of the Kimyal tribe in Irian Jaya, Indonesia, gave this unedited testimony of his experiencing new life in Christ.

Before, we at Korupun lived in extreme darkness. Living in darkness, we were utterly ignorant of God and His Word. We lived in absolute darkness. We knew nothing of doing good. We were ignorant of God's good news. Living life in which what we did were only dark things. Our ancestors also went on the dark and sinful path, and it is finished for them. . . . When Philip [the missionary] came bringing God's Word . . . we Korupun people here became God's children. (1992, 14)

---

9. Note A. Skevington Wood, *The Burning Heart. John Wesley: Evangelist*, Minneapolis: Bethany Fellowship, 1967, *passim*.

A Question

The Pope laments the tragedy of widespread indifferentism to mission based on "incorrect theological perspectives . . . characterized by a religious relativism which leads to the belief that 'one religion is as good as another'" (36). Part of the urgency of his task is the practical problem he is facing of the waning of missionary activity "to the nations" (2) to the extent that they are in danger of disappearing (79), a reality he considers to be a sign of crisis, both of faith (2), and of spiritual maturity (48).[10]

As we have seen, he sought to "clear up doubts" and prepare the Church for its evangelistic task. However, I feel the theological position he and the Church have taken, supported only by vague scriptural authority, borders on universalism, and is not likely to stem the indifference to mission that concerns him so deeply nor is it likely to rekindle the same enthusiasm for mission that sent Francis Xavier and others like him to the ends of the earth in a former day.

NEW EVANGELIZATION (MISSION *AD INTRA*)

The Pope turns from his discussion of the importance of mission *ad extra* to missionary activity *ad intra* (34). He describes this mission field as "entire groups of the baptized [who] have lost a living sense of the faith, or even no longer consider themselves members of the Church, and live a life far removed from Christ and his Gospel." Toward them he calls for a "new evangelization, or a re-evangelization" (33). He is painfully aware that the Churches "cannot be missionaries to non-Christians in other countries and continents unless they are seriously concerned about the non-Christians at home" (RM 34). His description fits much of the situation in Latin America today, home to 51 percent of the world's Roman Catholics (Vélez Vásquez 1993).

The Need of New Evangelization in Latin America

The Catholic faith arrived here with the conquistadors five hundred years ago. However, after half a millennium of mostly unchallenged ecclesiastical authority and spiritual influence, statistics reveal that all is not well. It was almost fifty years ago that Fr. John Considine argued for a massive sending of religious personnel, clerical and lay, for Latin America because of a dearth of native clergy and the deep spiritual need of the people (Cleary 1981, 9).[11] However, in spite of their efforts, at the present time Latin America represents the highest ratio of Catholics to priests in the world, and the gap is widening.[12]

Much of the problem of Roman Catholicism in Latin America is due to the kind of Christianity that was brought five hundred years ago. Some note that Spain molded a unique form of Christianity shaped by its own particular historical context.

---

10. In this context, it is interesting to remember Kenneth Scott Latourette's observation in his first volume of *A History of the Expansion of Christianity*, that another indication of vitality is the emergence of creative personalities who "become responsible for modifications in their inherited faith, attract to themselves followers, and are the founders of fresh groups. If in any faith they cease to appear, that faith is either somnolent or moribund" (1937, 3), something for Roman Catholics to keep in mind as they ponder both the lack of national clergy in Latin America and the explosion of the evangelical groups.

11. See John Considine, *A Call for Forty Thousand* (New York: Longmans Green, 1946) *passim*.

12. The *Statistical Yearbook of the Church* shows that in 1989 in Latin America this ratio was 1 : 7,208, up from 6,140 in 1979 (*Catholic International* 2:6:268).

The Protestant theologian, José Miguez Bonino, argues that Christianity as such never really took root in Latin America, that it was never Christian in the sense that Europe or even North America can be said to be so. He speaks of a colossal transplantation — the basic ecclesiastical structures, disciplines, and ministries were brought wholesale from Spain — a tremendous form without substance.

Pablo Alberto Deiros[13] dedicates fifteen pages in his work on the history of Christianity in Latin America to what he refers to as "Popular Catholicism." Among other characteristics, he notes that for many people Mary[14] and the saints are the source of power. Jesus "is one saint more, who helps the believer who seeks the miraculous to respond to the immediate needs of life." He notes the sense of plural figures: there are many "Christs" and many "Virgins" (Deiros 1992, 157).

Great changes have occurred in Latin America since John Mackay's *The Other Spanish Christ* appeared in 1933. People are now encouraged to read the Bible, the mass is celebrated in the vernacular, the charismatic movement has brought renewal to many, and Liberation Theology has created much greater sensitivity to the social needs of the poor. However, the Peruvian anthropologist and missiologist Tito Paredes wonders how many of these changes have filtered down to the "large multitudes of people who practice popular religiosity" (1992, 217).[15]

The Pope states that "some kind of communion, though imperfect, exists among all those who have received *Baptism* in Christ" (50; emphasis mine). As an evangelical I feel that the witness of the Catholic Church has been weakened through this sacramental approach. I share the concern of a Latin American reporter who complained:

> Our towns and villages overflow with baptized people. Are they Christians? . . .
> Many of them limit their participation to the rite [of baptism] and the parochial
> certificate of the saints. They lack a vital experience of God as Father. . . . Our
> baptized also lack a pattern of moral values according to the gospel. Their
> criteria of judgment, the goals for which they struggle, the models of life they
> pursue are divorced from the Lord's plan. (Vélez Vásquez 1993)

---

13. Pablo Alberto Deiros is pastor of the Evangelical Baptist Church and Director of the postgraduate program of the International Theological Baptist Seminary in Buenos Aires, Argentina. He holds a doctorate from the Southwestern Baptist Theological Seminary in the United States.

14. Although it is not a surprise, I feel it is unfortunate (and perhaps symbolic) that the Pope ends RM by referring to "Mary: the Church's Mother and model." With all due respect to the Pope's well-known personal devotion to the Virgin, I venture the following questions. First of all, why does he begin this encyclical by stressing Christ as central to our salvation and the mission of the Church, and then end with reference to Mary? The N.T. pattern, in the majority of cases, gives a model of ending epistles with a reference either to God the Father or Jesus (cf. Rom 16:25-27 as an example). Secondly, why does he mention her as a model of love? As evangelicals we are impressed with the Biblical reference to the love of God as the basis of mission (Jn 3:16) or Christ's love, which compelled Paul (2 Cor 5:14). Thirdly, after speaking of Christ as the only mediator, why does he close with a reference to Mary's mediation? This is of concern to us in Latin America where the figure of the Virgin becomes the de facto mediator and Jesus is seen as either an innocent child in her arms, a crucifix that inspires pity, or the coming judge (Paredes 1992, 216).

15. Note Tito Paredes's article on popular religiosity in Latin America including some of the current interpretations of the Andean forms (1992, 205-218).

The Expectation

Last October the Latin American Bishops (CELAM) met in Santo Domingo for three weeks with the Pope, where he called for stronger missionary efforts. The session issued a report, "New Evangelization, Human Promotion, Christian Culture: Jesus Christ Yesterday, Today, and Forever" (Serbin 1992, 46).[16]

Recently in my travels in Colombia, Peru, and Chile I have seen concrete evidence of the effort of the Church to bring renewal to local congregations and involve them in mission. I look with expectation to the long-term practical results.

The "Evangelical Sects"[17]

At the present time on this continent, both Catholic and Protestant observers note that we are witnessing an explosion of growth among evangelical denominations, particularly the Pentecostals. Peter Berger calls it a "global movement" of "enormous vitality" (1990, vii). According to a Colombian weekly news magazine, the Vatican calculates that "evangelical sects" now form 10 to 15 percent of the total population of Latin America (Vade Retro 1991, 50).[18]

Deiros gives the following description of the popular Protestantism that is growing so rapidly. The message of their preachers is simple, direct, and relevant. Humble lay people are encouraged to participate, and do. Contact with God is immediate and touches personal needs, including healing and deliverance from demon spirits (1992, 167-169). They speak of Jesus as personal Savior and Lord. The Bible is available, read, and studied by all. To most of them it was an unknown book before they became evangelicals.

Samuel Escobar gives evidence from both Catholic and Protestant authors to demonstrate that "the conspiracy theory" — the claim that the growth of popular Protestantism is due to financial and support from the United States for political ends — is unfounded (246). It is a movement deeply rooted in Latin American soil with its own enthusiastic leadership. David Martin,[19] provides the following sociological description of what he calls the evangelical "movement."

---

16. See also Alfred T. Hennelly, *Santo Domingo and Beyond: Documents & Commentaries from the Fourth General Conference of Latin American Bishops* (Maryknoll, N.Y.: Orbis, 1993).

17. The Pope speaks of "Christian and para-Christian sects" (RM 50). Undoubtedly he is applying one definition given by Webster: "a dissenting or schismatic religious body; esp: one regarded as extreme or heretical" (1979:1036). Undoubtedly the vast majority of evangelical groups, including Pentecostals, accept the conclusions of the early Ecumenical Councils and the Apostles' Creed, though they would "dissent" from some of the teachings of the Catholic Church. However, they seek to be faithful to Scripture, and thus feel it is patronizing for the Catholic Church to call them "heretical." They feel, rather, that it is the *Catholics* who have added doctrines not found in Scripture—and are thus "heretical!" Evangelicals reserve the term "sect" to refer to groups such as the Mormons or Jehovah's Witnesses.

18. The periodical, *International Urban Associates*, of which urbanologist Raymond J. Bakke is the executive director, noted in its Winter 1992 edition their projections that by the year 2,000 evangelicals will comprise the following percentage of the population in the following countries: Mexico 15 percent, Guatemala 58 percent, Brazil 29 percent, Chile 27 percent, and Argentina 17 percent.

19. David Martin, one of the world's leading authorities on the sociology of religion, is Emeritus Professor of Sociology at the London School of Economics, and author of *Tongues of Fire. The Explosion of Protestantism in Latin America*.

[It is] able to implant new disciplines, re-order priorities, counter corruption and destructive machismo, and reverse the indifferent and injurious hierarchies of the outside world. Within the enclosed haven of faith a fraternity can be instituted under firm leadership, which provides for release, for mutuality and warmth, and for the practice of new roles. (Martin 1990, 284)

Forty-three different evangelical mission agencies in Brazil have commissioned 1,898 cross-cultural missionaries, 788 of whom are serving in other countries (MARC 1993, 2), an illustration of tremendous spiritual vitality.[20]

According to a Colombian reporter, the subject that dominated the deliberations between the Pope and the College of Cardinals in their April 1991 meeting was the growth of the "religious sects" that affect above all Latin America (Vade Retro 1991, 50).[21] The Pope notes that:

Christian and para-Christian sects are sowing confusion by their activity. The expansion of these sects represents a threat for the Catholic Church and for all the Ecclesiastical Communities with which she is engaged in dialogue. (RM 50)

Undoubtedly he includes within this description the various Pentecostal groups, which account for about 75 percent of the evangelicals in Latin America (Deiros 1992:161). He is right. They are not particularly interested in dialogue. They are convinced they have a message to share that all need and are eager to call people to repentance and faith, regardless of their formal ecclesiastical affiliation.

The Pope expresses his belief in the work of the Holy Spirit in everyone, including devotees of religions hostile to Christianity. On other hand, Escobar laments that none of the Catholic missiologists he has read "look at popular Protestantism as one of the many movements that the Spirit of God has raised for the renewal of the church in the twenty centuries of Christian history" (1992, 247). I would like to encourage the Catholic hierarchy to appreciate the evidences of genuine Biblical spirituality within the various expressions of popular evangelical piety in Latin America. I would humbly suggest that nominal Catholics are being attracted to these evangelical groups because they are finding something legitimate they hunger for that they do not find at home.

CONCLUSION

I end my remarks as I began, by applauding the missionary spirit of Pope John Paul II and his concern for the extension of the gospel to all the nations of the world. Though I would prefer to believe, as he does, that "every man without any exception whatever — has been redeemed by Christ," I cannot find Biblical warrant for this

---

20. I do not intend this very brief description to be triumphalistic. As with any movement, popular Protestantism has its limitations in many spheres. For example, some would point out a certain shallowness of teaching, due to the lack of formal theological training of many of their leaders; others would like to see more social emphasis, criticizing that these groups become a "refuge of the masses" (see Lalive d'Epinay 1968: *passim*); and others describe their worship as mere emotionalism. My purpose is to stress its genuine spiritual vitality and growth. For a more complete contemporary analysis see Escobar (1992), Martin (1990) and Stoll (1990).

21. The author listed as the major causes of this attrition from the Catholic fold (1) lack of priests; (2) religious ignorance; (3) excessive ideological and political aspects of religious reflection; and (4) lack of close relationship among the religious societies.

optimism and suggest that it mitigates against the very missionary urgency and renewal he longs to promote.

I am grateful to God for the emphasis on New Evangelization on a continent where so much of traditional Christianity is "form without substance." I wish the Catholic Church well in their goal to bring renewal and encourage them rather than seeing the "evangelical sects" as a threat, to approach them as members of the same family who are under deep constraint to share the gospel, even if their enthusiastic activity be seen at the present time as "sowing confusion."[22]

---

22. Ricardo Pietrantionio, a pastor from Buenos Aires and a representative of the World Lutheran Federation, was one of the Protestant observers at the CELAM meetings in Santo Domingo. He gave the opinion that Catholic leaders have had the false assumption that Latin America was their "property." He added, "This world is going to have religious pluralism and the solution is to coexist, not combat" (Serbin 1992, 48).

BIBLIOGRAPHY

Berg, Mike and Pretiz, Paul. 1992. *The Gospel People*. Miami: Latin America Mission.

Berger, Peter. 1990. "Foreword," in David Martin, *Tongues of Fire. The Explosion of Protestantism in Latin America*. Oxford: Blackwell.

Blauw, Johannes. 1962. *The Missionary Nature of the Church. A Survey of the Biblical Theology of Mission*. New York: McGraw-Hill.

Bosch, David J. 1991. *Transforming Mission. Paradigm Shifts in Theology of Mission*. Maryknoll, N.Y.: Orbis.

Busab, Semmia. 1992. "What God Has Done at Korupun." Trans. Elinor Young. In *Church Planter's Link*. 3:314-316. Third Quarter

Cleary, Edward. 1981. *Crisis and Change. The Church in Latin America Today*. Maryknoll: Orbis.

Crockett, William V. 1991. "Will God Save Everyone in the End?" pp. 159-168 in Crockett and Sigounto (1991).

Crockett, William V. and Sigounto, James G. (eds.). 1991. *Through No Fault of Their Own?* Grand Rapids: Baker.

Deiros, Pablo Alberto. 1992. *Historia del Cristianismo en América Latina*. Buenos Aires: Fraternidad Teológical Latinoamericana.

Dialogue and Proclamation. 1992. In Scherer, James A., and Bevans, Stephen B., S.V.D. (eds.), *New Directions in Mission and Evangelization I. Basic Statements 1974-1991*, pp. 177-200. Maryknoll, N.Y.: Orbis.

Escobar, Samuel. 1992. "Mission in Latin America: An Evangelical Perspective," *Missiology*, 20:2:241-254. April.

Galilea, Segundo. 1981. *La Responsabilidad Misionera de America Latina*. Bogotá: Paulinas.

Gaudium et Spes. 1966. In Walter M. Abbott, S.J. (ed.), *The Documents of Vatican II*. New York: Guild.

Kalilombe, Bishop Patrick, W. F. 1991. "Reviving Mission *ad Gentes*" in *Catholic International*, 2:6:296-297, 15-31 March.

Knitter, Paul F. 1985. *No Other Name?: A Critical Survey of Christian Attitudes toward the World Religions*. Maryknoll, N.Y.: Orbis.

Lalive d'Epinay, Christian. 1968. *El Refugio de las Masas*. Santiago, Chile: Editorial del Pacifico.

Latourette, Kenneth Scott. 1937. *The First Five Centuries*. Volume 1 in *A History of the Expansion of Christianity*. Grand Rapids: Zondervan.

Lausanne Covenant. 1992. In Scherer, James A. and Bevans, Stephen B., S.V.D., *New*

Directions in Mission and Evangelization I. Basic Statements 1974-1991, pp. 253-259. Maryknoll: Orbis.

Lumen Gentium. 1966. In Walter M. Abbott, S.J. (ed.), *The Documents of Vatican II.* New York: Guild.

MARC Newsletter. March 1993.

Martin, David. 1990. *Tongues of Fire. The Explosion of Protestantism in Latin America.* Oxford: Blackwell.

Moo, Douglas. 1991. "Romans 2: Saved Apart from the Gospel?" pp. 137-145 in Crockett and Sigounto (1991).

Paredes, Tito. 1992. "Popular Religiosity: A Protestant Perspective," *Missiology* 20:2:205-220, April.

Parker, Percy Livingstone (ed.). n.d. *The Journal of John Wesley.* Chicago: Moody.

Serbin, Ken. 1992. "Catholic Bishops Renew Missionary Efforts to Stem Growth of 'Sects,'" *Christianity Today* 36:15:46. December 14.

Stoll, David. 1990. *Is Latin America Turning Protestant?* Berkeley: University of California Press.

Vade Retro. *Semana.* April 23, 1991, pp. 50-51.

Van Engen, Charles. 1991. "The Effect of Universalism," pp. 183-194 in Crockett and Sigounto (1991).

Velez Vasquez, Gustavo, "El Documento de Santo Domingo," *El Colombiano* (Medellín). 28 March 1993.

Webster's New Collegiate Dictionary. 1979. Springfield: G. & C. Merriam Company.

Wright, David. 1991. "The Watershed of Vatican II: Catholic Attitudes towards Other Religions," chapter 8 (pp. 153-171) in Andrew D. Clarke and Bruce W. Winter (eds.), *One God, One Lord in a World of Religious Pluralism.* Cambridge: Tyndale House.

4

Redemptoris Missio and Mission in India

Augustine Kanjamala, S.V.D.

Augustine Kanjamala is an Indian Divine Word Missionary priest assigned to the Ishvani Kendra National Missiological Institute in Pune, India. Ordained in 1970, Father Kanjamala holds a doctorate from the University of Lancaster, where he wrote on religion and the modernization process in India.

The purpose of this article is to illustrate that the Indian church has a distinctive response and reaction to the recent encyclical, *Redemptoris Missio.* I shall focus on the radically diverse missionary contexts exemplified in the various regions of India, analyzing the theology of the new document in relation to different types of people in India — for example, fundamentalist Hindus, oppressed Dalits (outcasts), and tribals. I shall attempt to explain why Indian theologians in general are unhappy with the theology of *Redemptoris Missio,* and in conclusion suggest alternative priorities.

THE INDIAN MISSIONARY SITUATION

After two thousand years of Christian presence and five hundred years of rather aggressive proselytization, starting from the beginning of the sixteenth century, Christian mission in India does not seem to have been a success if we evaluate it with the traditional ideal scheme of proclamation leading to conversion and baptism. At the end of the nineteenth century, when the mass conversion movement started in India among the Dalits and tribal peoples, only 0.7 percent of the population was Christian. Mass movement was responsible for the rapid growth of the Christian population from 0.7 to 2.6 percent in 1950 when India was constituted into a new republic. No significant growth has been recorded during the past forty-five years except in northeast India.

Christian missionaries arrived in India at different periods in history and initiated missionary activities in different areas among different ethnic and cultural groups. In terms of the results of their work, it may be significant to note that nearly 60 percent of the Christian population of India is concentrated in the four southern states (10,279,869, according to the 1981 census). Nearly half belong to the Oriental Church (Syro–Malabar Rite) who claim as their origin the missionary activity of St. Thomas the Apostle. The next concentration in Tamilnadu is the result of the missionary work started during the Padroado period. In the other states some successful missionary work was carried out during the last century.

With the aggressive missionary methods of the Portuguese missionaries, 40 percent of Goa was converted to Catholicism by the middle of the seventeenth century. Due to migration of the Catholics to other regions and the migration of other religious groups into Goa today the Christians constitute about 30 percent of the population. The rest of the Christian community in the Western region is the fruit of the past one hundred years of missionary activity, mainly among the Harijans and the tribals. According to the 1981 census 1,248,441 Christians in the area make 7.76 percent of India's Christian population.

One hundred and fifty years ago the German Lutheran missionaries, followed by the Jesuit missionaries, entered the Chotanagpur plateau. The Adivasis (aboriginal settlers of the land) had been exploited by the government officials, Hindu landlords, for several centuries; their ancestral land had been robbed and they were oppressed. When the missionaries, for example Fr. Constant Lievens, S.J., came to protect their land with the help of lawyers, around 70,000 people joined the Catholic Church in seven years. The two million Christians of Chotanagpur constitute 10 percent of Indian Christians and are living in fourteen districts spread over the southern part of Bihar, northern part of Orissa, eastern part of Madhya Pradesh, and western part of Bengal.

In spite of the missionary efforts of the Jesuits, Capuchins, and others for the past four hundred years in the Hindi belt, starting in 1580, conversion from Hinduism to Christianity is next to nil. A small number of Muslims were converted to Christianity in the eighteenth century because of the influence of a few Muslim converts from the ruling class, for example, the baptism of Begum Yohanna Samru, in Sardhana near Meerut in 1781. However, in the course of history, a good number of them went back to their original fold.

Nearly 75 percent of the Christians in the Hindi region are converts from the Adivasis in Chotanagpur and about 20 percent from the outcasts. This happened when missionaries, like Paul and Barnabas (Acts 13), after their unsuccessful work among the upper castes, turned their attention to the margin of the society at the end of the last century. The small number of Christians from other communities found in this region are those who came here as workers and soldiers during the colonial period and they are not culturally integrated into the local Church. Sixteen dioceses in North India have less than 15,000 Catholics each. In Upper Pradesh, the largest state with 120 million people (including 16 percent Muslims), the 0.15 percent Christian presence is like a drop in the ocean (A. Kanjamala, *Vidyajyoti*, May 1992).

The Christian presence in these small Hindi states, which are predominantly occupied by the Hindus, is very insignificant. Of the Christians in this area (61,000), 75 percent are concentrated in Delhi, most of whom have come from South India to the capital for employment. The number of Christians in the other states is almost negligible, with a small number of converts from the tribals and the Harijans. Jammu and Kashmir is a Muslim-dominated state with 64.1 percent Muslims, 32.2 percent Hindus, and 0.14 percent Christians. Muslim fundamentalism and militancy is fighting the Hindus. The Christians are a "tiny flock" indeed.

The region most responsive to the Christian mission during the past half a century is the northeast, which is predominantly tribal, belonging to the Chinese race. As a tribal population they were exploited both by the Muslim rulers as well as Hindu rulers. They were eager to become Christians when the Protestant missionaries entered the area a century ago. Though the Catholic missionaries came to Shillong in 1890 (the centenary was celebrated in 1990), successful missionary activities were carried out only in the post-independence period. Most of the credit for the conspicuous success here goes to the Salesian missionaries. Missionary activities in the traditional sense still continue with certain dynamism, which is not observed in other parts of India. The missiological thinking as well as missionary methods in the region are very much influenced by this success story. The 900,000 Catholics in the northeast constitute 25 percent of the Christians of the region. Today 17.7 percent of the Indian Christians are in the northeast, compared to 7.8 percent in 1951. This growth pattern shows that missionary activity is quite dynamic in this area and the response from the people is very encouraging.

In spite of sincere dedication, hard work, and admirable sacrifices by large numbers of European and American missionaries — Protestant and Catholic — the number of the Christians in the country today is small. Fewer than fourteen million (13,424,000) are Catholics. Nearly 50 percent belong to the Scheduled Caste and 25 percent belong to the Scheduled Tribe, most of whom were converted during the mass conversion movement. The failure of the Christian mission in terms of proclamation and baptism among high-caste Hindus and among Muslims and other religious groups (for example, the Sikhs) in India was a source of missiological debates and anxiety among missionaries for ages. Asia, with the exception of a few tribal belts, is the most difficult mission in the world. Given all this, what relevance has *Redemptoris Missio* for Asia in general and India in particular?

INTERPRETING THE CONTEXT OF *REDEMPTORIS MISSIO*

Crisis of Faith and Decline of Missionary Spirit

Pope John Paul II published RM to answer and clarify various issues and confusions regarding the nature and methods of understanding and carrying on mission that have grown up in the post-Vatican II period. While recognizing the growth of the missionary activity in "mission countries," it expresses itself as aware of serious decline of the missionary spirit, missionary personnel, and missionary activities (2).

On the global level, Christianity is on the decline in relation to the world population; it constitutes only 32.5 percent of the world population and the Catholic population is nearly 19 percent. A glance at the continents of the world shows the responses to mission varied from continent to continent. In Africa the Christian population grew from 9.2 percent (1900) to 45.4 percent today. In Europe, the Christian population has declined during the same period, from 97 percent to 84 percent. The Latin American situation is rather steady with 95 percent at the beginning of the century and 92 percent at the close of the century, and the Latin American church constitutes 40 percent of world Catholicism. In North America today's Christian population at 87 percent of total population is 10 percent less than at the turn of the century. Asia, the largest mission country in the world, has only 2 percent Christians. The Philippines is the only exception, with 84 percent Catholic population (Barrett 1982, 782-785).

Due to mass conversions resulting from intense missionary activities during the last hundred years, the center of world Christianity is gradually shifting from the Atlantic region toward the Pacific. In the beginning of the century 77 percent of the Catholic population and 85 percent of the Christians were found in the Northern Hemisphere. The Southern Hemisphere had only 15 percent of the Christian population and 23 percent of the Catholic population. By the year 1960 the Catholic population had declined to 52 percent in the North and increased to 48 percent in the South, due to successful missionary efforts. The trend of decline is continuing and, according to the predictions of W. Bühlmann, by the year 2,000 60 percent of the Christian population will be in the South and the remaining 40 percent in the North.

The power equation also is expected to shift along these lines (Bühlmann 1976, 86-87; 129-160).

The encyclical, from beginning to end, projects a sense of anxiety, not only because of the quantitative change in the world mission but primarily because of the decline of the quality of Catholic life in Europe and America. The anxiety may be well placed since, for example, fewer than 10 percent of the Catholics in Europe regularly attend Sunday liturgy. Pope John Paul expresses his anxiety: "Missionary drive has always been a sign of vitality. Just as its lessening is a sign of a crisis of faith" (2).

The Pope's Response

This anxiety for the fate of the church, particularly in traditional "mission-sending" countries, permeates the encyclical. Decline in the missionary drive is also seen as decline and crisis of faith (2). With the emergence of theological fashions unfavorable to missionary activity, there seems also to be a lull in Western Catholics' support of direct proclamation and of the necessity of being a visible member of the visible church. While Westerners express themselves as being "spiritual," fewer wish to identify with organized religion. The Pope summarizes the issue in a series of rhetorical questions that are not rhetorical for many Christians today:

As a result of the changes which have taken place in modern times and the spread of new theological ideas, some people wonder: *Is missionary work among the non-Christians still relevant?* Has it not been replaced by interreligious dialogue? Is not human development an adequate goal of the Church's mission? Does not respect for conscience and for freedom exclude all efforts at conversion? Is it not possible to attain salvation in any religion? *Why then should there be missionary activity?* (4; emphasis in original)

When one looks at the mission chronologically, three interrelated major models are marked: (1) the mission of Jesus, which was predominantly Kingdom-centered; (2) the apostolic mission, which was predominantly Christ-centered; (3) the post-Constantine mission, which was predominantly church-centered.

The main mission theology of *Redemptoris Missio* is found in the first three chapters of the encyclical. This section has also been taken as the Pope's attempt to clarify questions and to answer some missiological stances taken by the Indian theologians in recent times. The Holy Father's attempt to modify the historical model into a theological model is a serious attempt to reconcile the tensions that exist between different models operative in different parts of the world. From the historical perspective it is clear that whenever one model was dominant in a given situation, other models were less important. Below we shall discuss these elements from an Indian ecclesial and theological perspective, first by bringing into relief several elements of the Scriptural tradition on mission that seem particularly important from an Indian perspective.

THE TRINITARIAN BIBLICAL THEOLOGY OF MISSION

The Kingdom of God

It is evident that central message of the proclamation of Jesus, after receiving the Holy Spirit at baptism, was the Kingdom of God (Mk 1:14-15). The proclamation and establishment of the Kingdom are the purpose of his mission: "I was sent for this purpose" (Lk. 4:43). Further Jesus Himself was the "Good News" as he applied the words of Prophet Isaiah to himself. (Lk 4:14-21; Is 61:1). Jesus experienced and revealed that God is "Abba," Father. (Mk 14:36). St. John tells us that God is love (1 Jn 4:8, 16). When people "repent" and "believe" in God's merciful love (Lk 15:3-32) they are transformed by love. God's Kingdom is meant for all, especially the poor and oppressed. To show this he had table fellowship with the sinners and outcasts (Lk 5:30), and treated them as equals (Lk 7:34). Jesus was conscious of his mission, particularly to the poor (Lk 4:18) (Soares-Prabhu 1992, 140ff.).

Healing and forgiving characterize the physical and spiritual dimensions of his ministry also in RM (cf. 14). Acts of liberation from demonic possession are signs that "the Kingdom of God is come upon you" (Mt 28). The power of Satan is defeated. Humankind is restored to wholeness. The Kingdom aims at transforming human relationships. The whole law is summed up in the commandment of love (Mt 22:34-40). The "new commandment" is "Love one another as I have loved you" (Jn 13:34). Communion among all human beings and communion with God is the final goal of the Kingdom also in RM (15). When God's plan of reconciliation and loving communion is realized for all, the Kingdom of God will come. Even the new cosmic order — new heaven and new earth — is part of the Kingdom.

Christ-Centeredness

The experience of the Risen Lord, as recalled in RM, was so powerful that the apostles began to preach more about Christ and less about the Kingdom of God (16). For instance, Jesus spoke about the Kingdom about one hundred times. The apostles spoke of it about a dozen times. Peter said to the Jewish leaders, "There is no other name under heaven given to men by which we must be saved" (Acts 4:10, 12).

God's revelation is definitive and complete in his only begotten son, says Paul. "In many and various ways God spoke of old to our fathers by the prophets: but in these last days he has spoken to us by a son, whom he appointed the heir of all things, through whom he also created the world" (Heb 1:1-2). Christ is the only mediator between God and mankind. " For there is one God and there is one mediator between God and men, the man Christ Jesus who gave himself as a ransom for all" (1 Tim 2:5-7).

The prologue of St. John sees the universal aspect of his mission of grace, truth, and revelation (RM 5). "No one comes to the Father but by me" (Jn 14:6). A certain amount of controversy is involved in the contemporary theological debate on the following issues. What is the relation between the divine and human nature in incarnation? What is the nature of the union between the divine and human? Between the Word and Jesus Christ? What is the relation between "Jesus of history" and "Christ of faith?" (6). This christological controversy is not new; it is as old as the Church. The encyclical is reaffirming the unity, which is traditionally held. Christ is none other than Jesus (6).

The Pope further draws our attention to the tension between the proclamation of the Kingdom and the proclamation of Christ. In the Risen Christ, the Kingdom is inaugurated and proclaimed. "The preaching of the early Church was centered on the proclamation of Jesus Christ with whom the Kingdom was identified. . . . There is a need to unite *the proclamation of the Kingdom of God . . .* and *proclamation of the Christ-event* (the "kerygma" of the Apostles). The two proclamations are complementary" (16; emphasis in original). Many who speak about the Kingdom are silent about Christ, says the Pope (18). "Christ not only proclaimed the Kingdom, but in him the Kingdom itself became present and was fulfilled" (18). Detaching the Kingdom of God from Jesus Christ makes it impossible to understand the Kingdom he came to preach. The importance of RM at this period of the mission history is the

Holy Father's strong Christocentrism. It is significant to note that many theologians as well as missionaries maintain a studied silence about the proclamation of Christ.

Role of Holy Spirit

Chapter three of RM, on the Holy Spirit as the principal agent of mission, is both scripturally based and inspiring. The relation between the Spirit and the Church and Kingdom, the relation between Christ and Church is unique. Church is the "seed, sign and instrument of the Kingdom." Like her founder she is the servant of the Kingdom. The presence of the Kingdom of God outside the visible boundaries of the Church is upheld in RM because of the salvific functions of the Spirit in the whole world. This implies the provisionality of the Church, contrary to the high ecclesiology of RM, article 18.

The first three chapters of RM constitute the Trinitarian pattern of the mission. This pattern is also the source of tension in the missionary thinking and missionary methods. As an adequate understanding of the Trinity is not possible, so understanding Trinitarian missiology also is difficult. Hence there is bound to be a certain tension in missionary approaches.

The root cause of the contemporary missiological debate and missionary approaches is the inability of many to balance the dynamism and tensions of a Trinitarian thrust. To avoid this, many theologians and missionaries seek a solution that prefers one over the other.

HINDU RESPONSES TO CHRISTIAN MISSION

Yes to Jesus and No to Mission

During the eighteenth to the twentieth centuries, proclamation of Jesus Christ in India received two distinctive responses from Hinduism. Initially, many educated Hindus, who received Christian college educations, began to renounce the so-called superstitions of their own religion and began to appreciate Christianity and Western thought as a source of social change. For instance, Raja Ram Mohan Roy (1773-1833), founder of the Hindu renaissance, believed that the best ethical precepts for the reformation of Hinduism and India could be found in the teachings of Jesus Christ, particularly in the Sermon on the Mount. He published two books in English, *The Precepts of Jesus* and *Way to Peace and Happiness* (1820), with translations in Sanskrit and Bengali. He was the promoter of an "Ethical Christology," though he remained a Hindu. Other examples include K. C. Sen (1838-1884) and P. C. Mozoomdar, who, though not baptized, considered himself a disciple of Jesus and published the book *Oriental Christ*, in which he said: "My aspiration has been not to speculate on Christ but to be what Christ tells me to be" (Sharpe 1988, 8).

Among twentieth-century Hindu intellectuals and leaders Jesus is accorded a very special place, especially by Mahatma Gandhi (1869-1948), the leader of Indian independence and the father of the nation. Gandhi was never sympathetic to missionaries, whom he thought were collaborators with the mighty colonial power. But he was a great lover and admirer of Jesus. He read the Gospels regularly and it was obligatory for the members of his ashram to read scriptures of all religions.

According to philosopher and statesman S. Radhakrishnan (1888-1975) Jesus's life and teaching were closer to Eastern spirituality than to Western. For example, Jesus's teaching of "Eternal life" is mystical. An internal change and conversion is more important than the observance of the law. Again in his teaching on the Kingdom of God Jesus breaks away from the exclusivism of Judaism. The universality of

Jesus is seen in his attitude and relations to Romans, Greeks, Gentiles, and outcasts. Like a Hindu *sanyasi* Jesus is an ascetic.

No to Jesus and to Christian Mission

In contrast to the openness discussed above, organized opposition to the Christian mission in the modern times can be traced back to Dayanand Sarasvati (1824-1883) and his followers. In 1875 he founded "Arya Samaj" to fight missionaries and purify Hinduism. His motto was "back to the Vedas." He originated the Sudhi movement to reconvert Christian and Muslims back to Hinduism. Dr. Keshav Baliram Hedgewar (1889-1940) founded "Rashtrya Swayam-sevak Sangh" (RSS) to organize Hindus and to overthrow foreign rule as well as foreign missionaries. The main ideologist of RSS was Veer Savarkar (1893-1966). In his book *Hindutya* [Hindu Nationhood] he argued for Hindu *rashtgra* and ridiculed Western civilization and Western missionaries who were still living in the jungles when the great Indian civilization was flourishing. His policy was: "Hinduize all politics and militarize Hinduism."

There is, indeed, a wrong impression propagated by some Western scholars who have studied the Hindu scriptures, but not the history of Hinduism and Hindu culture, that Hinduism is a tolerant religion. This is false. Hinduism, like any other religion, becomes aggressive whenever its existence and identity are threatened.

RESPONSE OF THE TRIBALS AND DALITS — MASS CONVERSION

Proclaiming Jesus Christ to and obtaining conversions to the Christian community has been partially successful among the tribals and the Dalits of India. About 7.5 percent of India's population (65 million) are tribals, and among them about 5.5 percent converted to Christianity during the mass conversion. Fifteen percent of India's population (130 million) is classified as Scheduled Castes. Traditionally they were India's untouchables and outcasts because of the menial tasks they performed in the society. They were the slaves of Indian society, oppressed and inhumanly treated for more than three millennia. Today they prefer to be called "Dalits" [the oppressed]. When Christian missionaries preached love, equality, freedom, and human dignity, they embraced Christianity in large numbers in different parts of India. According to Stephen Fuchs social justice was the major factor that influenced mass conversion:

> And the reasons for the change of religion are evident: the refusal of the privileged class to grant social justice to the oppressed and exploited inferior communities. The conversion to Christian faith which preaches social justice and rejects economic exploitation could be fully justified. The dominating higher castes have to blame themselves for losing the aboriginals and the low castes to the Christian Churches since they continue to refuse the tribals and low castes their basic human rights. (Fuchs, 1972, 235)

Although the exact number of Dalit converts to Christianity is not available, it is estimated that about 8 percent of them have embraced Christianity and today they constitute half of the Catholic population. Among the Protestant churches the percentage is around 75 percent. During the last decades Dalit conversion is negligible. (Conversion of a few million Dalits to Buddhism in 1956 under the leadership of Ambedkar was also a protest movement and painful search for human dignity.) Nevertheless, high hopes and expectations for human dignity and equality are not always realized, since the caste system is still prevalent in the church (Raj 1992, 95ff.).

The biggest credit given to the Christian missionaries in India is for their selfless services among the tribals, Harijans, and backward communities. The missionaries should rejoice that the Gospel is preached to the poor (Lk 4:18). In the words of Jawaharlal Nehru, the first prime minister of India, in 1955:

> The Christian missionaries went to various tribal areas and some of them spent practically all their lives there . . . missionaries did very good work there and I am full of praise but, politically speaking, they did not particularly like the change in India.

K. M. Panikkar, a critic of Christian mission, observes the following:

> The work of the missionaries among the aboriginal tribes may be said to have created a tradition of social service which modern India has inherited. If the Indian Constitution includes special provisions for the welfare of the tribal communities and Adivasis, and if the Centre and the States are making concentrated efforts to bring them up to the general level of India, much of the credit for such activities must be given to the missionaries. (Panikkar 1963, 53).

AN INDIAN RESPONSE TO *REDEMPTORIS MISSIO*

With all the above as background, I turn to a more systematic response to *Redemptoris Mission* from within the Indian context.

One of the three parameters of mission *ad gentes* in RM is the so-called "territorial" frontier. As we have noted, by the end of the second millennium 60 percent of the world population will be in Asia, where only 2 percent of the population is Christian. Mission history shows that Indian mission is one of the most difficult missions in Asia. In the post-Vatican II period, Indian theologians are making a sincere effort to bring Christ and his Gospel to all strata of the society. It is within this context that they emphasize the theology of the Kingdom of God.

Their efforts to formulate a new christology — using Indian philosophy in a way parallel to the early church's adaptation of Hellenism and Greek philosophical categories in Nicene-Constantinopolian christology — is part of the same process. Indian theologians are aware that the second chapter of RM, on the Kingdom of God, is a criticism aimed at them. In that context, several observations from India on RM are perhaps apropos.

First, the tone of the encyclical tends to be aggressive in the sense that it is a powerful restatement of the traditional Christian mission theology. The Indian bishops, theologians, and missionaries, who are in constant touch with the non-Christian world (the *gentes* of *ad Gentes*), are — one might suggest — better judges of the missionary situation in India than the Western church. From an Indian point of view, pronouncements from the West are often permeated with outlooks derived from theoretical considerations that stem from mainly intellectual and not existential contact with Asian realities.

To many in Asia, RM appears to be primarily a response to the missionary crisis in Europe and America. It does not take seriously the Asian and Indian theological reflections. The meetings of the Federation of Asian Bishops' Conferences of 1974, 1979, and 1991, for instance, defined evangelization as a threefold dialogic process. Instead of integrating the visions and reflections of Asian bishops and theologians, the Vatican has come out with heavy criticism. In essence, however, this encyclical, despite its many good and valid points, only indirectly and then inadequately addresses the problems and life experience of Asia, home of all the major world religions. It voices, instead, primarily the anxieties of the traditional Catholic countries. A good number of theologians and people in the West are happy with *Redemptoris Missio*. Some in India are also quite happy with the teaching of the Holy Father. But by implicitly blaming Asian theologians for propagating new heresies and accusing India of being the epicenter of these heresies, Rome avoids the real problem of mission on its own doorstep. Why is the number of missionaries drastically declining in the West? Why is there a serious lack of mission spirit in Europe and North America? It is more urgent that the West put its own house in order before trying to enforce order in the East where there is greater religious as well as missionary spirit. By shifting the blame to the East, the West appears to be trying to escape fundamental theological and missiological problems and anxieties generated in modern Western culture.

Redemptoris Missio also introduces, perhaps unintentionally, a certain opposition between the mission of Christ, which is mediated in and through the church, and the work of the Holy Spirit, which is present and operative in a less visible manner outside the church in the religions and cultures of the world. This dichotomy may be the root cause of a certain reluctance for serious dialogue between Christianity and other religions — as if it were clear in one area and very mysterious in the other. Belief that "fullness of Revelation" (56) and "fullness of the means of salvation" (55) are present only in the church conveys the idea that the church has nothing seriously new to learn. Genuine dialogue — which is of primary importance in the Indian context — seems impossible with such a mindset.

A root cause for the misunderstanding between the Congregation for Evangelization of Peoples and Indian theologians is the problem of language. Most Western theologians are familiar only with a christology that is formulated with the help of Greek philosophy. In contrast, a majority of the Indian theologians are familiar both with Greek and Indian philosophy. When Indian theologians begin to use Indian concepts to formulate a new christology, most Western theologians — or at least those who appear to have helped the Holy Father draft RM — appear unable to understand new and unfamiliar formulation. Because these two philosophies develop from two different worldviews, they do not use a common vocabulary. Yet any theology that does not use Greek philosophical categories canonized in magisterial statements seems suspect and erroneous.

Another reason for the tension between Western and Eastern theology stems from diverse methods of theologizing. The Indian religious tradition is primarily concerned with the *experience* of God and of mystical unity between God and nature. Thus subjective experience is accorded centrality to a higher degree than "objective" truth and faithfulness to dogmatic formulae. Since the East emphasizes mysticism and the West emphasizes intellectualism, there is no easy solution. Those who uphold traditional missiology follow the so-called "theology from above." Most Asian theologians and a few Western theologians follow the methodology of "theologizing from below." Accordingly, answers to questions are bound to differ, since genuine theology should relate God's word to the realities of the world; but the context and realities of the West and the East virtually imply different worlds. They are radically different, and when representatives engage in the process of theologizing, they are bound to reach different conclusions — minimally they phrase even identical or analogous conclusions very differently.

Traditional mission theology and the emerging mission theology of India cannot be easily reconciled. This needs to be faced squarely. The relation between the Kingdom of God, the proclamation of Jesus Christ as universal savior, and the work of the Holy Spirit in both the church and in other religions, need to be clarified in search for mutual understanding. Perhaps some are fighting against a new

"Copernican revolution" in theology of mission. Indian theologians are seriously and genuinely searching for ways to express integral Christian faith. The freedom to make mistakes is a necessary part of the experiment.

Dialogue between Western and Indian theologians is one of the urgent missiological needs of our day. It is also unfortunate that Indian theologians are not called for a dialogue with the Congregation for the Evangelization of Peoples and the Congregation for the Doctrine of the Faith. There seems to be an actual lack of openness to engage in the dialogue that all profess to have. Both theologians and the stewards of the central Roman magisterium need to be open to correct their views of each other.

SEARCHING FOR AN ALTERNATIVE MODEL IN INDIA

The main emphasis of RM is on the traditional missionary model characterized by the following priorities: (1) Proclaiming Jesus Christ, converting, and baptizing non-Christians to the Catholic Church for their salvation; (2) planting the Church and ensuring its institutional strength; (3) interior transformation and new life in the Spirit.

India is searching for an alternative model of the mission. By an alternative model, I mean a new model of mission able:

• to reinterpret traditional mission theology with the help of Indian philosophical and cultural categories;
• to find a new way of organizing and relating as a Christian community to persons in other traditions; and
• to articulate new ways of feeling about mission, local peoples, and their culture.

Above all, the search is for new priorities in the realization of the various constitutive elements of mission. This should provide an integrated as well as a new vision of the mission, which will also demand a new lifestyle.

The alternative may be contrasted as a *qualitative* model of mission being striven for in India, one that reverses traditional *quantitative* models for measuring missionary success. It involves alterations as well as promoting new priorities. The future of the mission in India in all likelihood is not going to be marked by a great increase in quantitative results such as numbers of converts but in quality. How might we understand this principle?

First, proclamation and working for the realization of the Kingdom of God are the highest priorities in evangelization. However, it does not follow that the Kingdom of God is detached from Jesus Christ. In the Jesus who proclaimed the Kingdom, we have the concrete unfolding of the Kingdom and realization of the Kingdom in the course of history. Ours is a country that loves and respects the person of Jesus and his message of love, compassion, forgiveness, and selfless sacrifice. In a person-oriented mission thus announcing Jesus, and his Gospel whenever and wherever it is possible, should be understood as an integral part of the mission of the Church. The message of Jesus is universal.

Second, mission begins with the conversion of the heart of the missionary according to the values taught by Jesus. In the past, mission emphasized the conversion of the *object* of the mission — non-Christian people. In the future conversion must begin with the *subject* of the mission — missionaries. Missionaries who have not experienced God and are therefore unable to communicate an experience of God are not credible. In this regard, the last chapter of RM, "Missionary Spirituality," is especially noteworthy. The true missionary is a saint (90). The exhortation that "The missionary must be a contemplative in action" (91) is very appropriate in the Indian religious ethos.

Third, by providing an alternative vision of life, world, and society, Christian mission should continue to challenge Indian society as it did in the past. That is a prophetic role that many, perhaps because of their minority status, are afraid to exercise. By providing the model of action for the liberation of the Dalits, tribals, and other socially and economically marginalized communities, however, the Christians can contribute to creating a new social consciousness, one that reflects Kingdom values. Missionaries, particularly sisters, who live and work in the midst of the people play a significant role in this regard. This is true especially where sacramental life cannot be the primary focus because of the small number of Christians. The life, teaching, and example of Jesus — mirrored in the life of religious — can, however, inspire and motivate even a tiny flock.

Fourth, forming Christian communities and human communities that worship the one God of all humankind in spirit and truth goes hand in hand with mission-as-dialogue. Dialogue with people of different religious traditions and cultures should help to overcome Christian ethnocentrism — especially certain types of ecclesiocentrism. This can heal historical wounds and lead to mutual enrichment as different groups appreciate one another's spirituality and thus prepare the ground for universal brotherhood and sisterhood. All these together will lead many more Indians to salvation — the fullness of life, love, and light that Jesus promised.

BIBLIOGRAPHY

Anderson, Walter K. 1978. *The Brotherhood in Saffron, Rashtra Swayam Sevak and Hindu Revivalism*. New Delhi.
Barrett, David B. 1982. *World Christian Encyclopedia*. Oxford University Press.
Bose, A. 1988. *From Population to People*. New Delhi.
Bühlmann, W. 1976. *The Coming of the Third Church*. Liverpool.
Camps, A. 1983. *Partners in Dialogue*. New York.
C.B.C.I. 1990. *Catholic Directory of India, 1990*. New Delhi.
Fernando, W. 1990. *Indian Catholic Community, Pro Mundi Vita Dossiers*, January.
Fuchs, S. 1972. "A New Mission Method for India?" *Verbum*. Bonn.
John Paul II (Pope) 1990. Encyclical Letter *Redemptoris Missio*. December.
Jenkinson, W. (ed.) 1991. *Trends in Mission, towards the Third Millennium*. New York.
_____. 1992. "Future of the Mission in the Hindi Belt," *Vidyajyoti*, May. New Delhi.
_____. 1981. *Religion and Modernization of India*. Indore.
_____. 1990. "Understanding of Evangelization Today," *Conference of Religious India, National Assembly Report 1990*. Delhi.
Legrand, L. 1990. *Unity and Plurality, Mission in the Bible*. New York.
Neill, S. 1972. *The Story of the Christian Church in India and Pakistan*. Madras.
Neuner, J. 1992. "Mission in Ad Gentes and RM," *Vidyajyotia*. May.
Panikkar, K. M. 1963. *Foundations of New India*. New Delhi.
Statistical Handbook of India. 1991. Information Service Division, Madras.
Raj, A. 1992. "The Dalit Christian Reality in Tamilnadu," *Jeevadhara*. March.
Rajan, I. 1989. "Demographic Profile of Indian Christians: An Overview," *Indian Missiological Review*. April.
Soares–Prabhu, G. 1992. "The Table Fellowship of Jesus: Its Significance for Dalit Christians in India," *Jeevadhara*. Kottayam, March.
Sharpe, E. J. 1988. *Neo-Hindu View of Christianity*. New York.
Thomas, M. M. 1970. *The Acknowledged Christ of Indian Renaissance*. Madras.

5

A Lay Person's Perspective

Edwina Gateley

Edwina Gateley is an English laywoman who worked as a missionary in Africa and founded the Volunteer Mission Movement (VMM) to be a vehicle for her and her colleague's vision of a free association of men and women who would be at the service of the full range of needs felt and expressed by local churches and form members in a spirituality of prayer and service. Hundreds of VMM members have worked and continue to be active around the world. Ms. Gateley, no longer involved in the administration of VMM, pursues a life alternating between contemplative prayer in a midwestern hermitage and speaking to groups interested in mission and prayer.

Redemptoris Missio reaffirms for twentieth-century Christians the two-thousand-year-old mission mandate first articulated by Jesus of Nazareth after the Resurrection: "Go and teach all nations." Ever since that mandate was given to the first bewildered followers of Jesus, the church throughout the ages has struggled to define the meaning of mission and to put it into practice. *Redemptoris Missio* recognizes and acknowledges that the current malaise in missionary activity results from a complex variety of reasons, including sociological, political, and cultural problems as well as a growing attitude of "indifference" and "a lack of fervor [that] is all the more serious because it comes from within. It is manifested in fatigue, disenchantment, compromise, lack of interest, and above all lack of joy and hope" (EN 80). Nevertheless, RM urges the Christian community to continue to "fulfill its supreme duty to proclaim Christ to all peoples."

As a lifelong missionary I have no argument with that. The message of Christ is one of Good News — of hope, liberation, and love for all people. It is a message all people hunger for as they struggle amidst poverty, war, hunger, and oppression. *Redemptoris Missio* rightly affirms the essential nature of the church as missionary with the task of spreading the Good News of the Kingdom of God — "Every person has a right to hear the Good News" (46).

What the Good News may sound like and look like is where I have a problem with RM. The encyclical asserts that the primary reason for mission is conversion and baptism (46) and laments the modern tendency to question or pass over the call to conversion: "It is claimed that it is enough to help people become more human or more faithful to their own religion, that it is enough to build communities capable of working for justice, freedom, peace and solidarity" (46).

When I first went to Africa as a lay missionary nearly thirty years ago, it was with a strong sense and understanding of mission utterly consonant with all the statements since made in RM. I knew what mission was. I felt called and sent and my task was very clearly to preach the Good News of the Kingdom to those unfortunate souls who, for whatever reason, had not heard about it all yet. Perhaps what I did not take into account was the activity of the Holy Spirit who "blows where s/he wills" (cf. Jn 3:8). My first three years in Africa turned me upside down and shook what I had considered to be an unshakable understanding of mission. In Africa, I came not only to understand mission as a mutual process of conversion and growth, but also as an invitation to a gradual unfolding of faith *as a journey*. I came to understand the immensity of what I did not understand as I continued on this mission journey.

I returned to England with a disturbing notion of a God so much bigger than the one I had taken to Africa with me. I was already aware that being a missionary was a dangerous business. When we embark faithfully on the mission journey with prayer, zeal, joy, and hope there is no knowing where God will take us. But we can be fairly sure it will be a journey of faith in which God will constantly stretch us to an awareness of divine love and presence far beyond our tiny understanding.

As I continued this journey it was, perhaps, inevitable that I came across barriers set up (through well-meaning and innocent arrogance) that defined the meaning, boundaries, and aim of mission. One of my earlier experiences of such a well-intended but limiting barrier is actually still being raised thirty years later in RM. Chapter six concentrates on priestly and religious vocations as clearly being the special vocation of missionaries for life — the model of the church's missionary commitment (65).

Once again the laity is relegated to last place under the all-encompassing and generalizing title — "all the laity are missionaries by baptism" and "share" in spreading the faith "as co-operators." The missionary role of the laity is defined and limited to lay movements that "humbly seek to become part of the life of local Churches and are welcomed by Bishops and priests within diocesan and parish structures" (72). Only then is lay missionary activity "properly so-called" (72).

It was this clearly defined and limited role to which the laity was relegated that became a major obstacle in the struggles I faced in the late 1960s to found the now internationally-known and well-established Volunteer Missionary Movement (VMM). The church, faithful to definitions that limited the mission activity of laity, did *not* welcome the initiative of a new and different lay missionary movement — one that was run by lay people; one that proposed a whole new understanding of the laity's role in mission as lifelong; one that was to take responsibility for the spiritual and mission formation of its members; and one that was to be community based. This was a far wider mission mandate than the church has ever accorded laity — even to this date.

Yet, in spite of opposition, the VMM was founded in 1969 and has since sent well over a thousand missionaries to twenty-six different countries throughout the world. It now has centers in England, Scotland, Ireland, and the United States. Had I accepted the church's definition of my missionary role, I believe that a great disservice would have been done to the church's mandate to "go forth and teach all nations."

It is indeed "by their fruits that you will know them." The VMM has produced much fruit and continues to do so. As faithful missionary laity, we must in conscience challenge the repeated and limited categorization of our role and our mission. After founding and directing the VMM for ten years, I knew that I had to continue my journey of "mission unfolding" and that prayer and the Holy Spirit would lead me on this journey. I could not discover my role and mission as a laywoman through statements that came from a historically limited and hierarchical concept of mission.

This journey of trying to be faithful to mission *ad gentes* led me to the streets of Chicago, where I encountered prostitutes, pimps, winos, refugees, and homeless people. "Conversion and Baptism" seemed a far cry from the brothels and bars of the inner city. Yet I knew with utter conviction that I was on mission and that this mission was as meaningful and Spirit-filled as that of any priest or religious woman serving in the middle of Africa. Working with men and women who have been beaten, abused, and raped ever since they can remember, leads me to an understanding of mission that is about healing and nurturing. To heal even some of the bruises inflicted from childhood on those most poor of society can take years, a lifetime.

Conversion, if by that one means formal conversion to organized Catholicism, is not always appropriate in the context of this kind of urban mission. Loving and healing is often all we can do. There are rare exceptions when baptism might become a possibility after years of recovery. But in my ten years of street ministry I have witnessed only one baptism. I have, however, been involved in an ongoing process of personal conversion. Most of the people on the streets are not in need of conversion; they have many of the attributes of the Beatitudes already within them. I have been amazed — overawed by the inner beauty, the gentleness of spirit, the humility, the authenticity, and the forgiveness I have witnessed beneath the pain, the poverty, and the external hostility of many of the most abused and neglected of society.

I have come to believe that mission is first about conversion of the missionary; that we come to understand a little more who Jesus was and what the Kingdom of God is all about when we open our own hearts and lives to the saving action of God through the Holy Spirit. And Jesus is indeed our model for this.

Mission is inevitable and imperative if we are a Gospel people — whether we are lay, religious, or priest. Whether we are in Africa, Latin America, or the streets of Chicago, mission is a process of conversion that must not be limited by our attempts to control and define it.

Genesis House in Chicago, which I opened in 1984 to help prostitutes start a new life, has reached out to over seven thousand prostitutes. Like Mary Magdalene they recognize the face of Jesus in the lay community that cares for them. And, like Mary Magdalene, they, too, reflect the face of Jesus and share the Good News through a new way of life. They know "God is with us" in spite of all the pain and the darkness. Yes, there is "conversion" and there is "baptism." But on the streets of Chicago it looks different, and perhaps it can never really be defined and named.

It is unfortunate at another level that RM refers to the five hundredth anniversary of the evangelization of the Americas as a "major turning point" in the history of humanity and an encouragement to missionary outreach. A strong school of thought in the Americas (notably native American Indians) protests the terrible massacres and forced "conversions" that marked this "missionary outreach," not to mention the destruction of whole cultures and tribal religions. Protest against the five hundredth anniversary celebrations were held throughout the Untied States. Perhaps it is such out-of-touch and insensitive statements as those one reads in RM that result in the "indifference and disenchantment" that the Pope laments.

A missionary church — at this stage in global history, after so many crimes committed in the name of Christ — must learn from its ambiguous experience and from the Holy Spirit to be gentle and humble in its approach to mission, just as individual missionaries must learn this lesson. As RM states, "every person has the right to hear the Good News of the God who reveals and gives himself in Christ" (46). But the fruits of such a proclamation belong to the Spirit.

We are, as RM states clearly, to be witnesses — "the first and irreplaceable form of mission" (42). Perhaps, though, we have been so oriented toward results and concrete signs that the missionary church has charged in where angels feared to tread. It may do us well to ponder on our story and, in prayer and humility, do more of the witnessing and less of the planning and strategizing.

Redemptoris Missio, in chapter three, rightly emphasizes the primary importance of the Holy Spirit as the principal agent of mission as well as the necessity of an intimate communion with Christ, as a primary element of missionary spirituality (88). It goes on (90) to state that the call to mission is a commitment to holiness and that the "future of mission depends to a great extent on contemplation. Unless the missionary is a contemplative s/he cannot proclaim Christ in a credible way" (91). It is this call to holiness and contemplation that offers the greatest hope to the church's missionaries. To the degree that we try to respond to that call will be the degree to which we might be more faithful to Mission *ad Gentes*.

6

Ghanaian Reflections on Redemptoris Missio

Vincent Boi-Nai, S.V.D.

Vincent Boi-Nai is a member of the Society of the Divine Word and assistant director of the Tamale Institute for Cross-Cultural Studies in Ghana. He has a doctorate in ministry degree from Andover Newton Theological Seminary and is active in the formation of African Divine Word Missionaries, as well as in giving courses to and supervising the fieldwork and language learning of expatriate and indigenous Catholic and Protestant residents of the highly acclaimed Tamale program, which specializes in promoting the inculturation of Christianity in West Africa and dialogue with traditional African religions and Islam.

INTRODUCTION

The encyclical letter of Pope John Paul II, *Redemptoris Missio* calls upon the Catholic Church to renew her missionary commitment as she enters the third millennium. I see this letter as offering valuable guidance and clarification on the nature of mission and the task of evangelization given all Christians by Christ. In the following few pages, I wish to comment briefly on some of the key issues outlined in this important encyclical from a West African, chiefly Ghanaian perspective.

In article 3 of *Redemptoris Missio*, the Pope points out that "the moment has come to commit all of the Church's energies to a new evangelization and to the mission *ad gentes*." I think the Pope's call for a commitment to a new evangelization is a step in the right direction, because in the past, Christianity has been presented as a set of doctrines, rites, and cults of Western origin. As such, African people have often found it difficult to understand Christianity as involving a personal relationship with Jesus Christ. In addition, many Africans find Christianity to be too intellectual, a problem made worse when one considers the high rate of illiteracy in Africa. Then, too, despite much talk of liturgical inculturation and contextualization, people cannot really celebrate liturgically all that they actually live. In light of such factors, for a "new evangelization" to have meaning in Africa, it must address issues dealing with crisis situations — sudden death, sickness, witchcraft, fear of evil spirits, and so forth. In this respect, traditional religion through its diviners and Islam through its malaams provide answers that are psychologically fulfilling to the people.

The Holy Father emphasizes in article 5 that "Christ is the one Savior of all, the only one able to reveal God and lead to God." While African traditional religions recognize the divine origins of the universe, in contradistinction to the Christocentrism of Christianity (holding that Jesus Christ is the only mediator between God and humankind), African traditional religions generally affirm that God, after creating the universe, delegated authority to rule it to intermediary beings (divinities, ancestors, spirits), who intervene in the affairs of humankind. Below I shall discuss three Christological elements that I believe are essential for the kind of evangelization that the Pope speaks of to occur. And throughout, even though I do not raise the issue at every juncture, the question is posed: is Roman Catholicism prepared to allow Africans the liberty to create authentically African forms of Catholic Christianity?

ELEMENTS OF AN AFRICAN THEOLOGY OF EVANGELIZATION

The presence of ancestral cults and numerous shrines dedicated to various deities gives shape to the intermediary role that ancestors and divinities continue to play in the daily life of the people. From this perspective, I see African understanding of the message of Jesus constituting "good news" around which evangelization can coalesce comprising a threefold notion of Jesus as: (1) mediator between the living and the dead; (2) as savior and liberator from all that oppresses humankind; and (3) as the healer of physical sickness. We shall discuss each of these and attempt to tie them to the Pope's call for a new evangelization. Before doing so, however, it may be well to note that these elements and their development in an attempt to deepen and extend evangelization in an African context will differ enormously from what may be required in the West. One hears criticism about elements of the papal magisterium on mission that sometimes strikes Africans as rather "beside the point," since Western and African cultural and religious contexts are so diverse.

Jesus as Universal Mediator

The idea of a mediator is well understood by Africans. For example, among the various tribes of Ghana, the chief does not generally speak directly to his people, and the people also normally do not approach the chief directly except through the "linguist." The linguist, whose function is sometimes delineated by the English word "interpreter," receives and transmits the message from the chief to the people and vice versa. The social order expects this of everybody. The chief also mediates between the living and the ancestors; and the ancestors in turn mediate between the living and God. This idea, therefore, makes the intermediary role of Christ meaningful among African people.

This concept of Jesus Christ as a traditional intermediary who preserves due order in our approach to God is very different from the classical Christian idea of a mediator who not only provides channels of communication with God but also removes the barriers of sin and guilt that separate us from God. In this respect, the traditional African does not spontaneously see the mediatory role of Christ, including the office of pleading for human beings before God for the forgiveness of sin. Missionaries and pastors need to stress the expiatory role of Christ as they instruct people in the Christian faith. While I have the impression that many modern Western Christians find little attraction in aspects of New Testament Christology that touch on the expiatory role of Christ, in African contexts they can be extremely important, especially when linked to the notion that Christ functions as a common ancestor for all humankind in his act of expiation.

Nevertheless, this is not a move that is made without criticism. Raymond

Moloney argues that the model of ancestor of African tradition is clearly a human being, and promotion to a state of nearness to God suggests, if anything, adoptionism rather than full divinity. Further, Moloney points out that the shadowy nature of existence sometimes attributed to the ancestors seems closer to the biblical Sheol than to the Christian heaven. On account of these reasons, Moloney and other writers assert that the "ancestor model" is an imperfect comparison for Christian doctrine about Christ (Moloney 1987, 510).

In responding to such objections, African writers like Benezet Bujo maintain that Christ is ancestor in a unique sense — in the sense that he is "Proto-ancestor." As proto-ancestor, Christ becomes for us the unique source of life. Our new birth in Christ is a new creation that transcends the world of African ancestors, while embodying that salvation and life for which Africans have always yearned. Christ as proto-ancestor is the perfection and fulfillment of the ideals for which the God-fearing ancestors have always stood and longed (Moloney 1987, 511).

Jesus as Savior and Liberator

The main preoccupation of many Africans is redemption from physical threats and/or evil forces. The idea of deliverance is the commonest theme, for instance, in the hymns, prayers, and catechisms of indigenous African churches. These expressions of piety show Africans seeking complete individual and community deliverance from the forces of evil, witchcraft, death, drought, floods, and sickness. In this regard, the indigenous African churches and African traditional religion share similar ideas on the concept of deliverance. God in this context becomes the final arbiter to whom the African turns when all "help and comfort flee" (Parratt 1987, 71–72).

Further, God's saving power and response is acknowledged when the danger or the calamity is over and the need is provided. African languages abound in sayings and proverbs pregnant with evocations of God's saving power. In the area of justice, God is called to the side of the weak and the innocent. The following two Akan proverbs (see Parrat, 72) suffice to make the point: (1) *Onyankopon na oyam okoto kyekyere* "It is God who grinds the maize for the chicken"; and (2) *Aboa a omni dua no Onyame na opara no bo* "It is God who whisks the flies from the tailless animal."

In addition, the concept of saving is a very dynamic one and it is manifested in times of desperate need. It is this traditional African notion of God's intervention to rescue people which is firmly maintained by African Christians in their experience of the Savior. The theology of the Savior is expressed vividly in African hymns, for example, in *Maye koom na metwen Onyame* "I am calm awaiting my Lord" and in *Maye se abofra a wawo no* "I have become as calm as a newborn babe."

Jesus as Liberator

Liberation in Africa typically means removal of all that keeps one in bondage, all that makes persons less than what God intended them to be. It connotes the total idea of liberation from fear, uncertainty, sickness, evil powers, foreign domination and oppression, distortion of his or her humanity, poverty and want. In brief, it embraces religious, political, socioeconomic, spiritual, personal, and social concerns of the African convert. When the title "liberator" is ascribed to him, therefore, Jesus as Christ is believed to liberate Christians from all forces that hinder them from living fully as human beings. Jesus's self-identification with the poor and the needy makes his proclamation, "I have come that they may have life and have it more abundantly," more meaningful to the African Christian (Parratt 1987, 74–75).

Jesus as Healer

As far as African people are concerned, disease and misfortune have a mystical causation. To combat them, therefore, the cause must be found and uprooted. For the common people, religion is largely the means of reinforcing life, of proper precautions against powers that might destroy them. Jesus Christ is thus conceived of by many African Christians as the great physician, healer, and victor over worldly powers. To many, Jesus came that we might have life and have it more abundantly. But the question many people ask is: where is the abundant life when all around us we see suffering, disease, poverty, oppression, strife, envy, war, destruction? In answer to this question, the indigenous African Christian churches believe that total personal healing of human beings — spiritually, psychologically, and physically — is the gift of God, which pours on his believing community through Jesus Christ. Christ is seen as being more powerful than any evil power, even though African people recognize the existence of such evil powers. I must insist on saying that the indigenous African Christian churches' approach to healing does not aim at supplanting medical treatment, but supplementing it. The healing message through prayers, visions, dreams, use of consecrated water, and so forth in the church aims at dealing with practical problems of life. For Africans, Jesus Christ is the power by which they overcome their daily worries, concerns, and fears, and the source of their entire life.

REDEMPTORIS MISSIO AND AFRICA

Article 50 of the encyclical speaks of the need for ecumenical activity and harmonious witness to Jesus Christ by different churches and ecclesial communities so as to counteract the seed of confusion being sown by para-Christian sects. For this collaboration to work in Africa, I suspect that leaders of the traditional churches will have to change their attitudes of taking pride in and showing self-centered concern only for their own individual churches, believing and acting as if one's church is the only true church of Christ. To make ecumenism work, they must learn to respect each other's faith and develop the capacity to listen to others even if they disagree with them. Further, they need to promote common festivities like Easter picnics, organizing joint educational programs like workshops on Christian marriage and family life, holding non-denominational services during "Christian home-week" and "week of Christian unity."

In article 52 of *Redemptoris Missio*, inculturation is defined as the "intimate transformation of authentic cultural values through their integration in Christianity and the insertion of Christianity in the various human cultures." Keeping in mind this definition, I must say that much has been accomplished in terms of introducing drumming and dancing, not to speak of the singing of African songs, in the liturgy. Also, many liturgical texts have been translated into local languages. Nevertheless, more could be done to make our liturgical celebrations meaningful for the people. For instance, Africans like to communicate spontaneously and directly with God, hence there should be places in the eucharistic celebration for people to break into drumming and dancing spontaneously.

Another point I want to stress is that the inculturation of the Christian message demands the involvement of the whole Christian community. It is the duty of the African bishops to provide discernment and to encourage experimentation. Unfortunately, some bishops are very conservative and slow in giving permission for experimentation. Priests who have the courage to experiment are often criticized and accused of introducing "pagan practices" into the church. The matter is not an easy one to resolve.

In what may appear counterintuitive, but which in reality shows the complexity of the cultural scene in African Christian communities, many older African Christians do not show interest in matters of inculturation. They argue that before they became Christians they were asked to reject their traditional practices. This they did. Now they see no reason why they should fall back on the very practices they were made to reject.

In similar vein, forming basic ecclesial communities (which the encyclical calls for in article 51) has not been especially successful in cities and urban areas for several reasons, among which I would call attention to the following. First, people coming from rural areas to the cities claim that they find greater support in belonging to tribal associations operating in the towns and cities than in the church. From interviews I have personally conducted, I could see that members of tribal associations do help their "brothers" and "sisters" who are new to the cities. They do so by providing them with accommodation, giving them food, money, and helping them to find jobs as quickly as possible. Basic Christian ecclesial communities need to be at least this effective. In addition, through tribal associations, people are well informed regarding what is happening in their own villages and how their relatives are doing. As a result, they do not need to visit home frequently. In case of death, all members of the association come together to help the bereaved. For instance, they buy the coffin for the burial and bear transport expenses. People find it easer to interact with members of their own tribe than with people from other tribes who do not speak the same language. Pastors and missionaries working in towns and cities will thus have their work cut out for them in trying to help people to realize the importance of forming ecclesial basic communities that go beyond tribal lines. Evangelization in the cities will depend on such communities, but establishing them will not be easy.

In article 53, *Redemptoris Missio* calls upon missionaries to "immerse themselves in the cultural milieu of those to whom they are sent." It is my conviction that in answering the missionary call we must strive to develop the attitude of the missionary who is not only at the giving and teaching end but who is also able to receive and to learn from the people. By seeing themselves as learners, the missionaries will be able to appreciate the local culture and also able to share in the lifestyle of the people. Further, they will be able to build meaningful personal relationships and discern how God is already present in the cultural context.

In the same article 53, the Holy Father indicates that missionaries must learn the language of the place in which they work, become familiar with the most important expressions of the local culture, and discover its values through direct experience. In this direction, the Tamale Institute of Cross-Cultural Studies in Ghana — with which I am associated — offers courses on cross-cultural orientation, language- and culture-learning methodology, and an in-depth supervised field training. These courses prepare agents of ministry not only to respond appropriately to specific cross-cultural situations in Africa but also to develop attitudes, skills, and techniques needed to do ministry in a cross-cultural setting. Such courses, in my opinion, are absolutely essential for persons who wish to deepen the evangelization of African Christians.

It is stated in article 58 that people's development does not derive primarily from money, material assistance, or technological means, but from the formation of conscience and the gradual maturing of ways of thinking and patterns of behavior. In my experience, I have seen dedicated missionaries who have promoted development through schools, hospitals, printing presses, agricultural farms, provision of boreholes, wells, dams, and so forth. Many a time, some of these dedicated missionaries become so caught up in their development projects that they do not have enough time to spend in relationships that help form the conscience of people. They end up not ministering to the spiritual needs of those to whom they have come. Thus in the light of article 58, missionaries must not stress material development at the expense of spiritual progress. Development projects should come from the community, and not be imposed by bishops, pastors, and coordinators of development. Development should help the people to acquire attitudes of self-reliance, self-determination, dignity, and community building (Byrne 1993, 11).

In articles 73 and 74, the Pope touches on the important role catechists and other laypeople play in the church. Indeed, catechists in Africa deserve to be praised and appreciated for the work they do. Many of them have been teaching catechism for twenty years and more without pay. The reason is given often that the "church has no money." Other catechists have to travel from one outstation to another, conducting Sunday and weekday services, instructing catechumens in the faith, and preparing them to receive the sacraments. In the absence of a priest, catechists perform burial rites, bring communion to the sick, settle marriage problems, etc. Today, many pastors have recognized the work catechists are doing and they do make the effort to help them — organizing courses to help them improve upon their knowledge and leadership skills, and assisting them financially.

Likewise, since Vatican II, many laypeople have become fully alive to their responsibilities in the church. They no longer sit down and watch the priest do everything. They want to be involved in what is going on in the church. This change of attitude has come about as a result of ongoing formation programs organized in various parishes to educate the laity on their role in the church. Also, many parish priests have learned to entrust more responsibilities into the hands of responsible laypersons. On the other hand, there are some laypersons who do not participate fully in the life of the church. This is so, because these laypersons have not blessed their marriages in the church and often they feel ignored when people are being elected to serve on laity councils, parish councils, and other church committees. It is the task of parish priests to encourage these laypersons and to help them find solutions to their marriage problems.

In conclusion, I wish to say that Pope John Paul's encyclical letter *Redemptoris Missio* gives a clear and concise summary of the missionary life of the church. It clears up doubts and ambiguities regarding various aspects of missionary activity. It is my hope and belief that this important document will guide us all in our effort to carry on the process of new evangelization.

REFERENCES

Byrne, Fr. Tony. 1993 *Integral Development*. Ndola-Zambia: Mission Press.

Moloney, Raymond. 1987 "African Christianity," *Theological Studies* 48 (September), pp. 510–512.

Parratt, John, ed. 1987 *A Reader in African Christian Theology*. London: Latimer Trend & Co.

7

A Missionary's Misgivings: Reflections on Two Recent Documents

Anthony J. Gittins, C.S.Sp.

Anthony J. Gittins, member of the Congregation of the Holy Spirit, is profes-sor of theological anthropology at Catholic Theological Union, Chicago. Holding a doctorate in anthropology from the University of Edinburgh, Father Gittins has worked as a missionary in West Africa for eight years and as a member of the Volunteer Missionary Movement among street people in Chi-cago. Widely known as a lecturer on issues of mission and cultural adaptation, Gittins is the author of *Gifts and Strangers* (Paulist, 1990) and *Bread for the Journey* (Orbis, 1993).

INTRODUCTION

What follows is written by a teacher of missionaries, an anthropologist, and cross-cultural minister, who for the past decade has been in the United States, at-tempting to blend the work of the academy with Christian outreach *ad gentes* on the margins of Chicago. Aware that one can scarcely deal adequately with two such rich documents as *Redemptoris Missio* and *Dialogue and Proclamation* in a few pages, these lines involve, in fact, one person's perspective and some projection, a few responses but not a comprehensive critique.

"Missionary," we should know, is not a biblical word. The missionary component was, from the beginning, inseparable from the Christian lifestyle. Only much later, when established Christianity had fallen away from its early zeal, were missionaries institutionalized, as societies, orders, and other institutions were created specifically to undertake mission *ad gentes*. The word *missionary* dates from the early Jesuits in the sixteenth century.

REDEMPTORIS MISSIO

Ambitious and comprehensive, *Redemptoris Missio* tries to clarify the nature of "mission" from a Roman Catholic viewpoint. Four grounding theses constitute its bedrock: (1) All Christians are missionary; (2) the whole of the church's work is missionary; (3) the church is at the service of the kingdom; and (4) faith is a gift from God (Spirit). The theses seem legitimate, and the teasing out of their implications is surely desirable. Any "missionary" should be able to seek justification for and challenge to his or her activity. Yet much of the clarity afforded by these propositions is obscured by an underlying subtext and a particular understanding of "missionary." Taking them in order, we add a reconstituted subtext under four headings.

First, *all Christians are missionary . . . but some are more "missionary" than others.* Called to "mission" are the Twelve, the community of believers, then special envoys sent by the earliest Christian community at Antioch. From the start, "mission is seen as a community commitment, a responsibility of the local Church, which needs 'missionaries' in order to push forward toward new frontiers" (27). The theme is elaborated (61ff.), and one reason adduced for mission today is the "shortage of clergy" (62). The Pope's thinking is clear. The missionary is epitomized in the clergy; Jesus "gave the universal missionary mandate to the College of the Apostles with Peter as its head." From this principle the Pope derives his own missionary identity and responsibility: "my brother Bishops are directly responsible, together with me, for the evangelization of the world" (63).

The gravity with which Pope John Paul II takes this responsibility may explain the intensity of his personal life, and his motivation for writing. The "missionary" activity of Pope and bishops is seen as different from the commitment of other missionaries, notwithstanding their "special vocation" (65), which is "total" and "lifelong." If this were consequent on Baptism, it might be a rallying call to the whole Christian community. But the Pope has a much narrower focus. He is thinking of members of traditional "missionary" societies, orders, and similar institutions, who are engaged in activity *ad gentes.* Not only do subsequent paragraphs exclude laity and others, they accommodate a number of rather unexpected individuals, by ad hoc incorporation into the ranks of "missionaries" (66f.), defined in geographical terms as going beyond the borders of their own country. One wonders about "the nations" within their own country!

Priests, says the Pope, share concern for the church's mission. Yet in fact the majority of priests are not missionaries with a special vocation, and "concern for the church's mission" is not active engagement among the *gentes.* The notion of concern allows for the inclusion of all priests as missionaries, while the idea that they are called "by virtue of the Sacrament of Orders" (67) seems to have the effect of excluding all others from this call. Yet curiously, the special vocation is then extended to both "men and women missionaries," if they go to the *gentes* "for life" (66). This is a curiously narrow description of Christian mission today.

Missionary religious sisters (70) are mentioned, but though "other" priests are called to swell the ranks of missionaries, "other" sisters are not (cf. 67). Finally, the laity are embraced as missionaries — by virtue of their Baptism. But in articles 71-74, although ostensibly they are called to make a "specific contribution" (71) and have the "right" and the "obligation" to engage in mission, laity are effectively marginalized, apparently because they lack a "specific vocation." Why? Although it is not clear, it appears to be because they are presumably not committed for life (*ad vitam*), "because of their secular nature," and because "their own field [is] the world of politics, society, and economics" (72). This reduction of the People of God, and the view of religious activity not as embedded in human life but as compartmentalized and temporary, is controversial, even demeaning, a point borne out by Edwina Gateley's contribution to this volume.

The second theme regards the manner in which *the whole of the Church's work is missionary . . . but some "work" is more missionary than other work.* "Missionary" functions of the laity are itemized in apparently diminishing order of importance in articles 72 through 74. When all have been included, either everything is mission or a full-blown stratification has been established, in striking contrast to the Bible's organic images of the Body of Christ. Although the encyclical is to the whole church, it focuses on the imperative of (chiefly priestly?) missionary "vocations" (79). There is even a coda — an attempt to encourage "other forms of cooperation," specifically "visiting the missions" (82), a slip into old manners of thought on sending and receiving sides of the mission equation that not only betrays the geographical bias but trivializes the missionary vocation.

More positively, "true" mission *ad gentes* happens wherever Christ and the Gospel are not known or where the Christian faith is immature (33). It "is directed to people or groups who do not yet believe in Christ, who are far from Christ, in whom the Church has not yet taken root . . . and whose culture has not yet been influenced by the Gospel" (34). It has three constituents: proclamation, building up the local church, and promoting the values of the kingdom (ibid.). This "specifically missionary work" is to be distinguished from the overall mission of the whole people of God. The focus on "proper" missionary activity, however, excludes many people and much Christian activity. Confusingly, in the next sentence, the clearly-drawn lines are intentionally blurred, and the boundaries between pastoral care, new evangelization, and specific missionary activity are admitted to be not clearly definable; and it is said to be unthinkable that we should erect barriers between them or "put them into water-tight compartments."

Redemptoris Missio itself, I fear, contributes to the confusion. Its approach — statement, clarification, qualification, generalization, specification — becomes tedious. At the end of a paragraph we are assured that "missionary activity *ad intra* is a credible sign and a stimulus for missionary activity *ad extra* and vice versa"! But as soon as we note that "mission *ad gentes* knows no boundaries," boundaries are explicitly drawn (37). Again, "this mission [of Jesus, the Church, and the Apostles] is one and undivided . . . but within it, there are different tasks and kinds of activity" (31). And if this is not confusing, we read that witness is "the first and irreplaceable form of mission" (42ff.); yet the centrality of "proclamation," especially by the clergy, is emphasized time and time again.

Third, *the Church is at the service of the Kingdom . . . but the church determines how 'service' shall be done.* "The Church is effectively and concretely at the service of the kingdom . . . by establishing communities . . . by spreading throughout the world 'Gospel values,' . . . and by her intercession" (20). This is clear, noble, ennobling. But "[t]he Church is the sacrament of salvation for all mankind, and her activity is not limited only to those who accept her message" (20). This seems to run counter to the assurance that "[o]ne need not fear falling . . . into a form of 'ecclesiocentrism'" (19).

The encyclical insists on the inseparability of church and kingdom (17-19), but what can we say about the less salubrious periods of ecclesiastical history? One can hardly avoid the impression that ecclesiocentrism is the model underlying papal thinking in *Redemptoris Missio.* All the churches are appealed to for "vocations" (64), but the impression is unshakable that what is especially required are vocations of the clerical variety. Thus, in chapter five, the argument is focused on church, while the missionary element is tightly harnessed to "what the Church expects" (65), as interpreted by John Paul. The need for a visible communion of faith-filled Christians is not in dispute, but the "ecclesiofocal" perspective of the document leaves unacknowledged those people who may well long for a realm of justice and peace but are overlooked or condemned by the church, or who experience its unrepentant and sinful aspects. In attempting to control who of its members shall serve the kingdom and in what ways, *Redemptoris Missio* fails to convince one that its spirit is truly at the service of the kingdom. If it were, it might more explicitly cultivate a spirit of prophecy and trust, might not be reluctant to repent for egregious failure, and might call its members to practice vulnerability rather than a show of strength.

Fourth, *faith is a "gift from God"* . . . *but a gift in the hands of missionaries who promote conversion to the church.* God's Spirit works in "every person through the seeds of the Word, to be found in human initiatives." We are "obliged to hold that the Holy Spirit offers everyone the possibility of sharing in the Paschal Mystery in a manner known only to God"; "the Spirit's presence and activity affect not only individuals but also society and history, peoples, cultures and religions" (28). These words, borrowed from *Gaudium et Spes,* are among the most inspiring and encouraging in the whole document. But either they really carry meaning, or they remain empty. Given the emphases in *Redemptoris Missio* on the duty of missionaries and the place of the church, it is difficult not to conclude that we fail to trust God enough, but prefer to supplement the Spirit's work so that it is no longer "known only to God." "The Church opens her doors and becomes the house which all may enter, and in which all can feel at home, while keeping their own culture and traditions, provided these are not contrary to the Gospel" (24). But where in the world is this the norm? And by what criteria and by whom is "contrary to the Gospel" to be judged? Such statements, though articulating something apparently desirable, do not match the experience of many.

Other church documents have moving words about the Spirit's work in human lives: conversion is "the humble and penitent return of the heart to God in the desire to submit one's life more generously to him" (DP 11); and "the church seeks to convert solely through the divine power of the message she proclaims" (*Evangelii Nuntiandi* 18). Both these resist putting missionaries in control. *Redemptoris Missio* is less nuanced. It speaks, for example, of "Christian and para-Christian sects sowing confusion" and being "a threat to the Catholic Church" (51); the tenor is adversarial and touched by a proselytizing spirit, as when we read: "*Peoples everywhere, open the doors to Christ!*" (3; emphasis in original). This is clearly asking for acceptance of the Catholic Church, as "every human being needs Jesus Christ" (11), whom missionaries preach. How far from sensing the Spirit in all people and offering everyone a share in the paschal mystery in a manner known only to God!

One may feel frustration at a document that tries so hard to be comprehensive and creative but is sometimes disconnected from whole sections of the world and society. As in the time of Jesus, putative outcasts and sinners are all around. Some are victims of impersonal forces touching the circumstances of their lives. Others have been cast out or excluded by the church, or are self-excluded from an institution that does not seem holy or maternal or compassionate or welcoming. Faith is sometimes the one thing such people cling to when all else has turned to bile. But it is faith in God, in God's Spirit, and in Jesus: not faith in church or ministers, pomp, and rules. In defending the urgency of promoting Gospel values, the Pope focuses tightly on the institutional church, not admitting the sad and savage realities coloring the lives of so many. Proclamation and the call to conversion and baptism (44ff.) leave little room for a discreet or gentle approach to wounded and dejected souls, and do not mention building human dignity on the ruins of shattered lives.

So long as "the necessity of the Church for salvation" (9) retains an element of literalism, despite the qualification in favor of those who do not "explicitly believe in Christ" (10), we are unlikely to see the kingdom of God breaking in all around us. So long as Christians allow pessimism (35, 36) to block hope, or the arrogance of their own claims to ride roughshod over the sensibilities and memories of others, we are far from experiencing the kingdom, and far from seeing a church that persuades by a message that is incarnated in its membership.

DIALOGUE AND PROCLAMATION

A key element in living religiously is the attempt to seek "truth." A prime way to seek "truth" in a religiously plural world is in mutuality, by approaching the world and the "other" in a respectful and responsive movement. Or one might be more direct, trying to say the last word or create a blanket definition. The latter tactic lacks finesse and is unlikely to be successful or even helpful, because it is too fixed. A dialogical attitude is both more respectful and more likely to produce real insight. It also has the virtue of being open to modification, refinement, and improvement.

A mission document that promotes dialogue is more likely to convince by its modeling of that virtue than by being didactic. Perhaps in striving for clarity of definition and purpose, *Redemptoris Missio* is seriously compromised by its tone and style. A communication that seems not to trust its audience is unlikely to bring that audience to an attitude of trust; a style that strives to close rather than keep open a discourse is unlikely to convince others of the value of a dialogical approach. By contrast, *Dialogue and Proclamation* is less ambitious and shorter than the encyclical. *Dialogue and Proclamation* addresses in detail two major components of evangelization. It was almost completed when *Redemptoris Missio*, which deals more cursorily with the themes of dialogue and proclamation, was issued. The two documents differ greatly in style and tone. And since the authors do not strain under the burden that the Pope struggles to carry (RM 64), *Dialogue and Proclamation* is lighter and less beleaguered. Altogether, it reads as a more constructive and open-ended document.

Building on Vatican II, *Dialogue and Proclamation* is a brave attempt to craft a respectful argument about the presence of God and God's Spirit through all creation (DP 17). Its irenic tone is consistent with its theme. It explicitly states that "Christians, too, must allow themselves to be questioned," averring that there may be "need of purification" of the way some believers understand their religion and practice (32). Naturally, *Dialogue and Proclamation* represents a particular point of view, one that may well clash with certain other points of view. It helps to sustain the perception that openness and respect are part of today's missionary portfolio; nevertheless, it does not go far enough. It is not dispassionate about dialogue, nor ready to allow the dialogue to impinge radically on Christian consciousness.

To acknowledge the need for a respectful stance before others is important. To engage in a process of mutual questioning and the purification of religious attitudes may be a giant step forward. But true dialogue implies a willingness, not simply to allow the other to speak, but to hear and respond to the other. It demands admitting not simply the good will of others but their real insight, real wisdom, and real elements of the revelation of the God whom we say is present in all cultures. From a cross-cultural or ecumenical point of view then, the treatment of dialogue in this document is only partly successful. *Dialogue and Proclamation* talks about others, and even to others; it does not clearly envisage striving honestly to communicate *mutually* with others. It is a worthy, though partial view of reality. "The relationship between the Church and the Kingdom is mysterious and complex" (34); this will not help those at the margins or on the edges of "official" church structures. The assertions that "the Kingdom is inseparable from the Church because both are inseparable from the person and work of Jesus himself," and that it is "not possible to separate the Church from the Kingdom" (34) are redolent of *Redemptoris Missio* and opaque.

Both documents bespeak linear, systematic thinking, while the world spoken of is neither neat nor logical. What of "the Kingdom" before the institutionalization of the Church? Didn't Jesus say it was all around? If so, may we not be allowed to think that the Kingdom may sometimes be ahead of the Church or even where the Church is not? DP speaks timidly about "the inchoate reality" of the Kingdom, which can indeed be found "beyond the confines of the Church" (35), but then maintains that this reality "needs to find completion through being related to the Kingdom of Christ already present in the Church" (35) — such orthodoxy is often quite impracticable; certainly knowledge of what it means practically is unobtainable, as missionaries are only too well aware.

The theological foundations for religious dialogue are elaborated (38ff.), but the writers are attempting the impossible — to uphold freedom and autonomy of conscience and at the same time to argue that dialogue is an imperative for missionaries; to admit that "dialogue" must not coerce, yet to argue that everyone needs to be touched and changed by it. If, in great simplicity, the Church does "collaborate in God's plan," and if Christians unaffectedly "render to others true witness of Christ" (39), then the integrity of "the other" is not threatened and God remains responsible for the salvation of humanity. But if "God's call always passes through the mediation of Jesus Christ" (40), then explicit proclamation is necessary and justified, yet this does not solve much; we must still account for the fate of the "unreached." Also, those who lived before Jesus remain in theological limbo. It is as if the document cannot quite allow God to be God but wants to make salvation contingent on formal proclamation and visible ecclesial structures. Far from clarifying by its exactness, the language emphasizes the gap between missionary outreach (actual or potential), and the billions of effectively unreached peoples. Yet there are fine words about the gradual way in which Jesus revealed himself and the Kingdom to his followers, implying that partial or cumulative revelation is quite normal (69)! If this insight could be applied to the lives of those not reached (and never reachable) by missionaries, then without trivializing the missionary mandate or the importance of dialogue and proclamation, it may be possible to let God handle the destiny of those for whom the normal means of salvation is not the Church, rather than wrenching language until it fails to communicate.

In a similar vein, there are fine words also about justice (44ff.); but there are also unsavory episodes in the church's history. How much do we need to hunger for justice "at home"? The lack of contrition — or even candor — about the church's less-than-unblemished record reduces the impact of the language.

And when the document reiterates classic phrases about a Christianity that "supports many values found and lived in the wisdom and the rich heritage of cultures" and teaches that "attentive dialogue implies recognizing and accepting cultural values" (46), these words still cannot camouflage Roman inflexibility in relation to cultural adaptation, and particularly to the liturgy. There is contradiction, or inexactness (46f.), when support for dialogue is yoked to an injunction that we must remain firm in our belief about the uniqueness of Jesus Christ. If one's dialogue partner were to have as much personal commitment as is expected of the Christian, then dialogue, in the sense understood in the document, is likely to be stillborn.

We Christians should, of course, remember the treasure we hold and not treat our faith disrespectfully. But we may also need to be reminded of the creative tension that will obtain between openness to dialogue and respect for our own heritage. And we may need to cultivate mutual respect, trusting in God's grace in the lives of all and believing in a Spirit who breathes where it will. The document tries to separate proclamation from crude proselytizing. It is one thing to say in article 75 (quoting *Evangelii Nuntiandi*), that "salvation is offered to all as a gift of God's kindness and mercy," and to emphasize this by arguing that the "firm belief" of people of other faiths is "an effect of the Spirit of truth operating outside the visible confines of the Mystical Body" (26). It is quite another to insist that "proclamation is the foundation, center, and summit of evangelization" (EN 27; DP 10). At what point may one's respect for other people's firm belief allow us to keep a respectful silence before them, or try something more like dialogue than proclamation?

It is one thing to say that the Church's proclamation must "meet people's expectations" (76). It is quite another to claim that the Church's own expectations confer the unconditional right to proclamation, in a context in which people are trying respectfully to indicate that they do not wish to be subject to such proclamation.

CONCLUSION

Dialogue and Proclamation attempts to address the Christian imperatives to preach the Gospel and to respect freedom of conscience in others. It acknowledges (4c) that it cannot tie up every loose end and solve every practical problem. Consequently, one can engage with this document, defer to its insights, and acknowledge its limitations.

Redemptoris Missio is different. It tends to set up unattributed examples of "deviant" missionary praxis, which are then rather easily destroyed: "the temptation today is to reduce Christianity . . ."(11); "the Kingdom is much spoken of, but not always in a way consonant with the thinking of the Church" (17f.). In his encyclical, Pope John Paul II seems concerned to uphold the church's mission *ad gentes*, which he says "appears to be waning" (2). But he states other aims, including "to clear up doubts and ambiguities regarding missionary activity *ad gentes*" and "to encourage theologians to explore and expound systematically the various aspects of missionary activity."

The two aims listed above can in practice prove difficult to make simultaneously incompatible. And an attempt to systematize something as dynamic and creative as "mission" seems bound to run into an impasse. An "intellectualist" approach to mission seeks to define and clarify, to itemize and resolve. A more phenomenological approach would try to engage and experience, to wonder and to learn. There seems, then, to be real tension between a Spirit-led approach that is dialogical and respectful of others, and one resulting from dogmatic statements, formal propositions, and carefully planned tactics. That the strategy can be elucidated is unremarkable. But that all doubts and ambiguities can be clarified, and that personnel should receive their field orders in advance of living concretely with persons of different cultures and religious traditions, will strike many missionaries (and many adherents of other faiths) as arrogant and disrespectful, not to say impossible.

Christians should have great respect for authentic tradition. But if theologians, including "the faithful" in various local communities, as well as academic theologians, are to explore missionary activity, they will need to feel free to look, not narrowly at the perspectives and perceptions of Christians, but more broadly at the sensibilities and choices of the other parties in the experience and expression of mission. One detects papal hesitation to encourage research wholeheartedly in the encyclical. This gives the impression that the author does not really trust theologians or missionaries of a certain stripe.

An apparent papal "hermeneutic of suspicion" toward persons who see things differently turns the encyclical's potential as a statement of encouragement into one of admonition, and from dialogue into monologue. Thus a very comprehensive and at times profoundly insightful statement is robbed of pastoral effectiveness at a time when persons engaged in a variety of facets of Christian mission could use both guidance and encouragement in confronting both the nihilist intellectual trends and physical destruction of millions of lives in a heartless world.

8

Mission in China

Beatrice Leung, S.P.B.

Beatrice Leung is a member of the Sisters of the Precious Blood of Hong Kong and assistant professor in the Faculty of Social Sciences and Humanities at the University of Macau. She is the author of *Sino–Vatican Relations: Problems of Conflicting Authority* (Cambridge, 1992) and of many articles in other journals on church–state relations. Sister Beatrice maintains that the very conceptual dichotomization of relations between "church" and "state" is foreign to China and responsible for much of the misunderstanding that occurs.

OVERVIEW

In his encyclical letter *Redemptoris Missio*, Pope John Paul II has called for a revitalization of the mission effort of the church, and in *Centesimus Annus* he has expressed his negative views in regard to Communism, which finds its main upholders in China. Sino–Vatican rapprochement has not been possible in spite of the effort of so many over so many years; and the possibility of carrying on Christian mission in China is challenged in this sociopolitical context for all who are concerned with the evangelization of China. In these pages I discuss missionary work in China in the context of the current Sino–Vatican relations and the Pope's call for the Church's missionary revival.

Since the beginning of the 1990s, the whole world has been seeking light on how to create a new and more just global order in the wake of the crumbling of socialism in Eastern Europe, the disintegration of the Soviet Union, and the end of the Cold War. Economics is one of the major elements in these considerations. In that context, the Holy Father's encyclical *Centesimus Annus* eulogized the victory of capitalism over Communism, yet also reminded the world about the dangers of consumerism, which is the byproduct of capitalism. In RM, he turns his attention to church affairs and reminds Catholics about the urgency of missionary activity. The encyclical RM is an expression of his great concern, and in it he invites the whole church to renew her commitment to mission.

Many Christians anticipated that mission in states such as China could be revitalized once the political control over religion imposed by the atheist Communist

223

government is relaxed. However, it has also been reported that this has not been the case in Eastern Europe. When their sociopolitical life was released from its former controls, people appeared mainly to be busy trying to become rich, which left little time for religion. Meanwhile China, the only remaining major socialist state, has produced a different picture, allowing some forms of mission endeavor amidst tight governmental control. It is the aim of this article to discuss mission in China in a situation where the Chinese government demands that Catholic religious life be independent of the Holy See and where the government labors under fear that religious belief was a major force in driving out Communism in Eastern Europe.

THE BACKGROUND: CHURCH–STATE RELATIONS IN CHINA

Since 1949, Christian religious groups have had problems adjusting to the ruling Communist Party in China. This is partially due to Marxist distaste for religion in general and the particular suspicions of Chinese leaders about the political role of religion in Chinese life and of religious groups that have international linkages. In the case of the Roman Catholic Church, the difficulties were aggravated by the institutional nature of the Vatican, Sino–Vatican conflicts about teaching authority, the Vatican's continued diplomatic relations with Taiwan, and by Chinese belief that the Vatican served the ends of foreign imperialism.[1]

One of the most obvious results of the 1949 Revolution was the liquidation of the mission of the Roman Catholic Church in China. All ties with foreign countries were cut and missionaries were expelled. This had disastrous consequences for the 3.4 million Catholics in China. The establishment of the Catholic Patriotic Association (CPA) in 1957 produced a group acceptable to the Communist Government. The CPA became a line of demarcation between those loyal to the Holy See and those who are not, and positions taken in reference to the CPA caused a split of the church in China that has endured until today.[2]

Overtures from the Vatican aimed at effecting a Sino–Vatican reconciliation began with China's modernization program in 1979, when China implemented her open door policy, have still not yielded much fruit. Today the papal nuncio for China is still in Taiwan; and the People's Republic accuses the Holy See of intervening in the internal affairs of China whenever Chinese Catholics are assisted in their religious activities and social services by overseas Catholics.[3] In spite of political restraints resulting from tense Sino–Vatican relations and China's religious policy, the mission endeavor in China is growing.[4] This mission effort is not only the work of a "bridge church" as requested by the Holy Father in 1982 after the controversial appointment of Dominic Deng as the Archbishop of Guangzhou, but is also the manifestation of the mission effort of the whole church. In general, mission efforts can be divided into two fronts — namely religious activities and social services — which is very close to the suggestions of *Redemptoris Missio* and *Dialogue and Proclamation*. In implementing this missionary policy, there are problems that draw our attention to them even at this early stage of development.

---

1. For a full discussion of Sino–Vatican relations see Beatrice Leung, *Sino–Vatican Relations: Problems in Conflicting Authority (1976-86)* (Cambridge: Cambridge University Press, 1992).

2. For a detailed description of these events, see James Myers, *Enemies Without Guns: The Catholic Church in the People's Republic of China*, 1992.

3. See the Beijing-based official publication of the Catholic Patriotic Association, *Catholic Church in China* 4 (1992), pp. 18-23.

4. Leung, *Sino-Vatican Relations*. Appendices 2-6.

MISSION IN CHINA: AN UNORTHODOX APPROACH

Mission before 1949

In Christian tradition, rendering assistance and service on humanitarian grounds has long been a means of evangelizing. During the rule of the National Government in China, from the most prosperous city to the remotest rural site, whenever there was Catholic mission, Catholic social services in the form of nursery, orphanage, school, and medical services centers were found. It is recorded that in the period 1947 to 1948 Catholic mission services covered twenty provinces (Liaoling, Helongjiang, and Jilin were combined into one province—Manchuria). They included 254 orphanages, 216 hospitals, and 781 dispensaries.[5] In the field of education, there were 4,446 Catholic educational institutions in China; they included 3 Catholic universities, 542 junior technical schools, and 180 secondary schools. There were 319,414 students enrolled in Catholic educational institutions during that period. Most of these Catholic mission works were conducted by foreign missionaries and funded by mission societies based in Europe and America. After the Communist takeover, the Government kept a watchful eye on Catholic missions and their activities. Catholic education was a prime target for the suspicions of the Chinese Communist Party (CCP), since education was the major instrument by which the Party sought to mold the mind of youth. Thus mission educational institutions were confiscated. Christian mission came to a complete liquidation after the CCP promulgated the Three Self Movement in 1957, when foreign missionaries were condemned for "malpractice" in their mission services and were expelled. Accusations that infants had been killed in Catholic orphanages in Guangzhou in the 1950s are a good example of the kind of justifications commonly used for these takeovers. Canadian Sisters of the Immaculate Conception, who ran the orphanage in Guangzhou of Guangdong Province, were accused of killing infants in the orphanage and tried in public. They were found guilty and expelled. Some years later, the person who personally directed the case revealed the truth after he left China. He confessed that this false accusation was purposely devised by the CCP as a means to disgrace the Catholic Church and to justify expelling foreign missionaries.[6] Catholic educational, medical, and social services disappeared completely in China for nearly thirty years, until the dawn of the modernization era.

Catholic Mission in the Modernization Era

The reopening of churches for worship took place after the launching of the modernization program at the Party's Third Plenum of the Thirteenth Central Committee in December 1978. This modernization program allowed at least minimal religious activities to adherents of Christian churches. Chinese Catholics did not have the muscle to resume their mission service in education, medicine, and social welfare services as a means of evangelization, however, because the government did not want religions to flourish too publicly, since the CCP and religious beliefs were perceived to be rivals for the role of exercising teaching authority.[7]

---

5. The source of these statistics is *Annuaries de L'eglise Catholique en Chine 1949* (Shanghai: Bureau Sinologigue de Zi-Ka-Wei, 1949).

6. Xiao Feng, "Zong gong Zenyang Dueidul Jiaohui he Zongjiao Tu" [How Did the CCP Treat the Church and Religious Believers?], *Zhishi Fengi* (Xianggang) 65 (16 November 1970). The author of this article spent 1949 to 1959 working as a senior cadre in a provincial religious affairs bureau in South China.

7. Leung, *Sino–Vatican Relations*, pp. 302-345.

The crisis of faith in the Party itself and the collapse of Communism in Europe would have given Christianity the chance to flourish in China, but the competition for authority between the People's Republic of China and religion, although it has not been openly manifested, is implicit in the issuing of three major documents since 1984 (including one solely on Catholic policy) by the Party's Central Committee with the intention of putting all religious activities under the Party's aegis.[8]

For fear that it will not be able to control the revival and influence of religions, China allows neither foreign Catholic mission efforts to resume nor the subsidy of social and medical services, despite encouraging foreign investment in the economic sector.[9]

The lack of personnel and funds curbs the capacity of Chinese Catholics to resume their purveying of social services. However, such Catholic mission activities began to take place on a very small scale in 1981 and have moved into full swing since 1985. At this time, the continuance of Catholic mission efforts depends upon manifesting the church's good will and reassuring Chinese leaders with a view to getting China to consent to resuming the Sino–Vatican dialogue that was suspended after the Tiananmen Square incident.[10]

At the same time, mission efforts involving the collaboration of Catholics inside and outside China appear to have a new orientation vis-à-vis the leadership of the CCP. Being atheist Marxists of the initial revolutionary generation, CCP leaders who are at the pinnacle of power do not look with favor on any religion. As nationalists, they view foreign religions, including Catholicism, as forerunners of cultural imperialism. Thus, for political reasons, mission in China in the era of Deng must represent a break from the pre-1949 period.

Mission, we have noted, can be divided into two major divisions — namely social services and more purely religious church activities. Politically, however, these two aspects of mission are part of the same Vatican strategy in relation to China, the ultimate aim of which is to reconstruct the Chinese Roman Catholic Church. Religiously, mission may represent a response to the Holy Father's call for mission commitment in RM and DP. China has accepted Catholic social services as she has many of those offered by other foreign non-governmental organizations, but she frowns on evangelistic activities, fearing them as attempts at infiltration.

Characteristics of Mission in China Today

The first characteristic of contemporary Catholic mission in China is that it reflects Catholics from various walks of life and is not merely directed by or at the service of the official, clerical church. The universality of Catholicism is reflected in mission projects, when Catholics disregard race, ethnicity, social status, color, and nationality, all making their particular contributions. In the mission to China characteristic of the pre-1949 period, work seemed to be carried on only by men and women who were members of officially recognized missionary societies. Minimally, such societies took the lead, even when they were assisted by laity. The reopening of mission operations in China today has been marked by the leadership of laity who

8. Ibid., pp. 348-383. For commentary and documentation on China's monitoring of religious activities see: D. MacInnis, *Religion in China Today: Policy and Practice* (Maryknoll: Orbis, 1989).

9. In Document Number 3 (1989) of the Party's Central Committee, it is clearly stated that foreign donations for religious activities are not allowed.

10. From private sources from those near the Catholic authority, the author learned that right after the Tiananmen massacre, the Vatican postponed the dialogue with China aimed at leading to the Sino–Vatican rapprochement.

are supported by church officials and assisted by clergy and religious in middle-level administration. One thinks of the example of Catholic social service projects such as those launched by the German Miserior and Caritas International organizations. In them laity, religious, and clergy (both Chinese and non-Chinese) are involved in planning and organizing at their logistic bases in Germany, Hong Kong, and Macau. But the social services of various types rendered to underprivileged Chinese disregard the ideology, religion, and beliefs of the recipients and are conducted by the Chinese themselves.[11]

In spite of the fact that China frowns at communion between Chinese churches and the official organs of the Roman Catholic Church, Catholic social service projects constitute 34.3 percent of total social services rendered by foreign non-governmental organizations in China, and the amount of money ran up to $19,824,954 in 1991.

The second characteristic in the mission is the promotion of Gospel values rather than Christian doctrine at this stage of contact. The objective of social services, as expressed by the programs of Caritas, is to foster cooperation and mutual understanding through active participation in community affairs and to assist efforts in China's modernization programs in a true spirit of partnership, solidarity, and service. From a theological point of view, it seems that the orientation of DP has been used by Catholic social services to respond to the call of the Pope under the conditions in China today. In DP, for example, dialogue is understood as "reciprocal communication, leading to a common goal" — promoting "an attitude of respect and friendship" before it can go into a deeper level of "constructive . . . relations with individuals and communities of other faiths" (9).

The third characteristic of the mission in China is the immediate and short-term response to urgent needs. A book-sending project that can be put in the category of such assistance to the local church is a "second front" in Catholic mission strategy in China today. The project is a means for transmitting the Catholic faith in a situation where the ordained clergy are inadequate both in terms of quantity and the quality of their theological training. This self-financed project started humbly in 1984 when several volumes of essential religious literature such as prayer books and catechisms in simplified Chinese characters were reprinted. Chinese Catholics received these books with joy and gratitude because without such books their personal spiritual exercises could not be resumed after so much religious literature had been burned during the Cultural Revolution. The expansion of the book-printing project has proceeded until more than fifty titles have been printed, each of them numbering at least five thousand copies. The publication house that was founded in Hong Kong for various reasons is independent from the church hierarchical system, yet many clergy, religious, and laity in Hong Kong and overseas have contributed to this printing apostolate for mainland China. When the press of the Shanghai diocese (which was donated by German Catholic groups) was given permission to print religious literature, the older Hong Kong-based press contributed much to make the Shanghai printing apostolate a success.

Redemptoris Missio echoes the sentiment of *Lumen Gentium* when it suggests that in mission activity the cooperation between different parts of the Church "are bonds of intimate communion with regard to spiritual riches, apostolic workers and temporal assistance" (85). The printing mission is an authentic implementation of the teaching of the church in this respect by the laity who has the prophetic vision.

The crown of mission in China today is assistance rendered to the formation of clergy and religious. It includes projects providing books for their education and

---

11. See Beatrice Leung, "Hong Kong and Macau: Politics of Catholic Social Services in China," *American Asian Review* (forthcoming).

theological and philosophical lectures by qualified teachers from abroad. It is never an easy task to obtain permission to invite scholars to teach in Chinese seminaries. Shanghai took the lead and had two professors each semester brought in from outside China to lecture on various topics. In spite of the fact that things were made difficult for these overseas lecturers, they vowed to return if they were allowed to do so. This teacher-sending mission is vital to providing genuine seminary formation to future pastors who will be responsible for the transmission of authentic Catholic teaching at a time when qualified teachers and appropriate textbooks are very much lacking in China.

In general, mission efforts in China began to gather momentum as soon as the Party began to adopt the open door policy in 1979. Hong Kong, Macau, and Taiwan became the major channels for contacting China because of their proximity. One can witness ever-growing missionary activities in China in terms of quality and quantity. The variety of missionary endeavor takes place mostly in an informal manner. These stem from home visits of individual Catholics, occasional visits of overseas Chinese Catholic communities to mainland Catholic parishes, overseas theologians teaching at Catholic seminaries, and non-Chinese Catholic missionaries serving as professionals at institutes of tertiary education and commerce in China. Through contacts deriving from such activities, the apostolate among the Chinese has been increasing. According to the annual report of Bishop Zong Hueide, President of the Chinese Bishops Conference on the mushrooming of Chinese Catholic social-service activities as a means to contribute to the state's request for economic reconstruction, such works are the tip of the iceberg of Chinese mission endeavors.[12]

The role of "bridge churches" assigned by the Pope in 1982 to the churches in Hong Kong, Macau, and Taiwan came naturally to them. They have been active in China, at least partly because these churches are the major Chinese-speaking churches outside China. However, the experience of these Chinese mission endeavors reveals that they not only serve the purpose of advancing Sino–Vatican rapprochement, as the Vatican intended. Their efforts also serve the interest of these local churches. In the long run, they generate a variety of political effects in Hong Kong and Macau. Churches there have their own history of church–state relationships and they will have to deal with the Chinese Communist Government after it takes over Hong Kong and Macau in 1997 and 1999, respectively.

The experience of working for the Chinese mission enhances the capacity of Hong Kong and Macau Catholics to establish new relationships with the incoming Chinese government. For Catholics in Hong Kong and Macau who have traditionally had a smooth working relationship with the British and Portuguese governments, aid to projects in China is very valuable because they learn from Chinese Catholics how to deal with Communist officials. Moreover, the devotion of the Chinese to their faith in spite of constant oppression and discrimination are good lessons to prepare them for the Chinese takeover in 1997 and 1999.

As far as social services are concerned, Catholic social services in China provide good opportunities for the cooperation of mainland Chinese with Hong Kong and Macau Catholics.[13] Hong Kong has been frowned upon by Beijing as a bastion of subversion because of its support of the democratic movement in Tiananmen Square in 1989. In addition, the Hong Kong Catholic Church has been perceived as the base for Christian infiltration of China because of its aid to Chinese Catholics. In spite of mutual distrust and suspicion between Catholics in Hong Kong and the Beijing

---

12. See *Catholic Church in China* 4 (1992), pp. 10-18.

13. Beatrice Leung, "Hong Kong and Macau: Politics of Catholic Social Services in China," *American Asian Review* (forthcoming).

government, Hong Kong Catholics' contributions to Chinese socioeconomic reconstruction will improve their traditionally uneasy relations. In general, the benefits reaped from mission activities reconfirm the theory that mission is a matter not only of benefits gained from "giving to the missions but receiving from them as well" as is suggested by RM (85).

MISSION IN AN ACQUISITIVE SOCIETY

Redemptoris Missio suggests that "the evangelical witness which the world finds most appealing is that of concern for people, and of charity toward the poor, the weak and those who suffer. The complete generosity underlying this attitude and these actions stands in marked contrast to human selfishness. It raises questions which lead to God and to the Gospel" (42). Unfortunately for China, there is a spiritual vacuum left by the disappearance of faith in the Party, one which people try to fill by a "looking for money" mentality. The traditional good conscience of Chinese culture and religion has been weakened and there is little in its place.

The government is willing to accept Catholic social service but it is not prepared to treat Catholicism's ideas on social ethics in a kindly fashion. Meanwhile, at the grassroots level, local parishes are sometimes obsessed by the idea of getting financial gains. Thus they plunge into economic enterprises as if Catholic mission enterprise aimed at earning money rather than rendering services out of Christian love. Such social services by local Chinese Catholics may only serve the goals of the Beijing government, that the church not cause economic burdens for the Government. Such enterprises run the risk of becoming self-enrichment projects rather than serving to promote dialogue on basic human and religious values or the mission of the "evangelical witness which the world finds most appealing . . . that of concern for people, and of charity toward the poor, the weak and those who suffer . . . [showing a generosity] in marked contrast to human selfishness [and which] raises precise questions which lead to God and to the Gospel" (RM 42). Thus, one should ask what mission planners should look out for if China approves Catholic mission projects as she does foreign investment projects, which enable people to get rich. Should financial assistance continue when the recipients seek to get rich and forget the spiritual dimensions of mission projects?

Finally, there is a pitfall that does not lie in the nature of mission itself but from an the ideological preference that Pope John Paul expresses in *Centesimus Annus*. In this encyclical, the Pope embraces a political stance that denounces socialism and eulogizes the collapse of Communism in Eastern Europe. As the sole major socialist state left, China is very wary of the domino effect that the fall of socialism in Europe may be used to portend for China's own social and political system. As far as the Chinese Communist Party is concerned, Beijing will not be on good terms with those who work for and desire the final collapse of socialism in China. Papal remarks heralding the triumph of "the people" over socialism caused suspicion and distrust in China and it will block dialogue, the success of which requires respect and friendship, as is suggested in DP, article 9. The Pope perhaps has the problem of writing for several different audiences, but it is certain that his remarks on socialism, even if palatable in the West, have also been heard in China.

CONCLUSION

It has always been very difficult to translate church teaching into life practice. The teachings of RM and DP are no exception. The enthusiasm shown in mission in China reveals that the Holy Spirit still moves people toward mission. Mission in

China not only revitalizes the Chinese church but benefits those undertaking it as well. The preparation of churches in Hong Kong and Macau for the Chinese take-over in the near future is informed by their experiences in China. The characteristics of this mission with its breaks from the past were caused by the appearance of a government whose relationship with religion is not smooth because it perceives a conflict of authority between these two centers.

Today no one can anticipate in which direction China is heading. One thing we are aware of is this — Chinese society is the meeting point of the vices of both socialism and capitalism. The disappearance of social norms and morality that were once generated by the authority of the Communist Party results in an enormous number of socioeconomic problems and crimes. What is the role of the Catholic Church, the mystical body of Christ and a source of moral power, in confronting and understanding such social evils?

No matter the quality and timeliness of mission services, if everything is planned for and given to China from outsiders, results can only be ambiguous. It is vital to train local church leaders, both clergy and laity, who will have the vision to see the deepest needs of their church and take the lead in the new mission to China. Today, it sometimes seems that we are doing things in much the same way they were done in the pre-1949 period. But we are doing things differently from the past, especially in one way — we are trying to cooperate with local Catholics to train them to administer their own church with mature faith and to dialogue with their fellow Chinese with Christian values radiating from their own lives.

9

The Novelty of Redemptoris Missio

José Comblin

José Comblin, member of Mission Formation Center, Serra Redonda, Brazil, and Catholic University of Louvain, is the author of over forty books and articles, including the much-acclaimed *Retrieving the Human: A Christian Anthropology* (Orbis, 1990). The present article was translated by Lédice Lima, United Theological Seminary, Dayton, Ohio.

AN OVERVIEW

Redemptoris Missio (RM) bears the mark of almost all documents of the pontificate of John Paul II — the mark of an "aggressive voluntarism." The Pope seems to suppose that what is lacking to the Church is a longing for evangelizing, and the answer to the problem lies in inculcating this longing. He expresses his thoughts through strong exhortations. However, we can question whether voluntarism solves the problems.

The Pope points to Asia as the prime mission goal, but he does so without giving a historical analysis. He appears unconcerned about knowing the reasons for the failure of mission in Asia or what might constitute the grounds for an appropriate evangelization there. Instead, the Encyclical is written as if a strong desire for evangelizing were enough for the conversion of Asian peoples.

This characteristic is related to another — total indifference to the human sciences. From reading RM, one could get the impression that the Church bears in itself all knowledge to fulfill its mission. It does not need to know the history of the peoples who are to be the object of evangelizing efforts or to learn from the lessons of the history of Christian mission in relation to these peoples. It seems, indeed, that the Church does not need to pay attention to the sociocultural analysis, as if all of this is without importance to the mission enterprise.

For these reasons, we question whether this Encyclical is not destined to have the same fate of the Pope's appeals for a new evangelization of the lands of former Christendom. Until today the so-called "new evangelization" has largely remained at the level of pure speech without effect. There is no new evangelization going on. The prime reason for this is that the appeal for a new evangelization did not consider either the societal, social, psychological, and cultural conditions of the lands of former Christendom nor of its historical development. In RM, I suspect, we have a similar lack of analysis of what is necessarily involved in attempting to achieve evangelization, for the historical, social, psychological, and religious situation both of the Asians who are to be the objects of mission and of the Westerners whom the Pope would apparently summon to achieve his goals are not considered.

It appears that only such antimodern movements like Opus Dei or Communione and Liberazione — whose goal is to achieve an "integralist" rollback of post-Vatican II changes in the Church — will be suitable vehicles for the kind of mission effort the Pope envisages. Would such movements be appropriate instruments for evangelization of Asia? They did not, after all, get appreciable results in the new evangelization of the West, a failure that was foreseen by many. How can groups that refuse to dialogue with the modern world evangelize this same modern world? Or is Asia somehow considered premodern? How can such groups, which do not know Asian religious traditions, evangelize Asia? Are they going to evangelize the religious world of Asia utilizing the super-Western "universal catechism"? Or start from the new Code of Canon Law? And can this be carried out solely under the guidance of bishops chosen because of their subordination to Rome and general lack of creativity and spirit of initiative and adaptation?

For such reasons, we fear that RM's appeal to world mission will be totally without result. For it supposes that the evangelization of Asia will occur using mechanisms that have proved the near-total inefficacy over five centuries. What is recommended by the Pope, are the very same means that have been used without results since the sixteenth century.

Nevertheless, there have been attempts to renew mission and to find new ways different from those that have been revealed to be ineffective. RM even does not mention these attempts, as if all mission issues could be deduced from the abstract mode of the new universal catechism. But the history of the Church shows how success in the mission enterprise is closely related to attention to the historical, social, and cultural conditions of the peoples to whom missioners have gone. And all the missioners' good intentions and desires have remained ineffective when they face the obstacle of any of a number of adverse objective conditions. Christians did not receive a miraculous power from Christ. On the contrary, as Vatican II taught, they need to take into account the knowledge of the world and its conditions, finding ways to use the resources of their native intelligence enlightened by the Holy Spirit.

ANALYSIS OF THE ENCYCLICAL

Redemptoris Missio is a continuation of *Ad Gentes* of Vatican Council II and of *Evangelii Nuntiandi* of Pope Paul VI. Pope John Paul does not merely seek to repeat what was proposed by Vatican II or by Paul VI. Instead, he seeks to update their teaching and adapt it to new circumstances. This updating brings about, naturally, new elements, new viewpoints, new insistences. What, then, is new in this Encyclical?

First, this Encyclical is a reaffirmation of the necessity of mission in the face of objections to that enterprise from many quarters. In the past, it is fair to say, there were few objections *from Christians* to the mission *ad gentes*. Its warrants and their authority were pretty much accepted by all Christians. Liberal Protestants, it is true, had begun to be of several minds in the years between the two world wars. But for Catholics, the kind of objections to mission that have surfaced since Vatican Council II are something new indeed, and so one can say that the context of RM's writing *is* new.

Second, RM sets the mission *ad gentes* within the global mission of the Church. It starts from a new vision of the world. Third, RM attempts to integrate into its comprehensive doctrine of mission ecclesial experiences since Vatican II — base ecclesial communities, human promotion movements, and dialogue among world religions are all important in this integration.

A Defense of Mission

Chapters One and Two seek to defend the validity of mission *ad gentes*. Since the beginning of decolonization, which began with Indian independence in 1947 and the Bandung Conference in 1955, strong objections were raised in regard to Christian mission. Christians and non-Christians alike have criticized the notion of mission *ad gentes*. The Encyclical itself (in article 4) attempts to give an answer to several objections:

> *Is missionary work among non-Christians still relevant?* Has it not been replaced by interreligious dialogue? Is not human development an adequate goal of the Church's mission? Does not respect for conscience and for freedom exclude all efforts at conversion? Is it not possible to attain salvation in any religion? *Why then should there be missionary activity?*

These questions are actually found in the writings of contemporary theologians and missioners. And it is especially significant that they are found in authors who reflect upon mission to Asia. In RM, the Pope points to Asia as the greatest challenge for the present-day mission (37e). However, he does not relate the objections he lists to the specific difficulties of mission in Asia, and so RM has a peculiarly abstract character, since the "difficulties" obstructing the spread of Christianity in Asia are quite concrete. For example, Asia is the continent of great religions — Islam, Hinduism, and Buddhism. Except in exceptional circumstances (for example, among tribal peoples oppressed by Buddhist nobility), which students of mission understand well — Christianity has never successfully "converted" a major region where these religions hold sway. After centuries of mission, there have been few conversions of Muslims, Buddhists, and Hindus. In contrast, conversions of Christians *to these religions* have perhaps been large enough to offset the numbers of persons converting to Christianity *from these religions*. In addition, these religions denounce Christian mission as a form of colonialism, as a will to dominate the world by Christians.

In view of the impenetrability of Asian religious worlds, the renewal of these worlds, and the sometimes aggressive resistance of Asian religions to Christian mission, some Christian theologians have attempted to revise the very traditional theological doctrines that the Pope vigorously affirms.

It is important to note that large parts of Asia are practically closed to mission. This is the case of China and India, as well as the great swath of Muslim nations that includes Indonesia, Pakistan, the Arabic countries, Iran, and Afghanistan. Buddhist nations are scarcely different. Because of this, traditional forms of mission are not viable.

In Africa, mission is relatively easy — peoples from black Africa seek spontaneously a more universal religion that will connect them with the whole of humanity. But they find this in both Islam and Christianity. For Christian missioners in Africa, the field is ready. This is not the case in Asia.

The Pope's selection of Asia as an area for special missionary effort raises a question for missioners. How does one explain that many missioners are being supported in Latin America to preserve the establishment of Christendom when Asia almost lacks missionaries? Curiously, too, almost all missioners *ad gentes* coming from Latin America are directed to places such as Africa and Oceania, when the Pacific Ocean could easily take them to Asia?

The Pope criticizes those who lose heart because of the difficulty of mission in Asia. He appeals to new efforts and new attempts. Nevertheless, it is clear that mission in Asia requires serious adaptations and that it is not enough to transfer traditional structures from ancient Christendom to the Asian continent.

Quantitatively, according to Pope John Paul, mission is more urgent than ever, since the number of those who do not know Christ and do not take part in Church life is on the increase (3). The majority of these live in Asia and belong to one of the great Asian religions. It is evident that the number of missioners dedicated to evangelizing members of the great Asian religions is infinitesimal. Either there is something profoundly wrong in the present distribution of the missionary forces, or there is a fundamental error in the definition of the goals. *Redemptoris Missio* is a challenge to examine this question.

Mission ad gentes *and the New Evangelization*

The aim of RM in relation to mission *ad gentes* is clearly linked in the mind of the Pope to his new evangelization agenda for places such as Europe:

> I sense that the moment has come to commit all of the Church's energies to a new evangelization and to the mission *ad gentes*. No believer in Christ, no institution of the Church can avoid this supreme duty: to proclaim Christ to all peoples. (3)

New evangelization and mission *ad gentes* appear as two streams of the Church's general mission. Indeed, chapter four of RM offers a complex vision of the mission of the Church and sets the mission *ad gentes* within this mission. This chapter brings together the Pope's vision of both the contemporary world and the Church presence in it.

In view of factors in the world's contemporary evolution, some suggest that the old distinctions between mature churches and mission fields should be dropped. In this vision all lands are equally fields for mission. The view of the Pope in RM is that such an opinion is premature. For the Pope, the world is better divided into three different parts — each of which demands a specific kind of response from the Church. The first is that in which Christ and his gospel are not known and where there are no mature Christian communities to embody or to proclaim faith in a given setting. This is mission *ad gentes* properly so called (33).

The second is exemplified when Christian communities with solid ecclesial structures (33), able to "bear witness to the Gospel in their surroundings and have a sense of commitment to the universal mission. In these communities the Church carries out her activity and pastoral care" (33). The third field of mission is a kind of "intermediate situation" in the lands of a former Christendom, "where entire groups of the baptized have lost a living sense of the faith" (33). In this a "new evangelization" is required.

From these three situations, three Church tasks derive — caring pastorally for parishioners, a new evangelization, and "the specific missionary task" (34b). Each task is defined in RM by the distinction from other two. The Encyclical states that the limits between these tasks are not easily definable and that one should not erect artificial barriers and compartments between them (34b). This caveat is especially appropriate for Latin America, in which the three situations seem to coexistent and interpenetrate. Here there are complex and specific situations, different not only from those in other continents but also within the various countries and regions of the South American continent. Because of this the Church's task here will also be complex and diverse. Latin America is a mosaic comprised of many diverse situations in which almost universally are to be found all three "missionary" situations identified in RM.

According to the Encyclical, there are certain criteria for determining which specific tasks have priority. Thus the world and mission configurations become more precise, as do the tasks that arise from them. Article 37 discusses these ecclesial tasks. It is the most important article in RM in regard to the concrete way the Pope envisages mission should be carried on, offering in a limited way a theoretical basis for a missionary strategy. Although RM does not seek to present a detailed strategy for the various continents of the world, it nevertheless does offer principles that provide a frame of reference.

First there is *the geographical principle*, which remains valid if only to indicate the geographical frontiers in which the missionary activities should be carried on. The Encyclical sees the territorial principle counting above all in the Asian continent, where Christians are an insignificant minority. In Latin America, the geographical principle is less clear because diverse populations may coexist within the same geographical area. In Asia, however, the need to update the geographical principle is unquestionable.

Second, there is *the social principle*, which needs to be taken into account when the Church confronts entirely new social and social-psychological factors such as urbanization, the importance of youth, the manner in which migrations are changing the world's ethnic face, and poverty as it characterizes and mocks justice.

Throughout the world, mission *ad gentes*, says the Pope, needs to move beyond the rural areas that often confine it. In Brazil, for instance, 75 percent of the population is urban, and the large cities are mushrooming in size. Nothing we know today indicates that this revolution can be arrested. Nevertheless, the juridical structures, the content of preaching and catechesis, the social relation systems within the Church, the relationship between Church and world, and the priest's social position all speak of an origin in traditional European rural cultures. The Church still does not accept the urban world. It does not admit the world. The Church, it seems, does not want to acknowledge the reality of an entirely new world. Above all, the clergy resists adapting to the city. The Pope, to his credit, goes to the heart of the matter when he points out that the city is the most important place for contemporary mission, indeed, that cities are the future of the world.

The second major social context of mission dealt with in article 37 is the burgeoning of youth as a distinct entity. Is it churlish to recall that the Latin American bishops at Puebla already proposed a preferential option for youth? Yet twelve years have gone by and nothing of significance has been done. Even basic ecclesial communities are closed to youth in many regions. In Brazil, these twelve years were years of decay of public education, university, all levels of teaching; they were years of unemployment for youth, of killing delinquent adolescents, and multiplying street children. Youth is forsaken and Church initiatives to rescue youth have remained almost entirely on paper. Nevertheless, to his credit, the Pope insists that youth deserves priority as a focus of mission.

A third social factor to be taken into account, according to RM, is migration. One aspect is the arrival of non-Christians in traditionally Christian lands, bringing with them the possibility of occasions for cross-cultural contacts and dialogue, along with immense problems affecting migrants that can be alleviated by fraternal help from the Church. In Europe, migration affects Muslims but contact with Christians does not seem to have stimulated many conversions. Rather, it seems to have occasioned more conversions of Christians to Islam than conversions of Muslims to Christianity. Christian demonstrations of fraternity remain isolated phenomena in the context of a more generally Christian attitude of aggressive and arrogant behavior.

In Brazil, immigration is slight, but in the past, Brazil received large numbers of Buddhist immigrants from Japan and of Muslims from Arabic countries. Many Japanese converted to Christianity, more, it seems, than as the result of all missionary efforts in Japan. What were the reasons for this? There were some conversions within the Muslim community also, but never as many. Why?

> The last frontier affecting mission are the effects of poverty, often on an intolerable scale which have been created in not a few countries, and which are often the cause of mass migration. The community of believers in Christ is challenged by these inhuman situations: the proclamation of Christ and the Kingdom of God must become the means for restoring the human dignity of these people.

Cultural sectors, which the Pope terms "modern equivalents of the Areopagus" at which Paul preached the Gospel in Acts 17, comprise other major nodes of regional and global contact in the contemporary world. One such cultural sector are *the mass media*. The media are both an obstacle to Christian evangelization and Gospel life and a means of spreading the Gospel. In Latin America, Church presence in radio broadcast is significant, but in print and television media its presence is limited. Moreover, few people seem prepared for taking initiatives in these media.

Other areopagi are briefly mentioned — for instance, peacemaking, development and liberation movements (especially to benefit minorities), promotion of woman and child, the protection of nature, scientific research, the arts, and international relations.

The conclusion drawn from the Pope's survey of these phenomena and situations regards the comprehensiveness of Christian mission and the universality of the Gospel:

> the "ends of the earth" to which the Gospel must be brought are growing ever more distant. Tertullian's saying [in the *De praescriptione haereticorum*, XX: CCL I, 201f.], that the Gospel has been proclaimed to all the earth and to all peoples, is still very far from being a reality. The mission *ad gentes* is still in its infancy. New peoples appear on the world scene, and they too have a right to receive the proclamation of salvation. Population growth in non-Christian countries of the South and the East is constantly increasing the number of people who remain unaware of Christ's Redemption.
>
> We need therefore to direct our attention towards those geographical areas and cultural settings which still remain uninfluenced by the Gospel. All who believe in Christ should feel, as an integral part of their faith, an apostolic concern to pass on to others its light and joy. (40)

PATHS OF MISSION

Chapter five of RM deals with the paths of mission, restating and developing themes of *Evangelii Nuntiandi*. It is interesting to point out the development of some themes that were the great newness of *Evangelii Nuntiandi*. *Base ecclesial communities* were given official status in the Church by Pope Paul VI. Now, John Paul II not only confirms them but also strengthens them as a sign of vitality, an instrument for evangelization, and a worthy starting point for a new society (51).

The *goal of inculturating* the gospel in local cultures was a major theme in *Evangelii Nuntiandi*. In RM, John Paul II packs into three paragraphs basic aspects of his own teachings on inculturation. In short he sees inculturation as a necessity for evangelization and as an enrichment for the universal Church (52). While recognizing its necessity, the Pope gives exhortations for prudence and says its right develop-ment will stem from the observance of two principles: "compatibility with the Gos-pel and communion with the universal Church" (54a). In practice, however, we know that the Vatican does not readily give permission for experiments in new ways of expressing faith.

Promoting development and educating consciences were major fresh themes in *Evangelii Nuntiandi,* as was the insertion of a message of liberation in evangeliza-tion (EN 29-33). *Redemptoris Missio* is much more discreet on this topic. The Encyclical acknowledges that "mission *ad gentes* is still being carried out today, for the most part in the southern regions of the world, where action on behalf of integral development and liberation from all forms of oppression is most urgently needed" (58) but the call to action toward development and liberation is muted. The present Encyclical mainly presents basic considerations on gospel and development, without anything about liberation.

The Pope's text seems to reflect the evolution in thinking in the First World, where it is common to believe that the time for fighting for liberation is over; the Third World is considered a boring subject; and it seems that the Third World peoples are relegated to marginalization and the status of unimportance. But these are the First World views. What do the Third World peoples think about these issues?

AGENTS OF EVANGELIZATION

Chapter Four of RM deals with the agents of evangelization. There is no surprise in the paragraphs about bishops, priests, or religious, and none of these categories could be omitted. What is truly new in RM is the stress on laity, sign of an accelera-tive evolution. John Paul II recalls the teachings of recent Popes and Vatican Council II about the importance of the missionary activity of laity. He recalls the apostolic exhortation *Christifideles Laici,* which concluded the synod on laity. It is obvious that here laity is the issue. This is a sign of the times.

This level of consideration given to laity is important for Brazil, since after twenty years of military regimes, with bishops and priests becoming accustomed to being virtually the Church's only voice, the laity is very timid. Rather, the clergy gives its view on matters and the laity's initiatives in giving a religious reading of the times are very few. One might say that the clergy practices "an authoritarianism of love."

Besides the stress on laity, other aspects regarding the subjects of mission deserve attention. First, even in the realm of the laity new "ecclesial movements" such as the ones we mentioned above, are the star. The total silence in regard to the Catholic Action movement is striking. In the view of the Vatican, Catholic Action has disap-peared. In its place "ecclesial movements" are given special status. The Pope says,

I call to mind, as a new development occurring in many Churches in recent times, the rapid growth of "ecclesial movements" filled with missionary dyna-mism. When these movements humbly seek to become part of the life of local Churches and are welcomed by Bishops and priests within diocesan and parish structures, they represent a true gift of God both for new evangelization and for missionary activity properly so-called. I therefore recommend that they be spread, and that they be used to give fresh energy, especially among young people, to the Christian life and to evangelization, within a pluralistic view of the ways in which Christians can associate and express themselves. (72)

Elsewhere the Pope expresses his trust in these movements, again in relation to youth apostolates (37).

The Encyclical concludes with an optimistic view of the future of Christian mission, even though it is realistic about the problems and obstacles that confront it. The Pope notes that the Church's resources are limited which could justify pessimism. However, faith in God transforms this pessimism into optimism (cf. 86, 92). To that we can all say a sincere Amen.

Concluding Reflections

William R. Burrows

William R. Burrows, managing editor of Orbis Books, supervises acquisitions in the areas of mission and evangelization and theology of religions. He served as a Divine Word Missionary in Papua New Guinea for five years in the 1970s in rural stations and as a theology teacher in the national seminary in Port Moresby. While pursuing doctoral studies and writing a dissertation on the Catholic doctrine on other religious traditions at the University of Chicago, he was active in inner-city African-American parish work and published *New Ministries: The Global Context* (Orbis, 1980). He is currently working on a book on a postmodern theology of evangelization and Christian identity in a pluralistic age.

As I worked back and forth through the texts of RM and DP, the commentaries of Fathers Zago and Dupuis, and the nine reaction pieces, certain judgments began to firm up in my own mind. The first regards the ultimate timeliness of the discussion on *missio ad gentes* and on its nature. The second regards dialogue with theologians in a pluralistic Catholic Church and the limits of the genre of an encyclical or a statement of Vatican offices. The third discusses the need for an inclusive theology of mission that is open to non-traditional ministries. And finally, I was led to considerations on what could constitute grounds for a more adequate debate and discussion of the nature of mission, a conversation that would start from recognition that all theology is hermeneutical.

THE TIMELINESS OF THE TWO ROMAN DOCUMENTS

Although RM and DP have been greeted with as much hostility as acceptance, they are timely, important documents. The words "mission" and "dialogue" have come to mean whatever people want them to mean. Pope John Paul and the two Vatican dicasteries have attempted to inject a critical element into the debate over these terms, and in the process give the open-minded reader an invitation to look at the Roman magisterium's hermeneutics of the church's tradition concerning mission.

Missio ad gentes as an attempt to share the church's experience of life in Christ across the boundary of faith is an element of mission that since the Second Vatican Council has been treated with disdain by many in the progressive camp. Although it is painful for someone such as myself, who identifies theologically with progressive theology, it has often, in my judgment, been the case that progressives have bent so far backwards as to lose their Christian balance. The many just complaints of non-Christians about the practice of Christian mission have led many to want to drop words such as conversion from their vocabulary. Is this a case of liberals allowing themselves to be paralyzed by political and theological correctness? Are such complaints perhaps better dealt with by a purification of arrogant missionary praxis than by becoming so bland as to raise the question whether the salt has lost its tang? On the other hand, has the central authority of the church reflected sufficiently on the hackles it raises and the cloying character of its ornate prose and sometimes self-satisfied theology?

Still, conversion to the person of Jesus is at the core of Christianity and what it offers to the world, not something peripheral. RM and DP bring us back to that home truth. Moreover, I do not detect in any of the respondents significant reservation on that topic. That said, it is also true that most of the respondents are *critical*, even if — as in the case of Jack Voelkel — the central criticism is confined to wondering why RM is so vague about the evil from which humankind needs salvation. It is important, I suggest, to look very carefully at each of the nine reaction pieces. If the authors agree to the inmost core of the positions taken, why is their overall tone critical? In the following three sections of these concluding reflections, I offer ideas on this irony in the book as a whole.

THE CHURCH'S NEED FOR DIALOGUE WITH THEOLOGIANS

Eric Sharpe's article is, I believe, especially good in pointing to a very real set of problems in the diplomatic language of an "ecclesiastical state paper," which is what RM and DP are. Nuance and attention to scripture, as well as the need to cite precedents set by the teaching of other popes and the whole range of councils and synods, are useful at one level in RM and DP. But at a certain point they cloy. The reader, as Sharpe notes, detects in a string of such references what amounts to a claim that everything important has been said and understood in the past and that church authorities in the present are merely applying the self-evident lessons of the past. In reality, however, one mines the past to warrant a present conclusion. In so doing, one seeks to retrieve a "usable past," a past that *I* can use to make *my* point against *my* adversaries.

In such an enterprise, the key question is whether my selection of criteria is fairly arrived at. If my construal of historical evidence is to be fair, I need to say why I have chosen "A" and not "B," making the case that construal "A" of Christian identity, for instance, is more adequate. In that context, RM and DP choose, however, a theological line that has been consistently applied since the Council of Trent, one that has been marked since Vatican Council I as anti-modernist. That line may be fairly characterized as having great confidence that the institutions and laws of the Roman Catholic Church enjoy *de jure divino* authorization. It holds as a central element the doctrine that the Catholic Church is God's normal channel of grace, even if God operates richly elsewhere in manners known to Godself alone, God's purposes in the world being salvation, not condemnation (1 Tim 4:10; GS 22). Vatican Council II, in its use of "People of God" and other symbols, often taken from the early Christian literature commonly called "patristic," was perceived by many progressives to be opening the church to less restrictive understandings of salvation. My own research led me to believe that the official position was more ambiguous than many were calling it. Both toward other religious traditions and other Christian traditions, I argued in my dissertation, Vatican Council II's breakthrough was to validate a kind of irenic ambivalence toward others, not weaken the church's christocentric view of salvation.

During the pontificate of Pope Paul VI, Rome tried to keep anti-modernist canonical and institutional understandings in tension with mystical and more open-ended ("creatively vague"?) understandings of doctrines such as the universality and finality of Christ, the importance of the visible church in God's plan for salvation, and the goals of Christian mission. Conservatives accused Paul VI of fearing to crack down on impermissible dissent.

With the arrival of Pope John Paul II, the tendency has been to clarify ambiguities and say that the patristic images being used (by liberals) to warrant reformist agendas were wrong in their appeal to a vague "spirit of Vatican II." The Pope and his advisers, in effect, said that they alone were competent to interpret authoritatively what the Council meant. RM and DP are major theological interpretations of history and of the mission and ministry of the church in our day. While there are differences in emphasis and tone between the documents, they seek to give practical guidance and directives on how mission is to be carried on. As such, they display the results of a sequence of judgments on the part of Pope John Paul and his advisers; they do not merely apply *doctrina quam sancta mater ecclesia semper docuit* [doctrine that holy mother church has always taught] to our age. Yet the criteria on the basis of which judgments were made are not clear; one is left to infer their roots, as I have done in this and the preceding paragraph.

My judgment is that the encyclical seeks to counteract doctrines of certain theologians that have been prominently debated in recent years. For instance, I was able to recall phrases used in RM to epitomize what Pope John Paul considers erroneous opinions, phrases that occurred in books I have personally read over the years. Granted that popes and high-ranking cardinals view themselves not as debating theological fine points but teaching and applying the Good News to our day, it seems to me that a venue needs to be found for popes and cardinals to engage their theologians in the kind of dialogue that DP calls for; and then a literary genre that is less pretentious and more straightforward in putting forth findings of Roman authorities.

Although my own theological proclivities lie in directions pointed out by evoking the names Alfred North Whitehead, Mircea Eliade, Bernard Lonergan, David Tracy, Hans Küng, and Langdon Gilkey, I am also persuaded that the Pope is absolutely correct in fearing that a contemporary theological malaise threatens to paralyze the ability to give witness to the concrete uniqueness of the Way of Jesus of Nazareth, whom Christians believe to be God's Christ. Nor do I think that the church can responsibly turn the articulation of its identity to theologians. Theology is too often a *cursus honorum* for academic preferment, not a school of discipleship. On the other hand, the same could be said of advancement in the church. And thus today it is clear that large numbers of bishops and theologians do not trust members of their opposite ecclesial "order," if I may use that quaint word. But it is also clear that a new chapter in relations between the church and her theologians needs to be opened or the mission of the church will suffer.

RECOGNIZING NON-TRADITIONAL MODES OF MISSION

A second major theme began to emerge when I read carefully the critical responses to RM and DP. In one way and another, it was clear from the papers that came in and from reactions I got when theologian-friends found out I was editing a book on RM and DP, that RM raised people's defenses in ways DP did not, yet in every essential theological point DP agrees with RM, including the adoption of a very high christology, ecclesiology, and christocentric soteriology. "What," I asked, "is going on here?" My conclusion was that RM seeks to define "mission" canonically and restrictively; it seems unaware that what it ends up doing is putting up juridical fences that exclude persons engaged in "non-traditional" forms of mission and ministry from being considered fully "missionary." The viewpoint of RM, in other words — even when its *overt* theology is an expansive Kingdom-centered interpretation of Christian identity — is *implicitly* Romano-ecclesiocentric. Now a certain "ecclesiasticizing" of salvation certainly has ancient roots. By this I mean a complex of doctrines that see salvation mediated through belonging to the visible church and conceive of the church hierarchy as charged by Jesus with the role of making rules — including rules that define the meaning of words such as mission. Yet as Anthony Gittins observes in his article, "mission" is not a scriptural word. It is, that notwithstanding, a word that touches on a sense of total Christian vocation that many sincere disciples of Jesus find precious. I conclude that barrier-erection is far from the bridge-building that we Christians should be doing among our various centers in this age.

In the Gospel of Mark (10:38-41), the disciples want their teacher to rebuke an exorcist who is expelling demons in the name of Jesus. Jesus instead rebukes his own inner circle, apparently finding their narrowness of heart more troubling than rivals doing good works. RM is open to the accusation that it teaches that work done in the service of the Christ should only be done only under clear ecclesiastical direction. Several authors in *Redemption and Dialogue* disagree. Not a few Catholics appear to have embraced Tillich's Protestant principle in two regards: (1) the right to dissent, and (2) the right and obligation to bear witness in a manner one judges appropriate. Running through several articles, but emerging in full view in Edwina Gateley's, is the burgeoning of a laity that is not anti-clerical but that finds the clerical world rather beside the point. I found in neither RM or DP any clear willingness to confess that people could have had such bad experiences with the visible organized church that they could legitimately doubt that they could be good missionaries of Christ without having ecclesiastical recognition.

While traditional forms of mission, carried on under the aegis of religious orders, officially recognized lay groups, and diocesan bishops, following the prescriptions of the *Code of Canon Law*, have much to recommend them, the implication of RM is that such traditional modes of mission are the sole legitimate modes and that even lay participation in mission needs to be ecclesiastically approved. I want to state clearly that I think that groups such as the Maryknollers and the Society of the Divine Word, with which I am personally well acquainted, are wonderfully equipped to carry on Christian mission. Imbued with traditions of spirituality, formation, and support, they enable thousands of men and women to give themselves to Christian mission in ways that maximize their talents and reduce the damage untrammeled enthusiasm can inflict. But it is equally clear that membership in such groups no longer seems plausible to large numbers of Western youth for a variety of reasons. New modes of mission need to be pioneered. The Society of Jesus is, in one way and another, the inspiration for dozens of societies of men and women religious engaged in mission since the sixteenth century. It was also a radical break with the past when it was founded. José Comblin's essay raises the question whether such groups as Opus Dei or the Volunteer Missionary Movement are to be the paradigms of these new modalities. The Pope does seem to envisage the former rather than the latter. I am not sure I can see why.

TOWARD A NEW HERMENEUTIC OF MISSIONARY IDENTITY

If one reads the works of such theologians and philosophers as Paul Ricoeur, David Tracy, and Werner Jeanrond, one becomes aware of the need for new approaches to interpreting the Scriptures and to tradition. Already in the period before and after Vatican Council II, we were aware of the need to study the Bible and tradition in context. That has sometimes led to a mania for historical exegesis, as if we could solve present-day problems by piling up learned arguments.

Today, we should be aware that the great texts of tradition are not best used as mere sources for doctrinal statements, nor should we imagine that one can use the traditional dogmatic methods if only one takes care to use modern exegetical methods alongside them. In saying this, I am not attacking any doctrines espoused in RM or DP; I am merely making a point about what is effective *teaching*. What I drive at is this. Even doctrinal statements that are faithful articulations of meanings that Jesus or writers of classic Christian texts might find congenial will not solve the contemporary problem of Christians seeking light on mission and vocation. Why?

Classic texts function best when they excite the corporate religious imagination and, in new contexts, reveal worlds and possibilities that original authors might never have dreamed of. Such are the insights of the "new hermeneutics." When one sees displayed in *Redemptoris Missio* and in *Dialogue and Proclamation* central elements of Christian tradition, one is also face to face with the challenge of renewing living tradition to move into a future that a Moses, a Solomon, a Jesus, a Paul, a Mark, an Augustine, or an Aquinas could scarcely imagine. To get the full flavor of today's age, I suggest that we add the names of Shakyamuni Buddha, Muhammad, and Confucius, for these traditions also face futures their founders could scarcely have imagined. Today the futures of all these traditions are intertwined. In the mystery of redemption, it is in dialogue with the living spirits of such giants that we glimpse life-giving ways forward.

A great tradition moves ahead by coming to terms with and appropriating the dynamics of its founder, but ultimately it survives and grows only by embracing the risks of being creative in dealing with the future. In working with RM and DP and the commentaries and critiques of the authors of this book, what most struck me was the seeming reluctance of the two major documents to admit freely that we face futures whose outcomes we can scarcely imagine. Perhaps Christians need to recall Jesus's paradigmatic revelation of God, in his death on the cross.

If the dynamic of finding new life through death is the ultimate paradigm of Christian existence, then perhaps the death of Jesus is key to a Christian hermeneutic of mission in the contemporary world. The inadequacy of every human institution I know, including the church and other religious and secular traditions, call out to be recognized. Do they need to die in some significant way? Do RM and DP recognize that need? Should they have recognized it? There is, of course, a natural human desire — in the face of insecurity — to be reassured that everything will be okay. Still, when one purchases that reassurance at the price of ignoring problems, the paradise one builds in the sky is that of a fool.

Ultimately RM and DP challenge Christians to enter first into dialogue with Jesus and then to embrace the world dialogically as his followers. Dialogue, I believe, demands at least an act of bracketing one's convictions — a form of death — in order to entertain seriously what another is saying. RM and DP call for dialogue, to be sure. Do they understand the peculiar kind of liminality one experiences in dialogue? To their credit, both documents insist that mission and dialogue are intrinsically connected. For that we should be grateful.

Viewed from another perspective, dialogue does *not* mean giving up conviction, but placing two subjects in boundary situations, wherein they stretch to communicate across a threshold (a *limen*) of incommensurability and historical and linguistic complexity. I am not sure how or whether the staid language of an ecclesiastical state paper can capture that dynamism. I am sure, though, that Christian mission in service of a Nazarene peasant–carpenter–teacher entails dialogue.

In a section of his monumental *Transforming Mission* (Orbis Books, 1990, 222-226), David Bosch notes that the "missionary war" analogy is an element in the medieval Roman Catholic paradigm of mission that carries over into general Christian preunderstandings of mission. According to Bosch — and I think he is right — the image of mission mediated by history is of a kind of spiritual warfare. It has penetrated Christianity to the point that, whether consciously or unconsciously, mission is viewed as an enterprise where Christ conquers, much as an army on the battlefield. The result of mission purveyed even in very sophisticated Christian circles is to get pagans to embrace "Christian civilization."

Given the recoil of many of our morally most sensitive persons from the very notion of a Christian civilization, Christianity needs to rethink what mission, dialogue, and conversion really mean. Augustine Kanjamala as much as says that the Indian theologians and their fellow travelers — against whom many believe RM was principally written — are pioneering new ways of engaging in Christian mission. He believes the most vital challenge to Christianity lies in the West and that RM displaces its anxieties when it sees it in the East.

I first thought that Kanjamala overstated his case. When I spent more time turning his argument over, it began to seem fundamentally right. And when I then went back to the pieces by Beatrice Leung, Vincent Boi-Nai, and Laurenti Magesa, it struck me that all four indigenous third-world representatives in our volume were making the same point by their lives as well as their words. They are busy with the work of mission as inculturation and helping new churches grow under difficult circumstances. Indeed, when I finished editing Vincent Boi-Nai's chapter, I moved to an easy chair to sip a cup of coffee and saw by chance in the *New York Times* that hundreds had been injured and many killed in fighting near Tamale in Ghana, where his Cross-Cultural Center is located. I do not know how he and his associates have fared, but Vince is typical of a legion of large-hearted indigenous missionaries in Africa, Asia, and Latin America. Untroubled by many of the anxieties that paralyze us in the West, they simply carry on their master's work — in Vince Boi-Nai's case in dialogue with their fellow Christians, followers of African traditional ways, and Islam. No conquest, just incarnating Christ as best they can.

The image of an assertive Christianity in mission aiming at conquest is exactly what many non-Christian — and former Christians in the West — dislike most about Christianity. A Jewish colleague once called Christianity "relentless" in this characteristic. My suspicion is that the deeper we go into dialogue with other religious traditions, the more profoundly we Christians and our partners will realize that mission is not conquest. For this image of what mission is about to be exorcised, however, no small death will have to be endured, not least of all in ecclesiastical state papers that read as if someone knew the outcome of history. In saying this, I hope I do not sound like another Western Christian liberal engaged in breast-beating. What I do suggest is that we need to die to a certain kind of Christian identity mediated by our history in order to rise to new life. The life of third-world churches — wherein the rigid dichotomies of Western theology do not fit — may well be models of both Good Friday and Easter for all the church.